The
iPhoto™ 4
Book

The iPhoto™ 4 Book

Sam Crutsinger and David Plotkin,
Andy Ihnatko, Series Author

Wiley Publishing, Inc.

The iPhoto™ 4 Book

Published by
Wiley Publishing, Inc.
111 River Street
Hoboken, NJ 07030
www.wiley.com

Copyright © 2005 Wiley Publishing

Published by Wiley Publishing, Inc., Indianapolis, Indiana
Published simultaneously in Canada

Library of Congress Control Number: 2004102438

ISBN: 0-7645-6797-7

Manufactured in the United States of America

10 9 8 7 6 5 4 3 2 1

1V/RX/RR/QU/IN

This book is dedicated to the memory of Patches, who posed for many of the photos used in this book. Her puppies will miss her, as will Howard and Laura.

Credits

Acquisitions Editor
Michael Roney

Project Editor
Cricket Krengel

Technical Editors
Small Green Alien Productions

Copy Editors
Kim Heusel
Scott Tullis

Editorial Manager
Robyn Siesky

Vice President and Executive Group Publisher
Richard Swadley

Vice President and Publisher
Barry Pruett

Project Coordinator
Nancee Reeves

Graphics and Production Specialists
Amanda Carter
Sean Decker
Carrie A. Foster
Denny Hager
Jennifer Heleine
Lauren Goddard

Quality Control Technician
Susan Moritz

Proofreading
Laura L. Bowman

Indexing
Lynnzee Elze

Cover Design
Anthony Bunyan

Special Help
Maureen Spears

Preface

Preface written by Sam Crutsinger

(Take 2). Apparently I've never actually paid much attention to the preface of any of the books I've ever read because I was just told that my first preface wasn't actually a preface. I always thought it was that piece at the front of a book that was pretty much useless prattle from the author and could be skipped over so you could get to the inside pages you actually bought the book for. Apparently it's got more to do with telling you what this book is about. Who knew?

Well then. This book is about iPhoto. I'm hoping that much was glaringly obvious by the large lettering on the cover and spine. The reason this book had to be done is that nobody writes manuals any more and as a result people like me can write stuff like this and then people like you buy it and then companies like Wiley Publishing decide on whether or not they're going to ask me to do it all over again on another topic. Oh, that's probably not the level of honesty they're looking for now that I think about it.

iPhoto is of course one of Apple's drop-dead easy iApps that many people think is just a walk in the park. At its most basic level, it is. It has big colorful buttons and a relatively easy interface. Those *walk in the park* people usually have no clue about what kinds of stuff this puppy can actually do. They import some pictures and that's about it. Once you're done with this book, you'll know every nook and cranny of iPhoto and you'll be able to take pictures of those other people as they're walking in the park, import the photos into your computer, catalog all the shots, rate them, make a Web site out of them, email selects to other people, and then drop off a bundle to the *park people* that includes printouts, a photo CD, a DVD slideshow, and a hardback book of the whole park-walk experience.

However, if you use all of the knowledge in this book all at once like that on a person, he or she will either be gushingly flattered, or, and this is far more likely, the individual will take out a restraining order. It may not be such a good idea to use all this knowledge at once.

I'm relatively certain that we've managed to completely cover everything that iPhoto is capable of doing, and several things that popped into my head that you'd never want to do with iPhoto. Okay, so you might have noticed that I've got a bit of a habit drifting off the subject on occasion. My brain tends to run down some pretty odd avenues on occasion, but that's half the fun. Don't worry. Meds and extensive editing help keep the totally insane bits down to under 1% of the total content. I'm a firm believer that if you're bored you'll forget what I say in about 20 minutes, and I was not raised to be a boring person.

Preface

You'll note that my .Mac account address is plastered all over this book. It's *tackyshirt*, which is the name of my day job where I produce technical training videos. I bring that up for two reasons. The first reason is to pimp my company (DUH!). The second reason though is that *because* that address is all over this book, I'm resigned to the fact that it's about to become a very public thing and since that has an email address attached to it, **tackyshirt@mac.com**, I'm going to do a potentially stupid thing and ask for feedback. This is my first book, and I want to know what I did right and what I did wrong. I especially want to know if we let any errors slip through the cracks. Of course, if it's 2006 when you're reading this, odds are I've nailed all the problems by now, but end of 2004, early 2005, drop me a line and tell me what you think or where things went wrong. Send me suggestions for what you think might make the book more helpful or fun. I'll make a point of reading what comes in there, but don't expect any replies out of me unless you're like Anna Kournikova or Kirsten Dunst (and can prove it... then I might reply). It's a drop box, not a dialog, but it will certainly help me make future editions even better.

I'll also be posting a Homepage of several of the illustrations used in this book on my .Mac space so you can see what they look like in living color. Just head to **http://homepage.mac.com/tackyshirt/** and click on *The iPhoto Book* link in the wad of links at the top of the page.

Icons Used in This Book

So, how to get you started? First, let's introduce you to the unique structure of the book that you hold in your hands. There are a couple of book elements that you need to know about.

Sidebars

You'll notice these sidebars scattered here and there throughout the pages of the book. Sidebars are where I take the opportunity to digress. I share information that might enhance your understanding of the topic at hand, that adds new perspective, or that I just plain find interesting.

Notes

Periodically I might drop in a Note where I've spotted something that you might have been wondering about or where I think many people might go wrong without a little more information.

Tips

That's easy enough to figure out. These are little extras that might make your life easier or get the job done quicker.

Book Organization

This book is broken down into several parts that focus on different aspects of iPhoto. I'll start out with the very basics and get progressively more detailed until you've clicked on every button, slider, text field, and icon associated with iPhoto by the end of the book. To get the most out of the book you might want to be at the computer trying out the stuff I'm discussing on your own. I mean what's the point of learning all this stuff if you aren't going to actually use it?

Part I: The Basics

I start off the journey with a few hints to help you take good photos. Face it, iPhoto is a lot more fun and useful if you're working with pictures you can be proud of. Next you get a first glance at iPhoto just to familiarize yourselves with the general layout of the program, and then you'll look at various ways to get pictures into iPhoto.

Part II: Organizing Your Photos

Now it's time to organize your photos. In this part, you'll look at simple organizing techniques, some of which iPhoto does automatically. Then you'll get into albums. This is where most people start to realize that iPhoto is kinda keen. Chapter 6 is a bit more work but immensely important as it is where you go over adding titles, comments, and keywords to your pictures, which makes iPhoto 100x more useful than most people ever realize.

Part III: Editing Your Photos

When you find yourself needing to edit your pictures, you'll be reaching for Edit mode. These chapters introduce you to that area of iPhoto. After you have a look around, you start cropping, enhancing, and otherwise editing your photographs to make them better than ever. If you need more robust tools, you'll also look at how iPhoto interacts with other graphic applications.

Part IV: Getting It Out There: Sharing Your Photos

This part covers slideshows, which are a very simple way to show people a collection of pictures on your computer screen. It also delves into optimizing images for printing, and then how to print out some of your pictures on *your* printer. When *your* printer doesn't cut it, you can send your photos off for professional prints by the photo lab, which is also explained. You can use your pictures for your desktop image or for your screen saver. And I'll even show you how to make your pictures available to *other people's* screen savers. Finally, you will learn how to make QuickTime movies out of your shots, email pictures to friends, and how to make homepages to put your photo albums up where the world can view them.

Part V: Working with the iPhoto Book Feature

This part takes you step by step through Book creation starting with the settings that apply to the whole book. Then you zoom in a bit and work with the individual layouts. Then you zoom in a bit more and fix up the captions and comments fields so your pictures aren't all alone on the page. And then, you'll learn how to print your book and send it off to be professionally printed and bound as a hardback book you can be proud of. This chapter also covers some tips on how to modify the layout pages to make your own themes using Apple's Developer Tools.

Part VI: Using Other iLife Applications to Present Your Work

This part breaks away from iPhoto for a bit to look at some of the other applications in iLife that have deep ties to your photo collection, including iMovie and iDVD.

Part VII: Odds 'n Ends

In this single chapter, you'll have a peek at how iPhoto organizes your pictures on your hard drive. If you need to have more than one photo library, I'll show you how to get iPhoto to let you switch among several photo libraries.

Part VIII: Bonus Chapters from Andy Ihnatko

The last three chapters are a bonus selection of material from that Geek For All Seasons, Andy Ihnatko. The first chapter is one that I asked him to cover for me because, well, when you have a chance to let an AppleScript swami teach about AppleScript, you step back and let the master speak. In the next chapter Andy has a chat with his Aunt Estelle. That's a little Q & A section. In the final chapter Andy takes a look at features found in most digital cameras that many people don't pay attention to.

Acknowledgments

Sam Crutsinger

I met Andy Ihnatko when he came to be one of the stars of my first DVD at TackyShirt, and I can safely say he's a truly great and brilliant man. You should see his brain working live on the set prior to editing. Simply fantastic. He's pretty much like Dennis Miller in a hat and with more geeky historical references. I was giddy to get the message about helping out on one of the books. So, thanks, Andy, for letting me play along.

I've definitely got to thank David Plotkin for taking care of the mind-numbingly tedious click, click, click aspects of the book so I wouldn't have to spend so much time making sure I got the actual technical bits right. I'm not sure I could actually have pulled it off without that base. Not for my first book at any rate.

Thanks to my family and friends who donated photos to the cause. Your good pictures make me look fantastic.

Thanks to the Your Mac Life mailing list for springing to my aid when I posted bizarre questions about obscure uses of iPhoto and telling me "Lose that joke. It's not funny." when I bounced questionable material off the few hundred people who are subscribed there.

I want to give a special thanks to my parents for their support. After 35 years, I still don't know what I want to be when I grow up, but today I'm a writer. Their educational, financial, and legal support has allowed me to lead quite a meandering lifestyle up to now, and hopefully this book will get on Oprah's Book Club, sell millions of copies, and I can get my parents a nice summer home away from this Texas heat. It's the least I could do. (Oh and by legal, I mean with contracts, not the penal system.)

Thanks to Michael Roney for emailing me those fateful words "Wanna write a book?" (Okay, they weren't those words, but that was the gist.) As well, thank you to Cricket Krengel and Maureen Spears and all the other plethora of editors who pulled the answers out of me when I would manage to overlook the questions.

Lastly I'd like to apologize to Huge Systems for keeping that RAID array far longer than I should have. I wasn't being sneaky. I was just *really, really* busy. I'm sending it back now.

About the Authors

Sam Crutsinger is the President and Media Kingpin of TackyShirt. Sam's a native of Dallas, Texas, who was bitten by the Mac bug around the desktop publishing boom of the late '80s. He got a bachelor of science in audio engineering, but rather than stick just to sound design, he's constantly expanded into new areas, and now he's a professional audio engineer, video editor, video producer, graphic designer, videographer, photographer, writer, computer system designer, repair technician, and cat lover. This Emmy Award–winner has worked with film, video, and multimedia projects covering everything from music videos to presidential campaigns. Sam teaches everyone who'll listen how to get the most out of their Macintosh. Currently Sam's goal in life is to be the Straight Guy on an episode of *Queer Eye for the Straight Guy*. If you've been to his house, you'll understand why.

David Plotkin is a veteran Mac columnist and reviewer, computer book author, and digital photography expert.

Andy Ihnatko is America's 42nd Most-Beloved Industry Figure and has been a leading voice in the Macintosh community for over 15 years. He has been the monthly back-page opinion columnist for *Macworld* magazine and is currently a columnist (covering technology and the Internet) for *The Chicago Sun-Times*. He has also contributed frequently to *Playboy*, CNN.com, and too many online publications to adequately count. He lives in Boston with his two goldfish, Click and Drag. He invites you to visit his aptly named "Colossal Waste Of Bandwidth" at www. andyi.com.

Contents

PART I

The Basics

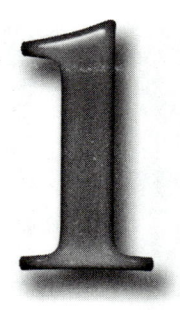

Taking Interesting Photos

In This Chapter

iPhoto lets you organize and fix up photos like never before, but there's only so much it can do. Hey, there's even only so much that the venerable Adobe Photoshop can do. The bottom line is that good photos start in the camera, not in the computer. Like the ancient Buddhist photographer monks like to say, "Garbage in, garbage out." If your picture is out of focus, the highlights are flared out, or the material just isn't interesting to begin with, there's not really much you can do to fix that in the computer. So, let's start off with a few pointers to help you take better pictures. The goal is to have shots that can be enhanced with a little bit of iPhoto magic to make them into photos you'll want to share.

FILL THE FRAME — BUT NOT TOO CLOSE!

You've all seen pictures in which the main subject is too far away or occupies such a small portion of the image that the picture simply isn't interesting (see Figure 1-1).

Make sure to fill a good part of the frame with your subject. Something out there got you to pull up your camera, so make it obvious what the viewer is supposed to be looking at.

Figure 1-1
Here are some of my buddies on a beach. I doubt even the CIA lab could tell who's who

Figure 1-2
Empty street. Big whoop

Figure 1-2 is a picture I took in Times Square in New York. Visually, this area is about as busy as it gets, but one thing in particular caught my eye in the midst of it all that made me want to snap the shot. The steam rising up from the intersection across the street, lit up by the car headlights (Figure 1-3) looked extremely cool, but I was in a hurry and didn't zoom in so I got a much less dramatic shot of the street. If I didn't tell you about the steam, you'd never have even noticed it was there.

Because I was zoomed out *so far,* I couldn't effectively crop the image without losing image quality. You start to see digital artifacts in the picture when it is enlarged to where it should have been zoomed into in the first place. Digital artifacts are what you'd call that blocky mosaic pattern you see when you zoom in too close on a digital picture. (They can also be seen around fine lines and details on pictures that are poorly compressed.) Obviously the fix here is to let your subject material fill a good part of the frame. You want someone to look at the picture and know why you took it. A rousing game of *Where's Waldo?* isn't usually the effect you're looking for in a picture.

Figure 1-3
Mysterious mist. Now that's got whoop

There are, however, reasons not to get *too* close to your subject, filling the frame completely.

First, be careful of a concept called *parallax.* This means that what you see when you look through an optical viewfinder isn't exactly what the lens is seeing because the optical viewfinder and the lens are separate. On most cameras, the optical viewfinder (where you compose the picture) is above and to one side of the lens where the light for the picture comes in. There are exceptions to this. Single-lens reflex (SLR) cameras (digital versions of which are finally starting to become affordable) combine the viewfinder and the lens into a single mechanism, which means that what your eye is seeing is the same as what the lens is seeing. So, if you compose the picture using the LCD on the back of a digital camera, you will get an accurate reading of what the picture will look like. But because using the LCD drains the battery quickly, some people continue to use the optical viewfinder. If your digital camera isn't an SLR type, and you attach a wide-angle or a telephoto lens to the camera, then you *have* to use the LCD. The image that is seen through the attached lens will be far different from the image seen through the optical viewfinder.

Another issue you will encounter when composing your shots has to do with aspect ratio. Most digital cameras take a photo that has a length-to-width ratio, which is called an *aspect ratio,* of 4 to 3. A common example of this is a standard screen resolution of 1024 by 768. This aspect ratio works well for images that will be used for your computer Desktop, screen backgrounds, onscreen slideshows, and the professional photo books you can create with iPhoto, but this aspect ratio does *not* work well with photos that you intend to print for framing. For example, a photo print size is 6 by 4 inches, which works out to an aspect ratio of 3 to 2. In order to prepare a standard digital photograph for printing, you'll need to crop a portion of the image to obtain the correct aspect ratio. Figure 1-4 shows an example of how you would need to crop a 4-to-3 aspect ratio image to turn it into a 3-to-2 aspect ratio image. iPhoto calls this aspect ratio *4 x 6 (Postcard)* and makes cropping easy to do, but it does mean that part of the picture will be thrown away, and you'd rather that it not be an important part!

PERILS OF PARALLAX

As a young boy I was really into stop-frame animation. Early in my career, at about age 9, I decided to immortalize a flip-book cartoon that I'd drawn in the margins of my parent's dictionary. I set up my 8mm film camera on the tripod. I set up some lights. I looked through the eyepiece. I focused on the page. I spent what seemed like hours tediously shooting page after page after page.

When I got it back from the photo lab, I threaded the film through the projector and watched in horror as a rather dull sequence of the kitchen countertop flickered onto the screen. Because the eyepiece was quite a bit higher than the camera lens, I'd *totally* missed my target.

Who knows? If it weren't for that devastating setback, I might be an executive at Pixar today.

Figure 1-4
The light areas around the edges will be cropped to change the aspect ratio of this image

SHOOT WIDE. FIX IT IN POST.

Since I've switched to shooting just digital pictures, I've gotten in the habit of shooting wide pretty much all the time, and then cropping it in the computer. Well, looking at Figure 1-2, I'm not in the habit of shooting that wide, but I do like to make sure I back off or zoom out a little just to make sure I've got plenty of picture to work with later. This trick of zooming out just a bit also takes care of that pesky parallax thing. There's nothing worse than pressing the button for the perfect shot and seeing that you've cut off part of your target, especially if your target is long gone when you see you missed it. Always shoot in high-resolution and a little wide to increase your odds of catching the shot. Sure, you lose a bit of resolution when you crop and zoom in, but if most of your pictures will be seen on a computer screen or on the Web, you've got resolution to burn.

▼ Note

If you don't crop the images to the correct printing aspect ratio before you take them to the drugstore to have them printed, the photo technician will decide which part of the image to crop. Don't let some stranger decide how to crop your pictures!

When you shoot pictures with a film camera and scan them into iPhoto, if you intend to print them out for framing, that will work fine, but you'll have to adjust the aspect ratio if you want to use the images for slideshows or Desktop pictures without the image distorting or getting cropped off willy nilly. Again, you'll be throwing away part of the image, so you need to keep that in mind when composing the picture.

MAKE EVERY PICTURE TELL A STORY

A good photo consists of one or more main subjects, as well as enough additional information to establish a context for the photograph. For example, you might take photos of family members during a vacation. The family member(s) are the main subject, but you should be able to see enough background to get an idea where the photo was taken. If you *aren't* careful about getting enough context, all your photos tend to end up looking the same. You've all seen those pictures. There's the family all standing in the same formation with their arms at their sides and the same tired smiles on their faces but with a different background in each shot. You shouldn't be in a rut when you take pictures. Take a look at Figure 1-5. I'm just riding on a train and looking out the window, but the layout of the image with the reflection in the glass and the blur of scenery streaking by makes this a much more dramatic picture.

Figure 1-5

Good composition can make a rainy train ride look cool

▼ **Note**

The obvious exception to including a lot of background is when you are taking portraits. With a portrait, the whole point is to get a good-quality image of an individual. Even with portraits, however, including some background that doesn't clash with the portrait can lead to a better picture. You can see an example of such a portrait in Figure 1-6.

YOUR OWN PERSONAL SERIES

You don't have to think of every picture as an island. Shoot a sequence of shots that work together. Use wide shots to establish the scenery, medium shots to show more details, and close-ups to show the highlights. With iPhoto, you can make slideshows or print books that really make a picture sequence work.

For example, some friends of mine took my camera over to Ground Zero in New York City several months after the September 11, 2001, terrorist attacks. They took a few pictures of the area that work together as shown in Figures 1-7, 1-8, and 1-9.

Figure 1-7
Ground Zero crater

Figure 1-6
Even portraits can have some interesting background

Figure 1-8
Memorial wall

Figure 1-9
Close-up of tributes

COMPOSE YOUR PHOTOS CAREFULLY

It can sometimes be hard to tell exactly what the photographer was trying to capture when he or she took the picture. You can help someone viewing the picture understand the subject by using parts of the background to guide the

viewer's eye toward the main subject(s). A line of trees, a road, railroad tracks, or other objects can guide the viewer's eye. Figure 1-10 uses a weathered fence on a beach on Maui to focus the viewer's attention right where I wanted it. The picturesque nature of the fence doesn't hurt, either!

Figure 1-10
Use elements in the picture to direct the viewer's attention where you want it

TAKE LOTS OF PICTURES

Digital pictures literally cost nothing to take, so don't be shy about pressing the button. Shooting several shots of the same subject comes in real handy when you aren't sure of the lighting. Take a picture using the camera's default settings, and then adjust the exposure compensation controls (assuming your cameras has these) and take more pictures using varying exposure settings. Later, you can look at them and choose the best one, or use a powerful tool such as Photoshop Elements to combine elements from multiple pictures to get a perfect shot. To paraphrase a cliché from the publishing industry: *The first picture you take with your camera costs $500. The second picture is free.*

 Tip

Taking lots of pictures uses up space on your memory cards, so get a large-capacity card or two. A 512MB card in a 3-megapixel camera at the largest JPEG setting has enough space for about 300 shots before you have to download your files to the computer. With a 5-megapixel camera you can get around 200. Load up on batteries, too, because you'll run out of juice long before you fill up a good-sized card in most cases. Oh, and yes, that 16MB card that comes with most cameras *is* a joke. It's just not a very *funny* joke. At the highest quality setting on my camera, that 16MB card will hold *one* picture. "Yeehaw! We're havin' fun now! Click. Oops. Gotta download."

CHECK YOUR WORK

Digital pictures may not cost anything to take, but get in the habit of reviewing your pictures in the LCD as often as possible. Those pictures get mighty expensive if you have to fly back to Paris because your camera was in a funky mode and every picture you took was totally underexposed. And, no, I don't think your boss will accept that excuse as a reason why you have to go back to Paris and double your vacation days.

Most cameras pull up the last picture on the LCD with the push of a single button, and then you can usually toggle through all the pictures on the card from there.

We've all seen that family reunion shot. (See Figure 1-11 for mine.) You know the one, where the naughty nephew

sticks out his tongue just as everybody else is saying "cheese." That nephew is the one who grows up to be the guy who puts up bunny ears behind people every chance he gets. You know who I'm talking about. I've got a couple of them in my own family.

Reviewing your photos immediately will help you head off problems like that. One thing to remember though is that the LCD does take up a fair amount of juice. It will run your battery down faster when you have the LCD turned on. Just how much faster depends on your camera. I prefer to load up on extra batteries and use the LCD all the time, but if you need to get the longest life out of your battery charge, use the LCD sparingly.

Figure 1-11
There's one in every family (I may have been *partly* to blame in this case though)

 Tip

To find little glitches like the family prankster just mentioned, you may have to zoom in on the picture in the LCD. It's pretty small and it doesn't give you much detail. However, on most cameras, just by pressing a few buttons, you can zoom in on part of the picture and then move around the image with the camera's navigation buttons.

PAY ATTENTION TO THE LIGHT

Most of today's digital cameras work great in auto mode where it takes care of all the exposure settings on the fly regardless of the conditions. There are times, however, when the camera won't catch what *you* want it to catch. Lighting sources are critical to making great pictures. Lighting sources are also responsible for a great deal of bad pictures.

Essentially, all cameras like lighting that is relatively even. If there is too much contrast between the brightest point in your picture and the darkest point, you'll end up losing something somewhere. Figure 1-12 is a shot I took in Zurich, Switzerland, in 1998 when there was a citywide art display called CowParade. The sculpture was under a shade tree, and the bright sun reflecting off the sidewalk dominated the picture. This was before I'd gone digital so I was going by the exposure meter in the camera and I got burned for it. The picture was underexposed and the *Harley-Davidson Motor Cycles* emblem on the cow's forehead is barely visible in the print. Care to guess what made me want to take that picture? Yup, the Harley emblem. DOH!

If I'd taken that picture with a digital camera instead of a film camera, I could have spotted the exposure problem in the LCD. I would have squatted down so the sidewalk would be out of the frame and the picture would have been what I was hoping for instead of what I ended up with.

There are a number of things you can do to combat uneven light. The first thing you can try is to use "open shade." Open shade is what you get when your subject stands in a big shadow but with plenty of ambient light around. Essentially you're just trying to get people out of direct sunlight so you don't have harsh shadows messing with you. As an added bonus, open shade will cut down on squinting shots big time!

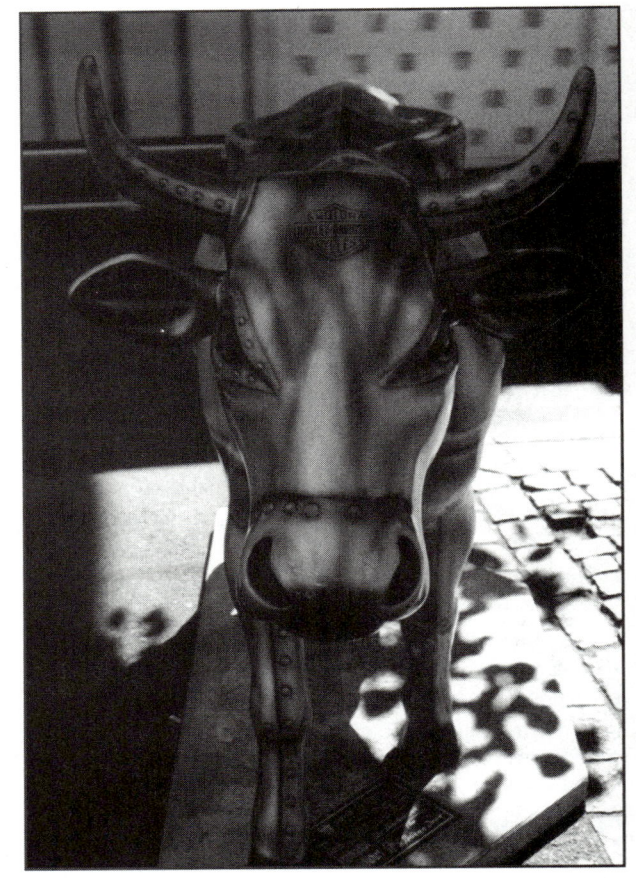

Figure 1-12
You can't always trust your automatic features

Another way to deal with uneven light — especially the harsh shadows around midday — is to use "fill flash." Basically, your camera has a flash that is meant to provide light on a subject when there is insufficient ambient light. But on most cameras, you can force the flash to fire even when there is sufficient light to take the picture. If your subject isn't too far away, the flash can fill in the shadows (hence the name fill flash). Be careful not to overdo it, however, because the flash can provide too much light. If that happens, try

LIGHT SPOTTING

Here's a fun activity you can do while watching your favorite TV show. Make a note of how many lamps on the set are turned on. Probably not many. Additional light sources in your shot kill your picture. The gaffer typically sets up the lights you do see in sitcoms and movies on dimmers so he can control the brightness in a typical 60-watt bulb. He probably will lower the output to something in the 5- to 15-watt range. Nightlights are usually about 4 watts. The lights that fill up the room are all out of frame so you don't see them in the picture.

When you see people sitting in a diner on a bright, sunny day by the window, the film crew has put up big sheets of tinting film that cover the windows to dim them. Without that window tinting, the director would have to choose either the people inside or the scene going on outside. Make the people look good and the outside is just a white field. Make the outside look good and the people are just black silhouettes. The window tinting evens out the light window so the director can see both the people and the background.

I'm assuming you don't have professional film crews working with you on your vacations, so the moral to this story is to keep away from putting people in front of bright windows or lamps. Position yourself so that windows and your light source (or the sun) are to the side or behind you and your pictures will work much better. Of course, there's nothing wrong with a nice silhouette shot if that's what you *want* to shoot. Just know what to expect.

In the shot in Figure 1-13, I wanted the sculpture and the torches to be completely in silhouette with the sunset filling the background. I used the high contrast for effect. Now why is the boy in the sculpture holding a sea turtle by the legs? That's another artist's statement. Don't ask me.

Figure 1-13
Silhouette can be sweet

backing up from your subject a bit to reduce the flash intensity and using the optical zoom to ensure that the subject is the size you want. Figures 1-14 and 1-15 show the differences between shooting a portrait without fill flash (1-14) and filling in the shadows with the flash (1-15).

Figure 1-14
Without fill flash, the setting sun puts the foreground all in shadow

Figure 1-15
Use fill flash to fill in the shadows and bring out the details of the image

COMPENSATE FOR A SLOW CAMERA

One big advantage old-school film cameras have over digital cameras is the quick draw. My camera takes a full 5 seconds to "boot up" when you turn it on. Those 5 seconds have cost me more hot shots than I care to admit. There's not really much I can do about it short of buying bigger and better equipment, but it is something to keep in mind when you like to *catch* shots instead of set up shots. A point-and-shoot camera would catch those shots but, hey, I've turned into an LCD junkie now. I can't imagine shooting photos without it. I'll stick with the occasional miss. I have gotten in the habit of flipping the power switch as soon as I touch the camera instead of after I get it up to my face. That shaves a little time off, but I could still use more.

On a related note, digital cameras usually go to sleep to save battery life. On mine, hitting any button will wake up the camera. Again, waking up takes time. In my case, 3 seconds. That's better, but I could still use more.

The place many people notice digital cameras lagging is when they actually take the picture. Mine has nearly a 2-second delay between the press of the button and the actual shutter click. Believe me, compared to the early consumer digital cameras, that is pretty darned good. But, this can drive you nuts on a moving target. That's a lesson you learn the hard way when you're trying to capture the cliff divers in Acapulco. Why are digital cameras so much slower than film cameras? There are two reasons. The first is that the camera has to focus on the subject and calculate the exposure. Most film cameras have to do that too, but many inexpensive film cameras can skip the focus step (which is what takes the longest) because they are fixed-focus cameras — anything farther away than about 6 feet is in focus. With a digital camera, by the time you get your subject in focus, the picture is gone. Using manual focus can cut your lag time in half, but manual focusing on a pocket camera is a pain and may not even be an option.

On the highest quality setting on my camera, it takes 6 seconds to save a picture to the card. It will let me fire off a second shot after about 3 seconds, but shooting off shots as fast as you can pull the trigger isn't an option. There are some cameras today that do have that ability, but they're up over the $1,000 mark, which is a bit out of reach of most consumers. Those cameras have a fast buffer that stores the pictures in memory so you don't have to wait for the buffer to finish dumping to the card. The buffer saves the shots to the card in the background and eventually catches up when you stop rapid firing, but that saving can take a while if you're shooting uncompressed TIFFs on a 5-megapixel camera. Those can be up around 14MB each. With most consumer digital cameras, while the camera is saving to the card, you're stuck watching a little flashing light and you can't do anything else.

If you use your noggin, you can beat all these lagging issues. Take that cliff diver, for example. You know he's coming, so you have your camera on and ready. Next, you have to deal with the autofocus. Most cameras will autofocus when you press the trigger button down halfway, so aim at the cliff wall and half press the trigger. Now the camera is on and focused off in the distance. After that it's a matter of getting the diver in the sweet spot when the camera takes the picture. This one was a bit of trial and error with an assistant spotter saying "He's juuuumpiiiiiiing NOW!" every time a diver took the plunge. Zooming out a tad so the frame covered more space helped increase the sweet spot (see Figure 1-16).

By contrast, in Figure 1-17 my buddies and I showed up when nobody was diving at all so we had to fake it. It's not much of an action shot, but the view was nice. On the bright side, my buddies were moving much slower than those free-falling divers, so I got that shot in one take.

Figure 1-16
Even the fast-moving cliff divers of Acapulco can be caught with a digital camera... just not on the first shot

Figure 1-17
The cliff divers weren't diving at this point, so we just had to do it ourselves

Lag time varies pretty wildly from camera to camera. When reviewing the specifications for a camera, this information is often provided. For example, the camera literature may mention the ability to take up to six pictures at two frames per second. If you tend to take a lot of action shots, you are going to want to give this specification more weight than someone who is mostly interested in shooting landscapes.

 Tip

Another way to capture a fast-moving subject is to tilt or pan the camera with the action. In the cliff divers example, tracking the camera down would keep the diver in the frame for a longer time. Provided you are using a fast shutter speed (which you should be for action shots), you should be able to freeze the action. Depending on how fast you're moving the camera, the background will tend to blur; but hey, nothing says fast-paced action and adventure like a bit of motion blur!

So there you go! All there is to know about photography in one little chapter! Yeah, I didn't think you'd buy that one. Photography is all about freezing the moving world around us. *Professional* photography is all about taking lots and lots and lots of pictures and never showing anybody the bad ones. I'm only half way joking there. To take a single picture you see in a magazine, the photographer might take two dozen pictures that look almost exactly the same just so he can get the eyes just right or the wind blowing the hair a certain way. Take lots of pictures. Even a bad picture will teach you what not to do. Digital cameras are very liberating. You don't have to worry about wasting film any more, so take lots and lots and lots of pictures. You don't have to show anybody the bad ones.

Getting Started with iPhoto

In This Chapter

Starting iPhoto • Understanding the workflow for editing and organizing images
Introducing each of the iPhoto modes • Setting up the iPhoto interface to suit your tastes
Setting the iPhoto preferences for the way you work

So iPhoto... what can it do for *you?* The short of it is that iPhoto imports images, keeps them organized, lets you do a smattering of editing, and then makes sharing your work in all sorts of ways a cinch. Sure it's got a lot of buttons, but iPhoto's not that intimidating once you get a feel for it. iPhoto has four modes, and parts of the interface change from mode to mode, but like all of Apple's iApps, it's pretty easy to work with. Lots of people *think* they know how to use iPhoto, but when I'm done with you, you'll *know* you know iPhoto.

LAUNCH IPHOTO

Just like any other application, you can fire up iPhoto in several ways:

- Open the Applications folder and double-click the iPhoto icon.

- If iPhoto is already installed in the Dock, you can single-click the icon there.

- If you've recently opened iPhoto, you can choose it from the Apple ➜ Recent Items menu.

> ### ▼ Note
>
> If iPhoto isn't already in your Dock, do yourself a favor and add it. At least keep it in there while you're working with this book because you'll want to play along for a lot of this. To make iPhoto a semipermanent fixture of your Dock, try one of these:
>
> - Drag the iPhoto icon in your Applications folder down to the Dock.
> - If iPhoto is already running, Control+click on the icon in the Dock and select Keep In Dock from the menu.
> - If iPhoto is already running, simply reposition the icon in the Dock to the left or right.
>
> Any of those tricks keeps that icon nice and handy until you drag the icon out of the Dock.

FIRST LAUNCH POP QUIZ

The first time you launch iPhoto, you get a dialog box you'll see only this once (see Figure 2-1). The top 80 percent of that dialog box is a bunch of promotional fluff welcoming you to iPhoto, but the bottom 20 percent is where you find the important stuff. This 20 percent determines what happens when you plug a camera into your computer. You have the following choices:

- If you select Use Other, iPhoto does *not* automatically launch when a camera is attached to your computer.

- Choosing Decide Later pulls up the question again at the next launch.

- If you choose Use iPhoto, when you connect a still camera to your computer, iPhoto automatically launches — if it's not already running — and switches into Import mode.

For most of you, curtain three is the ideal choice. If you want to change this behavior later, you can change the

setting with an application called Image Capture. I discuss Image Capture more in Chapter 3.

Figure 2-1
Welcome to iPhoto — time to do a little setup

UNDERSTAND THE IPHOTO MODES AND WORKFLOW

Let's break down using iPhoto a bit. The modes used by iPhoto are Import, Organize, Edit, and Book.

Import images

The first order of business is getting your pictures into iPhoto. You can bring them in from your hard drive or from a CD. With a little help from outside of iPhoto, you can even scan pictures in from prints and negatives. Of course, where iPhoto really shines is when it works with your digital camera (or its memory card, at any rate). The Import mode is dedicated to, well, importing stuff like that. Read more on Import in Chapter 3.

Organize your photos

Piles of unorganized pictures, either in the real world or inside your computer, aren't very helpful. Fortunately, iPhoto lets you sort and group your photos several different ways. You can add keywords to pictures to make them easier to find, and you can even rate your photos on a five-star rating system so you can quickly pick out your best work. Organization is covered in Chapters 4–6, but Organize mode is also where you share your pictures. Face it. The reason you take pictures is to show them to people. Well, I suppose some people take pictures to get paid not to show them to people, but none of us are like that, so I focus on getting your pictures out to the masses. With iPhoto, it's a cinch to package up your pictures and distribute them in a number of ways: You got your printer, your slideshow, your email, and even good old-fashioned lab prints. You can make Web pages. You can make DVDs for your TV. You can make a special slideshow for a .Mac account (if you have one, that is). Templates for all sorts of fun stuff are built into iPhoto. Sharing your pictures is where you really get your PC friends saying, "How'd you do that? That's awesome!" I go over all these sharing tools in Chapters 10–15.

Edit the images

I don't think I've ever seen a perfect picture right out of the camera. Most photographs can benefit from a slight bit of editing. In the Edit mode, iPhoto has the tools to tweak your images so they pop a little better. You can adjust the brightness and contrast, or paint out a freckle. You can crop out your ex-girlfriend. Edit mode is covered in Chapters 7 and 8.

Publish your own *book*

Apple includes a Book setup mode where you can work a collection of photos into several book template pages.

A QUICK BEEF

Personally, *I* think the major button headings should be Import, Organize, Edit, and Share. Printing out pictures isn't something that helps me organize my collection. Putting a picture on my Desktop or emailing it to a friend has nothing to do with organizing either. I'm sure an Apple executive decreed that iPhoto should steer everybody towards the book at all times because that button puts money in their pockets, but sticking the buttons that should go under Share in the Organize area just feels wrong to me. I'd feel much better if they'd compromise and have *five* buttons: Import, Organize, Edit, Share, and Book.

All right, there, I said my piece. (Now let's see if my editor takes issue with me working subliminal messages to the programmers at Apple into this book.)

[*If you can change the minds of a major corporation, good for you. You succeed with this, I'll contract you to get Congress to lower my taxes...-ed.*]

After you have the book designed, you can send it off to the printer with just a few clicks. In a matter of days, you'll be holding your very own hard-bound photo book. The book is cool. The book knocks 'em dead every time. I cover the Book mode in Chapters 16–19.

NAVIGATE IN IPHOTO

The iPhoto interface is simple and well laid out for the most part. You've got the four buttons near the bottom for Import, Organize, Edit, and Book. Each of those buttons brings up a different interface specially designed for that mode. Figure 2-2 shows how iPhoto looks in Organize mode, where you can arrange your photos, change their sort order, and make decisions about how to share them.

A PRIMER ON FILE TYPES

A lot of file types have evolved over the years; some are better than others for photographs. iPhoto can read many of the popular file types, and in most cases, iPhoto preserves the original file type when you edit the image. But which type of file should you use? Here is a brief explanation of the most popular image file types:

JPEG. JPEG is the file type of choice for most photographs. JPEGs can be opened and displayed by any browser. JPEG files are compressed when they are saved, so they do lose quality; however, you can control the degree of compression, balancing file size with the quality of the image. Large files (less compression) preserve more information (and therefore, photo quality), and smaller files are more compressed and can be visibly degraded. High-quality JPEGs take up far less room than TIFFs; but because JPEGs lose information each time they are saved, working on a photo as a TIFF file and then converting it to a JPEG file if you are going to email or post the photo on the Web is actually better (iPhoto does this conversion for you automatically — see Chapter 15).

CompuServe GIF. A GIF file is a good choice for clipart and other images that don't require more than the 256 colors that a GIF can handle. Smooth color gradations (such as in photographs) don't work well with GIFs because they simply don't have enough colors available. GIFs are also compressed when you save them, but unlike JPEGs, no information is lost during compression aside from the limited color palette.

TIFF. TIFF is also a good choice for storing photographs. But the files can be really huge, and browsers can't read TIFFs without a special plug-in. Fortunately, QuickTime is just the plug-in you need to read most (but not all) flavors of TIFF. Some multipage, funky fax TIFFs are out there that still won't work in QuickTime, but anything you get out of a photo-editing program shouldn't be a problem. TIFFs can also have multiple layers and other special info depending on how you save the file. If preserving all the picture quality is important, TIFFs work very well.

PSD. This is the native format for Photoshop and Photoshop Elements. This sophisticated file format preserves all the information needed by these programs, including layers and layer masks. Like TIFFs, PSD files get really, really big; but also like TIFFs, no information is lost when the file is saved.

RAW. Digital cameras have a special file format that preserves all the information recorded by the camera. This information can be used by special applications (supplied with the camera) to make very fine adjustments to the image, and convert the result into a more "normal" format. However, each camera manufacturer has its own RAW format, and iPhoto cannot read RAW files until you use the conversion program to, well, convert the file into JPEG, GIF, TIFF, or PSD. When set to take pictures in RAW mode, most cameras have the RAW file and also a second JPEG file the camera uses for quick reference. When you import the pictures with iPhoto, the program brings in the JPEGs and tells you it couldn't figure out the rest. Most mortals are just fine with the best JPEG setting, or with a TIFF if you're being anal. If you're reading this book, odds are RAW isn't really meant for you; but don't worry, it's not meant for me either.

Albums

Smart albums

Source pane

Display pane

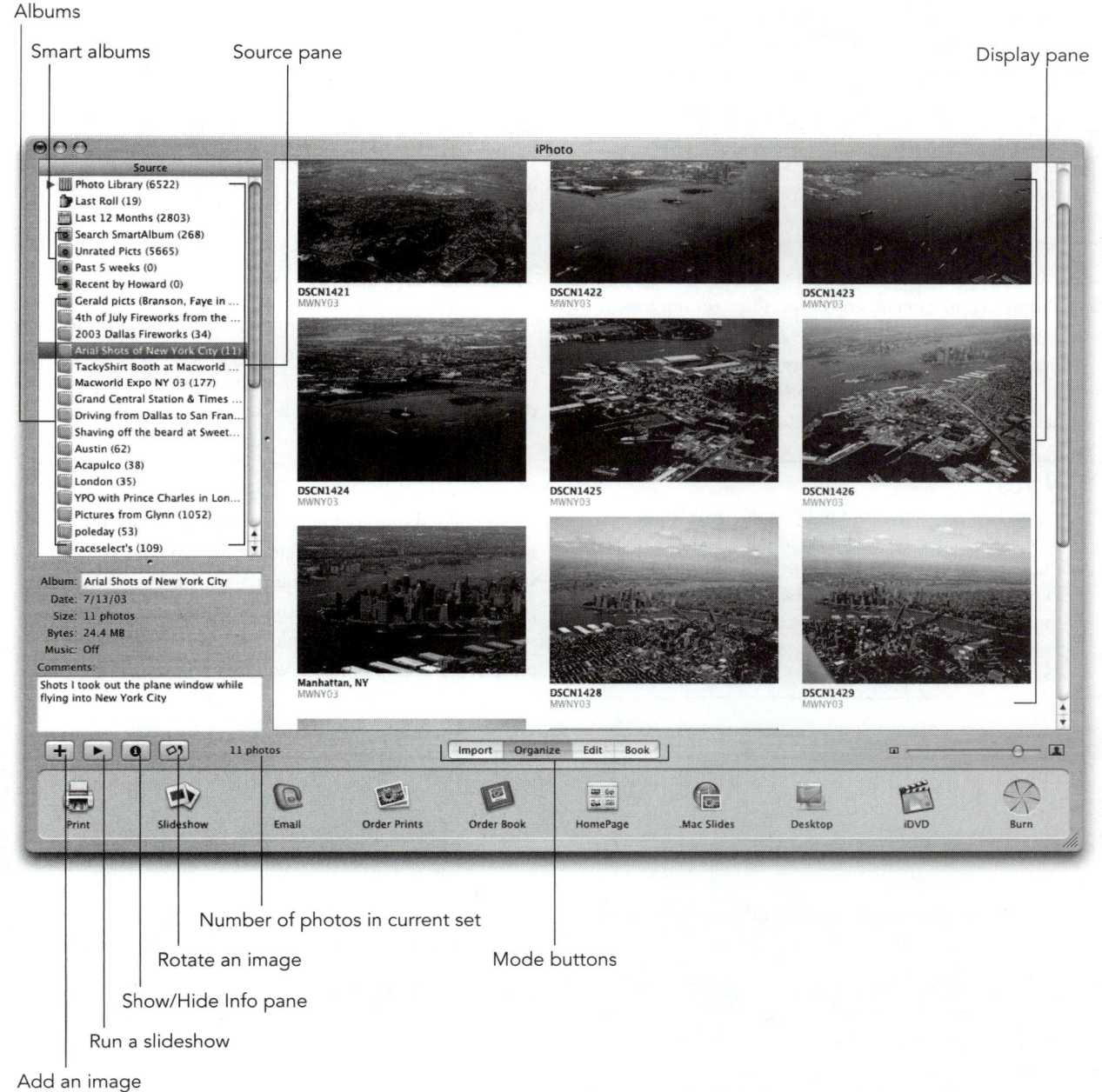

Number of photos in current set

Rotate an image

Mode buttons

Show/Hide Info pane

Run a slideshow

Add an image

Figure 2-2

The Organize mode interface shows the main elements for working in iPhoto

Edit mode is where you make the changes to your photos, so here you'll find editing tools for adjusting brightness and contrast, removing red-eye, and so on (see Figure 2-3).

▼ **Note**

Not many people know that you can also edit an image in a separate window. I cover that special version of the interface in Chapter 8.

You use Import mode to bring in photos from an external source, like a digital camera, an iPhoto share on the network, or a CD. The Import interface (see Figure 2-4) displays details about any connected cameras or card readers, a button to start the import, and a progress bar to show how much longer your import will take.

▼ **Note**

Except for importing from digital cameras, you don't have to be in the Import mode to import images into iPhoto. You can use File ➜ Import and choose the source from which to import. This technique is covered along with Import mode in Chapter 3. Then there's also that whole Mac way of life I like to call *drag and drop*.

In Book mode you get all the controls you need to turn a group of pictures into a book. You can choose from several different themes, arrange your pictures, and add display text and whatnot. When you're done, you can have the book professionally printed or print the pages out on your own printer. Figure 2-5 shows the special tools you use to work on these books.

TIPS AND TALKBACK

Apple hosts a Web page to provide hints and tips for using iPhoto (see Figure 2-6). The info on this site is fairly basic, but it does have a nice list of keyboard shortcuts. To access the Hot Tips Web page, make sure you are online and choose iPhoto ➜ iPhoto Hot Tips.

If you have your own ideas about how you think Apple could make iPhoto better, you can send in your opinions with the built-in link. Remember that you're a voice in a very large crowd, so keep your comments short and to the point. Apple is looking for trends: If thousands of people submit that the library should work better with more photos, for example, Apple will focus on fulfilling that

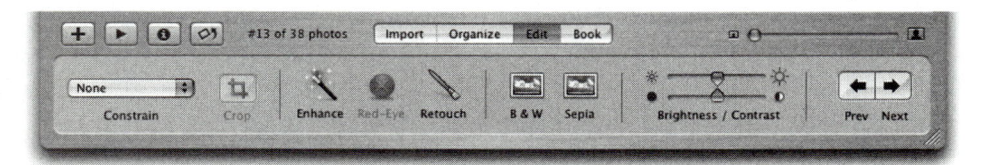

Figure 2-3

Use the tools in Edit mode to, well, edit your images

Figure 2-4

Import images from external sources with Import mode

Page thumbnails

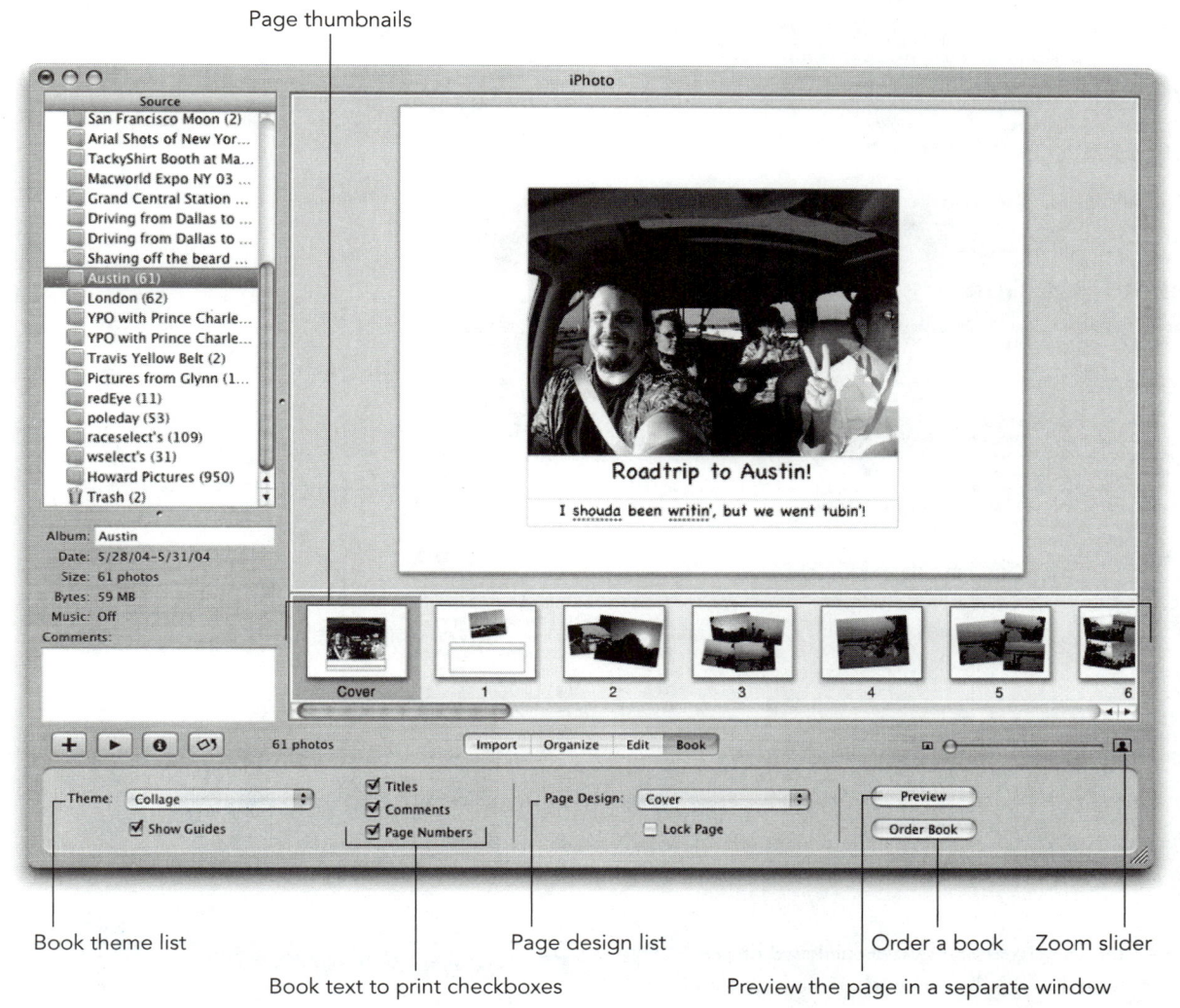

Book theme list

Book text to print checkboxes

Page design list

Order a book   Zoom slider

Preview the page in a separate window

Figure 2-5

Construct a book suitable for printing and giving as a gift with Book mode

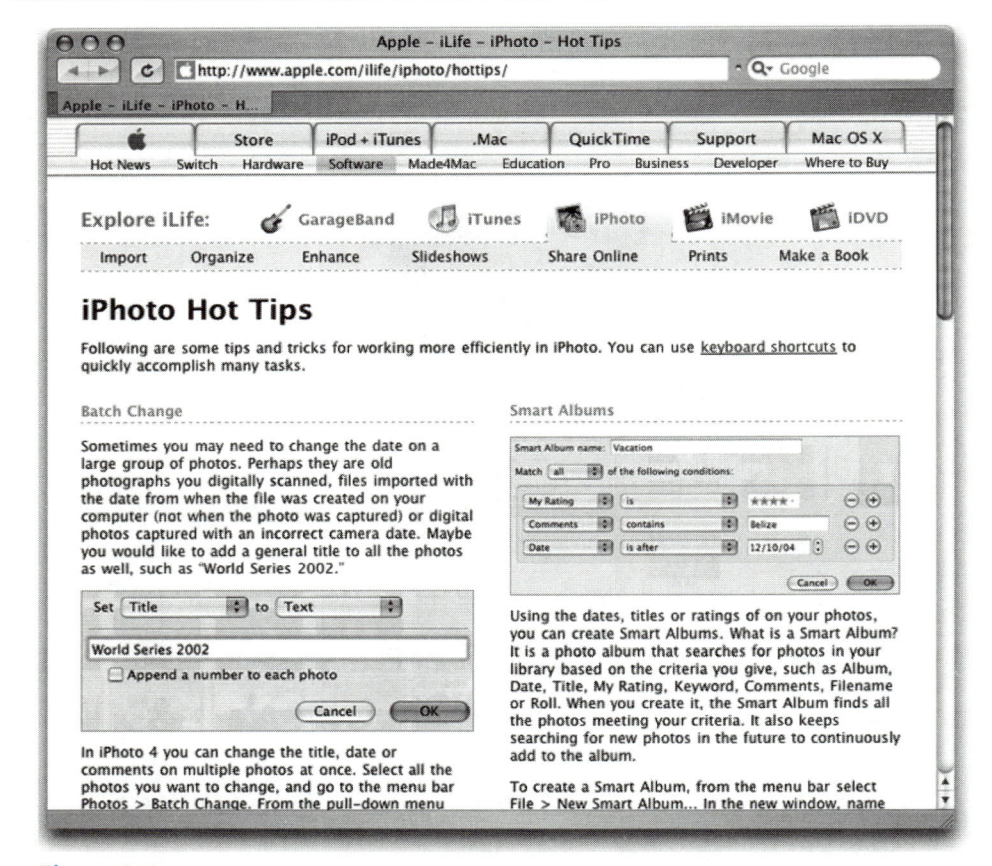

Figure 2-6

Check Apple's idea of "hot tips" for iPhoto on the Internet

request — and they fixed that exact issue based on feedback for version 4. Apple listens to what you have to say, but don't expect a reply. You won't get one.

To give Apple feedback on bugs or improvements you'd like to see, make sure you are connected to the Internet and choose iPhoto Provide iPhoto Feedback. This opens the iPhoto Feedback Web page (see Figure 2-7), where you can fill in your information, record your suggestions, and submit your ideas to Apple.

▼ **Note**

Unfortunately, Apple doesn't publicly keep a list of the top 10 beefs people have reported with iPhoto. Just because you don't know if you're in tune with the rest of the users doesn't mean you shouldn't make suggestions. Many of the improvements in iLife '04 came from people who used the software and weren't quite satisfied with it. At any rate, sometimes it just feels good to rage against the machine! Don't bottle up those feelings. Let Apple know how you feel!

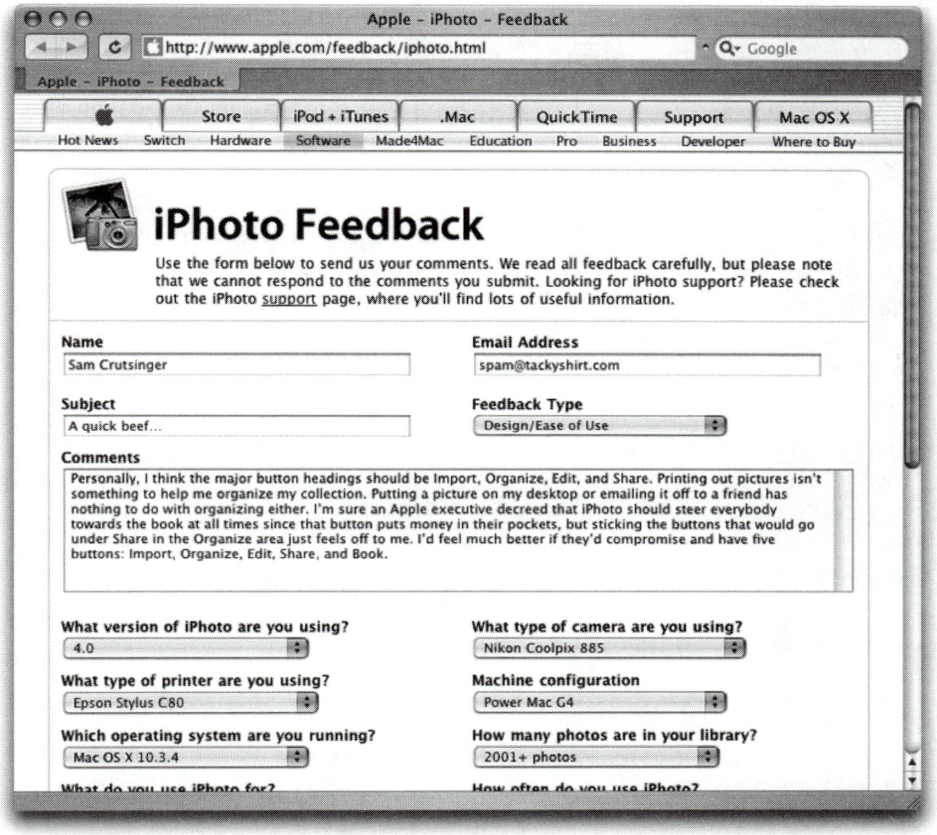

Figure 2-7

Send your good ideas to Apple via the iPhoto Feedback Web page

REGISTER IPHOTO

Product registration has gotten a bit of a bad rap. Many places just use registration to collect personal data so they can sell it to annoying telemarketers and spammers. Apple isn't one of those places.

I *always* register all my Apple products. That track history really comes in handy when you have problems later. Face it, when you're calling for support and they see a long registration history of new Macs, purchases of every OS

upgrade, and several software packages and peripherals, that just says to the person on the other end that you're a loyal customer, not some thieving pirate.

When dealing with a bum installer on another application, my diligent registration habit let me skip over a bunch of red tape because the guy said, "It's okay. I see here that you've got registrations for every version back to version 1.0, and two on version 2.0. Don't worry about it. I'll get that replacement disk out to you today." Without my good record, I'd have had to fax in all sorts of receipts and other documents. I'm sure if I gave out that person's name, they'd get in trouble for taking a shortcut in my case; but people are people, and that guy cut me a break because of product registrations. Your mileage may vary, but registering doesn't hurt, and as long as you uncheck that box for Apple to send you updates and notices, you won't get pestered.

Oh yeah, and send yourself an email with your Apple ID info so you don't forget what email address you gave them when you made the account (like I did). If you create a new Apple ID because you forgot your old one, you just started over, and all that old track history won't do you any good.

To register iPhoto, make sure you're on the Net, and then choose iPhoto ➡ Register iPhoto to open the Apple Product Registration Web page. From there, do the following steps:

1. **Choose your language and location (country).** The page automatically switches to a page where you can log in with your Apple ID (see Figure 2-8).

Hyperlink

Figure 2-8

Register any Apple product on the Apple Product Registration Web page

2. **If you don't have an Apple ID, you can create one.** You do this by clicking on the *create one* hyperlink in the second paragraph on the right and filling in your information.

3. **Follow the screen prompts to register any Apple product you have.**

 **Tip**

Because you can't avail yourself of many of iPhoto's capabilities without an Apple ID, creating one and registering the product isn't a bad idea.

The registration process is pretty self-explanatory until you get to Step 5 (see Figure 2-9). The Marketing Part Number requested when registering iLife '04 is the number on the label on the bottom of the box with a bar code. It should be something along the lines of: M5432LL/A.

CONFIGURE THE INTERFACE

iPhoto offers a few options for customizing the interface so you can get your work done faster. First of all, you can change the width of the Source pane on the left side of the screen (which also changes the width of the Info pane located just below it).

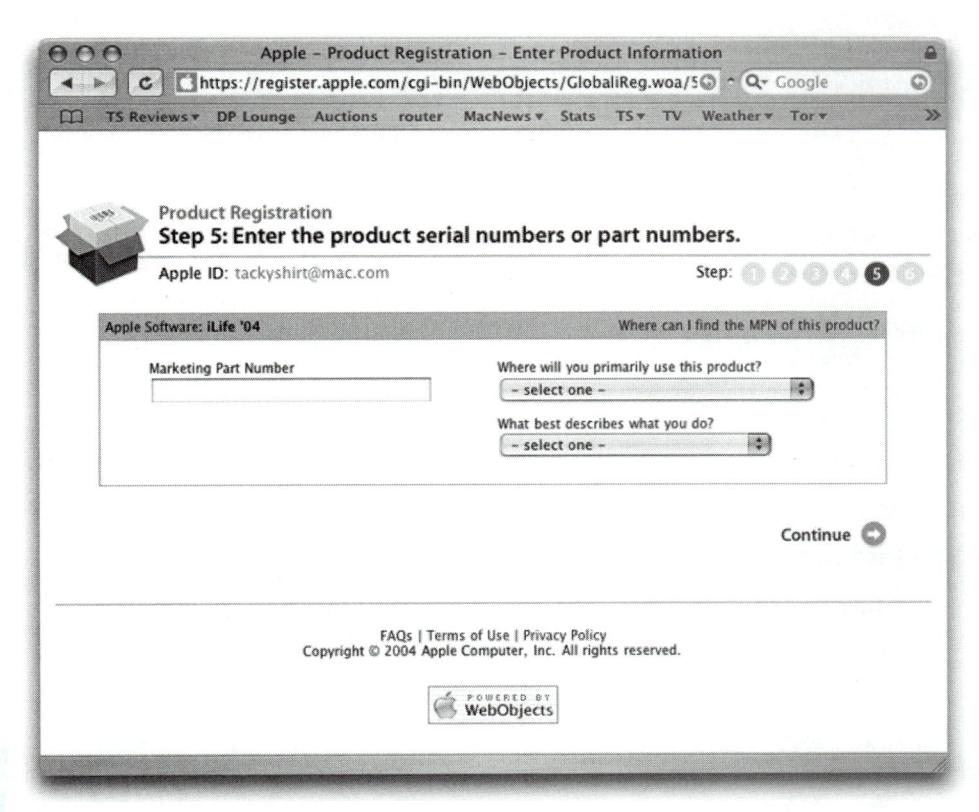

Figure 2-9
Step 5 can be confusing

Resize the Source pane

The Source pane is full of wonderful info which is all good and well when you need it, but sometimes you just want it to get out of the way so you can see more of your pretty pictures onscreen at once. Not a problem.

To resize the Source pane:

1. **Move the mouse pointer over the bar separating the Source pane and the Display pane.** The pointer becomes a double-headed arrow (see Figure 2-10).

2. **Click and drag the divider to the left or right to adjust the split between the panes.**

   - **Dragging the divider to the right makes the Source and Info panes wider.** This gives you more room to view long album names and the full contents of the fields in the Info pane (such as the picture title and the date).

   - **Dragging to the left makes the Source and Info panes slimmer, enlarging the Display pane.** This enables you to see more thumbnails in Organize mode, more of a selected picture in Edit mode, and more book page thumbnails and individual pages in Book mode.

3. **When you have the panes sized the way you want, release the mouse button.**

Adjust the Source pane and Info pane split

Those of you who get chatty in the Info pane might need more than a line or two of space to see all you have to say. That window is also adjustable.

You can also adjust the split between the Source pane and the Info pane:

1. **Move the mouse pointer over the bar that separates the two panes (see Figure 2-11).** The pointer becomes a double-headed arrow.

2. **Click and drag the bar up or down to adjust the split between the panes.**

   - **Dragging down increases the height of the Source pane.** This shows you more albums without the need to scroll up and down.

   - **Dragging up increases the height of the Info pane and the size of the Comments field.** This allows you to see longer comments without the need to scroll through the contents of the Comments field.

3. **When you have the panes sized the way you want, release the mouse button.**

You can also control the size and content of the Info pane using the Show/Hide Info pane button (the button with the *i* on it near the lower-left side of the window). Each click of this button adjusts the size of the Info pane. The three sizes are

- **Large.** Shows all the fields in the Info pane, including the Comments field. Figure 2-11 shows the Info pane in its large size.

- **Small.** Shows only Album, Date, Size, Bytes, and Music. The Comments field is hidden.

- **Hidden.** The Info pane is not visible; the Source pane extends all the way down the left side of the window.

Click and drag to adjust the Source pane display width.

Figure 2-10
Adjust the split between the Source pane and the Display pane to give yourself the space you need

MAKE IPHOTO MYPHOTO WITH GENERAL PREFERENCES

The general preferences let you personalize the way iPhoto works and what it shows you. This is where you configure the special albums at the top of the Source pane. It's where you tell iPhoto what external application you

want to use for editing pictures and what email application you prefer to use.

To set the iPhoto general preferences, choose iPhoto ➔ Preferences to open the Preferences dialog box. Then click the General button to display the General dialog box (see Figure 2-12).

Click and drag to adjust the Source pane height

Show/Hide Info pane

Figure 2-11

You can give up album space to see longer comments when you adjust the size of the Source and Info panes

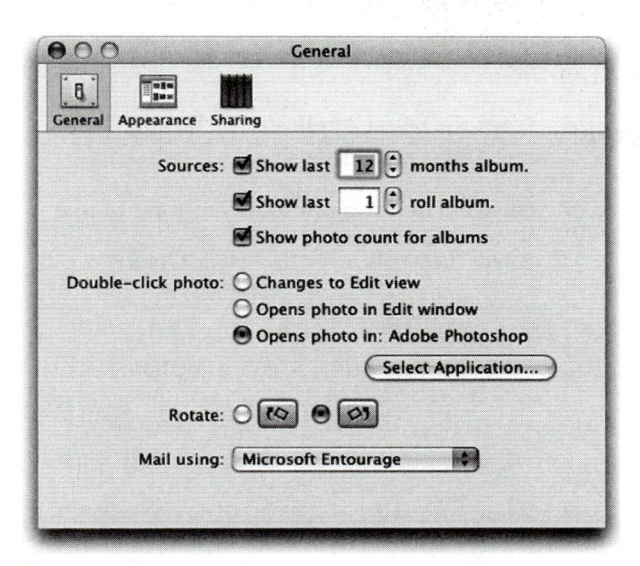

Figure 2-12
Use the General pane of the Preferences dialog box to set the general preferences

 Tip

Changes made to your preferences take effect immediately; you can see the changes without closing the window. You can even leave the Preferences dialog box open and work with iPhoto, opening images for editing, doing imports, and other operations (although why you would want to do that is beyond me).

The four main areas under General are Sources, Double-click photo, Rotate, and Mail.

Sources controls what you see in the Source pane on the left side of iPhoto.

- **Show last... months album.** Select this checkbox to display an album that contains pictures taken within the number of months you specify in the field. The default is 12 months (Figure 2-12). Uncheck the box to remove the album from the Source pane.

- **Show last... roll album.** Check this box to display an album that contains pictures from the most recent imports, called *film rolls* in iPhotospeak. See Chapter 4 for more information on film rolls; but basically, a new film roll is created whenever you import pictures into iPhoto. The default value is only the last roll (the field is set to 1), and this album is visible in the Source pane in Figure 2-12. Deselecting this checkbox removes the album from the Source pane.

- **Show photo count for albums.** Select this checkbox to display the number of images in each source (Photo Library, Last Roll, Smart Albums, Albums, and the Trash) in the Source pane (see Figure 2-13).

Figure 2-13
Display the number of images in each album and the photo library

The options for **Double-click photo** tell iPhoto what you want to happen when you double-click on a picture in Organize mode:

- **Changes to Edit View.** The picture comes up in the Display pane and the tools appear along the bottom as iPhoto switches to Edit mode.

- **Opens photo in Edit window.** The picture opens in a separate window with a configurable toolbar along the top of the window. Using this option enables you to have several images open for editing at once.

- **Opens photo in:** Opens the image in an external photo editor like Adobe Photoshop (regular, or the unleaded version, Elements), Macromedia Fireworks, or whatever application you prefer to use for futzing

SHOOTING IN LANDSCAPE VERSUS PORTRAIT MODE

With very few exceptions, cameras just don't take square pictures. They take rectangles. All of your pictures will be wider than they are tall unless you rotate the camera. If it's wider than tall, that's a *landscape* picture. Think of it as a wide landscape portrait hanging over a sofa. Ever see one of those that's taller than wide? No, because landscapes are wide by definition.

If the picture is more wide than tall, that's a *portrait* picture. Go pull out your yearbook. See all those pimply portraits? Tall and narrow.

Now, can you take a portrait in landscape mode or vice versa? Of course you can. Tall buildings, like Big Ben, scream for portrait orientation; and depending on the background, a landscape-oriented portrait can be amazing.

When you import your pictures, all your portrait-oriented pictures will be laying sideways, so click the image and then click the rotate button to spin the picture 90 degrees in the direction indicated on the arrow.

with photos. These applications give you *many* more options and tools than the basic ones that come in iPhoto. After you make your changes, close the image in the other program (saving changes as you do); you'll be returned to iPhoto, and the image thumbnail

will even update. To specify the external photo editor to use:

1. **Click the Select Application... button.** This opens the Open dialog box.

2. **Navigate to the application you want to use.**

3. **Select the application and click Open.**

 Note

When you Control+click (or right-click if you have a two-button mouse) a thumbnail in Organize mode, the contextual menu enables you to select any of three ways of opening an image for editing: Edit, Edit in Separate Window, and Edit in External Editor. However, the Edit in External Editor item is grayed out and unavailable until you specify an external editor in the General Preferences dialog box.

The two **Rotate** options control which direction an image turns when you click the Rotate button, which is located just below the Info pane. Rotating an image is handy if you had to turn the camera from landscape to portrait to get a good picture.

▼ **Tip**

Take a note of how you hold the camera when you turn it sideways. I turn mine clockwise so the top is to the right; with the LCD, this just feels more natural to me. If you're using the viewfinder though, turning it the other way may feel better. Neither is right or wrong, but if you always find yourself doing the Rotate, Rotate, Rotate dance, swapping the Rotate preference will simplify things (because two wrongs don't make a right, but three lefts do).

Finally, the **Mail** pop-up list lets you pick the email program to use when you want to email photos (see Chapter 14). The pop-up list includes America Online, Eudora, Mail (Apple), and Microsoft Entourage. However, if you don't have a particular email program installed on your Mac, that option is grayed out and the pop-up list is unavailable. The program you select here will determine what icon appears for the Email button in Organize mode. I personally use Entourage for my email, which is why my system has a purple "e" down there instead of the birdie postage stamp of Apple's Mail application (see Figure 2-14).

Figure 2-14
iPhoto nabs your email application's icon

SET THE IPHOTO APPEARANCE PREFERENCES

The Appearance preferences control the cosmetic look of iPhoto. This is where you can add an outline or drop shadow to the pictures in the Display pane. You can also change the background if white is just too bright for your sensitive eyes. You can tell iPhoto to arrange your pictures in straight columns, reverse the sort order, and manipulate the size of the source text in this pane.

To set the Appearance preferences, click the Appearance button in the Preferences dialog box (see Figure 2-15).

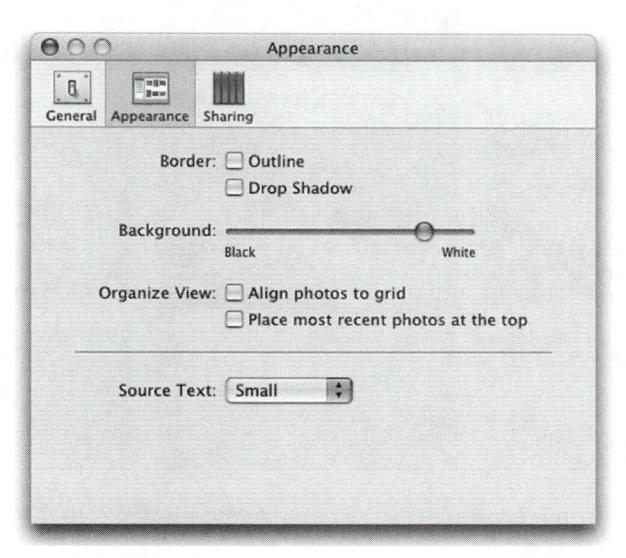

Figure 2-15
Set the Appearance options for iPhoto's behavior with the Appearance preferences dialog box

The four main areas in the Appearance dialog box are Border, Background, Organize View, and Source Text.

Use the **Border** section of the Appearance dialog box to choose the type of border you want pictures to have in Organize mode. You can add an outline and a drop shadow to the thumbnails by checking these boxes. Figure 2-16 shows how the Drop Shadow and Outline options look. You can use either, both, or none. Whatever floats your boat.

None
Outline
Drop Shadow
Outline and Drop Shadow

Figure 2-16
Frame your pictures like you like it

 Note

Displaying a drop shadow or a border may slow down both scrolling and the display of the thumbnails.

The **Background** slider controls the color of the background, ranging from pure white (all the way to the right) to pure black (all the way to the left). Figure 2-17 shows a white vs. dark background.

You have two options for the **Organize View.** Click the Align photos to grid checkbox to place the photos in a grid in which the widest photo sets the size of the grid (see Figure 2-18). This takes up more space than if you unclick the Align photos to grid checkbox (see Figure 2-19). Some people get the feeling that there's order in the universe when they have their pictures all in nice straight columns. I'm more of a chaos theory guy myself, so I like that I can see more stuff at a glance with Align photos to grid turned off.

By default, images in Organize mode are displayed with the oldest pictures at the top. To reverse this order and place the most recent pictures first, select the Place most recent photos at the top checkbox. Interestingly enough, if you choose to view the pictures by title (choose View ➜ Arrange Photos ➜ by Title), selecting this checkbox arranges the images in reverse alphabetical order.

The **Source Text** option simply allows you to choose the size any text appears in the Display pane.

Figure 2-17
A dark background really makes the thumbnails stand out

SET THE IPHOTO SHARING PREFERENCES

One of the more recent features to come to iPhoto is the ability to share your pictures over the local network with other Macs. For those of us with more than one Mac in the house, or in my case, half a dozen, this feature lets you peruse through the pictures that are in the photo libraries on your other computers as long as they're currently running iPhoto and they're on the same local network.

To set the Sharing preferences, click the Sharing button in the Preferences dialog box (see Figure 2-20). This allows you to set the preferences for sharing photos with other Macs on a network.

Click the Look for shared photos option to access copies of iPhoto that are sharing pictures on your network. Any shared albums appear in the Source pane, nested under the shared name specified on the other computer.

To share *all* of your photos with other computers on the network, follow these steps:

1. **Click the Share my photos checkbox.**

2. **Click the Share entire library option.**

To share just *selected albums* (including Smart albums), follow these steps:

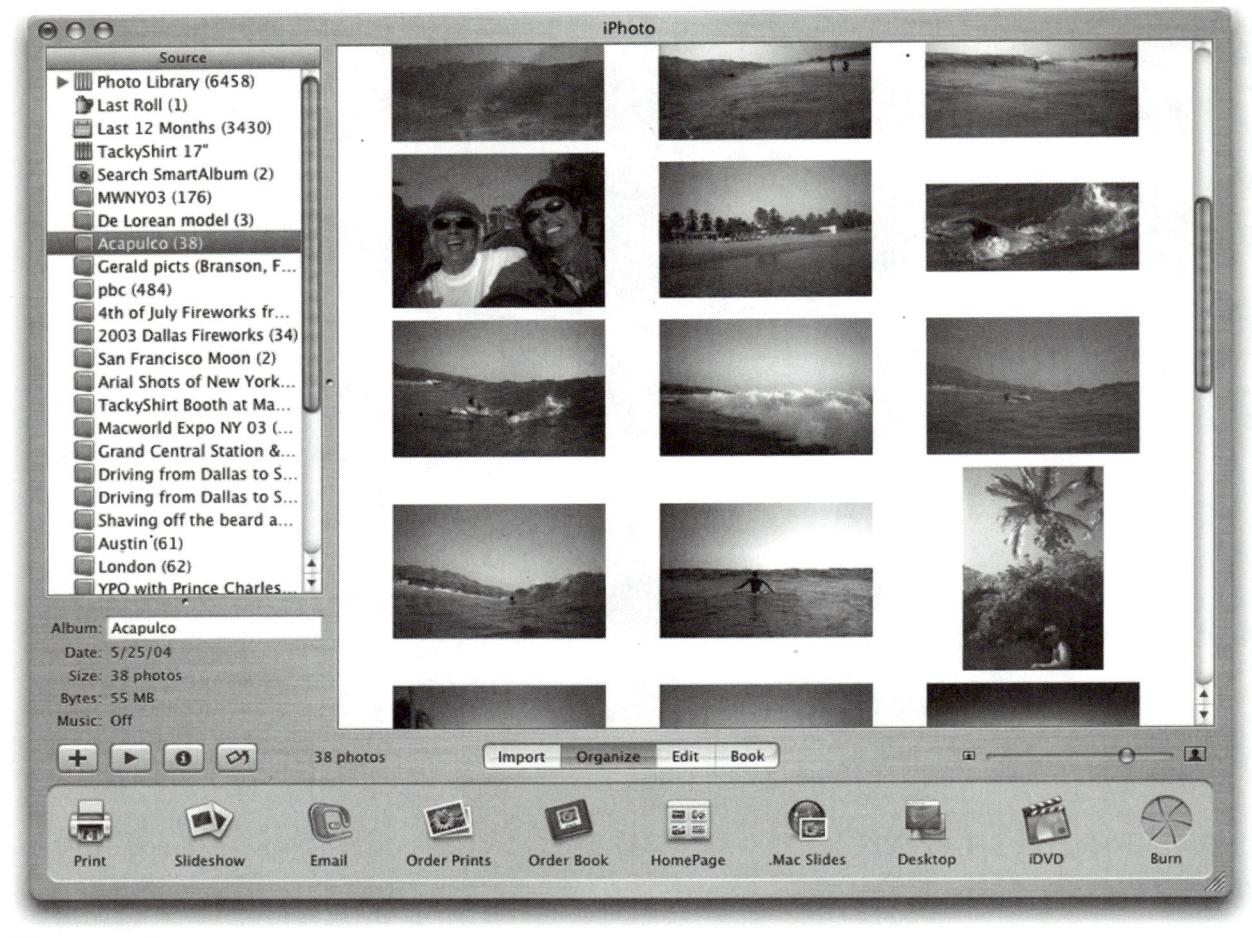

Figure 2-18
Turning on Align photos to grid produces a nice and tidy grid of images

1. **Click the Share my photos checkbox.**

2. **Click the Share selected albums option.**

3. **In the scrolling list of albums, click the checkboxes next to the albums you want to share.**

If you want only users with the correct password to be able to see your photos, follow these steps:

1. **Click the Share my photos checkbox.**

2. **Click either the Share entire library option or the Share selected albums option.** If you click the Share selected albums option, click the checkboxes next to the albums you want to share.

3. **Click the Required password checkbox.**

4. **Type the password into the adjacent field.**

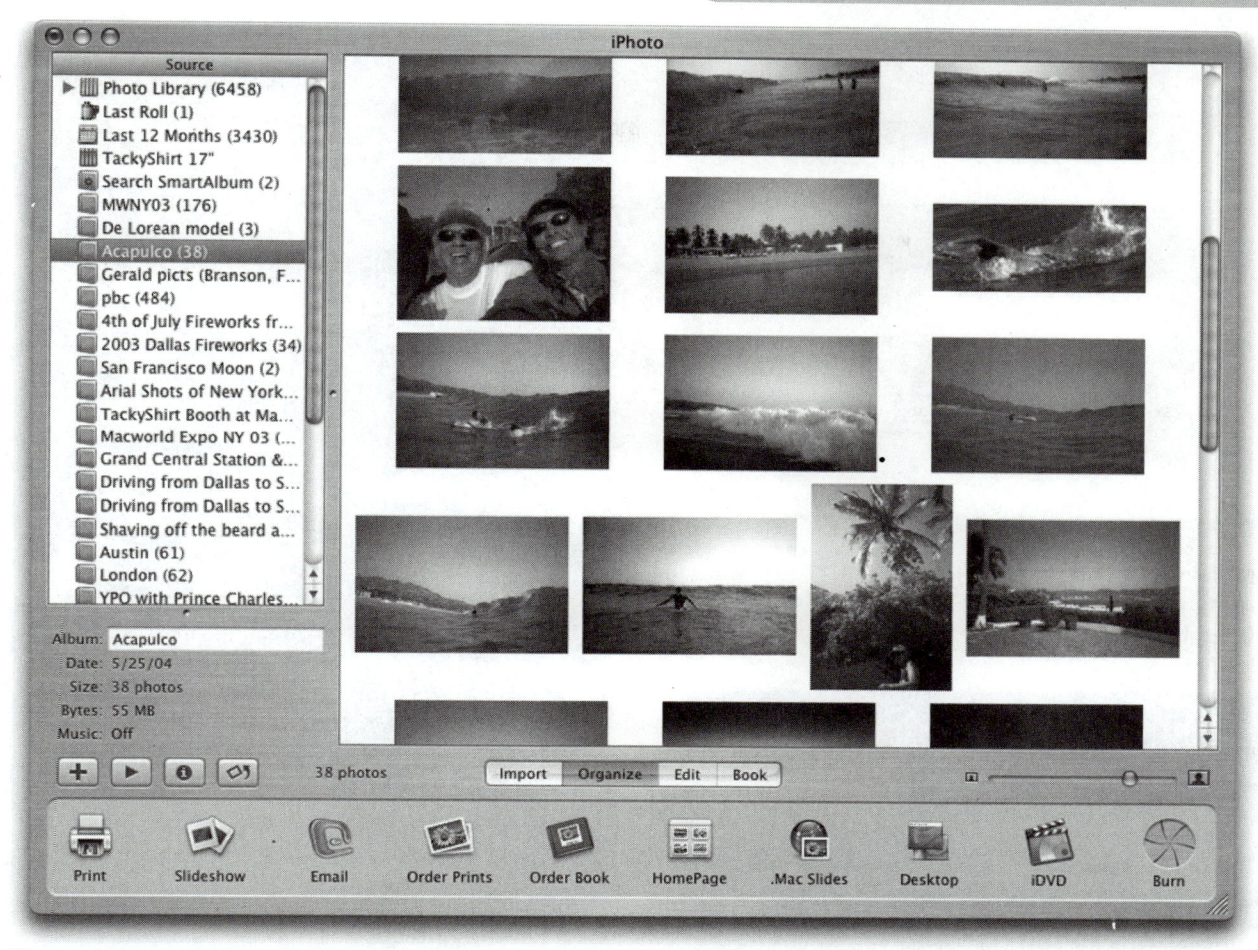

Figure 2-19

Turning off Align photos to grid uses space more efficiently

You can specify the shared name for your albums by typing the name into the Shared name field. Your albums appear on other computers nested under the shared name, identifying those albums as having come from your computer.

You should at least be comfortable with poking around at this point. You may not know what you're poking yet, but things should be a tad less intimidating right now. The

iPhoto preferences are pretty simple, but that's because iPhoto itself is pretty simple. Up to now you've just been warming up the engine and adjusting the mirrors. Now that you've got the seat tilted at just the right angle, it's time to put this thing in gear. In the next chapter you'll work on getting pictures into iPhoto. That's what you've been waiting for, so I'll just shut up now and let you turn the page.

Figure 2-20
Sharing preferences houses the options for how iPhoto shares the love over a network

SHARING YOUR PRIVATE MOMENTS

Sharing iPhoto over the network is extremely cool, but hey, every silver lining has a gray cloud. Make sure you PowerBook and iBook users are careful with this feature when you head out on the road. When you use a hotel's broadband, anybody else who fires up iPhoto in that hotel, even if he or she is 15 floors away, has access to what you're sharing if they're on the same subnet.

If any of you have pictures that you may not want other people to see, or maybe pictures that you promised somebody else that *no one would ever see*, then you may just want to make sure you turn sharing off. Not only can shared albums be seen, but they can be copied and then perhaps posted to the Internet as well.

Hey, what you do with your camera is your business. I'm just trying to make sure it stays that way.

SHARING AND SUBNETS

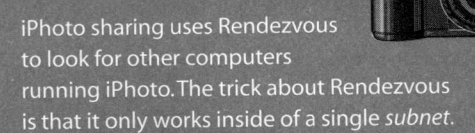

iPhoto sharing uses Rendezvous to look for other computers running iPhoto. The trick about Rendezvous is that it only works inside of a single *subnet*.

Right. I know. Eighty percent of you just glassed over and said "Aw man! He's speaking geek again."

It's not that hard. Your computer has an IP address that you can see in your Network System Preferences. If you have several computers at home on a single network, then odds are your IP addresses will all be the same except for the last number, for example, 10.0.1.3, 10.0.1.55, 10.0.1.200.

As long as the subnet mask is 255.255.255.0, you can be anywhere from 0–255 on that last number and if the rest all matches up, you're on the same subnet. I'm really oversimplifying this because it's just not the sort of thing I'm looking to cover in this book, but it might come in handy to know if you want to share and it's not working.

Most offices will have one subnet for the whole network. In this case you will see everybody who has iPhoto Sharing turned on in the whole office. If part of the network is on one subnet and part is on another, then Rendezvous won't see anybody who's on the other subnet.

Also, since Rendezvous only works on one local subnet, you can't use iPhoto Sharing to look at pictures on your home system from the office. They're on different subnets. Clear as mud? Good.

Bringing It In:
Importing Pictures

In This Chapter

Import from a digital camera or memory card • Add photos to iPhoto from your hard drive, DVD, or CD
Import photos from an iPhoto disc • Discard and recover photos from the Trash

The first time you fire up iPhoto, well, it's empty. That's about as fun as swimming in a pool with no water. It doesn't matter if you've got millions of pictures on your hard drive. Until you import them into iPhoto, you can't do squat. Fortunately, it is easy to import images from a digital camera, a memory card, your hard drive, a CD-ROM, or a DVD, among other sources.

 Note

Importing images into iPhoto *copies* the images to iPhoto's photo library on your hard drive — even if the image is already on your hard drive. Every image you import from your hard drive exists in two places on your drive and takes up twice the space. Once you import an image and you're sure it's in iPhoto, you can delete the original to free up some drive space. You won't be losing anything because iPhoto has a perfect clone in its folders.

GETTING IPHOTO IN AN IMPORT MODE MOOD

iPhoto has a special Import mode for bringing pictures into the program. You can manually tell it to switch to that mode and there are several ways it automatically switches itself.

Hook up a camera. When a camera is attached to the computer, iPhoto launches — if it's not running — and switches into Import mode. (You can disable this in Image Capture. See the next section for details.)

Place a memory card in a card reader. Just like hooking up a camera, placing a memory card into a card reader attached to your Mac launches iPhoto in Import mode.

Choose File ➔ Import. Choosing File ➔ Import (⌘+Shift+I) pulls up an open dialog box so you can pick images from your hard drive or any other mounted volume.

Import with Drag and Drop. The more Mac-way of getting the job done is just to drag and drop photos or folders full of photos into iPhoto. Different things will happen depending on where you let them drop.

CHANGING THE DIGITAL CAMERA APPLICATION

If you choose Use Other when you first launch iPhoto, or you want to change which application opens when you connect a digital camera, use the following steps:

1. **Open the Image Capture utility.** (It's in your Applications folder.)

2. **Choose Image Capture ➔ Preferences.** This opens the Image Capture Preferences dialog box (Figure 3-1).

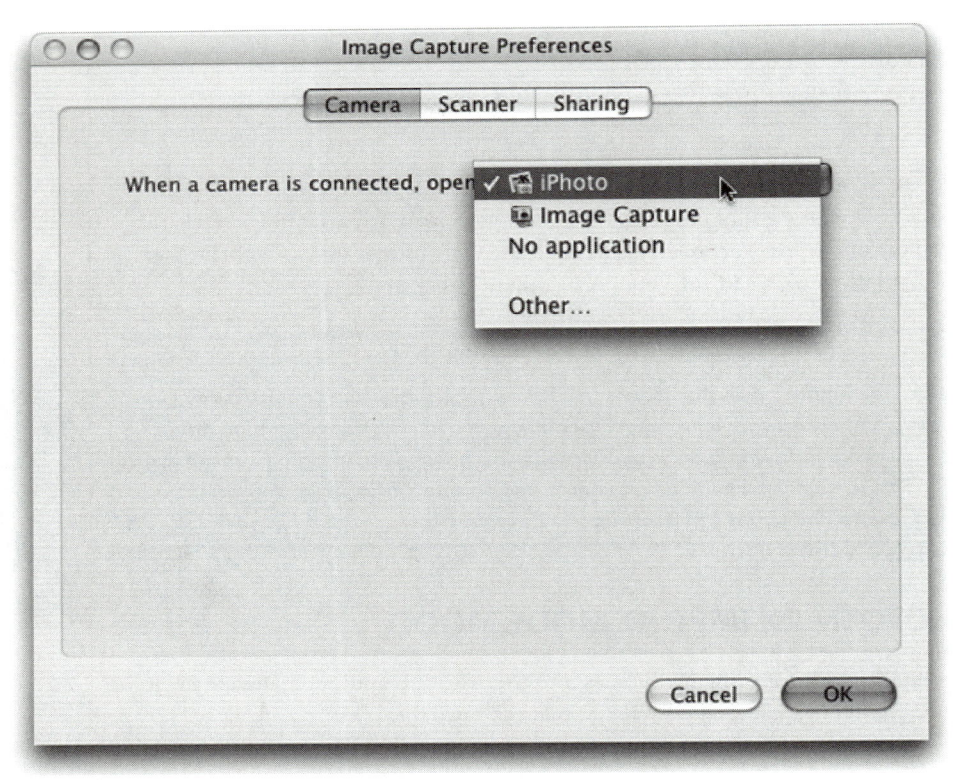

Figure 3-1
Use the Image Capture Preferences dialog box to set which application opens when you connect a digital camera

3. **Select Camera from the buttons along the top.**

4. **Choose the application to fire up under the *When a camera is connected, open* pop-up list.**

If you choose Other from the pop-up list, you'll have an opportunity to pick the application that opens. If you don't want any application to open automatically when a digital camera is connected, choose No application from the pop-up list.

DEALING WITH DUPLICATES

When you import pictures, odds are that eventually you'll end up trying to import pictures that are already in your iPhoto library. There's a safeguard in iPhoto to keep you from filling up your drive with duplicate pictures of your latest vacation. When you tell iPhoto to import a photo that's already in your library, a dialog box opens (see Figure 3-2) that asks you how you want it handled. This also works if you're importing several photos at a time. You can either click Yes (import the image) or No (skip that image) for each photo, or click the Applies to all duplicates option and *then* click Yes or No. That automatically applies that response to every duplicate it encounters. If you click Yes, then iPhoto will add "_1" onto the duplicate file names (for example, monkey_1.jpg). If you import it *again,* then it will rename it again (monkey_2.jpg).

If you have two different pictures with the same name, iPhoto recognizes them as different pictures and imports them both. If you have two of the same picture but with different file names, iPhoto will also say they're different and import them both.

Figure 3-2
iPhoto warns you if you try to import a duplicate image

 Note

iPhoto stores photos according to date taken (or when that is missing, the import date) down to the granularity of the day. Within a given day, iPhoto identifies duplicates by file name, so it is possible for iPhoto to identify two files as duplicates that are not (although that doesn't happen often). Use the thumbnails in the Duplicate Photo dialog box to determine whether two files are actually duplicates; if they are not, go ahead and import the "duplicate" file.

FOILED FATHER'S POCKET PICTURE BOOK

They say the road to somewhere or other is paved with good intentions. I'm chock full of good intentions.

When my dad got a digital camera and I was hooking him up with iPhoto, I saw that he had hundreds of pictures in the camera from all sorts of reunions and trips, but at the time, I was trying to grab the last few pictures taken of the family after a holiday meal. I did him a favor and imported all of the pictures into iPhoto and wiped them off of the card.

Little did I realize that he'd been using the camera as a pocket picture book. He would pull up pictures he took of my 102-year-old Aunt Faye and show them to people who couldn't get down to see her at her birthday party. He'd show his mother pictures of her great-grandkids because she doesn't have a computer to pull up a picture Web page.

At that time, iPhoto didn't deal with duplicates at all. It just imported everything. If you imported everything a second time with one extra picture tacked on, you ended up with two of everything plus one.

Today, he can import from his camera, leave the pictures on the card, and because he can tell iPhoto not to import the duplicates, it will only import the new pictures he's taken since he last imported.

▼ **Note**

If your camera does mount in the Finder (MSC mode), you might want to rename your card to something other than NO_NAME or CF or the various other cryptic names that the card takes on by default. If you see the removable media on your Desktop, just rename it like you would any folder. If you're not configured to see removable volumes on your Desktop, press ⌘+Shift+C to go to the Computer window. You can rename the card in there. You can't rename drives by clicking on their listing in the side bar in Panther. Be aware, though, that if you erase the card in the camera, the name will most likely be blown away; in my case, back to NO_NAME. I find it helpful to have personalized names on mine because I have more than one card.

IMPORT FROM A DIGITAL CAMERA

I think every iPhoto promo picture has a camera tethered to a Mac by a USB cord. This is obviously the cool, sexy way to import photos.

Now that you're a few years into this twenty-first century, any digital camera you buy will be able to connect to a computer with a USB connection. The cable you need comes with the camera. It usually has USB on one end and some funky proprietary connection on the camera end. Hooking the camera up to the computer is a piece of cake.

1. **Connect the camera to the Mac via the custom cable.** iPhoto launches if it's not running and switches to Import mode automatically.

▼ **Note**

Step 1 assumes that you selected Use iPhoto when you first launched the application. If you didn't, you can still import into iPhoto, but you have to manually launch the program. Once iPhoto is running, it switches into Import mode automatically, indexes the images in the camera, and displays the number of images it is ready to import, as seen in Figure 3-3.

2. **Click the Import button.** Wait while the pictures download from the camera into the iPhoto photo library.

3. **Dismount the camera in the Finder if necessary.** (See the sidebar "Photo Transfer Protocol (PTP) vs. Mass Storage Class (MSC).")

4. **Disconnect the camera and you're done.**

PHOTO TRANSFER PROTOCOL (PTP) VS. MASS STORAGE CLASS (MSC)

Most cameras work in a mode called PTP, which allows the camera to transfer pictures without any need for drivers and mounting in the Finder. Some cameras have the option to use either PTP or MSC. MSC mounts in the Finder as a hard drive. In this mode, you can navigate through your memory card like you do any other disk drive. You can copy items to the card even if they have nothing to do with pictures. This is handy for carrying around secret documents, for you James Bond or Sydney Bristow types.

If you use a card reader, which I'll cover here in a bit, you're in MSC mode. As much as I'd love to have a card reader that has a PTP option, I haven't seen one yet.

The downside of MSC mode is that when you're done importing your pictures, you still have to dismount (eject) the volume before you shut off the camera or yank the cord. If you don't, your Mac throws a warning box at you. For that reason, I prefer to have the camera in PTP mode. I don't like it when my computer yells at me.

The official policy is that you *must* go to the Finder and eject the volume like you do any CD, FireWire drive, or network server. I'm just not that patient sometimes. I've been known to occasionally just pull the card out and dismiss the warning box. I mean, come on. It's an empty card at that point, but still, perhaps something *could* go wrong if you don't dismount it. Maybe I've just been very fortunate. You might not be so lucky. I'm just saying, don't come crying to me if you break your card after I told you that you *should* dismount it first, even if I often don't. If OS does yell at you for yanking the card, don't panic. Reinsert the card and then eject it properly. Or you can live dangerously and dismiss the dialog box, which you should never do because it's there for your own protection even though I do it all the time. So there. (Don't sue me.)

In most cases that's it. If you have iPhoto set up to automatically launch when a camera is attached, you don't even need to have anything open. When you plug in the camera, iPhoto launches in Import mode (see Figure 3-3). Some cameras aren't quite as friendly. You have to switch a few into Transfer mode or some similarly named state on the camera before the camera talks to the computer. Consult your camera manual if it doesn't *just work* when you plug it in.

The Import button on the right side of the Import mode window is only available if a camera, card reader, or other device that looks like a camera to your Mac is plugged in and has importable photographs. Importing proceeds until all the pictures have been imported into iPhoto or you click Stop. If you stop the import, iPhoto opens a dialog box, where you can choose whether to keep the already imported photos or to discard them.

Figure 3-3
Connect a digital camera to your Mac and download its contents straight into iPhoto

PRINCE OF A SHOT

While I was in London on a con-ference, selected people were whisked away to hang out with Prince Charles. I wasn't one of the whisked, but when they got back, the photographer handed me a short stack of memory cards and told me to be *very* careful, because hanging out with Prince Charles was a dream come true and those pictures were *extremely* impor-tant to him. As I offloaded the memory cards into iPhoto, he was perched on my shoulder like a buzzard. I imported them *without* the autodelete feature just to be safe. When I handed the card back to the photogra-pher, he asked me if I was sure it was safe for him to erase the card. Then he asked me if I was *sure* it was safe. Then he asked me if I knew what he meant by "being sure." Then he asked me if I knew what would happen to me if I was wrong.

After reassuring him that I knew what I was doing and showing him the pictures on the screen, he stuck the card in his pocket, pictures still on it, and walked away looking at me askew. I think he waited until he got back to the States a week later before he erased that card.

He was a big fan of the Royal Family.

You can have iPhoto erase the images in the camera after you import them by clicking the Erase camera contents after transfer option. Whether you choose this option depends on how important your pictures are to you. If it's a series of pic-tures of your cat sleeping in a funny pose, it's probably safe to delete the images off the card when downloading is com-plete. If you're loading pictures of your audience with the queen of England, I would personally *not* check that box. I've never personally been hosed by this feature, but computers being the moody creatures that they are, you never know.

To make sure the import worked correctly, click the Last Roll icon in the Source pane. You should see the images you just imported from the camera. If you can't see Last

Roll in your Source column, switch it back on in the pref-erences (see Chapter 2).

(see Chapter 2)

▼ Note

There are a couple of things you should keep in mind when importing pictures directly from the camera. First of all, don't wait too long after connect-ing the camera to start the import process. Many cameras will power down to conserve battery power, breaking the USB connection and causing your Mac to complain that you removed the device improp-erly. If this happens, you'll have to turn the camera back on and start over. Also, transferring.... images..... from...... most.... cameras.... is..... slooooow. Make sure you either connect the camera to an AC adapter or have a full battery charge so that the camera doesn't run out of juice in the middle of the transfer!

IMPORT FROM A MEMORY CARD

About every digital camera you buy today uses a removable memory card to store images. There are several competing formats out there. Check your camera manual to see what format your camera requires. Most cameras come with something like a 16MB card, which is pretty much useless, but at least it gives you something to hold up to the sales guy at the electronics store so you know you're getting the right kind of card.

While you're buying that respectable replacement card, do yourself another favor and get a card reader. Card readers are almost always going to move your pictures faster than plugging the camera directly into the computer, but speed is only one benefit.

Basically, there are three popular kinds of card reader: PC Card, USB, and FireWire.

- **PC Card.** If you're using a PowerBook with a PC Card slot (also known as PCMCIA), a PC Card Adapter is a great way to go. You pull the card out of the camera and slide it into the back of the adapter card, and then slide the adapter card into the slot on the side of your PowerBook. The card is about the size of a short stack of business cards so it's easy to carry. Most of the time I keep mine in the slot. You can find them for under $10 if you look around. This is probably the fastest way to download pictures right now, but only PowerBook users have these slots.

- **USB.** USB card readers are the most popular devices to use if you don't have a PC Card slot. The best thing about them is that most read about any format you can find. You may only need Compact Flash for *your* camera, but when friends or family stop by with their cameras, it's really nice to have access to something that works with their equipment. I have one that reads Compact Flash types I and II, Secure Digital, MMC, Memory Stick, Memory Stick Pro, and Smart-Media, all in a little box smaller than a kid's-meal cheeseburger, and all for about $30. If anybody stops by with any format card, I'm covered.

The USB readers will be either USB (USB 1.1) or USB 2.0. The 2.0 variety is a faster standard that works fine with the older USB, but at the slower USB 1.1 speed. In 2004, Apple started putting USB 2.0 in its computers. Either flavor works on your Mac, but new Macs will take advantage of the faster throughput.

- **FireWire.** If speed is what you need, and you're willing to spend a little more, get a FireWire card reader. Those are about $50 right now, but pictures *fly* off of your cards when you use one of those things compared to the USB 1.1 readers.

When you hook up any sort of card reader to the Mac and insert your memory card, it shows up in the Finder as a volume and also triggers iPhoto and goes into Import mode unless you tell it not to. If it doesn't, you can click the Import mode button below the Display pane to manually switch into Import mode. Simply click the Import button in the lower-right corner to start the process and import all the images from the memory card.

CARD SPEED

Not all memory cards are created equal. The cheapest ones have much slower transfer speeds than the higher end cards. Different brands use different ways to mark their products, so you might have to do a bit of research. Lexar has adopted the CD-ROM transfer speed numbers where 1x is 150KB/s. So the 4x would be 600KB/s and the 80X is up to 12MB/s. San-Disk uses different names for their speed ratings. The Ultra II is their high-speed card. Kingston calls theirs the Elite Pro.

There's not really a standard you can rely on other than digging out the actual numbers. My main card works at about 1.5MB/s but it was the cheapest 256MB card they had back when I bought it so I'm happy it gets up to even that fast. Today the prices are really coming down on cards. Even the higher-speed ones are only about a $20 premium over their slower counterparts.

If you tend to take pictures in small clusters of a dozen or so pictures at a time, then the speed won't really matter for you, but when you find yourself loading off a whole week of Hawaiian paradise pictures, a slow card will add a few minutes to your import times.

Oh, and capacities are up to 8GB now, but those cards are nearly $2,000. I suggest you have two to three smaller cards (256MB or 512MB). They're good for 100 or so pictures each, and they're small, so they're easy to carry. Many professional photographers use multiple cards so they can keep shooting while the filled card is importing into the computer.

▼ Note

Because the memory card appears on the Desktop as another drive, you can import individual images from the card by using the Finder, as discussed in the next section.

When you finish importing images from the memory card, eject the card by choosing Eject from the card's contextual menu. Once you eject the card, you can remove it from the memory card reader or the PC Card slot.

IMPORT PHOTOS DIALOG BOX

You can use the Import Photos dialog box (see Figure 3-4) to import pictures if you're the type who likes dialog boxes. This lets you import from basically anything you can mount in the Finder like your hard drive, CD-ROM, DVD, network drive, Internet drive (iDisk), or memory card.

CAMERA OR CARD READER?

If you want my advice, get a card reader as soon as possible and stick your camera's USB cable in a drawer where it can collect dust and wither away. A camera is for taking pictures. A card reader is for getting them into your computer. Most cameras make pretty crappy card readers.

Here's the problem I ran into when I bought my camera. My Nikon uses an external battery charger. The AC adapter was sold separately, a fact that rated about a 7.2 on my personal annoy-o-meter. I took a few pictures with the flash, fiddled with the settings for a while, and ended up draining the battery. I got the urge to offload my pictures, and because I only had my camera and the USB cable to get the job done, that dead battery totally shut me down. I had to put the battery on the charger and wait until the next morning to get my pictures into the computer. That day I bought a card reader and have never looked back.

With a separate card reader, you can shut off the camera, put your battery on the charger, and load up your pictures right away. Me? I have three readers. One stays in my PowerBook. One stays on my desk. One stays in my backpack for emergency card-reading purposes.

1. **Choose File ➔ Import.** The Import Photos dialog box opens.

2. **Use the columns in the dialog box to navigate to the volume and folder containing your images.**

3. **Select the images you want to import.**

4. **Click Import to import the images into iPhoto.**

 Note

The images are imported only into the photo library. They are not placed in any albums, even if you have an album selected when you choose File ➔ Import.

DRAG AND DROP IMPORT

Here's how I prefer to play when I'm importing from a disc or network volume. You can click and drag a picture, a group of pictures, or a folder of pictures into iPhoto with a simple drag and drop:

1. **Locate the images in the Finder.**

2. **Select one or more images or a folder containing images.**

3. **Click and drag that selection over the iPhoto window and release the mouse button.** How the photo imports depends on where you release the mouse button:

   ▪ **Importing the image only.** Releasing over the main Display pane while the photo library is selected in the Source column just imports the images.

   ▪ **Importing into a displayed album.** Releasing over the main Display pane while an album is selected in the Source column imports the images and adds them to that album, as seen in Figure 3-5.

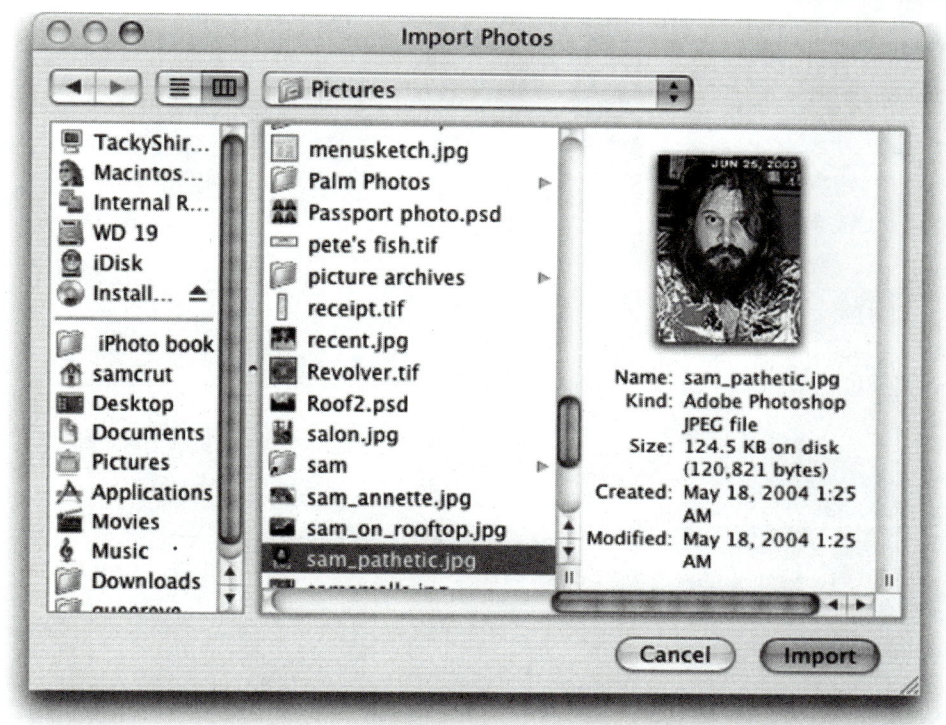

Figure 3-4
Use the Import Photos dialog box to select images and import them into iPhoto

- **Importing into an undisplayed album.** Releasing with the pointer over an album name in the Source column imports the images and adds them to that album even if it's not currently displayed, as seen in Figure 3-6.

- **Importing and creating an album.** Releasing with the pointer over the Source column but *not over an album name* (Figure 3-7) creates a new album, imports the images, and adds them to that new album. If you're dragging in a folder and you do this, the new album takes the name of the folder you drop.

This is just so much faster and more flexible than using the Import menu, in my opinion, but hey, you do what works for you.

 Note

When you add images to iPhoto, they are *always* added to the photo library (visible at the top of the album pane), which contains all the pictures in iPhoto. If you use one of the techniques described here to also add them to an existing album or to create a new album, the images appear in that album as well as the photo library.

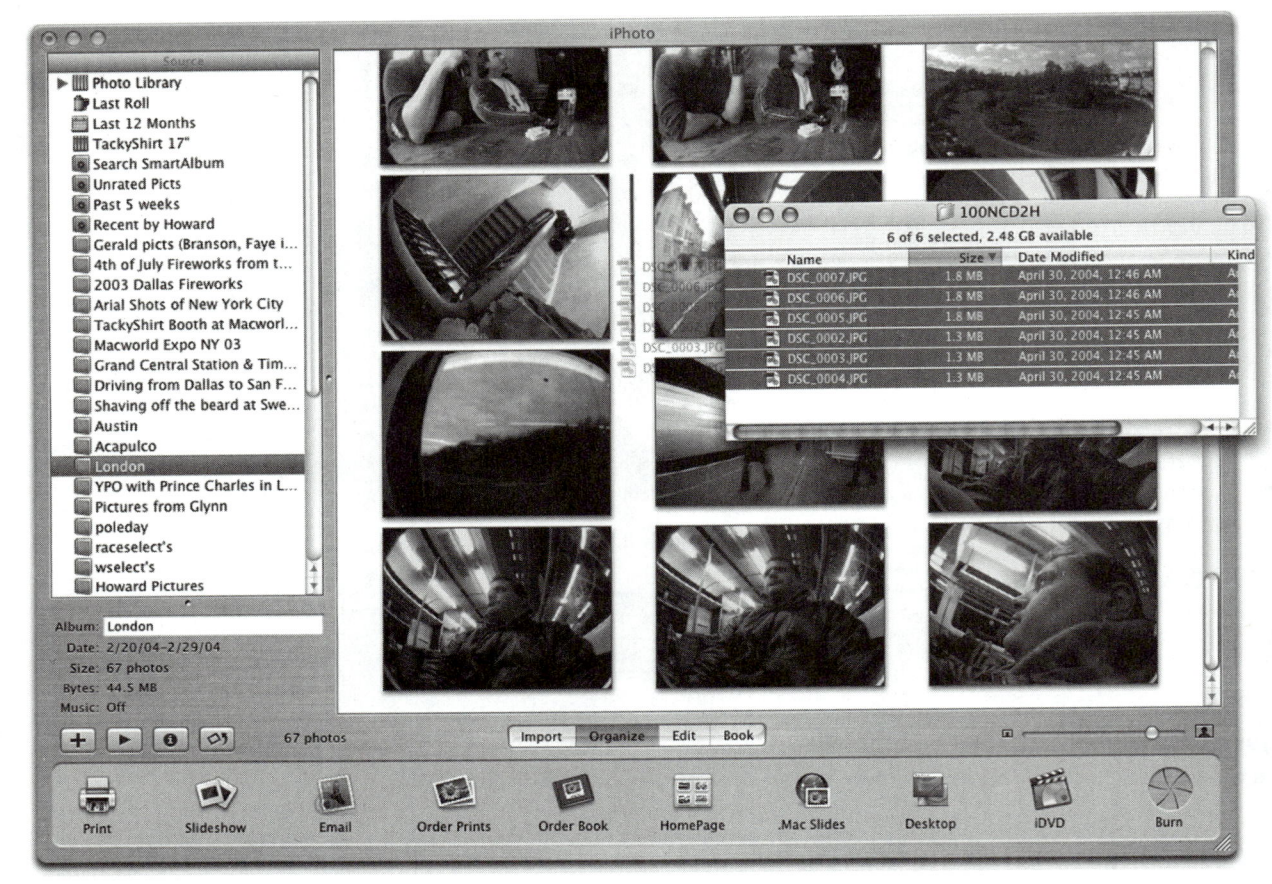

Figure 3-5

Drag one or more images into the Display pane to add them to the open album

▼ Note

If you click and drag pictures into the display window while an album is displayed, you'll see a black bar indicating where those pictures should go (see Figure 3-5). Well, I think that was the idea anyway. In truth, that black bar doesn't do anything. This is a bug. It deposits the picture at the bottom of the pane if you're in Manual sorting mode or in its appropriate sorting position if you're in any other sort mode. In the main photo library, this insert bar doesn't appear.

Similarly, if you click and drag to just below the photo library, you'll see a horizontal insert bar that typically indicates that your import would create an album between photo library and Last Roll. Another bug. That just imports the picture(s) into the main photo library. If these don't do what I just described, odds are they've put out an update and fixed these bugs, so never mind.

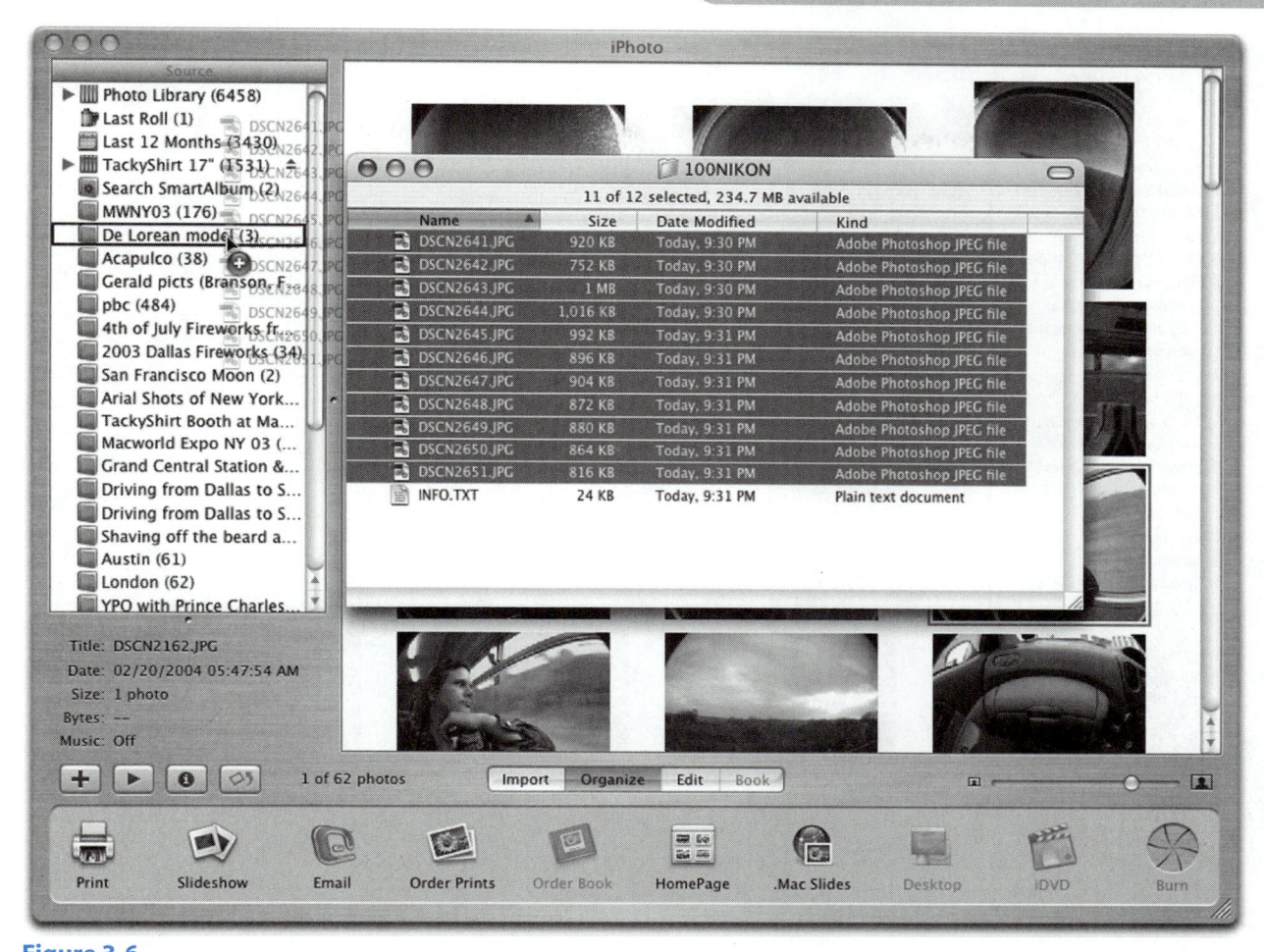

Figure 3-6
Drag images to an album to add them to that album automatically

SELECTING IN THE FINDER

When selecting images in the Finder, there are a couple techniques you might keep in mind depending on what you want to select:

- To select multiple individual images, click the first image, hold down the ⌘ key, and click the other images to select them. Clicking an image a second time (with the ⌘ key still held down) deselects the image.

- To select a range of images, click the first image, hold down the Shift key, and click the last image in the range. All the images in between are selected. You can hold down the ⌘ key and click one or more images in the range, deselecting them. You can also add images to the range by ⌘+clicking images outside the selected range.

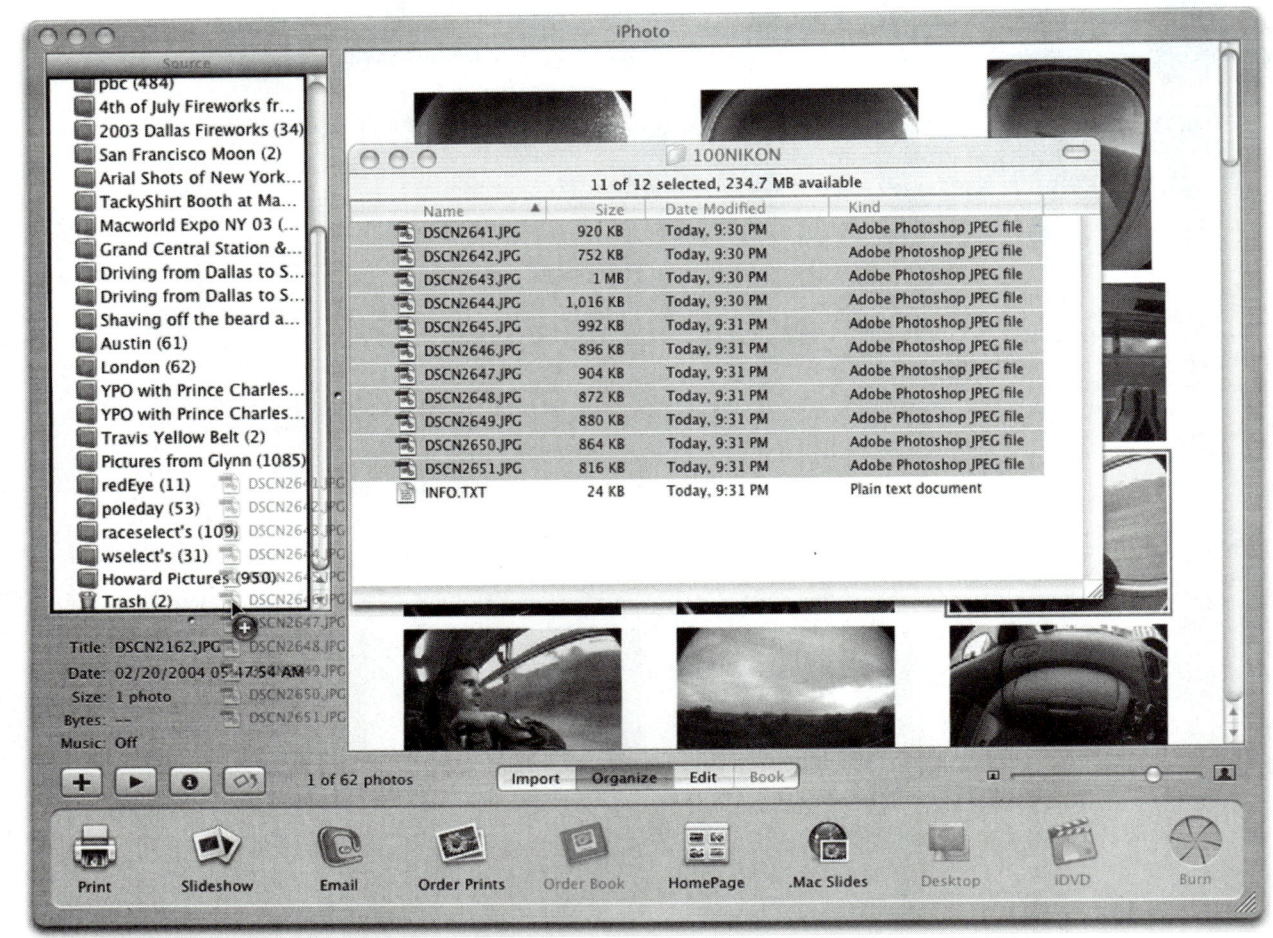

Figure 3-7
Drag images to a blank spot in the album pane to create a new album at the same time you import the images into iPhoto

IMPORT FROM AN IPHOTO DISC

As you'll see in Chapter 14, it is easy to back up your iPhoto photo library (including albums, titles, and comments) by burning a CD or DVD within iPhoto. This is an excellent way to share your photos with another iPhoto user. If someone gives you a CD/DVD he or she created by backing up all or part of an iPhoto photo library, you can import the contents of the disc into iPhoto.

The picture CDs made by iPhoto can automatically launch iPhoto when one is inserted. This setting is configured in the Mac OS X System Preferences under CDs & DVDs, where it says, "When you insert a picture CD select iPhoto if you want the program to launch automatically." Click Ignore if you don't want anything to trigger.

To import images from a picture CD or DVD:

1. **Insert the CD or DVD into the drive on your Mac.** The contents of the disc appear in the album pane as a new photo library. To see the albums nested below the photo library, click the arrowhead to the left of the new photo library. See Figure 3-8 for an example.

2. **Click either the disc's photo library or one of the albums.** This displays the images in the Display pane.

3. **Click and drag one or more images to the Source pane to import the image(s).** As discussed earlier in this chapter, you can drag the images to the photo library, to an existing album, or to a blank area of the album pane to create a new album.

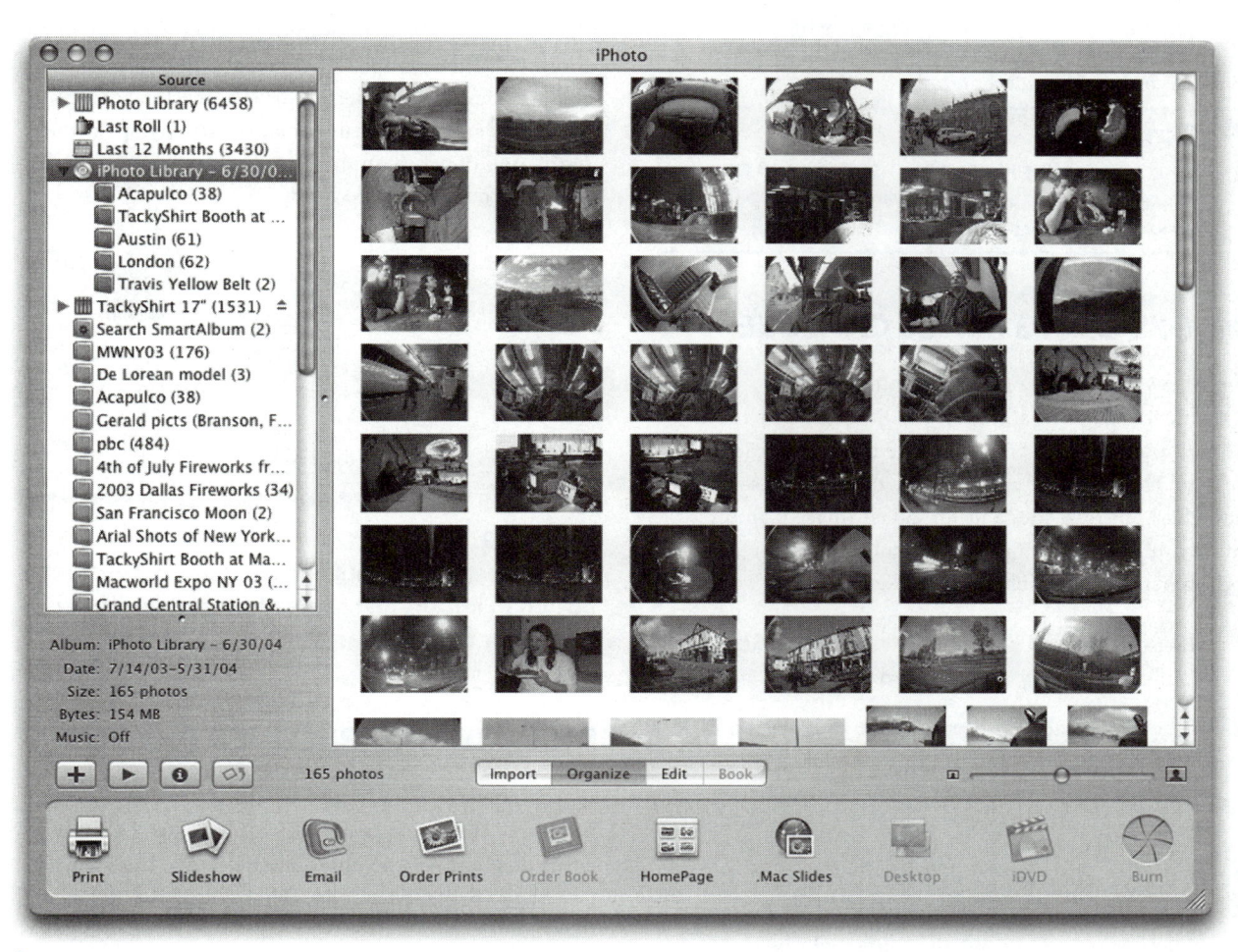

Figure 3-8
An iPhoto disc appears as a separate photo library in the album pane

Note

You can import an entire album from a picture disc by clicking and dragging the album to an empty area of the Source column. If you want to import the entire CD/DVD, then drag the CD/DVD icon to an empty area of the Source column and a new album with the same name as that disc is created and all the images go in that album. However, you lose the other albums on the disc when you do this. For best results, drag all the albums instead of the disc itself so you can keep it organized.

▼ Tip

You can eject the iPhoto disc by pressing Ctrl and clicking the disc's photo library in the album pane. Next, choose Eject from the contextual menu.

IMPORT USING IMAGE CAPTURE

One of the limitations of importing images from a camera or memory card using iPhoto is that it is an all-or-nothing proposition. You must import all the images; you can't pick and choose the images to import. There is a solution, however. Apple provides a utility called Image Capture, which you *can* use to import just a subset of the images in your camera. Use the following steps:

1. **Start the Image Capture utility.** You'll find it in the Applications folder on your hard drive.

2. **Insert a memory card or connect your digital camera.** Image Capture indexes the contents of the device and displays that information in a dialog box (see Figure 3-9).

3. **If desired, click the Download To pop-up list, choose Other, and select the destination directory (where you want to put the imported photos) from the resulting dialog box.** Then click Open.

4. **Click Download Some to open a new version of the dialog box (see Figure 3-10).** This displays a list of the images on the device. Use the View buttons in the upper-left corner to switch between viewing the contents as a text list or as thumbnails.

5. **Select the images you want to import and click Download.**

Once the images have been imported to the destination directory, you can import them into iPhoto using the Finder as described earlier in this chapter. Image Capture makes this very easy because it automatically opens the destination directory in the Finder, making it easy to drag and drop the images into iPhoto.

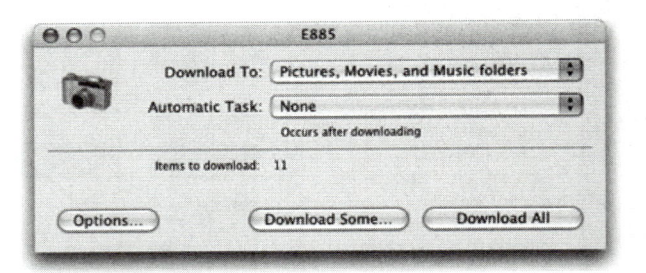

Figure 3-9
The Image Capture utility dialog box provides the option to import just some of the images in your camera or memory card

DISCARD AND RECOVER PHOTOS

iPhoto provides a Trash can that is always available at the bottom of the album pane. You can drag images from either an album or the photo library to the Trash can (see Figure 3-11). As you do, iPhoto displays a red icon that indicates the number of images you are sending to the Trash.

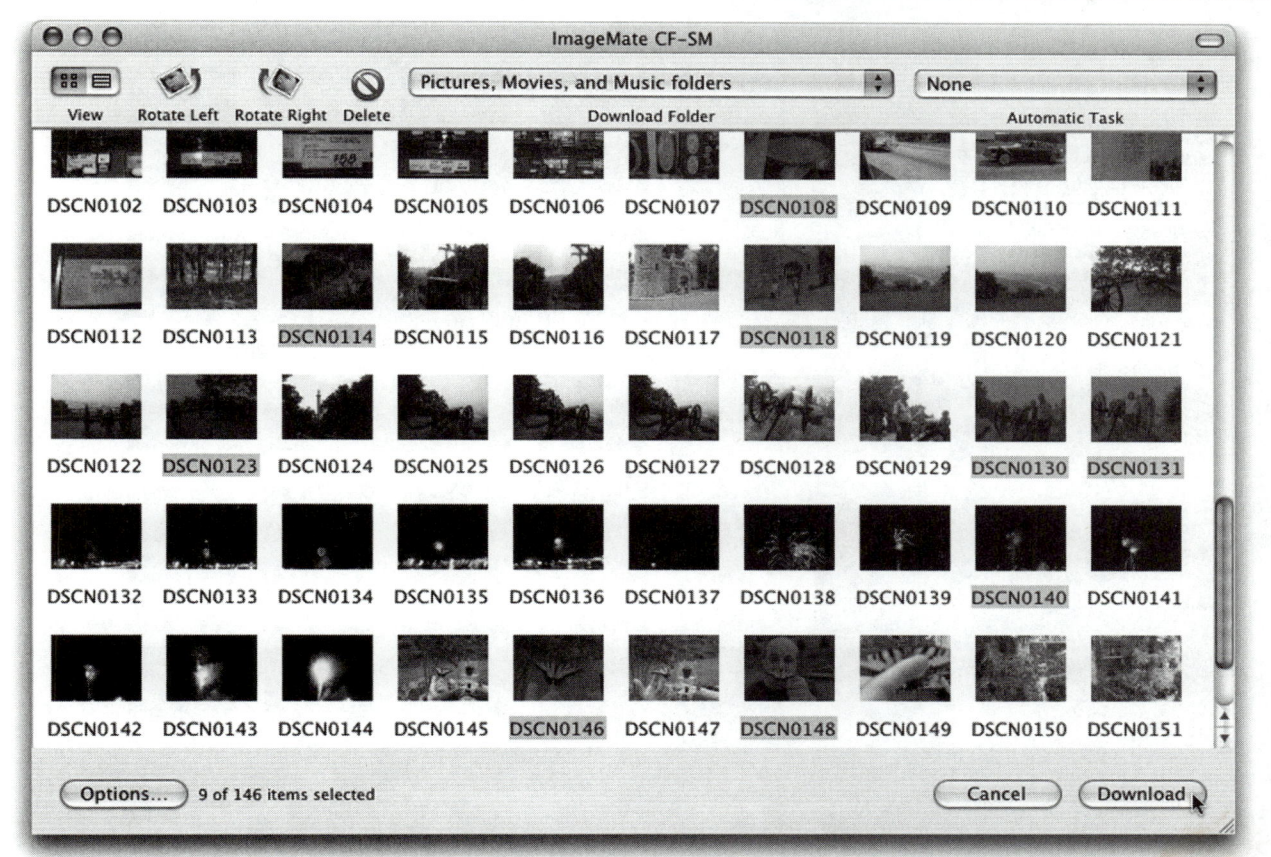

Figure 3-10
Select the images you want to import from the device and click Download to start the process

The Trash can is actually an album (see Chapter 6) and serves two purposes: removing images from an album and discarding an image from the photo library:

- **Removing an image.** To remove an image from an album, click and drag the image from the album's Display pane to the Trash can, or choose Remove from Album from the image contextual menu. This does *not* delete the image from the photo library; it only removes it from the album. To add the image

back to the album, switch to the photo library and drag the image thumbnail to the album. You can also choose Edit ➜ Undo Move to Trash (or press ⌘+Z).

- **Discarding an image.** To discard an image, select the photo library in the Source pane, then drag the image thumbnail to the Trash can, or choose Move to Trash from the contextual menu, or just press the Delete key. This removes the image from the photo library as well as any albums that include the image. It also *adds* the image to the Trash can.

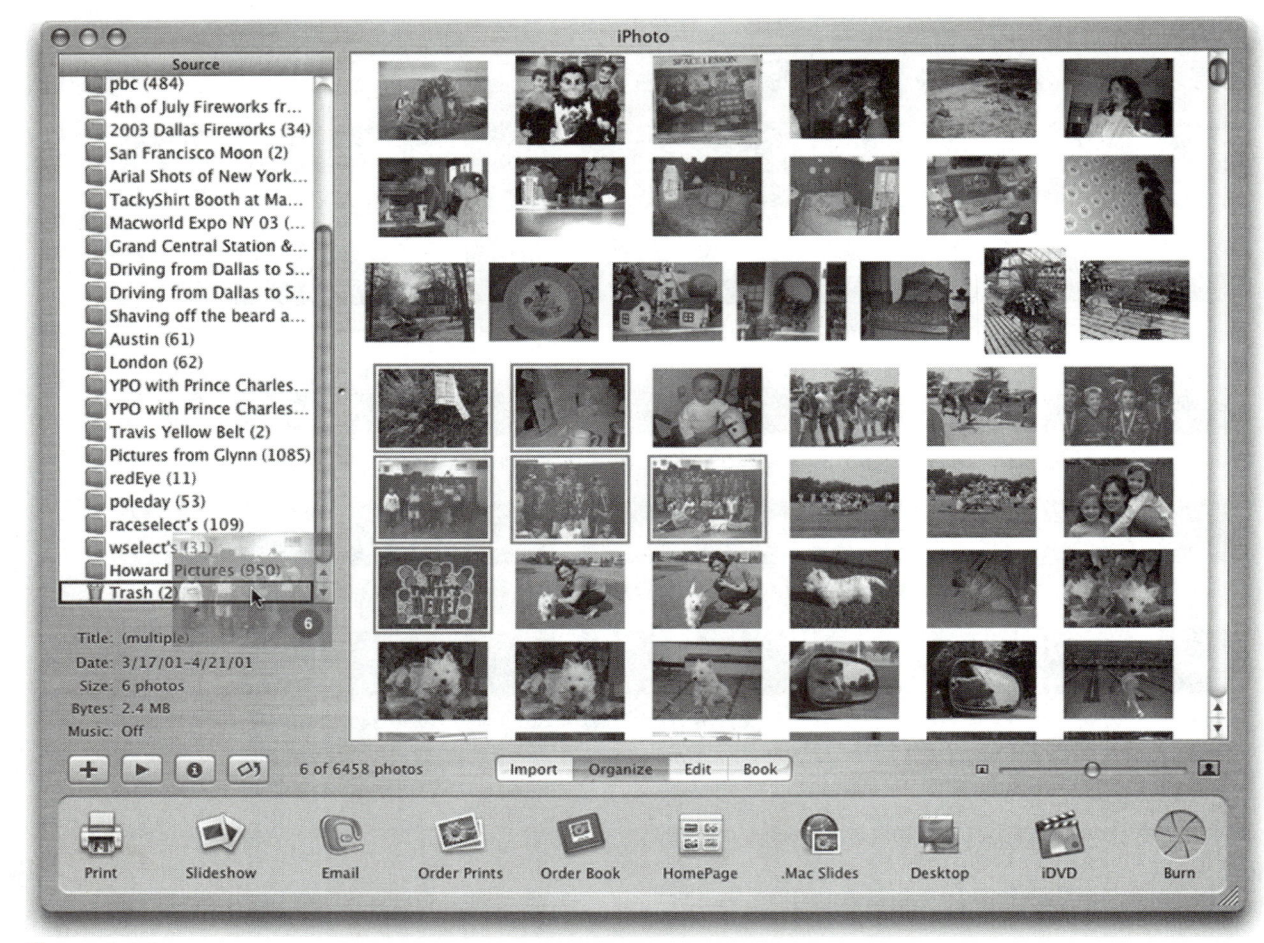

Figure 3-11

As you drag images to the Trash can in iPhoto, you can see how many images you are discarding

Because the Trash can is actually an album, you can view all the images you have placed there. To do so, click the Trash can. iPhoto displays all images in the Trash in the Display pane. This also makes it easy to restore an image to the photo library. Simply Ctrl+click an image and choose Restore to Photo Library from the contextual menu. Doing so not only restores the image to the photo library, it also adds the photo back into any albums it was in *and* removes it from the Trash can.

▼ **Note**

What you *can't* do when you just remove an image from an album is retrieve the image from the Trash can. Because you didn't really discard an image (you only removed it from an album), the image does not appear in the Trash can. However, if it was the last thing you did, ⌘+Z brings it back.

Now things are getting fun. I remember the first time I saw a digital picture I'd taken with my own hands and then immediately loaded into my computer. I was giggling like a schoolgirl. Then again, it was much more impressive back in 1995 with that old QuickTake 100 camera. Now it's old hat. Trust me. You got it good these days.

The one import method I haven't really discussed is scanning in your old prints. iPhoto doesn't handle that itself. You'll have to get a flatbed scanner and use the software that comes with it to bring your hard copy pictures into the computer, and then into iPhoto. How that gets done is a bit past the scope of this book because the software varies quite a bit from scanner to scanner, but I just wanted to make sure you knew that it could be done, just not with iPhoto alone.

So now that you've got your pictures into iPhoto, what are you going to do with them? Read on shutterbug!

PART II

Organizing Your Photos

Organizing Your Pictures: The Basics

In This Chapter

Working with film rolls in the photo library • Changing the displayed information for the thumbnails
Sorting your photos in the photo library • Changing how you see the pictures
Scrolling through your images

Chapter 3 covered importing pictures into iPhoto; now let's have a look at how to arrange and organize them. Organize mode has lots of features to help you make sense of your collection. Some of those features enable you to organize and arrange your photos with just a few clicks, or even less in some cases. (I'm lazy, so less is definitely a good thing.)

Importing anything into iPhoto creates a *film roll,* which groups all of the pictures from that import session together. Film rolls give you a bit of organization without you ever having to lift a finger. iPhoto also has special groups it maintains behind the scenes: Last 12 Months and Last Roll give you an easy way to view just your recent shots or what you just imported. All of that is totally automatic. When you first use iPhoto, you may feel that this is enough organizing. But, after your picture collection starts growing like a wild pack of dandelion weeds, you'll outgrow this thinking and be ready for Chapter 5, which discusses *albums.*

This chapter covers the basics of Organize mode. Organize mode has a heck of a lot crammed into it, and this is where you'll probably spend most of your time. You can sort your pictures by name, date, and various other traits. You'll see how to turn various display info on and off in the display pane and how to see hundreds of pictures at a glance or zoom in on one picture at a time. Get used to Organize mode because you'll be digging around in it's features for several more chapters.

ENTER ORGANIZE MODE

Many of the things I'll be talking about in this chapter, like everything over in the Source pane, will be accessible from the other modes, but Organize mode is where you work with those items. Organize mode is pretty much the catch-all mode for iPhoto. I think they decided that if you're not importing, editing a single picture, or making one of their swanky books, then you must be organizing! You can get into Organize mode in a few ways. They are:

- **Click the Organize button.** The simplest way to enter Organize mode is to click the Organize button below the Display pane. This switches you from any other mode (Import, Edit, or Book) to Organize mode.

- **Click another album.** If you are in Edit mode, click another album in the Source pane to switch to that album in Organize mode. If you are in Book mode (see Chapter 17), clicking another album switches to that album but leaves you in Book mode; you need to Option+click another album to switch to that album in Organize mode. This also works in reverse: If you are in Organize mode and Option+click another album, you'll switch to that album in Book mode.

- **Click the Photo Library album.** If you are not already viewing the photo library, click the Photo Library album to switch to it in Organize mode.

UNDERSTANDING FILM ROLLS, ALBUMS, AND THE PHOTO LIBRARY

When you import images into iPhoto, each image is placed in the photo library, which is visible at the top of the Source pane. To see the entire contents of the photo library, click on its icon to display the thumbnails in the Display pane (see Figure 4-1).

AIRING YOUR DIRTY LAUNDRY IN THE PHOTO LIBRARY

One thing that took me a little while to understand was that *everything* is in the photo library. Every single picture you have in iPhoto is in the main library. You can't have a picture *not* in the photo library if it's in iPhoto. If confidential shots of a new invention for a patent application, or pictures of you testing out your macro lens by shooting extreme close-ups of your nose hair are in iPhoto, they're all out there on the line with the rest of your laundry in the photo library. You can hide some things by collapsing film rolls, but when you turn off film rolls, all that dirty laundry is back up on the line for everyone at your computer to see.

You can work around this little hole, but the methods are pretty drastic and involve completely separate photo libraries, a remedy that smells a bit like duct tape to me. I'll be getting to such advanced things later on in the book. I just wanted to drive the point home that if it's in iPhoto, it's in the photo library, and there's no use fighting it.

As mentioned earlier, importing one or more images into iPhoto results in a film roll. Each film roll has a name, the date on which it was imported, and the number of photos included in the roll. If you imported individual images, the default film roll name is "Roll xx," where xx is a number. However, if you imported an entire folder of images, the film roll is set to the folder name, so providing meaningful names for a folder of images prior to importing it makes sense.

 Note

If you import a folder that contains nested folders, iPhoto creates a film roll for each folder.

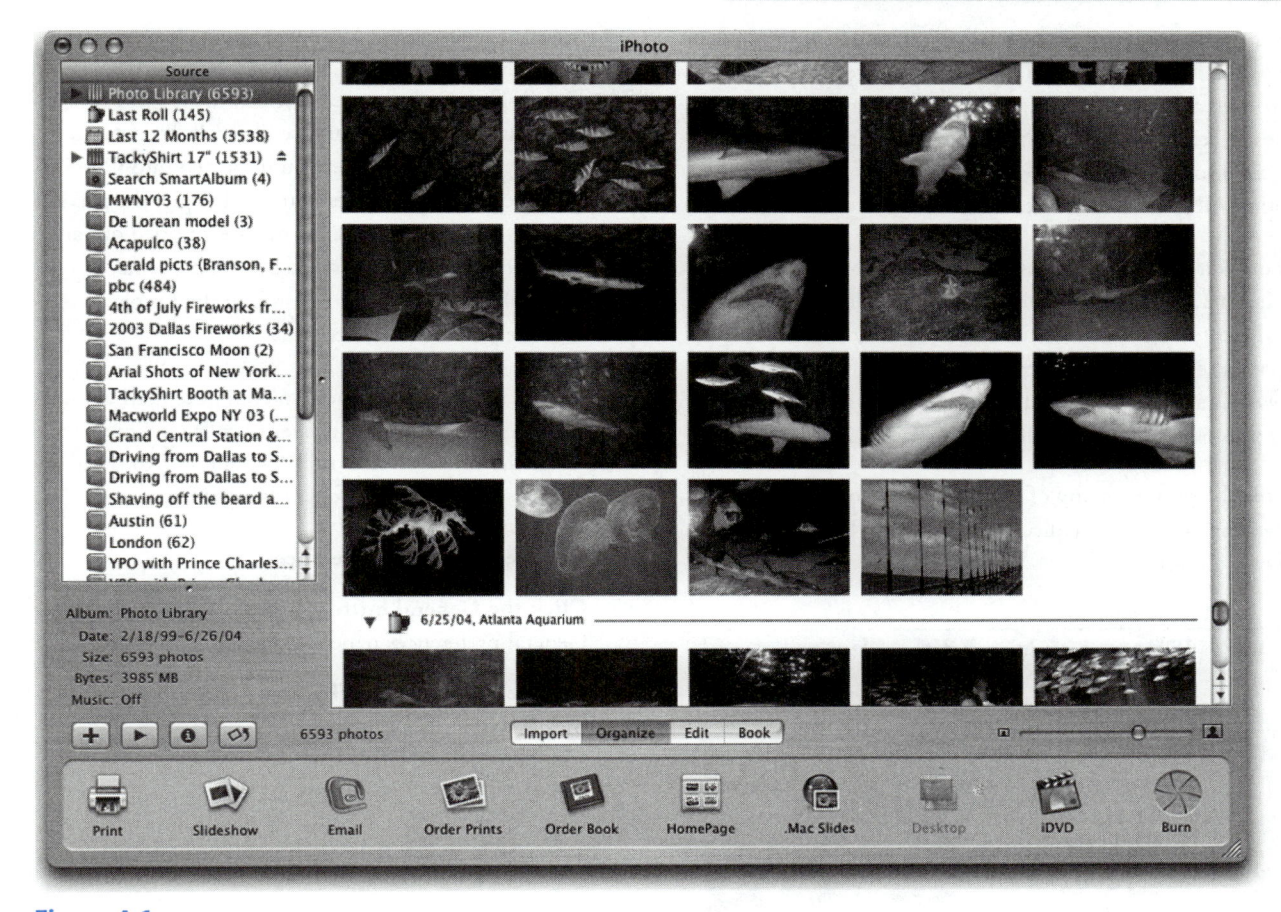

Figure 4-1
View the entire contents of the photo library in the Display pane

Film rolls provide a modicum of organization, but they're definitely not enough. For one thing, film rolls are only visible in the photo library. In addition, you cannot rearrange photos by dragging them from one film roll to another, nor can you change the order of images in the film roll or the order of the film rolls themselves.

 Note

As described later in this chapter, you can change the sort order of the entire photo library using the View ➜ Arrange Photos hierarchical menu. However, the film rolls disappear if you do.

To truly organize your image collection, you'll need to use *albums*. Albums are collections of images over which you have a great deal of control. You can create and delete albums, set their order in the album pane, add photos to the albums, and arrange the order of images within each album. Albums are discussed in Chapter 5.

iPhoto automatically breaks up the images by year, starting with 2001. To view the yearly collections, click the arrowhead located to the left of the Photo Library album. This expands the photo library to display the yearly collections, as well as a collection called Early Photos, which contains any photos taken before 2001 (see Figure 4-2).

To see the photos in any of the collections in the Display pane, click one of the collections under the Photo Library album.

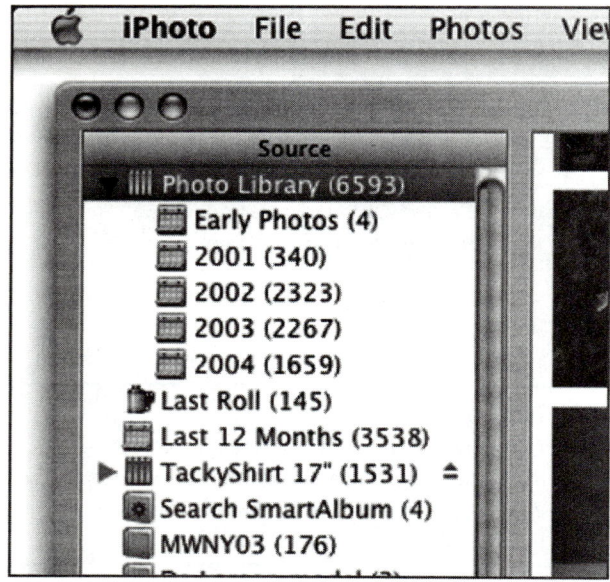

Figure 4-2
View the collections in the photo library by clicking the Photo Library arrowhead

THE LAST ROLL

The Last Roll film roll (located just below the Photo Library album) is a special purpose film roll. By default, it contains the last set of pictures you imported into iPhoto. Each time you import another batch of images, the previous contents of the Last Roll film roll are emptied out and replaced by the current import. To see the contents (thumbnails) of the Last Roll film roll in the Display pane, just click the roll in the Source pane.

You can use iPhoto's preferences to configure the Last Roll film roll to contain the last number of rolls you imported. To change the Last Roll film roll (for example, to show the last two rolls or three rolls), follow these steps:

1. **Choose iPhoto ➡ Preferences.**

2. **Click the General button.** This switches to the General preferences pane (see Figure 4-3).

3. **Use the Show last... roll album field to set the number of rolls to include.**

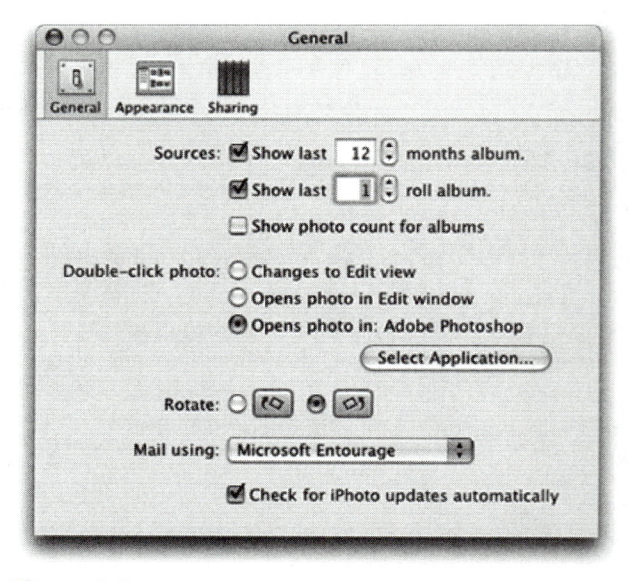

Figure 4-3
General preferences pane

You can also turn off the Last Roll icon in the Source pane by unclicking the Show last... roll album checkbox. If you change the value in the field, the icon in the Source pane changes to reflect how many film rolls are included. For example, Figure 4-4 shows how the Last Roll icon looks when you set it to contain the last three film rolls imported.

Figure 4-4
Setting the Last Roll film roll to contain more than just one roll affects the icon in the Source pane

The Last Roll film roll (at its default setting of 1) can be especially handy when you have a batch of images to import that will not all go into the same folder. For example, I recently returned from a trip to both Sydney (my first stop) and London (my second stop) with a digital camera full of images. I imported these pictures from the digital camera all at once, but I wanted them to be in two separate folders. No problem; I just clicked on the Last Roll film roll to display all the thumbnails in the Display pane, then clicked and dragged the images into their respective folders.

> **Tip**
> Make sure to do this rearranging before importing the next batch of pictures because the Last Roll(s) album changes every time you import more pictures.

LAST 12 MONTHS

Last 12 Months is another collection of pictures in the Source pane. Strictly speaking, it isn't really a film roll, nor is it an album (for example, you can't make a book out of it); it behaves much like the date subcategories under the Photo Library album. By default, this collection of images contains pictures taken in the last 12 months. To view these pictures in the Display pane, click the Last 12 Months icon in the Source pane.

You can use iPhoto's preferences to configure the Last 12 Months collection so that it contains pictures that are either more recent or older than the last year. To change the Last 12 Months (for example, to show the last 9 months, or the last 14 months), follow these steps:

1. Choose iPhoto ➜ Preferences.

2. Click the General button to switch to the General preferences.

3. Use the Show last __ months album field to set the number of months you want to include.

You can also turn off the Last 12 Months icon in the Source pane by unclicking the Show last __ months album checkbox. If you change the value in the field, the icon in the Source pane changes to reflect how many months are included.

SORTING YOUR PHOTOS

You can look at your pictures in any order you like and iPhoto does a nice job of sorting your snapshots in various ways, whether you want them by date, alphabetical by title, by film roll, by rating, or in your own personal order if you want to manually arrange them. You can independently set the sort order for each album and the photo library. To establish the order of your photographs, choose View ➡ Arrange Photos, and then pick one of the hierarchical menu items:

- **By Film Roll.** Sorts the images by film roll — that is, in the order they were imported into iPhoto. Within each film roll, the images are sorted by date. However, film rolls are not visible in the albums, so sorting by film roll may lead to a sort order in the albums that you may find confusing.

▼ **Tip**

You can toggle the visibility of the film rolls in the photo library by choosing View ➡ Film Rolls. Turning off the visibility of the film rolls does *not* change the sort order. Film rolls break up your display area. If you want to scan through thousands of pictures, it might be easier to view without the film rolls breaks.

- **By Date.** Sorts the images according to the date they were taken, or if that date is not available, the date on which the file was created. If you are viewing the photo library, choosing to sort according to date hides the film rolls.

- **By Title.** Sorts the images according to the title of the file. This is initially the file name, but you can change the title if you wish, as described in Chapter 6. If you are viewing the photo library, choosing to sort according to title hides the film rolls.

- **By Rating.** You can rate your images from one to five stars by selecting one or more images and choosing a rating from Photos ➡ My Rating (see Figure 4-5), or by selecting My Rating from the image contextual menu. After you've set up the ratings for images, you can sort the images according to these ratings (highest to lowest).

- **Manually.** This option is only available for albums (see Chapter 5); you can't use it for the photo library. With this option, you can drag and drop a thumbnail to a new location within an album. A heavy black line shows where the image will be located when you release the mouse button. You can drag and drop multiple images and a red icon indicates how many images you are relocating (see Figure 4-6). Dragging and dropping images automatically switches the View ➡ Arrange Photos hierarchical menu item to Manually.

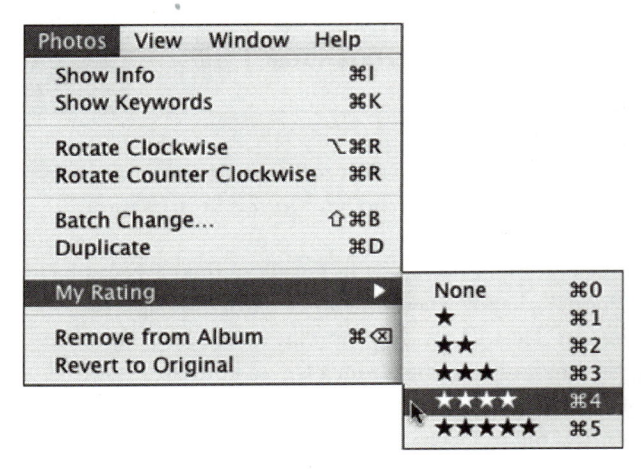

Figure 4-5
Set a rating from one to five stars to rate the quality of your images

Figure 4-6

Drag and drop multiple images to rearrange the order of the album

▼ **Tip**

After you arrange your photos manually, you can switch to another sort order (by Film Roll, Date, or Title) to re-sort the images in one of those orders. If you then switch back to Manually, iPhoto remembers the manual sort order you specified and displays the images in that order.

▼ **Note**

The ability to specify the order of the images in an album becomes very important when you build a book (see Chapter 16), because books are created and printed in the same order that the images appear in the album.

CHANGE YOUR VIEW

You always want to see your photos in iPhoto, but sometimes you may or may not want to see the additional info that goes along with each photo. Each image has a title, which defaults to the file name; I'll discuss how to change the title in Chapter 6. As mentioned previously, you can rate your images, and you can also assign keywords to each image, as I'll also discuss in Chapter 6. You can view any combination of titles, keywords, and ratings in Organize mode. To turn on the titles, choose View ➡ Titles. Figure 4-7 shows an album in Organize mode with the titles turned on.

If you've assigned keywords to an image (see Chapter 6), you can view those in Organize mode as well. To do so, choose View ➡ Keywords (see Figure 4-8). As with View ➡ Titles, this menu item is a toggle: Selecting it again removes the check mark and turns off the keywords.

 Note

Turning on the keywords is of limited usefulness, as you can only see the first few keywords of each image.

Finally, you can view your ratings by choosing View ➡ My Rating (see Figure 4-9). As with View ➡ Titles, this menu item is a toggle: Selecting it again removes the check mark and turns off the ratings.

FIVE-STAR PHOTOGRAPHY

iPhoto allows you to add a rating from one to five stars for your photographs. If you want to know the truth, I only really use the five-star ranking. I had to add all sorts of ratings to the pictures you're seeing in these example shots you're seeing just to show what it looks like with different ratings.

I mean, think about it: How often am I really going to go off in search of that two-star picture I took that time? If it were a one-star photo, I probably wouldn't want to waste the drive space to house that photo. Of course, we all use our computers our own way. Maybe you want to show a photography class samples of how *not* to take pictures. I suppose then a one- or two-star rating could come in handy.

The moral here is that you need to look at how you expect to use iPhoto and label, rate, classify, and name your pictures accordingly.

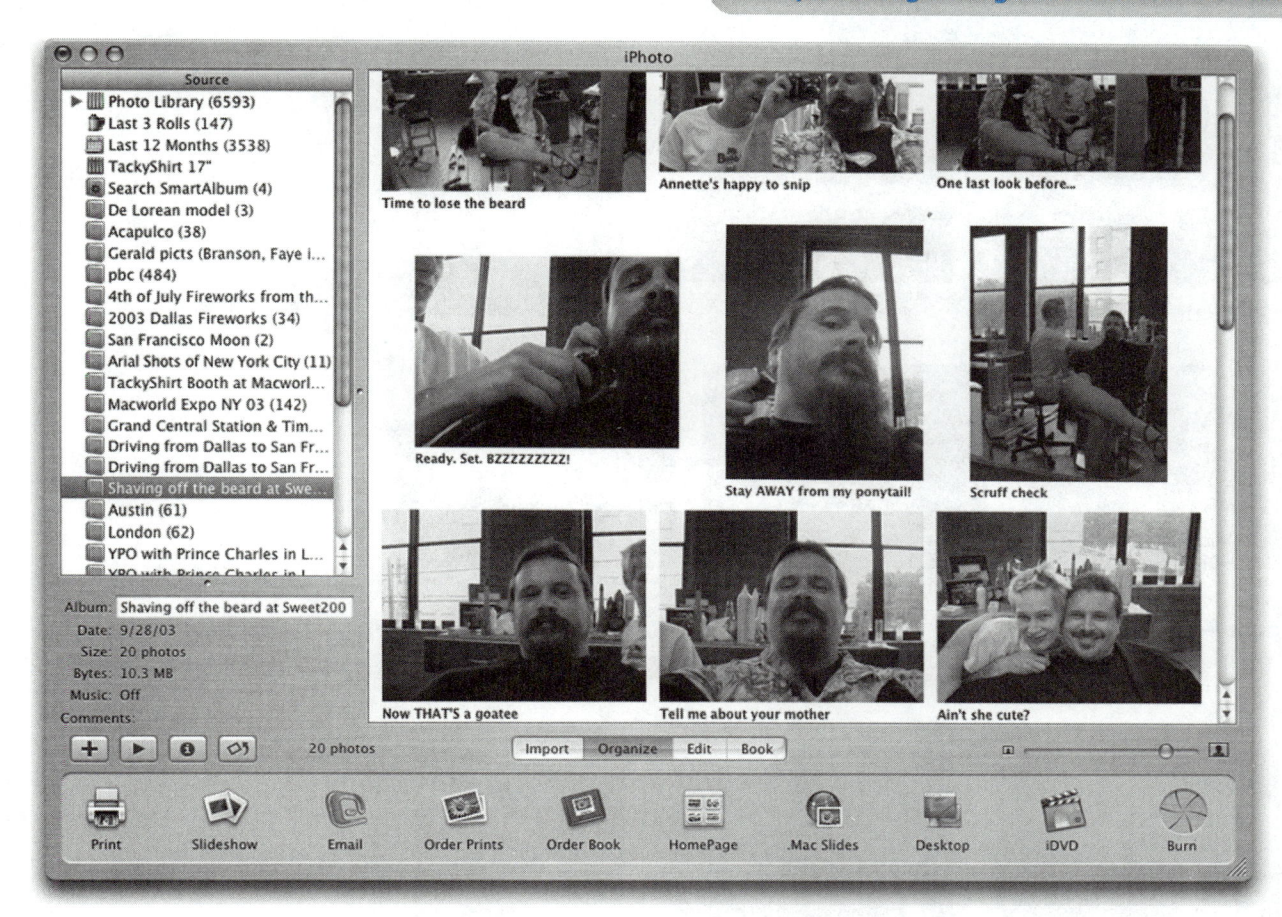

Figure 4-7

Turn on Titles to see image titles in Organize mode

Karl Under the light thingie
Vacation, Karl Kimbro, Austin

Oasis Sunset 8:13:19 PM
Vacation, Austin

Checked in at the downtown A...
Vacation, Jonathan Corns, Raymo...

Jonathan nailed a $20 win on a $5 scratch...
Vacation, Jonathan Corns, Austin

Raymond eating Oasis munchies
Vacation, Austin, Raymond Martin

River Prep. Slather on the SPF30. I missed ...
Vacation, Austin, Karl Kimbro, Jonathan Corns

Figure 4-8

Turn on Keywords to see them below the images they are assigned to

Karl Under the light thingie
★★★
Vacation, Karl Kimbro, Austin

Oasis Sunset 8:13:19 PM
★★★★★
Vacation, Austin

Checked in at the downtown A...
★★
Vacation, Jonathan Corns, Raymo...

Jonathan nailed a $20 win on a $5 scratch...
★★
Vacation, Jonathan Corns, Austin

Raymond eating Oasis munchies
★
Vacation, Austin, Raymond Martin

River Prep. Slather on the SPF30. I missed ...
★★
Vacation, Austin, Karl Kimbro, Jonathan Corns

Figure 4-9

Turn on My Rating to show ratings under the images

SCROLL THROUGH THE DISPLAY PANE

As you can imagine, the photo library (and some albums) can get quite large and include a lot of thumbnails. You'll need to scroll through the thumbnails to view them. Here are some of the ways you can do this:

- **Use the Up and Down Arrow keys.** Click on a thumbnail and use the Up and Down Arrow keys to move up and down through the rows of thumbnails. The thumbnails scroll automatically when you reach the upper or lower edge of the Display pane.

- **Use the Page Up and Page Down keys.** Press the Page Up key to scroll up one page of thumbnails. Press the Page Down key to scroll down one page of thumbnails.

- **Use the Home and End keys.** Press the Home key to jump to the first image in the photo library or album. Press the End key to jump to the last image in the photo library or album.

- **Click the scroll bar.** Click the scroll bar located at the right edge of the Display pane to scroll the thumbnails up (click above the scroll indicator) or down (click below the scroll indicator) one page at a time.

- **Option+click the scroll bar.** To jump to a particular section of thumbnails, Option+click in the scroll bar. The scroll indicator jumps to that spot, and the corresponding thumbnails are visible in the Display pane.

- **Click the scroll arrows.** Click the up arrow to scroll up by one row of thumbnails. Click the down arrow to scroll down by one row of thumbnails.

The location of the scroll arrows depends on how you have your Mac configured. The two choices are either to have both arrows at the bottom of the scroll bar, or to have the up arrow above the scroll bar and the down arrow below the scroll bar (this is how I have my Mac configured). To adjust the location of the scroll arrows, follow these steps:

1. **Open System Preferences.**

2. **Click General in the Personal section of the System Preferences dialog box.**

3. **Select one of the Place scroll arrows options.** The two options are At top and bottom and Together.

VIEW AND EDIT FILM ROLLS

As I mentioned earlier, each time you import images, iPhoto creates a film roll which is visible in the photo library (if the film rolls are not visible, choose View ➜ Film Rolls). If you import a folder, the film roll is named for the folder. Further, if the folder contains other folders, a separate film roll is created for each folder. For example, Figure 4-10 shows the result when a folder called Hunter-Soccer was imported. iPhoto creates a separate film roll for each subfolder too. If you have a folder with five subfolders that you drag into iPhoto, you'll end up with a separate roll for each of those subfolders and a roll for the folder you're dragging if there are pictures in there with those subfolders.

You can expand or collapse the contents of a film roll by clicking the triangle alongside the film roll icon. For example, in Figure 4-11, the H&T CincoDeMayo film roll is expanded. Clicking the triangle alongside the film roll icon collapses the contents. Below H&T CincoDeMayo, you can see several other film rolls that are collapsed.

▼ **Tip**

Option+click the triangle next to a film roll to expand or collapse *all* the film rolls in the photo library.

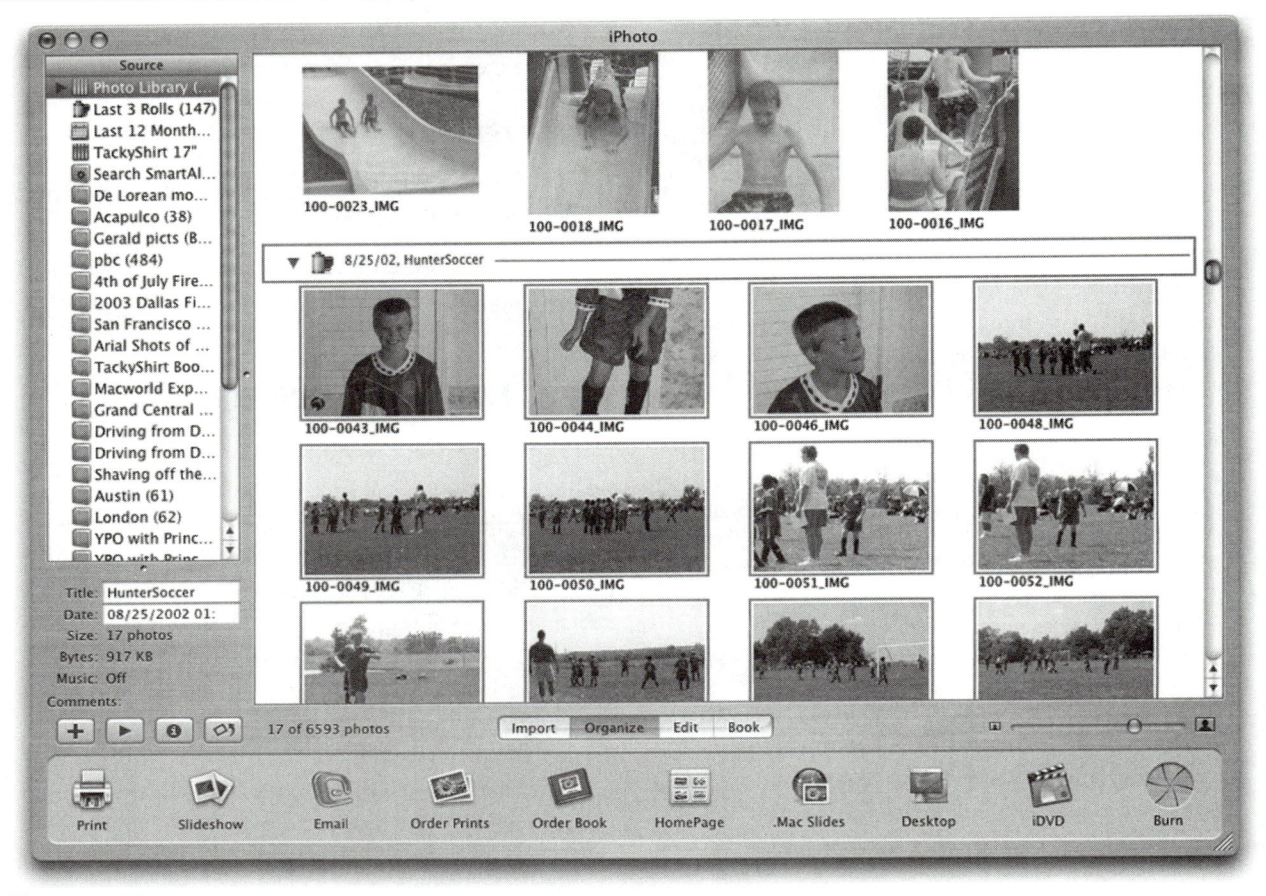

Figure 4-10
If you import folders, the film rolls are named for the folders

If you went to the trouble of naming a folder before importing it, the film roll reflects the name of the folder. But what if you imported a collection of pictures? In that case, the film roll has a name like Roll 29, or something equally uninformative. However, you can fix this by renaming film rolls. Just follow these steps:

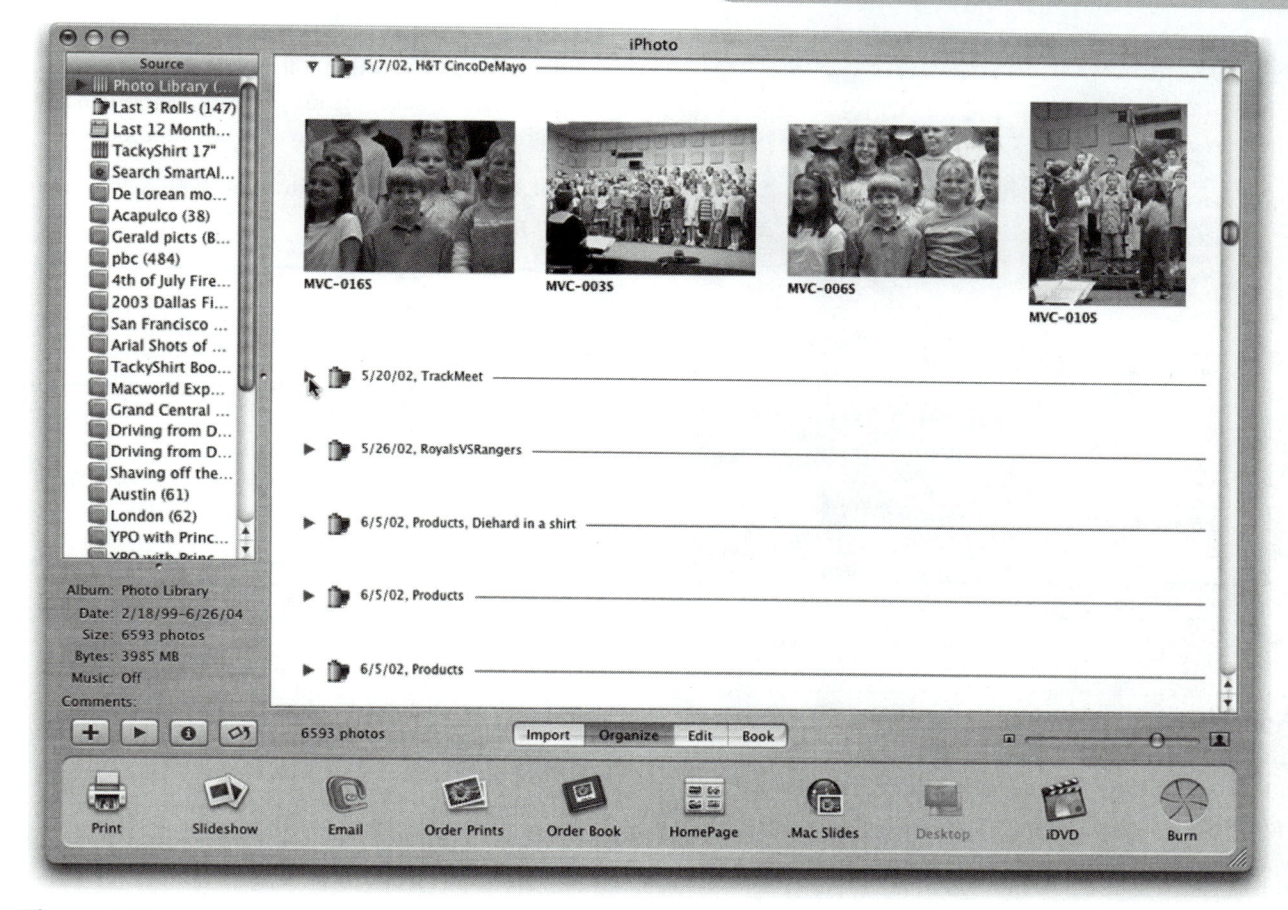

Figure 4-11
Collapse (hide) the contents of a film roll by clicking the triangle alongside the film roll icon

1. **Click the film roll icon.** This places the title and date in the Info pane (see Figure 4-12).

2. **Type over the title or date and replace them with your own values.**

3. **You can even add comments explaining what the images are.** You can do this by typing the comments into the (can you guess?) Comments field in the Info pane.

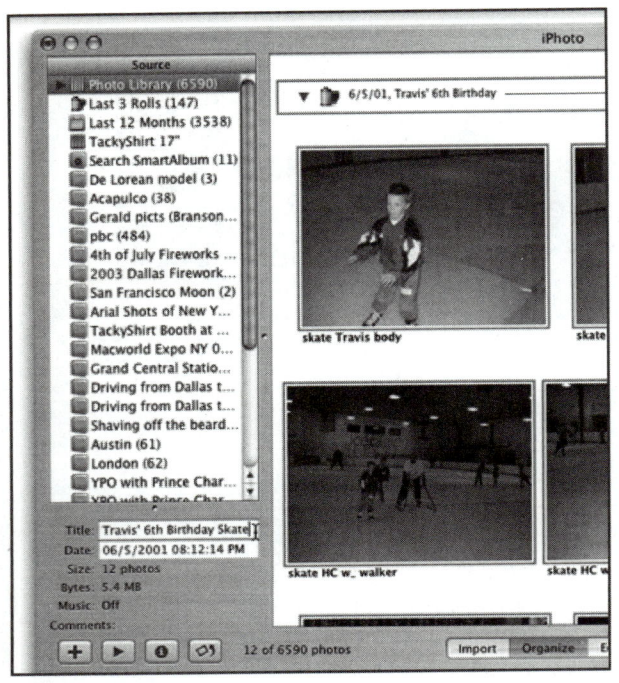

Figure 4-12
Change the title and date for a film roll in the Info pane; in this case, I wanted to add "Skate" to the roll title

You can also create a new film roll from images in the photo library. To do so, follow these steps:

1. **Select the images you want to include in the new film roll.**

2. **Choose File → New Film Roll from Selection.**
   Alternatively, you can right-click in an empty area of the Source pane and choose New Film Roll from

Selection from the contextual menu. Either way, iPhoto creates a new film roll with the selected images, and removes the images from their original film roll (an image can be in only one film roll).

3. **Type a meaningful name into the Title field in the Info pane.**

▼ **Tip**

To select all the images in a film roll, click the film roll icon or the film roll name.

▼ **Note**

The Source pane contextual menu is only available if empty space exists in the Source pane. That is, if the Source pane is completely filled with albums, you can't use the Source pane contextual menu.

Starting to get the hang of how this operation is working? One thing you might be noticing is that iPhoto really starts to come in handy when you keep adding names and such to your pictures and film rolls. It's much easier to let the computer just pull up something by name than it is to skim through pictures looking for that shot of your cousin at that picnic... Let's see... it was hot so that narrows it down to between May and September... Oh, there's a picture of the puppies. It was before they were born... Backing up... Wait, what year was that? Two or three years ago?

I'll get more into ways to make your pictures easier to find in later chapters, but how about using Organize mode to actually, oh, I dunno, *organize* your pictures! Next stop, Albums.

WHAT'S IN A NAME? AS MUCH AS YOU WANT.

At first I named my film rolls with terse little titles that were pretty cryptic to anybody but me. Then something dawned on me: I was stuck in an old computer file name rut. You know what I'm talking about. Back in the day you had to name things with stuff like "FIREWKS." Later I could go from eight-letter names to 32 characters, but I still tried to keep them short like "7-4-03 Fireworks."

When naming film rolls, you can say all you want to say (see Figure 4-13). There isn't really any limit to how long a film roll name can be, but there is a limit to how much you can see. The film roll name doesn't wrap to a second line, so you do want to keep your names shorter than your screen is wide; however, the type size in iPhoto is pretty small, so give your film rolls meaningful names that adequately describe what's in there. Something like 100 characters is a good bogus maximum, just to make sure you don't run off the page. That last sentence is exactly 100 characters. That's plenty of room to make a point without getting too deep into shorthand like "Fourth of July Fireworks 2003 shot from the Trinity spillway in Dallas." (That one's 70 characters.)

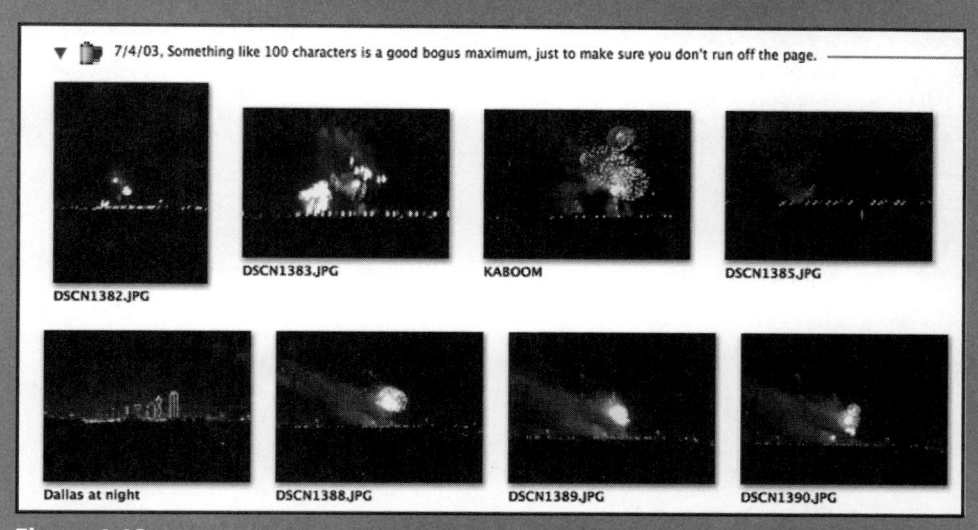

Figure 4-13
You can use plenty of text in your film roll names

Leveraging the Power of Albums

The idea of the photo album probably dates back to about two minutes after Louis-Jacques-Mandé Daguerre, the inventor of the permanent photograph, found himself staring at a stack of a dozen or so Daguerreotypes. I'm sure he was thinking they'd be even cooler in a nice book with captions. Okay, maybe not. Those first pictures were shot on sheets of copper instead of paper. That'd be one heavy book.

When you hear the word "album," most of you think about black vinyl disks with groovy tunes on them, but when you hear "*photo* album," you think about sticking pictures to sheets of tacky cardboard covered in peel-away cellophane. Rearranging the pictures was a royal pain, and adding captions meant cutting up little strips of paper to place with the pictures. Fagetaboutit! Those days are over.

An album in iPhoto is a dream to work with. You can add, remove, rearrange, and title your pictures in no time. Plus, because they don't fill up bookshelves like old-school albums, you can make as many as you like. Sometimes you want to make an album of a particular event, like a Fourth of July picnic. In iPhoto, you can make albums based on certain rules, like maybe anything with your mother in the picture, or any picture you rate as a five-star image. Try that with tacky cardboard and cellophane! Those special albums are called Smart Albums, and they tap into ratings, keywords, comments, titles, and other criteria that you assign to your pictures. Any picture that meets the criteria is automatically added to the album. That's pretty sweet.

THE IMPORTANCE OF ALBUMS

When you first start working with iPhoto and you have a few dozen pictures in the photo library, you will probably find yourself simply scanning around in the big pile for pictures instead of using many of the organizational features (like Albums). That's how it was with me.

I found myself with several hundred photos before I really started to see the benefits of organizing my work. Actually, it was a rapid progression up to thousands of pictures, and suddenly I had tons of pictures with no keywords, albums, or descriptions. Thankfully, the fact that the date and time get recorded on all pictures gave me half a chance of dealing with this train wreck.

Trust me, the sooner you get in the habit of naming your film rolls, creating albums, and adding keywords and comments, the better off you'll be in the long run. I'm not sure if I'll ever manage to get caught up on my personal collection. Learn from my mistakes.

On the bright side, after you start using iPhoto to share your travel pictures on the Web, you'll start to feel good about titling and organizing your pictures as quickly as you load them (so you can show your friends what a great time you had on your trip).

UNDERSTAND ALBUMS

Albums are your most valuable tools for organizing your photo collection. Essentially, an album is a collection of images. You can:

- Create albums
- Delete albums
- Add pictures to albums
- Remove pictures from albums
- Rearrange the pictures within an album

Albums are also very valuable tools in constructing slideshows (see Chapter 10) and books (see Chapter 16) because both slideshows and books use the entire contents of an album as their source. Each album is visible in the Source pane at the left side of the iPhoto window. To view the contents of an album in the Display pane, simply click the album's icon.

▼ Tip

You can ⌘+click multiple albums to see their combined contents in the Display pane.

CREATE NEW ALBUMS

The three ways to create a new, empty album are:

- Choose File ➜ New Album (⌘+N).
- Click the New Album button (+) located just below the Info pane.
- Control+click a blank area in the Source pane, and pick New Album from the contextual menu.

Whichever method you choose, the New Album dialog box appears (see Figure 5-1). Type the name of the new album into the dialog box and click OK. The new album appears in the Source pane.

You can create a new album and populate it with images from the Display pane. These images can be in the photo

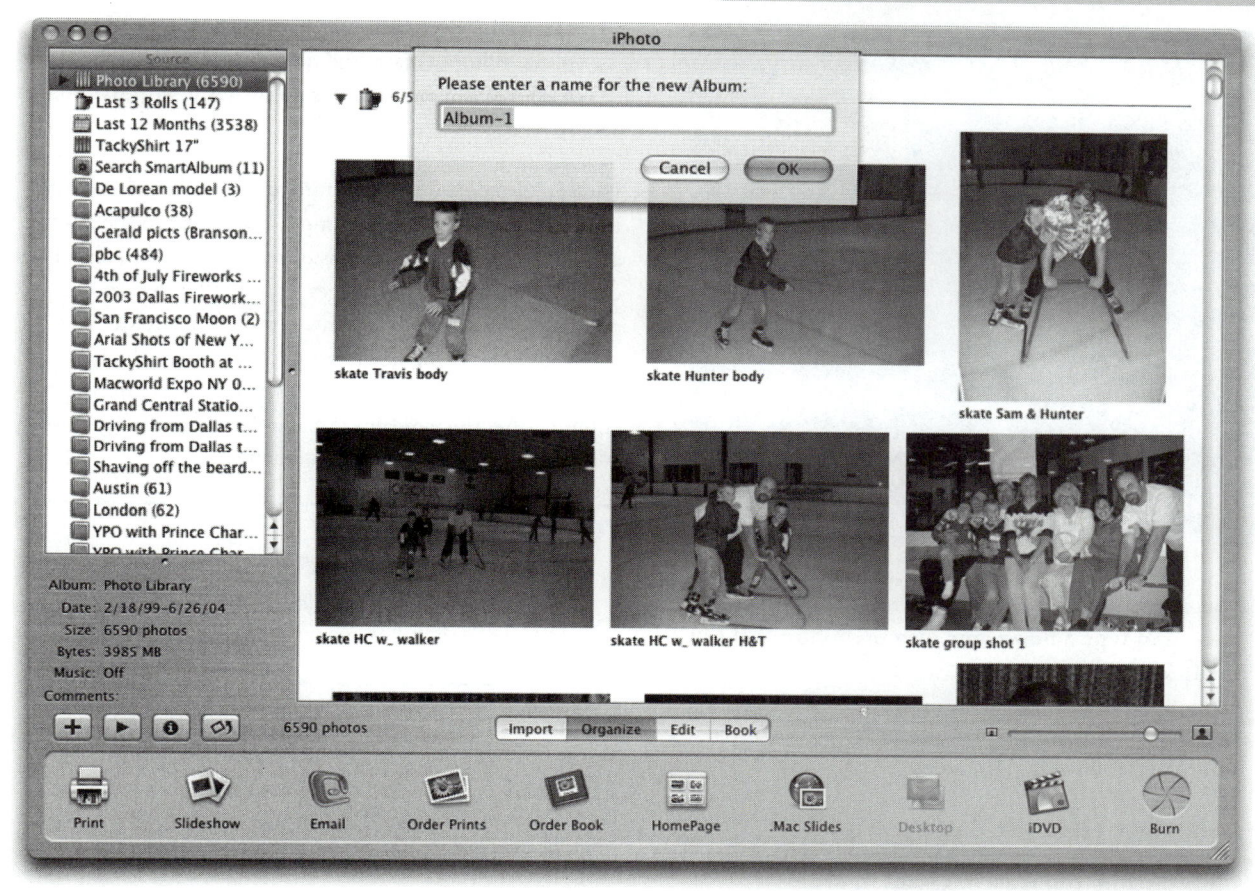

Figure 5-1

Type the name of your new album into the New Album dialog box

library, one of the yearly collections under the photo library, the Last Roll film roll, the Last 12 Months collection, or an album. To add images to a new album from the Display pane, follow these steps:

1. **Select one or more images in the Display pane.**

2. **Choose File ➜ New Album From Selection.**

3. **Type the name of the album into the New Album dialog box that appears.**

There is another way to create a new album and pre-populate it with images from the Display pane: Follow these steps:

1. **Select one or more images in the Display pane.**

2. **Drag the images to an empty spot in the Source pane.** iPhoto creates a new album (with the default name) and populates the album with the selected images.

ALBUM NAME GAME

Album names can be as long as you want them to be, but short album names work better in the typically narrow Source pane. One thing to keep in mind though is that the name you choose now may be used elsewhere later on. If you make a homepage in iPhoto, for example, the title of the album is the headline at the top of the Web page. Although the album name can be longer, the homepage headline only displays around 40 characters or so, but that's plenty.

If you want to really get deep into detail on what's in that album, use the Comments field at the bottom of the Source column.

3. **Make sure the new album is selected in the Source pane, and type a new name into the Album field in the Info pane.**

Finally, you can also create a new album from the contents of a film roll by following these steps:

1. **Click Photo Library in the Source pane.**

2. **Click the film roll icon you want to use.**

3. **Drag the film roll to an empty spot in the Source pane.** iPhoto creates the new album, gives it the same name as the film roll, and populates it with the images from the selected film roll.

You can also create a new album automatically during the import process, adding the imported images to the album at the same time the album is created. To do this, simply drag a folder or a set of images from the Finder into an empty area in the Source pane. If you drag a folder into the Source pane, the newly created album has the same name as the folder. If you drag a set of images into the Album pane, the new album has a default name (such as Album-1), which you can then change.

▼ Note

On occasion, dragging a folder into the Album pane creates a new album with a default name and *not* the name of the folder. This bug appears randomly. If it happens to you, just rename the album.

You may run into difficulties creating a new album if you already have a large number of albums, because no blank space exists in the Source pane for you to drag images, folders, or film rolls to. You can work around this in two

DON'T BE STINGY ON THE ALBUMS

Making albums is way too easy in iPhoto. It's something you should get in the habit of doing as you import pictures. Eventually you'll wean yourself off of working so much in the main pile and start focusing on working in albums, because there you can scroll around without having all those other thousands of pictures cluttering up the room.

Go ahead and make an album any time you see a cluster of pictures that should be grouped together. It only takes a few seconds to select a cluster of pictures, drag it over to the Source pane, and type **Trick or Treating Halloween 2004**. There! Now you at least have fast access to where those pictures are.

Naming individual pictures, although I think it's a blast, is a bit of work. Adding keywords can also be a bit awkward. I can understand if you end up with thousands of pictures named DSCN12345 and the like, but making albums for your pictures is so easy there's no real excuse for not creating as many as you need.

ways. The first way is to create a new, empty album (choose File ➜ New Album), rename it, and then drag the images to the new album. A more efficient way is to drag the images, folder, or film roll to a spot either directly above or below the Trash album. When you do, a black rectangle appears around the entire Source pane (see Figure 5-2). When you release the mouse button, the new album is created automatically.

Too many albums about the same thing? You can create a new album by merging the contents of multiple albums. To do so, follow these steps:

1. **In the Source pane, select the albums you want to merge.** iPhoto displays the contents of all the selected albums in the Display pane.

Figure 5-2
Create a new album when the Source pane is full by dragging images just above or below the Trash album

2. **Select all the images in the Display pane.** The easiest way to do this is to click in the Display pane, and then choose Edit ➜ Select All.

3. **Click one of the highlighted thumbnails and drag it to an empty area of the Source pane.** This creates a new album containing all the selected thumbnails.

RENAME ALBUMS AND ADD COMMENTS

You can rename an album at any time using the following steps:

1. **Select the album in the Source pane.** This places the name of the album in the Album field in the Info pane.

2. **Select the existing contents of the Album field.**

3. **Type in the new name.**

You can also type comments describing the contents of the album into the Comments field. Double clicking an album's name, icon, or anywhere in that row in the Source column also allows you to change the album name.

 Note

If you already have a picture selected when you try to name your album in the field below the Source column, the information *for that picture* displays, not for the album. You have to click in the background space around the picture before you see the album's Title field and Comments field.

If you're zoomed in all the way in Organize mode when you click on an album, iPhoto has the currently displayed picture in that album selected. Again, click off of the picture to view the album name and comments.

DUPLICATE AND DELETE ALBUMS

Duplicating an album is not only easy to do, but extremely handy. For example, say you want to build two books from the contents of a single album, but you want the images to be in a different order for each book. Or perhaps you want to create two slideshows from a single album, but you want to leave out a few images in one of the slideshows. The problem is that both books and slideshows use the entire contents of an album in the same order the images appear in the album. So the easiest way to achieve the effects you want is to duplicate the album, and then make minor modifications to the duplicate album (such as rearranging the images or deleting a few images).

To duplicate an album, select the album in the Source pane. Then choose Photos ➜ Duplicate, or choose Duplicate from the Album contextual menu. The duplicated album has the same name as the original, with a sequence number appended. For example, the duplicate of the London 2003 album has the name London 2003-1.

 Note

You can select multiple albums before choosing Duplicate; all the albums get duplicated.

Deleting an album is just as easy as duplicating one. Select the album you no longer need and choose Photos ➜ Delete Album, choose Delete Album from the Album contextual menu, or just press the Delete key and then press Enter or Return when the sheet drops down to ask you if you *really, really* want to delete that album. Remember that this only deletes the album; it doesn't delete the images from the photo library.

ALBUM ORDER

You can change the order of albums in the Source pane. To do so, click and drag an album. As you do, a heavy black line appears where the album will be located when you release the mouse button (see Figure 5-3).

 Note

Although you can rearrange the order of Smart Albums by clicking and dragging a Smart Album (see "Build a Smart Album," later in this chapter, for more on Smart Albums), you cannot intersperse Smart Albums with regular albums in the Source pane.

Smart Albums must remain near the top of the Source pane, just below the Photo Library album, Last Roll film roll, and Last 12 Months collection (if you have these turned on in Preferences).

ADD PHOTOS TO AN ALBUM

You've seen how to create new, empty albums, as well as albums that contain an initial set of images. But you can

Figure 5-3
Drag albums in the Source pane to change their order

add new pictures to albums any time you want. For example, you might create an album for a trip, and later discover another roll of film that also contains pictures from that trip. As described in Chapter 3, you can directly import the images into an album from a CD, hard drive, or digital camera. But you can also copy pictures from one album to another, or from the Photo Album to a newly created album.

 ### Note

Even if you add the same image to 7,822 different albums, iPhoto only stores the image once. Essentially, each album contains a set of references (pointers) to the actual images. What this means is that if you change anything about an image, such as the title, or edit the image in any way, the change occurs in the photo library *and* in all the albums in which the image is included.

To copy images from one album to another, follow these steps:

1. **Select the album containing the pictures you want to copy.**

2. **Select the images in the Display pane.**

3. **Drag the images on top of the target album.** A black rectangle indicates the target album, and a red icon shows how many pictures will be added to the target album (see Figure 5-4).

Dragging images also works with pictures from the photo library, its subcategories, the Last 12 Months collection, or the Last Roll film roll. Of course, good old cut and paste also works. Follow these steps to cut and paste an image:

1. **Find the pictures you want to copy and select them.**

2. **Press ⌘+C (or choose Edit ➜ Copy) to copy.**

3. **Select the album where you want to put the picture.**

4. **Press ⌘+V (or choose Edit ➜ Paste) to paste.**

If you want to move a picture from one album to another (instead of copying it), follow these steps:

1. **Select the pictures in the source album.**

2. **Choose Edit ➜ Cut, or choose Cut from the thumbnail contextual menu.**

3. **Click on the target album.**

4. **Choose Edit ➜ Paste, or choose Paste from the thumbnail contextual menu.**

REMOVE PHOTOS FROM AN ALBUM

You can remove an image from an album by selecting the image(s) and using one of the following options:

- Choose Cut from the contextual menu.
- Choose Remove From Album from the contextual menu.
- Choose Edit ➜ Cut.
- Press the Delete key.
- Drag the image to the Trash album.

Removing an image from an album doesn't actually delete the image; the image is just no longer part of the album. The picture is still available in the photo library, and you can add the image back into the album (or any other album) by dragging it from the photo library to the album. Just a reminder: If you delete the image from the photo library, it's really gone. All instances of that image in all your albums vanish too.

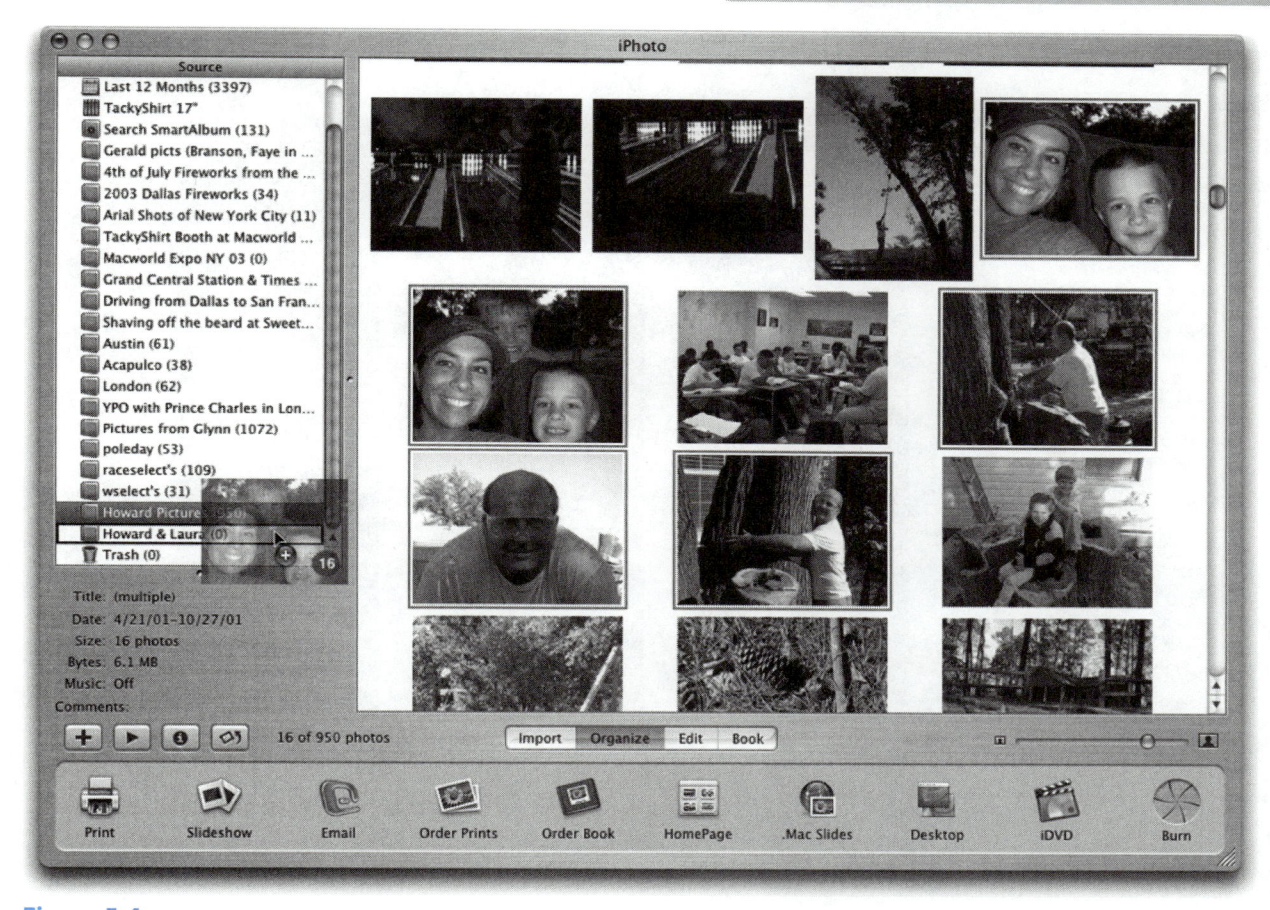

Figure 5-4

Drag images from one album to another to copy the pictures into the target album

BUILD A SMART ALBUM

A Smart Album is a special kind of album that iPhoto maintains for you. The contents of a Smart Album are all the images in the photo library that match the criteria you specify. For example, you can build a Smart Album that contains all pictures that have not been rated, or an album of all the pictures that have been given the keyword *family*.

You can combine multiple criteria to specify the images to include. For example, you can create a Smart Album that contains all pictures with the keyword *family* and that are rated four stars. The more information you feed into iPhoto about your pictures, the more useful Smart Albums become. A Smart Album appears in the Source pane as a purple book with a gear wheel on the cover (see Figure 5-5). They are always located near the top of the Source pane.

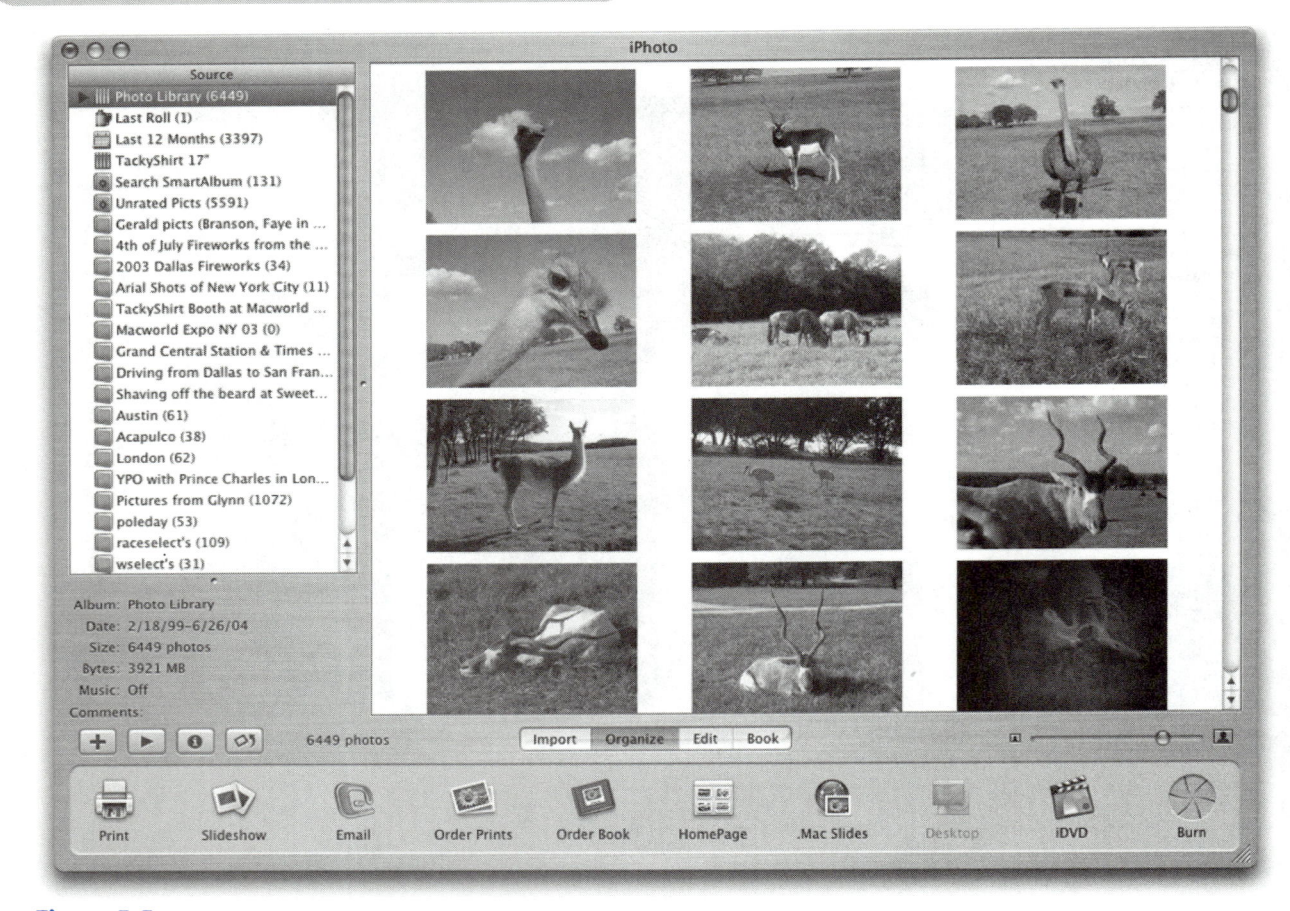

Figure 5-5
Smart Albums are easy to distinguish from regular albums: They are purple and have a gear wheel

Although you can sort the contents of a Smart Album by date, title, or rating (choose an option from View ➜ Arrange Photos), you cannot rearrange the images manually. That is, clicking and dragging an image to a different location within a Smart Album doesn't do anything.

To create a Smart Album, follow these steps:

1. **Choose File ➜ New Smart Album, or choose New Smart Album from the Source pane contextual menu.** iPhoto displays a drop-down box (see Figure 5-6).

2. **Name the album (type a name into the Smart Album name field).**

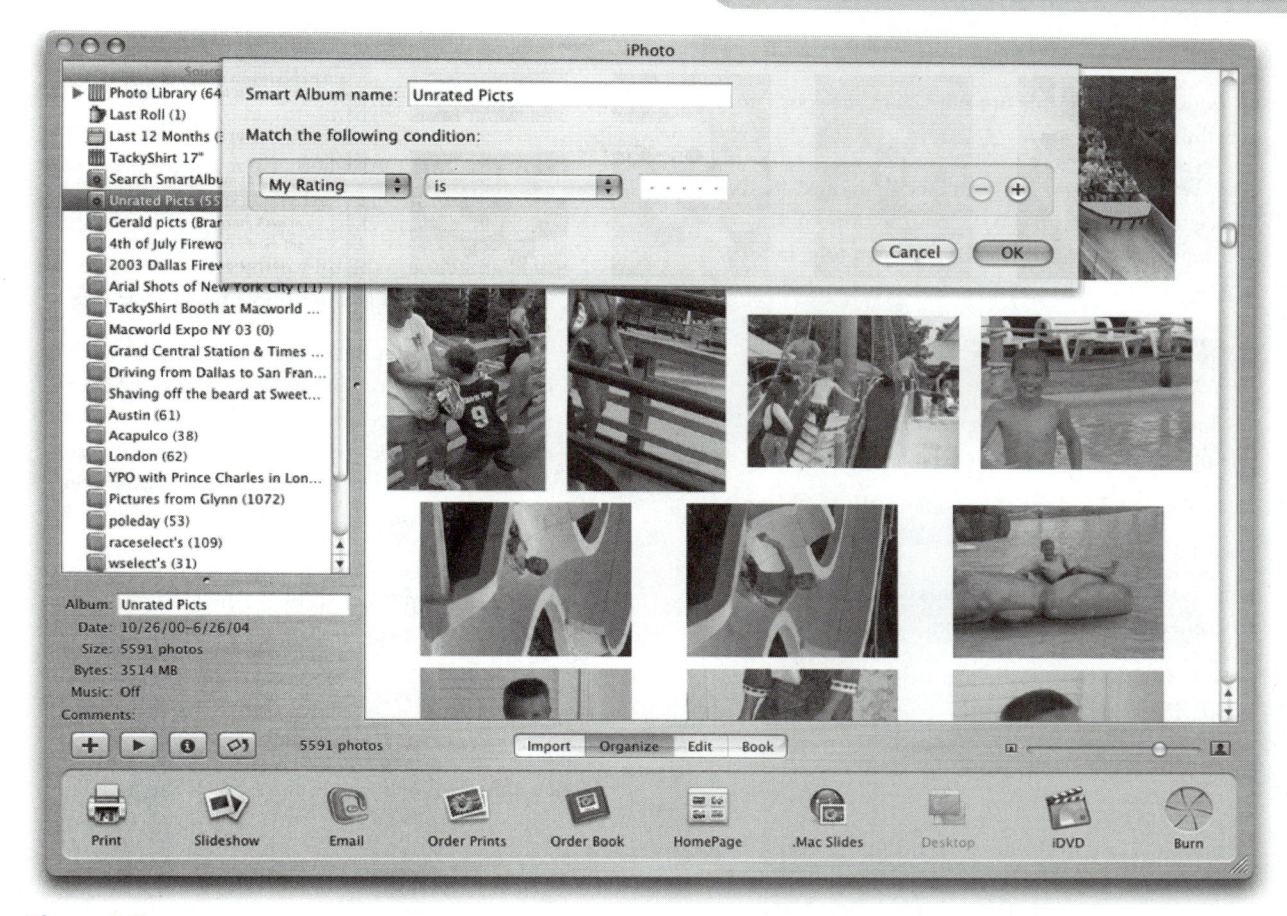

Figure 5-6
Name your Smart Album and specify the conditions for images to be included in the Smart Album

3. **Specify the condition(s).** Any image that matches the condition(s) is included in the Smart Album.

To specify a condition for a Smart Album, follow these steps:

1. **On the left, choose the attribute you want to look for** (such as Date, Title, File Name, etc.).

2. **Next to that choose how you want to compare that attribute** (such as Contains, Does Not Contain, etc.).

3. **On the right, enter the word, name, date, or whatever you want to use for the search.**

The image properties you can use are

● **Album.** The album that the image appears in (or does not appear in). Select from a list of albums in the rightmost pop-up list, as well as the value Any, meaning that the image is present in any album. The compare functions are

- **is.** The image is present in the specified album.

- **is not.** The image is not present in the specified album.

○ **Any Text.** Compares the contents of any text field associated with the image (such as the title, comments, file name, or keyword) to whatever you type into the rightmost field. The compare functions include

- **contains.** The specified text appears somewhere in the text fields.

- **does not contain.** The specified text does not appear anywhere in any of the text fields.

- **is.** One of the text fields contains the exact contents of the specified text.

- **is not.** None of the text fields contains the exact contents of the specified text.

- **starts with.** One of the text fields starts with the specified text.

- **ends with.** One of the text fields ends with the specified text.

○ **Comments.** Compares the contents of the Comments field to whatever you type into the rightmost field. The compare functions are the same as the Any Text option.

○ **Date.** Compares the date associated with the image to the specified date, date range, or elapsed time. The compare functions are

- **is.** The image date matches the specified date. Specify the date in the rightmost field.

- **is not.** The image date does not match the specified date. Specify the date that the image date must *not* match in the rightmost field.

- **is after.** The image date is after the specified date. Specify the date the image date must be later than in the rightmost field.

- **is before.** The image date is before the specified date. Specify the date the image date must be earlier than in the rightmost field.

- **is in the last.** Tests whether the image date is more recent than the specified elapsed time. To set the elapsed time, type a numeric value into the text field and choose the unit of measure (days, weeks, or months) from the rightmost pop-up list (see Figure 5-7).

- **is not in the last.** Tests whether the image date is not within the specified elapsed time. To set the elapsed time, type a numeric value into the text field and choose the unit of measure (days, weeks, or months) from the rightmost pop-up list.

- **is in the range.** Tests whether the image date is between two dates. Specify the beginning date in the first (left) field, and the end date in the second (right) field.

○ **Filename.** Compares the contents of the Filename field to whatever you type into the rightmost field. The compare functions are the same as the Any Text option.

○ **Keyword.** Compares any of the keywords associated with the image to whatever you type into the rightmost field. The compare functions are the same as the Any Text option.

○ **My Rating.** Compares the image rating (stars) to the number of stars specified in the rightmost field. The compare functions are

- **is.** The image rating is exactly equal to the specified number of stars.

- **is not.** The image rating is not equal to the specified number of stars.

- **is greater than.** The image rating is greater than the specified number of stars.

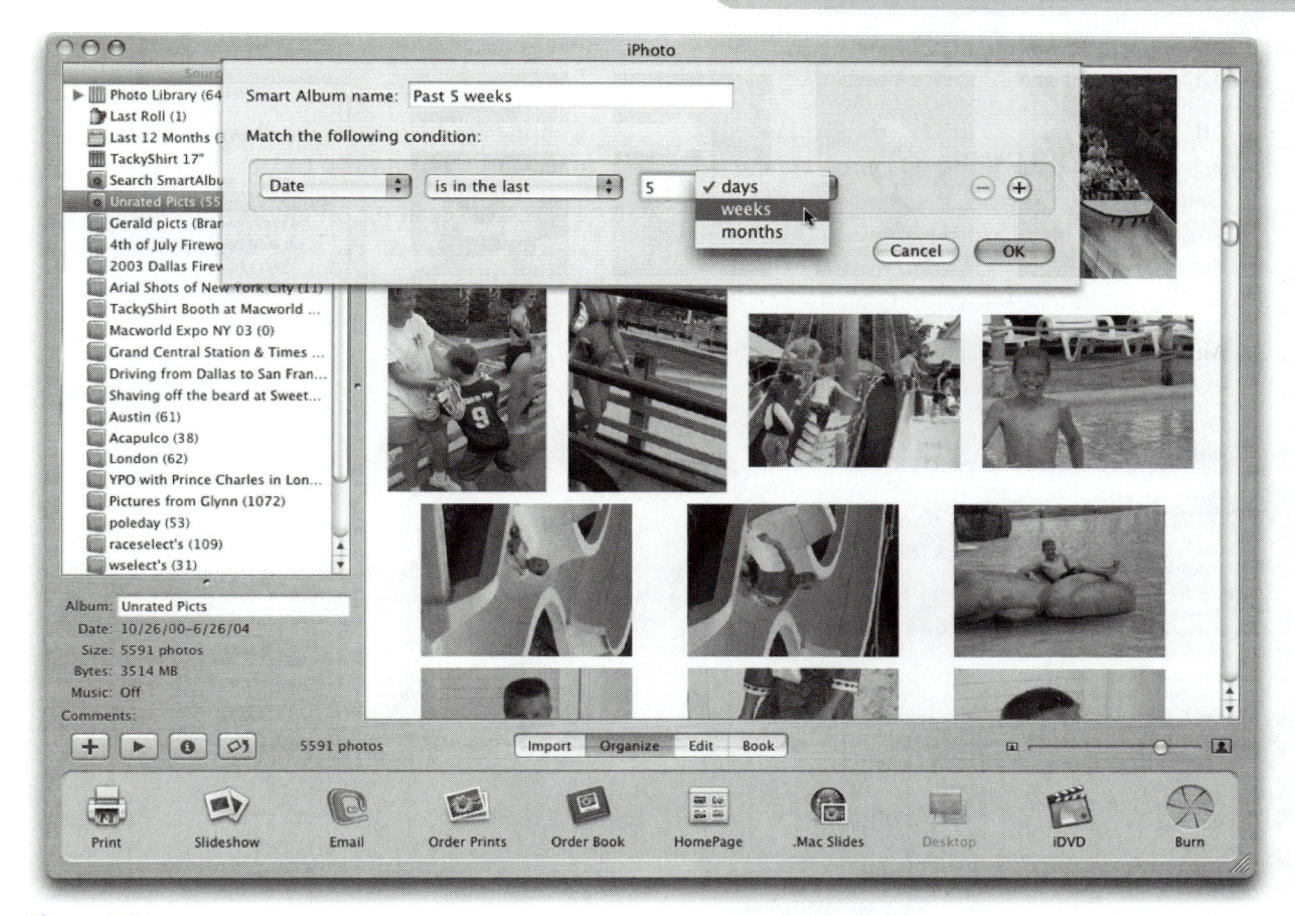

Figure 5-7
Specify how recently a picture must have been taken to be included in the Smart Album

is less than. The image rating is less than the specified number of stars.

is in the range. The image rating is in the range given by the two rating fields. The leftmost field specifies the lower end of the range, and the rightmost field specifies the higher end of the range.

● **Roll.** Tests whether the film roll containing the image is in the last or is not in the last number of rolls you type in the rightmost field.

● **Title.** Compares the contents of the Title field to whatever you type in the rightmost field. The compare functions are the same as the Any Text option.

After you're done specifying the first condition, you can add more conditions by following these steps:

1. **Click the plus sign (+) button at the right edge of the Smart Album drop-down box.** A new condition line appears below the line in which you clicked the plus sign.

2. **Select an option from the Match pop-up list.** The available options are

   ■ **All.** The images must match all conditions in order to be included in the Smart Album. For example, Figure 5-8 shows a Smart Album in which the pictures must not only have a keyword that contains the words *shot by Howard Crutsinger* but must also be dated in the last 30 days.

   ■ **Any.** The image must match at least one condition in order to be included in the Smart Album.

3. **Fill in the additional criteria in the new condition line.**

4. **Continue adding criteria until you are done, and then click OK.**

5. **To remove any of the conditions, click the minus sign (-) button near the right edge of the Smart Album drop-down box.**

Figure 5-8
Combine multiple criteria to filter the images that appear in the Smart Album

SMART USE OF SMART ALBUMS

Smart Albums both rock *and* roll. I mean come on! Think about all the stuff you can do with that feature! As long as you enter enough data for your pictures, Smart Albums can feed up all sorts of fun. Here are a few ideas to help you get in the mood for how sweet they can be.

When you're adding keywords, use some broad ones as well as more specific ones. Let's say you just took a trip to London. Tag those pictures with the keyword **vacation** and you can have a Smart Album of every trip you've imported. Tag those pictures with **vacation** and **London,** and now you can see all your vacations or just pictures you've taken in London. Add more and more keywords and then you can pull up just pictures from **London** on **vacation** that have your buddy **Dave** in them. Now every time you have a pint with Dave in London on vacation, the pictures you tag as such are magically added to the group. Been there a few times to see good ol' Dave? Narrow it down further and you can see just pictures from that one year. That is so cool!

Smart Albums come in handy for maintenance purposes. My camera names all my pictures something like DSCN0123.jpg. If I'm in a naming mood, I can just pull up my Smart Album that says "Title Contains DSCN," and there you go. That's pretty much all of my pictures that I haven't named yet.

The one thing that Smart Albums don't do well is serve as the source for a book, or for other print options where the order of the images is important. This is because you can't manually rearrange the images in a Smart Album. To fix that:

1. **Select the Smart Album.**

2. **Select all the pictures in that album.**

3. **Press ⌘+Shift+N to make a new album from that selection.**

You can do whatever you want to that new album, though this does mean that the new album won't auto-update based on the old Smart Album's rules. The new album is just a snapshot of what the Smart Album was at that point.

 Note

You can adjust the conditions for a Smart Album at any time by selecting the Smart Album in the Source pane and choosing File ➜ Edit Smart Album, or by choosing Edit Smart Album from the Smart Album's contextual menu.

Smart Albums are dynamic; that is, if you change the properties of an image so that its conditions match the conditions to be included in a Smart Album, iPhoto places the picture into the Smart Album automatically. Removing a photo from a Smart Album is just as automatic; if you modify the image properties so that its conditions no

longer fall under the rules set for that Smart Album, the picture simply blinks away. Depending on your computer speed, it may take a little bit for iPhoto to realize that one of these images is not like the others.

Albums are one of the most important aspects of iPhoto as you can well imagine. Albums and Smart Albums are where you start to wrangle your pictures into something that finally makes sense. It can be easy to go a little overboard with the albums though. Your Source pane can only show so many albums before it runs them off the bottom of the window. That's why it's important to also use the other features of iPhoto to tag and describe your pictures so they'll be easy to find even without an album.

Remember when I was saying you'd outgrow the film roll method of keeping up with your pictures pretty quickly? Albums take a bit longer to outgrow. You have to get past a couple of dozen *events* before you start to notice where relying on albums falls apart. That's when you see that you can't see all those albums at once any more. You also see that you have lots of albums cluttering up the column that you don't remember making and you're not really sure why you made them to begin with.

Luckily, you're reading this book instead of going through the natural progress of outgrowing each stage. That means that you can check out the next chapter and learn about titles, comments, and keywords so your pictures will be so much easier to keep up with than *my* old collection of untitled, unmarked pictures with no way to pull them out of the pile other than scanning through thousands of tiny thumbnails. You kids have it so much better now than I did!

Assigning Titles, Comments, and Keywords to Images

In This Chapter

Adding titles and comments to images • Viewing photo data
Assigning keywords to photos • Locating photos with keywords
Searching for photos using titles and comments

A picture may be worth a thousand words, but a few *select* words attached to a picture go a long way toward making sure the viewer picks the *right* thousand words. This part of iPhoto may seem a little bit like actual work, but the payoff for you is great. In this chapter, you're going to get into how to add all sorts of descriptive info to your photographs like titles, keywords, comments, and even a very cool chunk of info you probably didn't know you already had in your picture files just because you used a digital camera to take JPEG pictures. After you type enough info, you can make obedient little Smart Albums that display information about any group of pictures at any time.

ASSIGN TITLES TO PHOTOS

When you first import a file into iPhoto, the file name on your hard drive is what it uses for the picture's title. Of course DSCN1031 doesn't really do you much good. You can change the name to something a tad more useful like, oh, "Kitty napping on monitor." Titling your pictures also gets used later when you make Web pages or build a photo book because these titles are what iPhoto uses for the default captions that ride alongside the picture. Changing the title doesn't change the file name on your hard drive. You can still tell iPhoto to show you the picture with the file name of DSCN1031.jpg, but you can also tell it to pull up the picture with the title "Kitty napping on monitor" and get the same picture. To change the name:

1. Click the thumbnail so that the existing title is displayed in the Title field of the Info pane (Figure 6-1).

2. Select the title.

3. Type in the new text.

You can also change the title of one or more images automatically. The basic steps are:

1. Choose Photos ➜ Batch Change…, or choose Batch Change from the thumbnail contextual menu. iPhoto displays a drop-down sheet where you make batch changes to the title (see Figure 6-2).

2. Make sure that Title is selected in the left pop-up list.

3. On the right pop-up list, select what you want to change the title to (such as Text).

4. Some items (Text & Date/Time) will ask for additional input in the lower part of this sheet. Fill in that info.

5. Click OK to change the titles of the selected images.

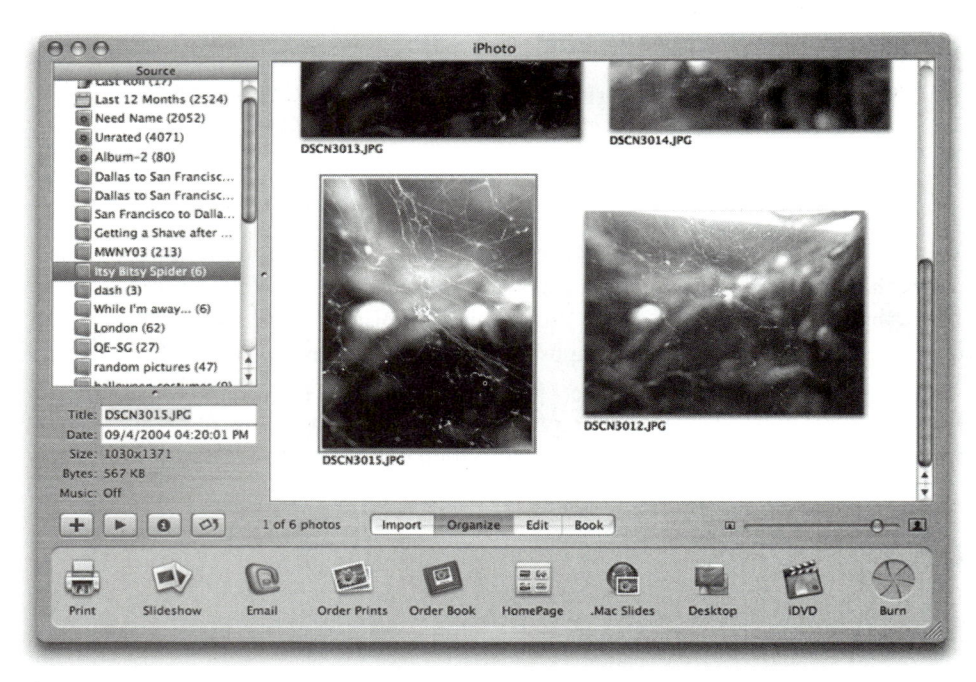

Figure 6-1
Change picture titles in the Info pane

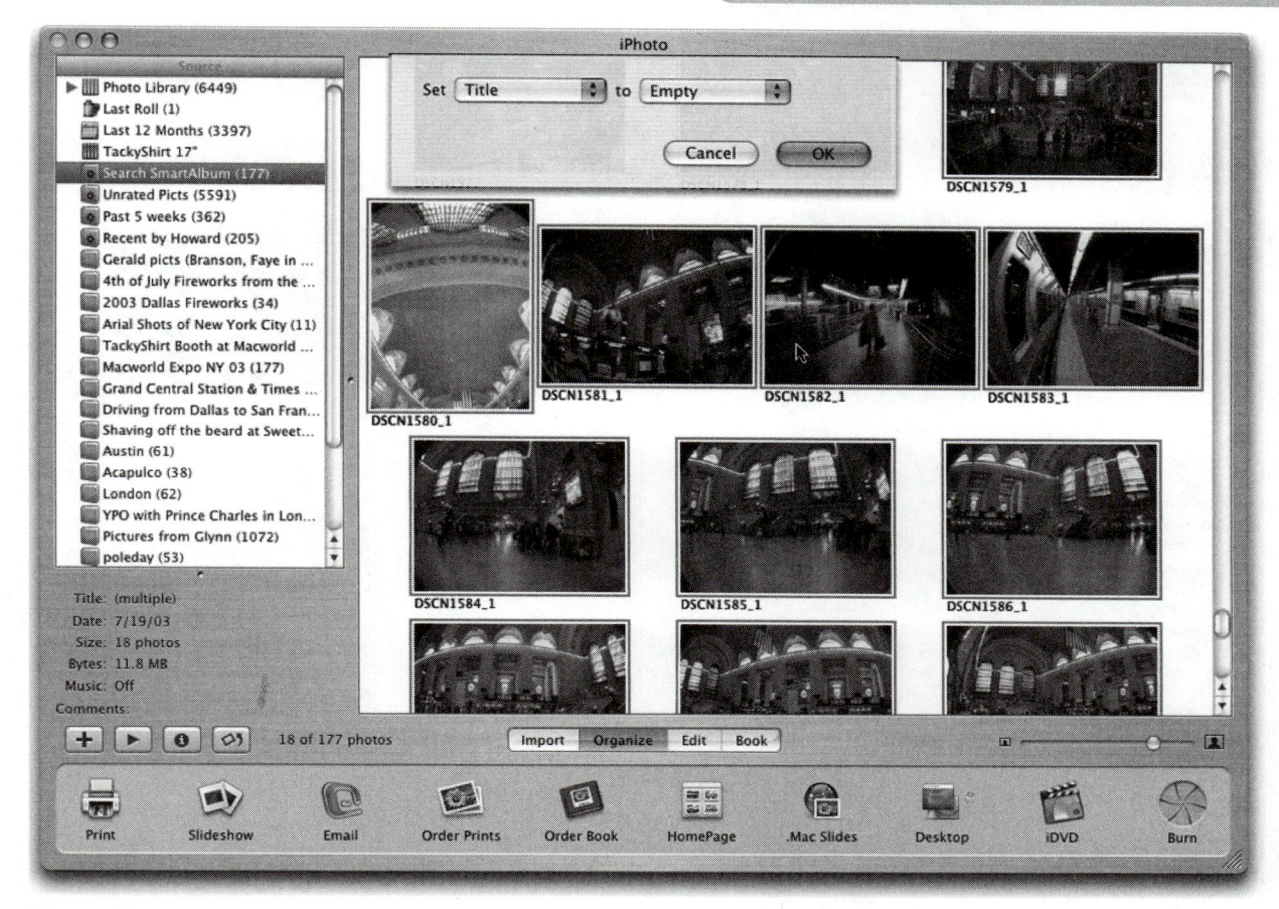

Figure 6-2
Make batch changes to the title using this drop-down sheet

▼ Note

You can also use this drop-down sheet to make batch changes to the date and comments, as discussed in the next few sections.

The available title options are:

- **Empty.** As you might imagine, this option deletes the title and leaves the field empty.

- **Text.** This sets the title to the text you type in the text field located below the pop-up lists (see Figure 6-3). If you want to append a number to the block of text, click the Append a number to each photo checkbox (for example, Sasquach-1, Sasquach-2, Sasquach-3).

- **Roll Info.** This sets the title of the image(s) to the same name as the film roll, followed by a sequence number. This option is especially useful when applied to all the images in a film roll.

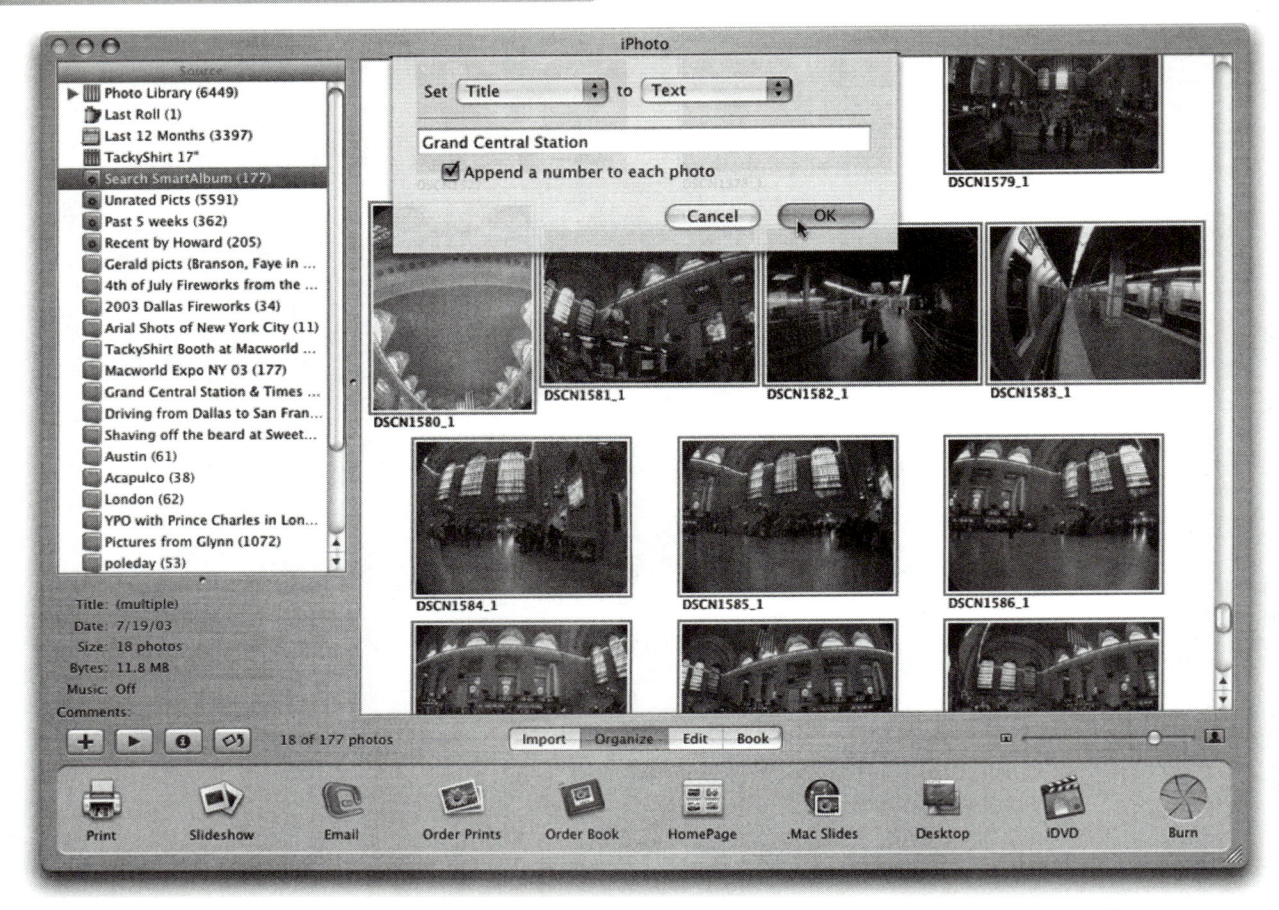

Figure 6-3
Type in the text to use as the title for each of the selected images

- **File Name.** This option sets the title of the image to it's file name (the default title).

- **Date/Time.** You can use the date and (optionally) the time to provide a title for an image. When you select this option, iPhoto modifies the drop-down sheet so you can set the format to use for the title (see Figure 6-4). Your options include whether to include the date (select the Include Date checkbox), whether to

include the time (select the Include Time checkbox), and the format to use for the date and time. A sample of the file title is displayed at the bottom of the dialog box. The date formats include the following:

- **Short.** Includes just the numeric date, abbreviation for the month, and the four-digit year. For example, 31 Dec 2003.

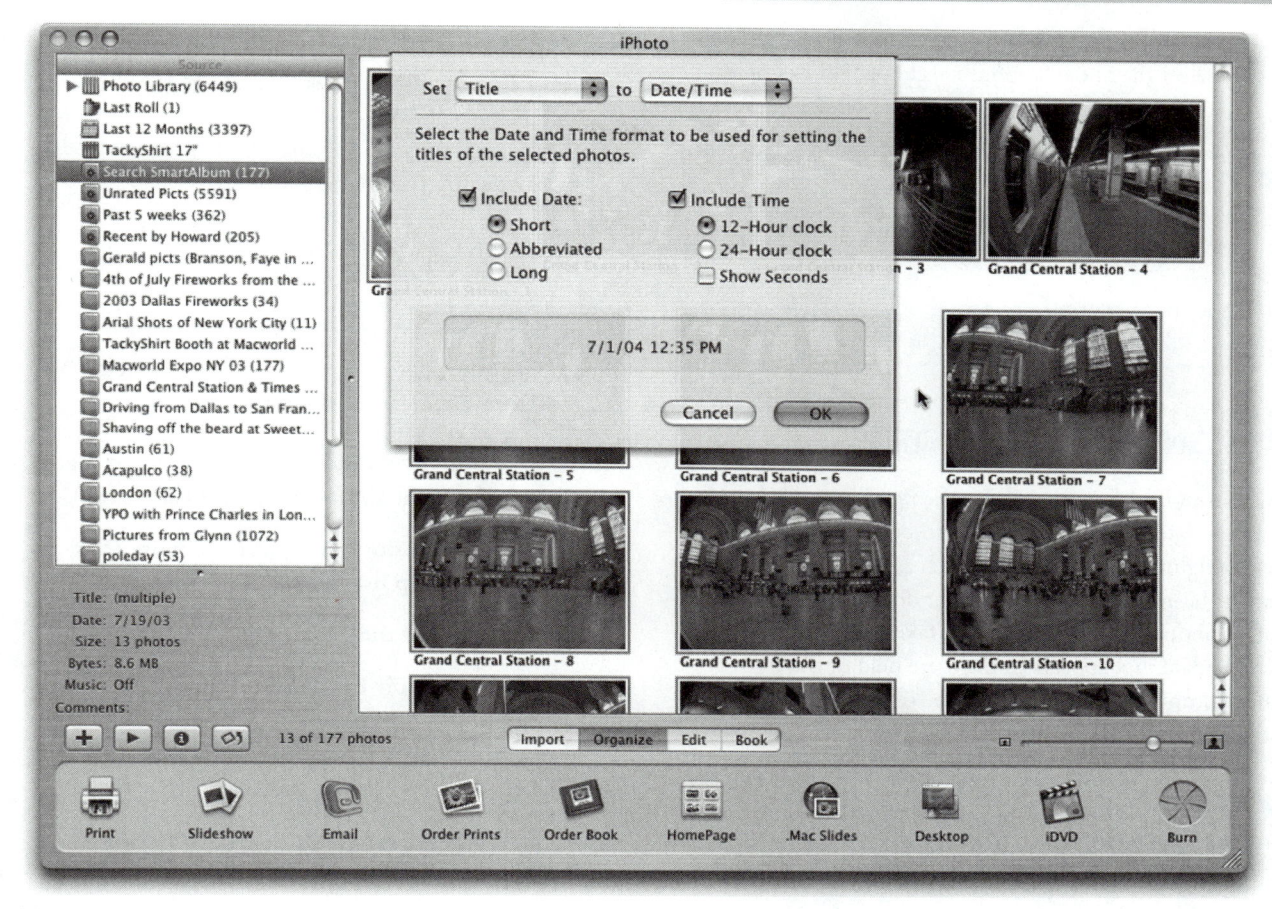

Figure 6-4
Specify the date and time formats to use for a file title with the Set Title To Date/Time dialog box

- **Abbreviated.** Includes the day of the week, the abbreviation for the month, the numeric date, and the four-digit year. For example, Wed, Dec 31, 2003.

- **Long.** Includes the day of the week, the month fully spelled out, the numeric date, and the four-digit year. For example, Wednesday, December 31, 2003.

The time formats include the following:

- **12-Hour clock.** Shows the time using the 12-hour clock, including AM/PM. For example, 09:01 PM.

- **24-Hour clock.** Shows the time using the 24-hour clock (military or European time format). For example, 21:01.

● **Show Seconds.** If you want to include the seconds, select the Show Seconds checkbox. For example, 09:01:50 PM.

 Tip

You can assign titles to all the images in a film roll. To do so, Control+click the film roll in the photo library, choose Batch Change from the contextual menu, and then select the option for setting the title as described previously in this section.

ASSIGN DATES TO PHOTOS

In addition to titles, you can use the fields in the Info pane to assign dates to an image. This can be handy when the image originates from a source (such as a scan or an image that has been heavily modified) that doesn't preserve information about when the photo was taken; in a case like this, the date that appears in the Date field of the Info pane is simply the file creation date. To change the date, select it and type in the new date.

 Tip

Another good time to change the date is when you are taking digital pictures during international travel. For example, I neglected to adjust the time on my camera when I went to London recently. As a result, the date and time attached to each picture was off by 8 hours; so my pictures — which were clearly taken in daylight — carried a time of 4:00 a.m.! Fortunately, going back and adjusting the time was easy.

 Note

The date you type must be a complete and correct date and time. If you type in an invalid or incomplete date, the results can be somewhat unpredictable. For example, if you leave out the time, iPhoto fills in 12:00:00 PM as the time. And if you type in an invalid date (such as Oct 32, 2003), iPhoto converts it to some other date (such as 02 Oct 2003). So be careful about what you type in the Date field.

You can apply a batch change to dates of the selected images. To do so, follow these steps:

1. **Choose Photos ➜ Batch Change (or choose Batch Change from the thumbnail contextual menu).**

2. **In the resulting drop-down sheet, choose Date from the pop-up list (see Figure 6-5).**

3. **Set the date and time using the fields.**

4. **Click OK to apply the date and time.**

If you want the time incremented for each photo, follow these steps:

1. **Choose Photos ➜ Batch Change (or choose Batch Change from the thumbnail contextual menu).**

2. **Click the Add checkbox (see Figure 6-5).**

3. **Specify the increment in the field located to the right of the checkbox.**

4. **Choose the time increment (Second, Minute, Hour, or Day) from the pop-up list and click OK.**

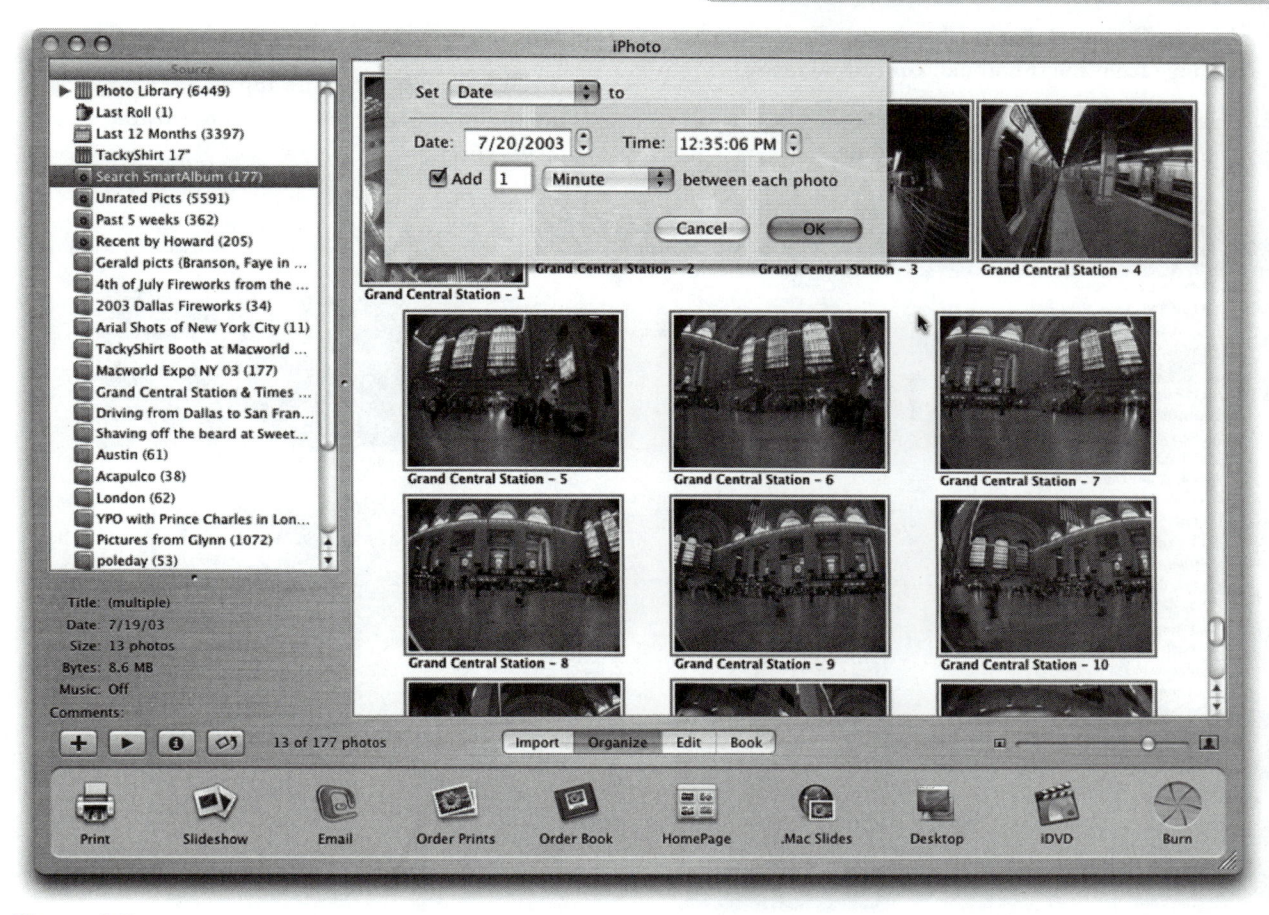

Figure 6-5
Apply batch changes to image dates, including incrementing the time for each image

ASSIGN COMMENTS TO PHOTOS

Photo titles tend to be short for several reasons. For one thing, the title field in the Info pane itself is short, so your tendency is to keep the titles short as well. This is actually a good idea, because long titles get cut off when you build a book, giving the result a rather amateurish look. But if you really want to describe a photo with a lengthier block of text, you can use the Comments field in the Info pane.

You can type as much text as you want, but the Comments field does not provide a scroll bar, so you need to click in the Comments field and use the arrow keys to scroll up and down to view and edit your text. Well, you can resize the field by dragging up in the space above the Title field too.

You can apply a batch change to the comments of selected images. To do so, follow these steps:

1. Choose Photos ➜ Batch Change (or choose Batch Change from the thumbnail contextual menu).

2. In the resulting drop-down list, choose Comments from the pop-up list (see Figure 6-6).

3. Type the comment in the text field.

4. If you want this text to be appended to any existing comment, click the Append to existing Comments checkbox.

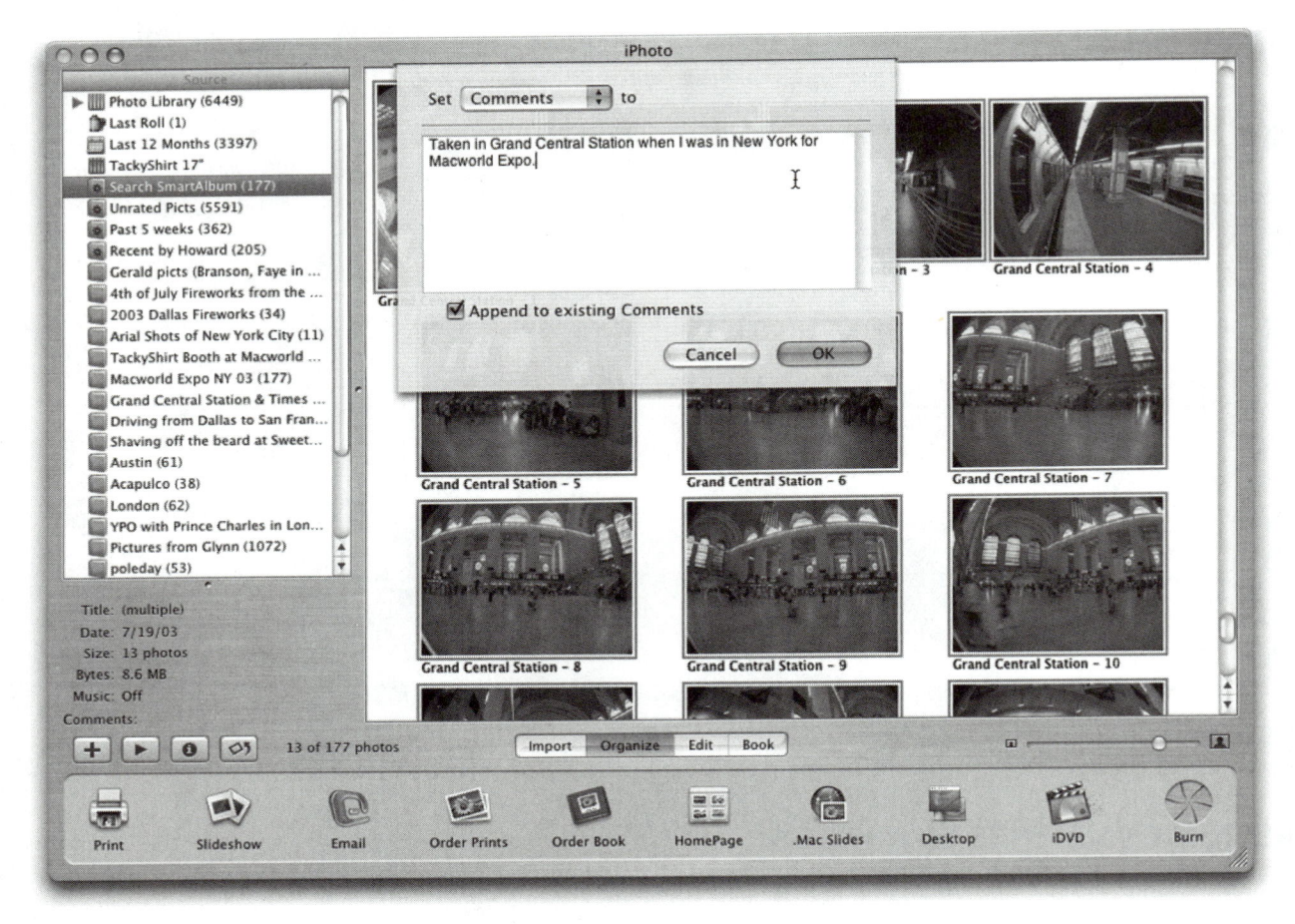

Figure 6-6

Apply batch changes to image comments, including appending the batch comment to the existing comment

BATCH CHANGE IS YOUR BUDDY

Batch is a hot little feature in iPhoto, particularly when it comes to the Comments field. That little checkbox for Append to existing Comments makes batch changes particularly sweet, because the Comments field can hold just about anything you want to put in there. I tend to use the Comments field as an extended keyword repository. Keywords have their place in the world, but under Comments, I can put more specific info.

When it comes to Comments, Batch Change won't add a leading or trailing return when you're appending to other comments. Hello little buggy wug! If you already have some comments in there, Batch Change sticks the new comments onto the end of that same line of comments. You *can* have carriage returns inside your comment, but if you type **[return, return, return] Photographer: Sam Crutsinger[return]Mardi Gras in New Orleans[return]**, the first and last returns are ignored, and the middle one survives. The comment ends up looking like this:

[prior comments blah, blah, blah] Photographer: Sam Crutsinger

Mardi Gras in New Orleans

VIEW PHOTO INFORMATION

Many digital cameras record quite a bit of information about a picture. This information may include the time and date, the exposure used, the height and width of the image, the zoom setting, any exposure correction, whether the flash was used, the aperture and shutter speed, the ISO film speed, and even the type of camera used. This information is stored in a special format called EXIF (Exchangeable Image Format).

You can view some of this data in iPhoto by choosing Photos ➜ Show Info, or by choosing Show Info from the photo's contextual menu. Either of these actions opens the Photo Info dialog box. The two tabs in this dialog box are the Photo tab (see Figure 6-7), which includes basic information about dates, sizes, and the camera; and the Exposure tab (see Figure 6-8), which contains a wealth of information about the camera settings at the time the picture was taken.

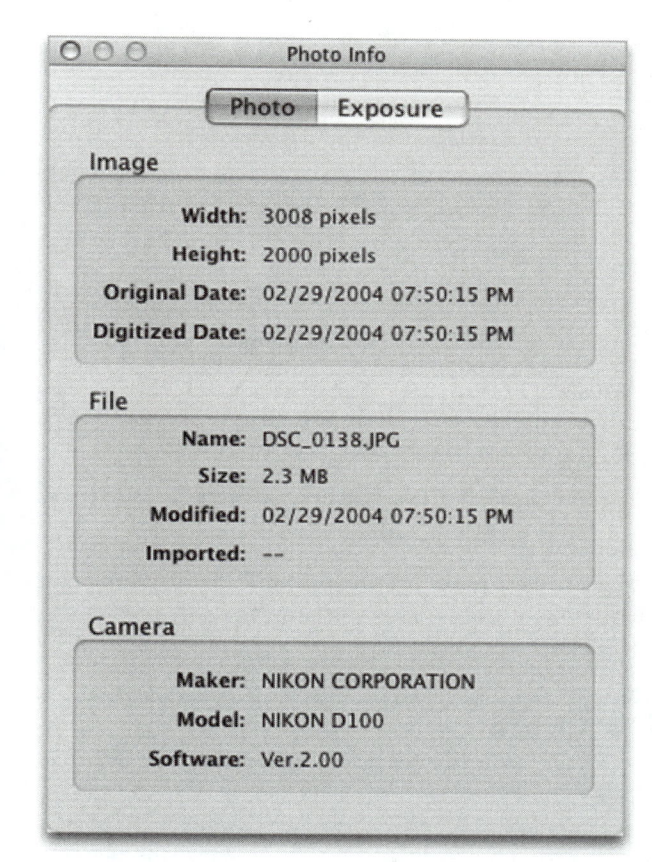

Figure 6-7

The Photo tab in the Photo Info dialog box gives you information about the image size, file, and camera

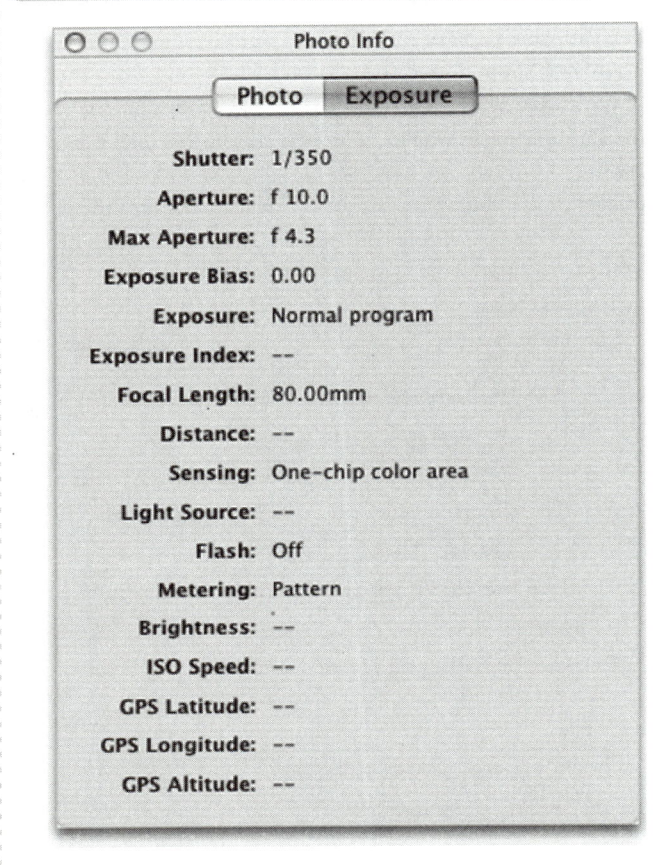

Figure 6-8
The Exposure tab in the Photo Info dialog box gives you information about the camera's settings when the picture was taken

 Note

Not all cameras record EXIF information, and the amount and type of information recorded vary by camera. Keep in mind that if you use iPhoto (or some other photo-editing software) to change the picture type to some other format, like PNG, the EXIF information is lost. EXIF info can be found embedded in JPEG, TIFF, RAW, and Adobe Photoshop (since version 7) files. As time passes, other formats, such as PNG, will likely begin to incorporate this data.

MANAGE YOUR KEYWORDS

Keywords provide a way to find photographs that match certain characteristics. For example, if you assign the keyword *mother* to every picture that contains a picture of your mother, iPhoto makes viewing these pictures later much easier. Working with keywords involves three main steps:

1. **Setting up a list of the keywords you want to use**.

2. **Assigning the keywords to the appropriate photos.**

3. **Using iPhoto's search capabilities to locate photographs that have certain keywords attached.**

To create a new keyword, follow these steps:

1. **Choose Photos ➜ Show Keywords to open the Keywords dialog box, shown in Figure 6-9.**

2. **Choose New from the pop-up menu at the top of the dialog box.** This creates a keyword labeled untitled, ready for you to edit.

3. **Type in the new keyword; your text replaces the untitled text.**

4. **Click anywhere in iPhoto outside of that text block to finish editing the keyword.**

To change an existing keyword (for example, if you misspelled a keyword), follow these steps:

1. **Choose Photos ➜ Show Keywords to open the Keywords dialog box.**

2. **In the list, click the keyword you want to change.**

3. **Choose Rename from the pop-up menu at the top of the dialog box to make the keyword editable.**

4. **Type in the new keyword.**

EXIF WILL JUST GET MORE *EXCELLENT!*

When I first saw all the info my camera had been saving into my pictures, I was floored. Even the pictures I took with the still-shot feature on my DV camcorder had the EXIF info in there. To be honest, this info isn't all that useful beyond knowing the date/time of each shot, and maybe what camera you used when you took the picture; but just knowing it's there is extremely cool, at least to me.

EXIF even has fields in it for GPS Latitude, Longitude, and Altitude. GPS is short for Global Positioning Satellite, and involves a bunch of low-orbit satellites up overhead that a little receiver can listen to and then spit out information about where you're standing on the planet (to within about 10 meters). That just sends a shiver up my spine because it's just the coolest thing since ice.

Right now it's rare for a camera to have a GPS built in, but some cameras do have GPS connectivity. Some high-end cameras have an RS-232 port you can use to attach an external GPS unit. Some cameras are starting to come out with a card slot for nice, compact GPS upgrades that don't have clumsy cables tripping you up. After you're jacked into the GPS, every time you take a picture, your location information is added to the EXIF data, so you can later see just where you were standing when you took the shot.

Here's one that I'm not sure anyone's thought about. The FCC is forcing all cellular phones in the US to have GPS location built in by 2005, so the new E-911 emergency systems can locate the growing number of emergency calls being made on wireless phones. This is so they can *know* your location instead of having to deal with, "I don't know. Somewhere on I-35. Oh, there's a Texaco station over there. Does that help?"

Okay, so what if those camera phones could tap into that GPS and stamp all of your camera phone pictures? If someone's not already doing it, I predict they will be very soon.

When I'm looking at a picture, "*Where* was that taken?" is usually my first question. Hopefully, before too long, you'll be able to keep track of that as easily as you can tell *when* it was taken.

5. Click anywhere in iPhoto outside of that text block to finish editing the keyword.

One thing to keep in mind is that if a keyword is assigned to pictures when you modify that keyword, you'll be updating that keyword everywhere. In other words, if you have several pictures with the keyword "Donna Hogan" and then Donna marries my brother later, changing that one keyword listing to "Donna Crutsinger" will update that keyword everywhere it's used. (See the next section for more information on associating a keyword with an image.)

Finally, you can remove a keyword from the list. Maybe you created a temporary keyword or something and now you have no use for it. There's not much reason to delete keywords though except that the Keyword window might get a tad cluttered. Some programmer forgot to make that window resizable, so you can only see 13 keywords at a time. Anyway, follow these steps:

1. Choose Photos ➔ Show Keywords to open the Keywords dialog box.

2. Select the keyword.

ASSIGN KEYWORDS TO PHOTOS

After you create a set of keywords, you can assign one or more keywords to images. No matter where you assign a keyword to a picture, that keyword gets assigned to that picture everywhere it lives even if it's in 50 other photo albums. To assign keywords to images, follow these steps:

1. **Make sure the Keywords dialog box is open (choose Photos → Show Keywords).**

2. **Select the images in iPhoto to which you want to associate one or more keywords.** You can pick the images from individual albums or from the photo library, and you can pick multiple images using the techniques discussed earlier in this book. For example, you can select all the pictures of fountains by clicking the first fountain thumbnail, holding down the ⌘ key, and clicking all the other fountain pictures. Each selected image displays a light blue border around the thumbnail.

3. **Click the keywords you want to associate with the selected images from the Keywords dialog box.** You can pick multiple keywords if you want. Each keyword you pick is highlighted in blue.

4. **Click Assign.** When you do, the selected keywords are highlighted in gray (see Figure 6-10).

Figure 6-9
Set up the keywords you want to use in the Keywords dialog box

3. **Choose Delete from the pop-up menu at the top of the dialog box.** The keyword is removed from the list, as well as from any images to which the keyword had been associated.

KEYWORDS VERSUS COMMENTS

Both keywords and comments let you do very similar things, but in different ways. They both let you assign words to a picture that can be used as markers for finding the picture later on. Here is a list of some of the differences:

- Keywords lock you down to a word list, which can prevent some problems, unlike comments where you may call someone Mike in one comment and then Michael in another. Also, if you're not the only one labeling the pictures, the Keywords option shows a Keyword list so that the other person knows what your system is. Comments, on the other hand, are more freestyle. You type in whatever you want.

- With keywords, you're sure to always get the spelling right (or at least consistently wrong), but comments require that you type in material that matches previous comments if you're going to get a picture to come up with the others that match.

- Keywords can be seen in the Display pane under each picture, and comments are only visible for the selected picture.

- Comments have a decent-sized window to type full sentences into. Keywords *can* be long, but are typically limited to just a few short words.

- Comments can be included with pictures you email out. Keywords can't.

- When making a photo book or exporting a Web page, comments can be included, but keywords can't.

- You find pictures according to keyword by using the Keywords window to show only matching pictures. To find pictures with comments that have a common word, you have to use a Smart Album.

They both have their moments, but, personally, I tend to lean in favor of using meaningful comments. Comments are more free and right-brained, and keywords are more rigid and left-brained. Sure, I may use "That's my mom" for one picture comment, and "My mother and her new 15in PowerBook!" for another picture, but I can always tell the Smart Album to catch *mom* and *mother* and *Carla* and anything else I may have called her in a comment, so it's somewhat of a wash in the search department.

Comments are referenced in more sharing situations, which makes them useful, but if you were to use *just* comments to mark your pictures, you'd get really tired of seeing "Taken in Acapulco" in the comments on every single picture you took on that trip. How you tag your pictures is up to you; just make sure you think ahead to what you'll want to do with that data and enter it accordingly.

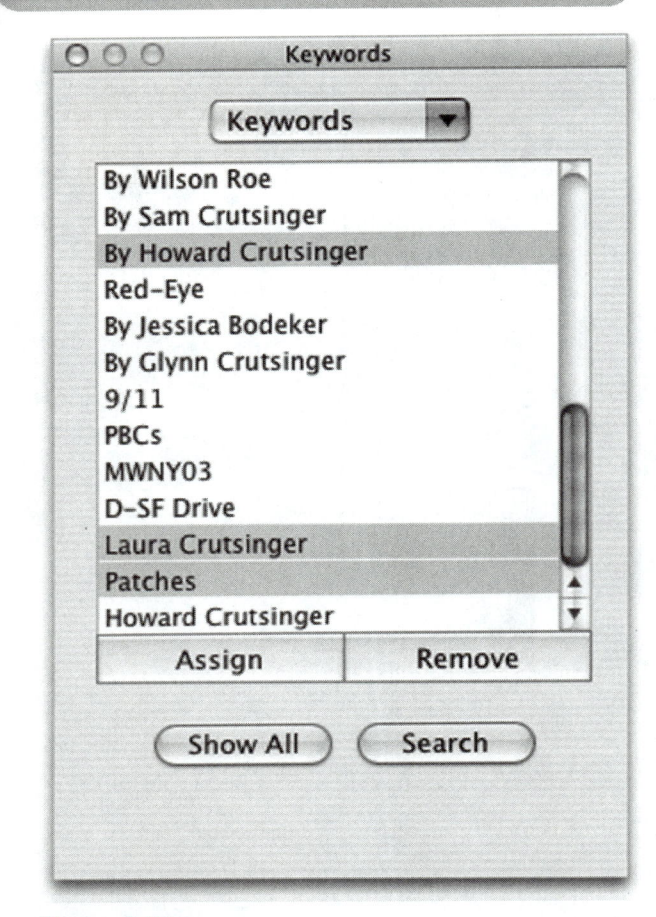

Figure 6-10
Keywords highlighted in gray are assigned to the selected images

You can check which keywords are assigned to images by making sure the Keywords dialog box is open and clicking a thumbnail; any associated keywords are highlighted in gray. You can also display the keywords in Organize mode by choosing View ➡ Keywords to display any associated keywords below the image thumbnail (see Figure 6-11).

 Note

If you select multiple images while the Keywords/Search dialog box is open, *all* the keywords associated with *all* the selected images are highlighted in gray in the Keywords dialog box. So remember that not all of the highlighted keywords are assigned to every image.

SEARCH FOR A PHOTO USING KEYWORDS

Some of you might be saying, "But Sam, why am I spending all this time assigning keywords to all these pictures?" Because keywords make it a piece of cake to find pictures later. For example, if you assign the keyword *fountains* to all the pictures you've taken of fountains, you can easily find those pictures and display them in Organize mode (where you can then use them to perhaps create a Smart Album and build a book of all the fountains you've visited from Bethesda Fountain in Central Park to Jet d'Eau in Geneva).

To find all the images in the photo library or in an album that have certain keywords associated with them, follow these steps:

1. **Switch to the album or photo library.**

2. **Choose Photos ➡ Show Keywords to open the Keywords dialog box.**

3. **Click the keyword you want to search for and click Search. (Double clicking a keyword in the list also works.)** iPhoto displays only those images that are associated with the selected keyword (see Figure 6-12).

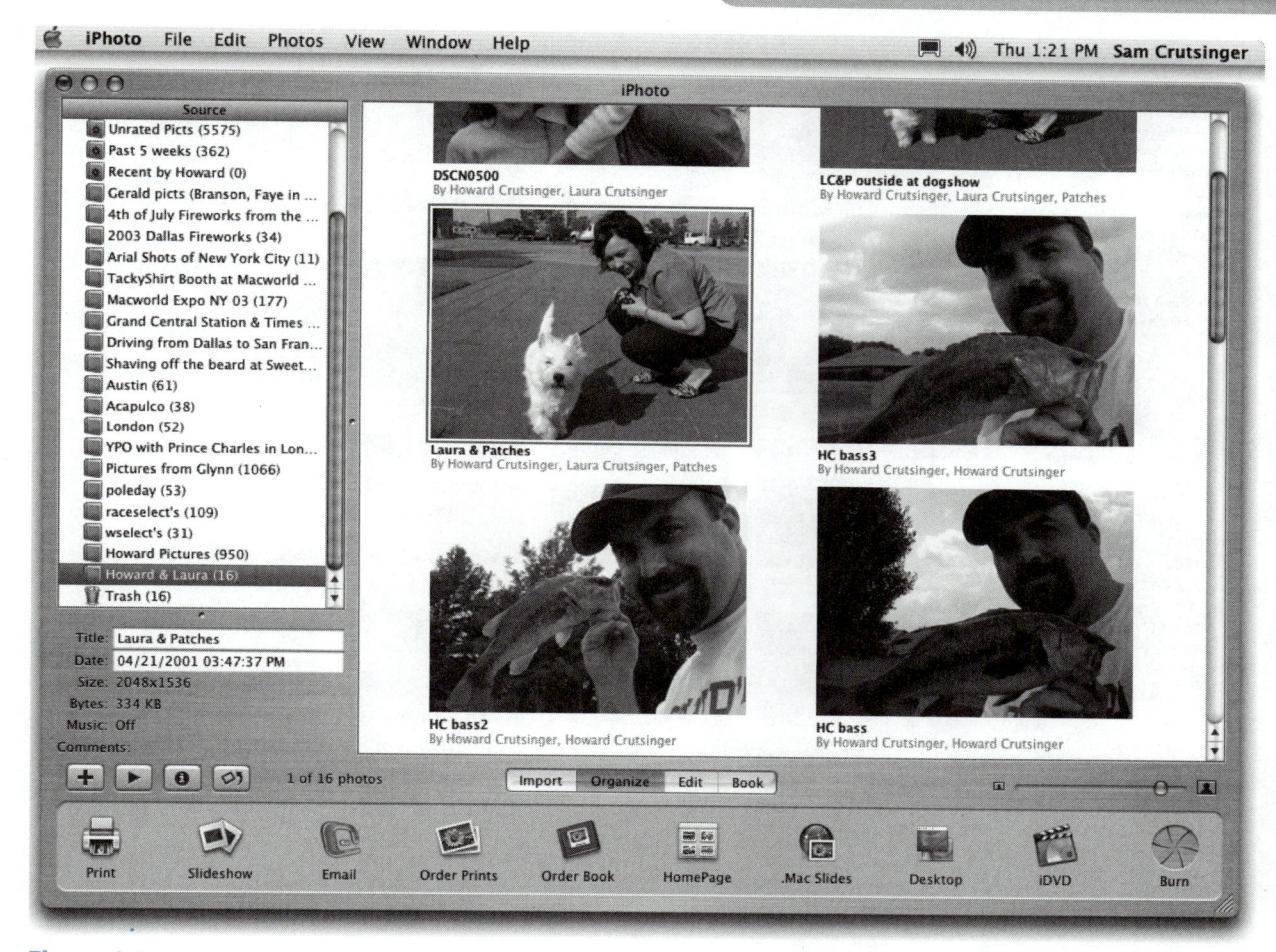

Figure 6-11
Choose View ➜ Keywords to see an image's keywords in Organize mode

4. **To find the images that are associated with multiple keywords, select all the keywords you want from the Keywords dialog box (⌘+click to pick multiple keywords), and then click Search.** Only those images that are associated with *all* the selected keywords are displayed in the result.

Figure 6-12

Find images associated with keywords by simply picking the keywords and then clicking Search in the Keywords dialog box

REMOVE KEYWORDS FROM PHOTOS

If you change your mind about assigning a keyword to an image, removing the keyword association from the image is easy. Simply click the image(s) from which you want to remove the keyword(s), and proceed using one of these two techniques:

- To remove *all* keywords from the selected image(s), click the Remove button in the Keyword pane. The gray-highlighted keywords are all deselected, and no keywords are associated with the image(s).

- To remove only specific keywords from the selected image(s), click the keywords in the Keywords dialog box list — highlighting the keywords in blue — and then click the Remove button. Only the

USING THE CHECK MARK KEYWORD

You may have noticed an item in the Keyword list that is simply a check mark. Not much of a key-*word* per se. This "keyword" can be handy for temporarily flagging a set of images you want to use later (perhaps to create a new album). To associate the check mark with a set of images, follow these steps:

1. **Select the images.**

2. **Click the check mark keyword.**

3. **Click the Assign button.**

After you're done working with this temporary set of images, you'll probably want to remove the check mark keyword from the images so it will be available when you need to mark a different set of images. To remove it, follow these steps:

1. **Search for all images that have the check mark keyword associated with them.**

2. **Click the check mark in the Keywords dialog box.**

3. **Click Remove.**

blue-highlighted keywords are disassociated from the image(s), the other keywords (which are highlighted in gray) are left alone and remain associated with the image(s).

Keywords, comments, and titles are like seeds you plant now so you can have a... no, that's not it.

Keywords, comments, and titles are like children. You raise them now and they support you in... nope.

[Strike two. —ed]

(Whoops! Three bad metaphors and I've got to take a mandatory nap. Hmmmm.... Okay.)

Keywords, comments, and titles are the frame, the boards that hold up your iPhoto house. (Not bad, but hey, that one was a *simile,* not a metaphor, so ppttttthh!)

What I'm failing to find a flowery way to say is that keywords, comments, and titles are what make iPhoto immensely useful once you get 10,000+ pictures in your collection. Is it a pain in the prat to enter all that data? Usually, yes, but it's one of those situations where you put in a little bit of work here and there so you'll have smooth sailing later on. An ounce of prevention is worth a pound of cure. A stitch in time saves nine. A... [That's it. You're done. —ed]

PART III

Editing Your Photos

127 + 178 mm = 5 × 7

Understanding the Edit Tools

In This Chapter

Entering Edit mode • Understanding the Edit tools
Customizing the Edit toolbar • Editing in the Display pane
Editing in a separate window

It doesn't matter if you're John Q. Public or a celebrity photographer like Annie Leibovitz: Every picture has *something* you can improve. Maybe you want to crop the picture so the balance is better. Maybe you want to erase a distant airplane from the sky of your otherwise totally pure slice-of-nature picture. This chapter introduces you to the Edit mode, which is where you fix your pictures. The specific details for each Edit tool are covered in Chapter 8, and Chapter 9 shows you how to use other photo-editing tools in concert with iPhoto.

WHAT CAN YOU DO IN EDIT MODE?

Briefly, here is what you can accomplish with the Editing tools:

- **Rotate.** If you scanned your image upside down, or rotated the camera (from landscape to portrait mode), you can use the Rotate function to correct the situation.

- **Retouch.** The Retouch brush enables you to paint out small imperfections, such as dust spots, blemishes, and scratches.

- **Crop.** The cropping tool enables you to remove unwanted portions of the picture to improve the composition, or adjust the aspect ratio for printing or creating a slideshow.

- **Enhance.** With a single click, iPhoto attempts to improve your photo by adjusting the brightness, contrast, and color saturation of the image. The result is not always an improvement on the original, however.

- **Fix Red-Eye.** This tool removes red-eye, the red color that sometimes appears in people's eyes when you're using a flash.

- **Adjust Brightness/Contrast.** These sliders enable you to make small adjustments to increase or decrease the brightness or contrast of the image. You can make the adjustments independently of each other, giving you a great deal of control over the final result.

- **Convert to Black and White.** Converts your color image to black and white.

- **Convert to Sepia.** Converts your color image to old-fashioned sepia tones, which use shades of brown to render the picture.

GET INTO EDIT MODE

You can switch into Edit mode in three ways. The first way is to select the image you want to edit in whatever mode you happen to be in, and then click the Edit button (the third of the four buttons located just below the Display pane).

The second way to enter Edit mode is to double-click an image's thumbnail in Organize mode. Depending on how you set up your iPhoto double-click preferences, the image opens in the Display pane, a separate window, or the selected external photo editor you chose.

The last way to enter Edit mode (and my favorite because it offers the greatest degree of control) is to Control+click the image in Organize mode, and then choose one of the options from the context menu:

- **Edit.** Opens the image in the Display pane.

- **Edit in separate window.** Opens the image in a separate window.

- **Edit in external editor.** Launches the external photo editor, which in turn opens the photo.

UNDERSTANDING THE EDIT TOOLS IN THE DISPLAY PANE

If you open an image for editing in the Display pane, the edit tools appear across the bottom of the iPhoto window (see Figure 7-1). You can use the zoom slider to zoom in and out of the image you're editing. If you'd like to zoom in on a particular portion of the image, click and drag with the mouse pointer to select that part of the image before starting to zoom. If you do this, iPhoto moves the selected part of the image to the center of the Display pane as it zooms in. For more details on selecting part of the image, see "Select Parts of a Photo" in Chapter 8.

 Note

If you enlarge the image so that it is larger than the Display pane, you can use the horizontal and vertical scroll bars to scroll around in the image. You can also hold down the ⌘ key, and then click and drag with the mouse pointer to scroll the image.

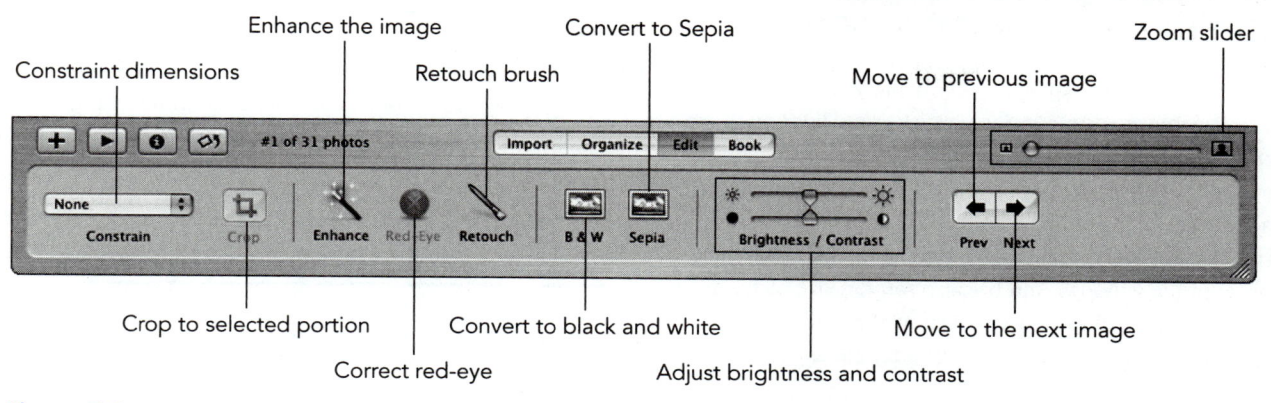

Figure 7-1
The edit tools appear below the Display pane

USE THE DISPLAY PANE CONTEXT MENU

When editing an image in the Display pane, the context menu (Control+click the image) provides a number of useful options (see Figure 7-2). In addition to the editing tools (Enhance, Red-Eye, Retouch, B & W, Sepia, and Crop), you can do the following:

- **Next/Previous:** Move to the next or previous image.

- **Duplicate:** Duplicates an image. I'll discuss the reasons for duplicating images in Chapter 8.

- **Show Info:** Display the detailed photo information.

- **Rotate:** Rotate the image clockwise or counterclockwise.

- **Revert to Original:** Revert an edited image to the original version.

- **Edit in separate window/external editor:** Open the image in a separate window, or open the image in an external photo editor.

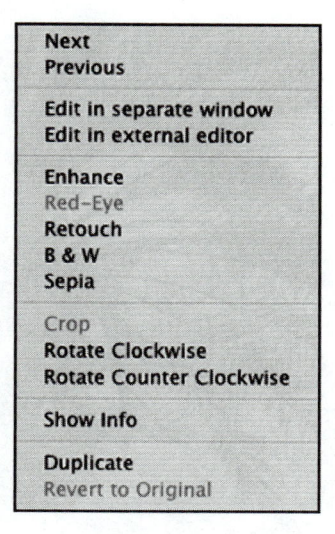

Figure 7-2
Use the Display pane's Edit context menu to choose tools and switch editing modes

EDIT IN A SEPARATE WINDOW

Editing images in a separate window provides some distinct advantages over editing in the Display pane. For one thing, you can have more than one image open for editing at a time. For example, Figure 7-3 shows three Edit windows, each with a different image in it. You can independently size each window by clicking and dragging the lower-right corner of the window. And because you can size each separate window to fill the entire screen, you can see the overall image at a larger size than in the Display pane.

 Tip

To switch between multiple open Edit windows, use the Window menu in the menu bar to select the image you want to work with (bring to the front). You can also press ⌘+` (the key with the ~, just below ESC) to cycle through all the open windows in iPhoto. That keyboard shortcut actually works in many applications, but few people know about it.

Figure 7-3
Open multiple images for editing in separate windows

Note

As with the Display pane, if you zoom the image larger than the separate window (using the toolbar zoom tool described in the next section), you can use the horizontal and vertical scroll bars to scroll around in the image. You can also hold down ⌘, and then click and drag with the mouse pointer to scroll the image.

 Tip

To hide the toolbar (and thus see more of the image in the window), click the button in the upper-right corner of the Edit window. To reopen the toolbar, click that same button again.

Editing in a separate window versus editing in the Display pane has one disadvantage: When you make changes to an image in the Display pane, you can undo those changes by choosing Edit ➜ Undo even after you've switched to another mode. To back out of multiple changes, just continue choosing Edit ➜ Undo. You can undo changes when you edit in a separate window as well, but after you close the separate window, your undo options vanish. Your only undo option is to revert to the original, which loses *all* changes you made to the image since importing it into iPhoto.

CUSTOMIZE THE EDIT WINDOW TOOLS

When you edit an image in a separate window, the editing tools appear in a toolbar across the top of the window. Figure 7-4 shows the default version of this toolbar.

Most of the tools should look familiar because they are the same as the edit tools available in the Display pane, but there are a few differences:

- **Zoom:** Instead of using the zoom slider (in the lower-right corner of the Display pane), you must zoom in and out of the image using the zoom buttons located at the left end of the toolbar. As with the zoom slider in the Display pane, however, you can select part of an image prior to zooming, and iPhoto moves the selected section to the center of the window as you zoom in.

- **Fit:** If you've zoomed in or out, you can fit the image back to the window size by clicking the Fit button. If you do this, you can then click and drag the lower-right corner of the window to resize the window and automatically resize the image as well; that is, if you make the window larger, you automatically zoom in on the image because you are making the image

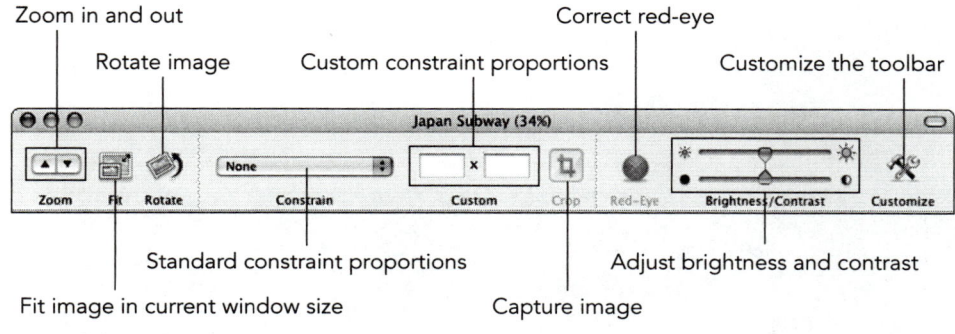

Figure 7-4

The Edit toolbar for editing in a separate window is different from the Display pane — and you can customize it

larger. If you decrease the size of the window, you automatically shrink the image.

- **Custom constraint:** In addition to the standard constrain dimensions available from the Constrain pop-up list, you can type in custom values in the two Custom fields. You should enter these values before selecting part of the image for cropping.

As you may have noticed, several tools appear to be missing from the Edit toolbar. For example, neither the Retouch brush nor the Enhance tool is visible! Fortunately, you can customize the toolbar to add or remove tools, as well as rearrange the order of the tools. To customize the toolbar, either click the Customize button (at the right end of the default toolbar) or Control+click the toolbar and choose Customize from the context menu. Either will open the customize panel (see Figure 7-5).

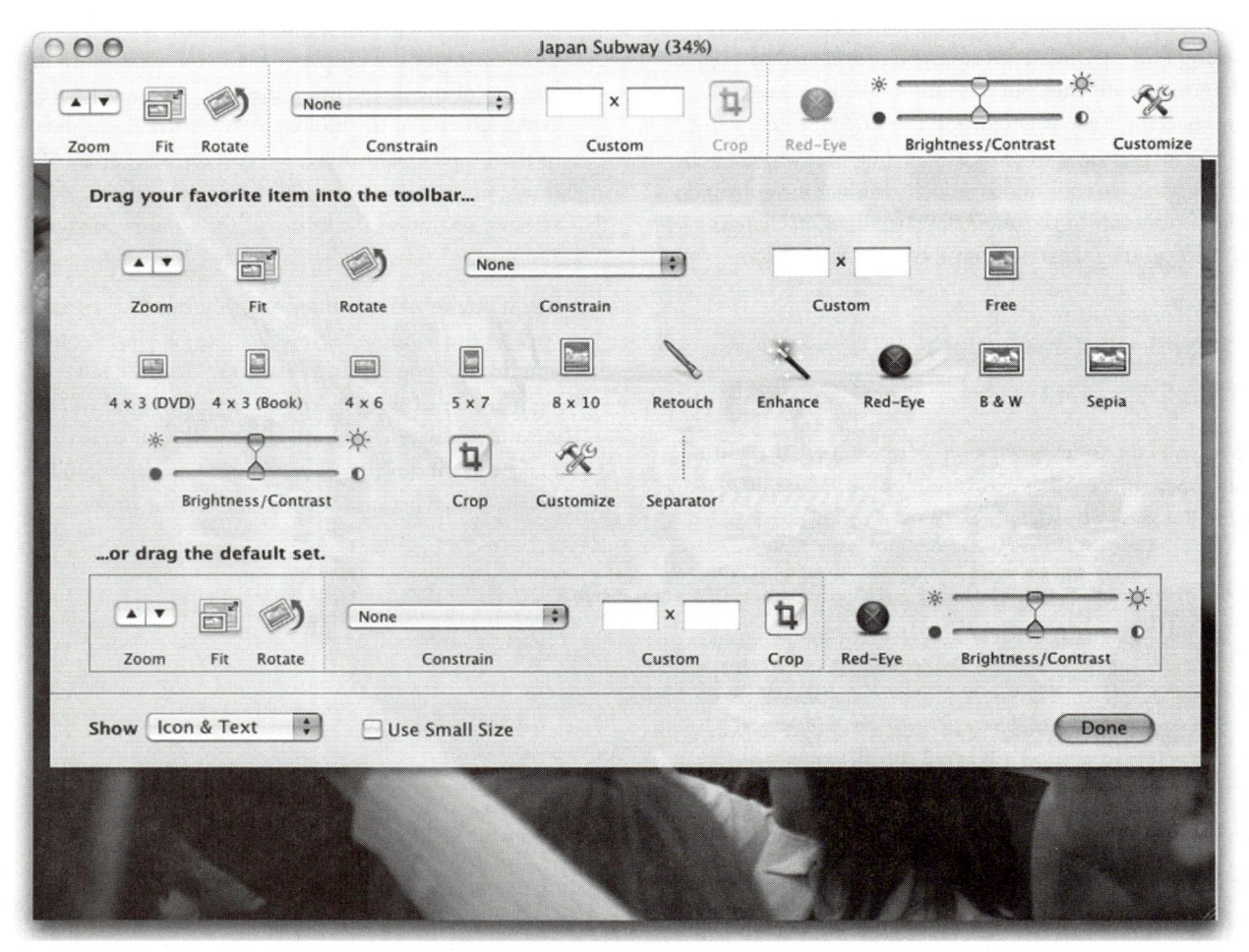

Figure 7-5
Use the customize panel to change the layout of the Edit toolbar

REMOVING AND ADDING EDIT TOOLBAR TOOLS

To remove a tool from the toolbar, click and drag the tool from the toolbar. The remaining tools move to the left to close the gap.

To add a tool to the toolbar, click the tool in the customize panel and drag it into the toolbar, positioning the tool where you want it (the B&W tool is being dragged in Figure 7-6).

To rearrange the tools in the toolbar, simply click and drag a tool to its new position.

To reset the toolbar to its default configuration, click anywhere inside the default toolbar section in the customize panel (labeled "...or drag the default set.") and drag it over the toolbar.

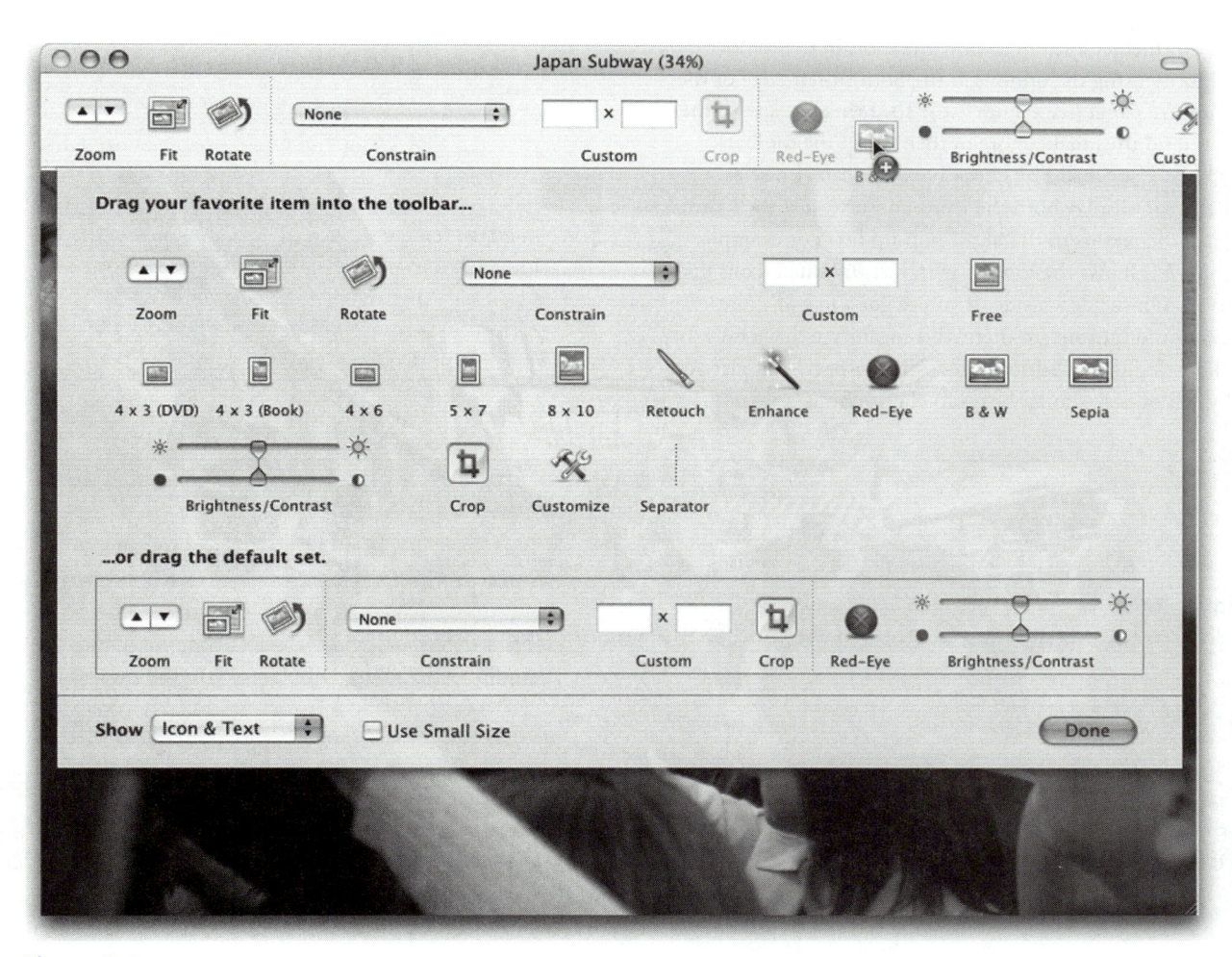

Figure 7-6
Click and drag a tool onto the toolbar

To add a separator between sets of tools, click the Separator tool in the customize panel and drag it into the toolbar.

If you find that you use a specific aspect ratio quite a bit (for example, 4 x 6 or 5 x 7 for printing snapshots), select one or more of these aspect ratio tools and drag them into the toolbar. To select a portion of the image with that aspect ratio (see "Select parts of a photo" in Chapter 8 for more information on selecting parts of an image), simply click the aspect ratio in the toolbar (see Figure 7-7).

You can further customize how the tools in the toolbar appear by using the options at the bottom-left edge of the customize panel (see Figure 7-6). To shrink the size of the icons (and thus make more of them fit in the toolbar), click the Use Small Size check box. You can also select whether to display both the icons and text, just the icons, or just the text from the Show pop-up list. For example, Figure 7-8 shows the toolbar with just the small icons displayed. On the down side, if you've got a few of those aspect ratio buttons up there, this means you have no way of knowing which button is for which aspect. You just get a bunch of very similar boxes to choose from.

After you're done customizing the toolbar, click the Done button in the customize panel.

If the window is too narrow to show the entire contents of the toolbar, a pair of right chevrons appear at the right end of the toolbar. To view and use any tools that are not visible in the toolbar, click the chevrons to display a list of the "missing" tools (see Figure 7-9). To choose one of these tools, select it from the list.

▼ Note

You cannot use some tools — such as Constrain, Custom, and Brightness/Contrast — from the list displayed when you click the double chevrons, so they'll be grayed out. This is because you must enter information for these tools to work, and there is nowhere to do so in the list. To use these tools, you need to increase the size of the image so that the toolbar has room to display the tools. You can also move those items to the left side of the toolbar where they won't so easily fall off the right edge into that overflow.

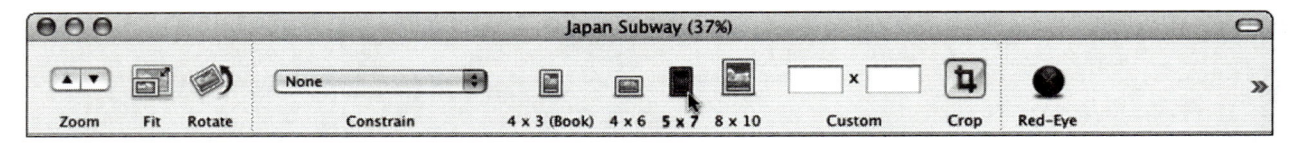

Figure 7-7
Add aspect ratio shortcut buttons to the toolbar that you use frequently

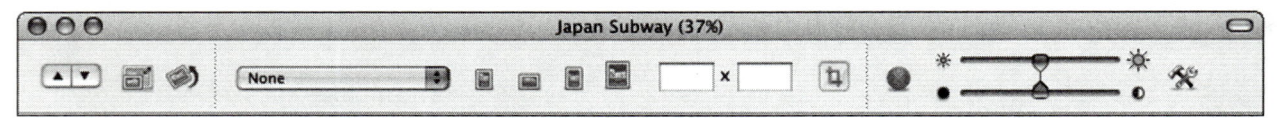

Figure 7-8
Fit more tools in the toolbar by shrinking the icons and hiding the text

Figure 7-9
Click the double chevrons to display a list of missing tools in the Edit toolbar

You can customize the Edit toolbar even without opening the customize panel. To do so, hold down ⌘ and use the following techniques:

- **Remove a tool from the toolbar.** Click and drag the tool off the toolbar. You can also Control+click the tool and choose Remove Item from the context menu.

- **Rearrange the tools.** Click and drag the tool to a new location.

▼ **Tip**

Because you can choose to customize the toolbar from the toolbar context menu, wasting space by placing the Customize icon on the toolbar is unnecessary. In addition, you should place the most-often-used tools at the left end of the toolbar so they won't "fall off" the right edge, becoming accessible only by clicking the double chevrons. And, of course, you should place tools at the left end that won't work from the double-chevrons list!

SPICING UP YOUR FOOD PHOTOS

Listen, I've got a sidebar quota to maintain here, and frankly I'm drawing a blank on any pithy anecdotes or pearls of photographic wisdom for this chapter. So instead, here's a little secret recipe I picked up while dating this spunky blue-eyed waitress who worked at a local haunt called The Angry Dog. Every table in there had three shakers on it: salt, pepper, and "fry salt." The first two are easy enough, but the "fry salt" is what makes their fries some of the best in Texas. It's a simple little mixture, but very effective. Okay, you ready? They'd probably ban me from the joint if they knew I was telling you this. Right, then...

- One part salt
- One part garlic powder
- One part paprika
- One part cayenne pepper

That's it. Equal parts of those four ingredients and then blend, shake, fold, or whatever you gotta do to get it all mixed together evenly; then sprinkle that yummy red powder onto French fries, burgers, breakfast burritos, or anything else you may otherwise use salt on, and prepare for a flavor party. Oh, and don't worry about the cayenne pepper if you're not into spicy foods. This doesn't come across as hot at all. It's just a mild kick. It's not a five-alarm whoopin' kind of spice.

And now we return to our regularly scheduled photo-editing chapter already in progress.

It's good to get in there and customize iPhoto so you can get the tools you use most where you can get at them faster. Esh much moore ehishent to... oh <gulp>. Sorry. Typing with my mouth full. After that sidebar I had to go make a big beefy burrito and smother it in that fry salt. Oh, um, no. I didn't make enough for everybody.

This chapter was just the appetizer, or setting the table.... Wait, I'm not going down that road again. Those Wiley Publishing security guards are a lot stronger than they look. I've still got bruises from the last chapter.

The separate window editing toolbar is really the only place you get to customize the iPhoto interface, and most people never actually realize that they can do that separate window trick to begin with. That's one of those things you can show somebody who's been using iPhoto for a while and they'll say, "Whoa! What did you just do? It can do that?" which is nice if the person's a know-it-all. If that doesn't work, ask them if their computer has "LRF Support." Egg them on. "If you don't even know that, what good are you?" Whatever you do, don't tell them that LRF stands for *little rubber feet.* It will drive them up the wall that you hit them with a techie term they don't know.

All right already. Let's get to some actual editing!

Better Photography through Editing

In This Chapter

Cropping and rotating your photos • Fixing red-eye • Enhancing a photo
Retouching a photo • Selecting part of a photo • Undoing your changes

iPhoto's editing tools are very limited compared to the big dogs of photo editing, but the truth is that the vast majority of what most photos need can be accomplished with these simple tools. As long as you're taking decent pictures in the first place, this stuff can take your picture up a notch and turn "decent" into "Oooh! I like this one. Did you take that?"

You can crop your pictures to make the composition better. You can adjust the brightness and contrast to bring out the details a bit more. There's even a magic wand that you can use; fortunately, the wand in question tends to lean toward making pictures better rather than making them into toads, but that's not to say that it won't turn your picture green given the right set of circumstances.

SELECT PARTS OF A PHOTO

Selecting just a portion of an image is important in a number of instances. For example, the best way to correct red-eye (see the "Correct Red-Eye" section for more on red-eye) is to select just the area around the eye. To crop a photo (see "Crop a Photo" later in this chapter), you'll need to select just the portion of the photo that you want to keep.

To select a portion of a photo, move the mouse pointer to a spot you want as one of the corners of your selection and drag a rectangle in any direction. The area outside the rectangle is "dimmed out" to show that it is not part of the selection (see Figure 8-1).

 Note

To reselect the entire photo (perhaps so you can start over selecting a portion of the photo), simply click in the dimmed-out portion of the image.

Figure 8-1

The dimmed out area outside the rectangle is not included in the selected part of the image

ASPECT RATIOS

Pictures come in any number of *aspect ratios*. For those of you who can still remember back to your geometry lessons, that's the relationship between the height and the width of the image. Normal photograph prints are typically 5" x 7" or 4" x 6", but what they typically fail to mention is that those aren't just different print sizes, but *different shapes* as well. Now let's muck it up a bit more with the fact that digital cameras are based on a 3:4 ratio which most likely has something to do with the fact that the technology is sort of an offshoot of the video camera, and TV is a 3:4 medium. Mostly. Now everything is moving to wide-screen TVs that are 16:9. There are even wide-screen displays on some of the Macs now, but those are different. They're 16:10 displays.

You don't even want to know about all the different film aspect ratios they use in movies (see Figure 8-2)!

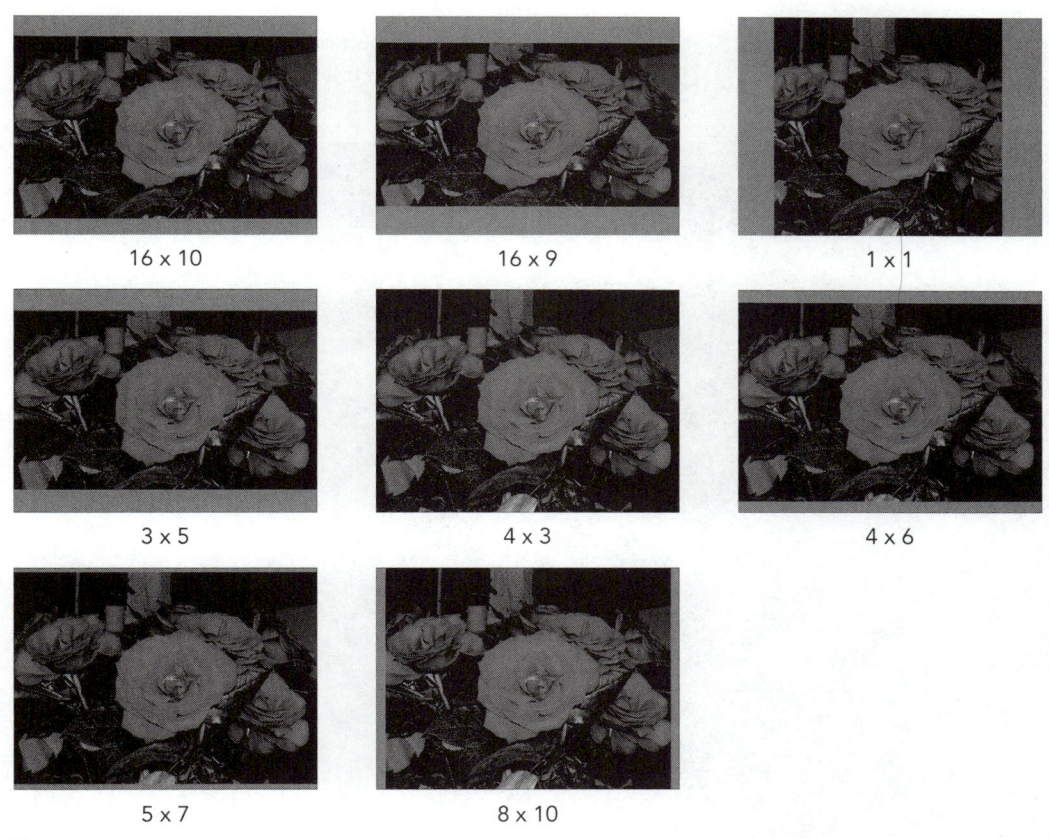

16 x 10   16 x 9   1 x 1

3 x 5   4 x 3   4 x 6

5 x 7   8 x 10

Figure 8-2
Different aspect ratios whittle away at your picture

The deal is that depending on what you want to do with your photograph, you might have to slice off bits and pieces to make the photo the correct shape, the correct aspect ratio, for the job. That's why movies are shown in *letterbox format* most of the time. Those black bars at the top and bottom of your TV aren't something they put there to annoy you. They're there because the movie image is short and really wide when you're in the theater. They're just cramming a wide rectangle into a square, and that leaves extra space above and below the picture. Or they fill the frame from top to bottom, and that crops off the sides so you only see maybe half of the whole image on your TV. Us film guys refer to that as *very, very bad,* but the official term the video guys use is "pan & scan" because the video frame has to move all over the place to center on the action since you only get to see part of the image, and lots of stuff happens over on the edges you'd miss otherwise.

Okay, I'm a bit off the path here but I've heard way too many people say "I hate it when they put those black bars on movies." So consider this tangent a public service announcement. Okay, back to pictures....

An aspect ratio of 4 x 6 for a *landscape* image (wider than it is tall) results in a picture that is 4 inches high by 6 inches wide — or 8 inches high by 12 inches wide, and so on (Figure 8-3). An aspect ratio of 4 x 6 for a *portrait*-oriented image (taller than it is wide) results in a picture that

Figure 8-3
The 4 x 6 landscape aspect ratio is wider than it is tall...

is 4 inches wide by 6 inches tall — or 8 inches wide by 12 inches tall, and so on (Figure 8-4). The figures show the 4 x 6 aspect ratio applied first to a landscape image (4 inches high by 6 inches wide), and second to a portrait image (4 inches wide by 6 inches high).

Figure 8-4
...and the 4 x 6 portrait aspect ratio is taller than it is wide

Picking the correct aspect ratio for how you want to use the picture is very important. For example, a picture with a 4 x 6 aspect ratio looks terrible if you use it in a slideshow. Black bars appear on top and bottom of the image because it doesn't fit the screen properly. On the other hand, an image with a 4 x 3 aspect ratio works much better for a slideshow if your screen resolution is set to 1024 x 768 because this resolution fits the 4 x 3 ratio. Here are some guidelines on what aspect ratios to use for a particular purpose:

- **1280 x 854.** This first entry in the Constrain pop-up list varies depending on your display resolution. 1280 x 854 is, obviously, the best ratio to use for slideshows for your computer.

- **2 x 3.** This aspect ratio matches wallet-sized photos, so use it if you intend to print out small photos.

- **3 x 5.** I'm not really sure what this aspect ratio is good for. It's close to one of the standard photo sizes (3½ x 5), but not exactly, so using this aspect ratio leaves you with white areas on the print. (For making flash cards?)

- **4 x 3 Book and 4 x 3 DVD.** This aspect ratio matches the "normal" aspect ratios from the period before Apple started stretching the screens. Thus, this aspect ratio is good for images designed to be displayed on screens with resolutions such as 640 x 480, 800 x 600, 1024 x 768, and 1280 x 1024 — the sort of screen resolutions that most of your PC-owning friends regularly use. This aspect ratio also works well for slideshows you burn onto a DVD to show on a TV screen because "normal" (non-HDTV) screens also have a 4 x 3 aspect ratio. Finally, this aspect ratio works well for pages in iPhoto books because these pages are also close to 4 x 3. The difference between 4 x 3 Book and 4 x 3 DVD is that DVD is locked to landscape orientation while Book can be switched to portrait orientation if you like.

- **4 x 6 (Postcard).** Works well for snapshots you either print yourself (you can buy 4 x 6 paper) or have printed at the drugstore. Because this is considered a standard-size photo, purchasing mattes and frames in this size is easy.

- **5 x 7 (L, 2L).** Works well for snapshots you either print yourself or have printed at the drugstore. Like 4 x 6, this is another standard size you can order commercially printed, and it is also easy to purchase mattes and frames in this size.

- **8 x 10.** Like 4 x 6 and 5 x 7, this is a standard photo size, suitable for commercial printing and matting/framing.

- **16 x 20.** Another standard photo size.

- **20 x 30 (Poster).** As the name implies, this is a standard size for printing posters. Your images have to have a very high resolution to make a suitable print at such a large size.

- **Square.** As you may imagine from the name, this aspect ratio results in a square picture. Square pictures are easier to place on a Web page or other page where you want to create an arbitrary layout of images.

- **Constrain as portrait.** This option appears when you are working with a landscape-oriented image. The aspect ratio for a landscape image normally places the longer dimension as the width. If you would rather have the longer dimension as the height, click the

DON'T GET CAUGHT UP IN CONSTRAINTS

One thing I'd like to suggest is that you not get stuck on making sure your pictures are always locked into those preset crop constraints. If you're just sending your pictures out in emails or posting them on the Web, feel free to get a little crazy with cropping if the picture looks like it's asking for it.

On a drive from Dallas to San Francisco, I came across a long row of windmills. I shot the picture, shown in Figure 8-5. When I got home and looked at the picture, it just wasn't very dramatic looking because of the boring traffic in the foreground and the vacant sky covering the top two thirds of the image. Cropping the image down to a short and extremely wide aspect ratio made the picture focus a lot more on what it was that got me to take the picture in the first place (see Figure 8-6).

Constrain as portrait option (it shows a check mark in the pop-up list). This option is a toggle: Select it again to turn it off.

- **Constrain as landscape.** This option appears when you are working with a portrait-oriented image. As mentioned earlier, the aspect ratio for a portrait image normally places the longer dimension as the height. If you would rather have the longer dimension as the width, select the Constrain as landscape option (it shows a check mark in the pop-up list). This option is a toggle: Select it again to turn it off.

Figure 8-5
Traffic and too much sky were ruining this picture

Figure 8-6
Cropping to the extreme totally changed the picture

CONSTRAIN YOUR SELECTION

To constrain a selection to a particular aspect ratio, you can select the ratio in one of the following ways:

- In the Display pane, choose the ratio from the Constrain pop-up list (see Figure 8-7), and then click and drag. iPhoto maintains the selected ratio of height to width.

- From the separate Edit window, follow these steps:

  1. **Type the height into the left-hand Custom field.**

  2. **Type the width into the right-hand Custom field.**

  3. **Click and drag the rectangle.** iPhoto maintains the selected ratio of height to width.

Figure 8-7
Choose a value from the Constrain pop-up list to set the aspect ratio of the selected rectangle

If you've already clicked and dragged a rectangle to select a portion of the image, you can adjust the aspect ratio by changing the value in either the Constrain pop-up list or the Custom fields. This change modifies the height-to-width ratio of the selected rectangle.

▼ **Tip**

To remove a constraint, simply select None from the Constrain pop-up list.

▼ **Note**

The aspect ratio tools work with the original aspect ratio of the image. For example, if the image is landscape (wider than it is tall), then the aspect ratio tool uses the larger dimension (for example, 6) for the width and the smaller dimension (for example, 4) for the height. If the image is portrait (taller than it is wide), then the aspect ratio tool uses the larger dimension for the height and the smaller dimension for the width.

iPhoto also provides an easy way to temporarily override a constraint setting. Click and drag to start selecting the rectangle, and then hold down the ⌘ key. You can now select any rectangle you want, regardless of the constraint settings.

You can move the selection rectangle after you draw it. Move the mouse pointer **over the rectangle** (the pointer becomes a pointing hand), and then click and drag to relocate the rectangle.

You can also adjust the dimensions of the rectangle. Move the mouse pointer close to the edge of the rectangle (the pointer becomes a pointing arrow), and then click and drag to make the rectangle larger or smaller. When you have an aspect ratio constraint set, dragging one edge (for example, to adjust the width) also adjusts the other dimension (for example, the height).

As discussed in Chapter 7, when you first apply a constraint to an image, the aspect ratio matches the image

orientation as much as possible. For example, if you apply a 4 x 6 aspect ratio constraint to a landscape-oriented image (wider than it is tall), the 6-inch dimension is used for the width, and the 4-inch dimension is used for the height. However, turning the aspect ratio 90 degrees is possible — meaning that the 6-inch dimension is used for the height and the 4-inch dimension is used for the width. To do this, follow these steps:

1. **Move the mouse pointer to the edge of the selected rectangle (the pointer becomes a pointing arrow).**

2. **Click and begin to drag the edge.**

3. **While still holding down the mouse button, press the Option key.** The selected rectangle rotates 90 degrees.

CORRECT RED-EYE

One of the biggest issues with using flash photography is the problem of *red-eye*. Basically, instead of someone's eyes showing their true color, the eyes come out glowing red. For example, even in black and white, the weird glowing red eyes are apparent (see Figure 8-8). Red-eye is caused by a combination of several all-too-common factors. The first is that the flash is located very close to the camera lens. This causes the light from the flash to bounce off the back of the retina of the subject, showing the red color created by the blood vessels in the back of the eye. Of course, with small cameras, the flash is virtually *always* located very close to the lens.

The second factor that can cause red-eye is when the iris (the center of the eye) is dilated to allow more light into the eye. This is exactly what happens when the ambient light level is low — the usual conditions when you want to use a flash! When the iris is dilated, the light from the flash has more area to enter the eye and cause the bounce effect discussed in the previous paragraph.

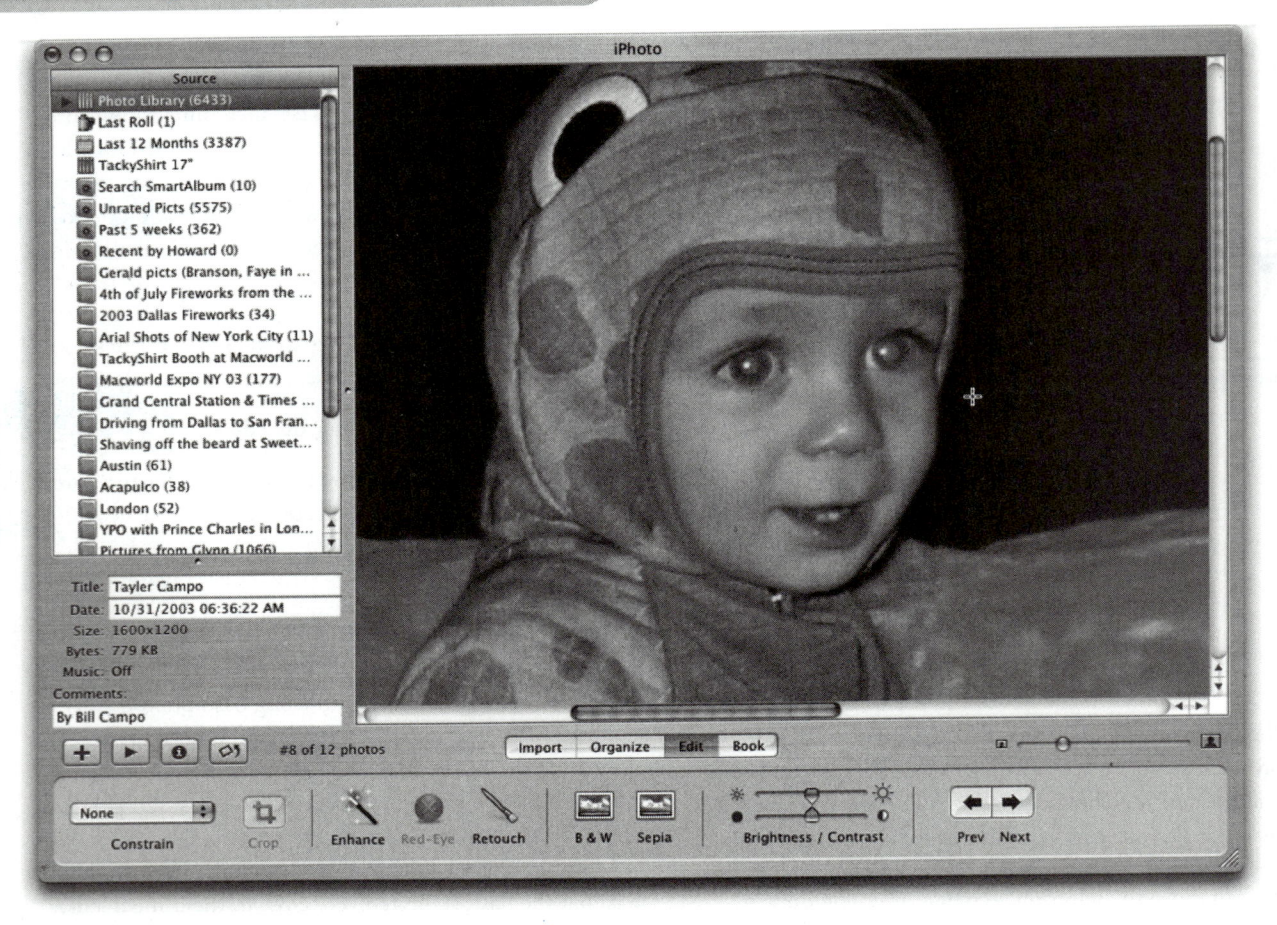

Figure 8-8
Red-eye is a pervasive problem when using a flash

The final factor that aggravates red-eye is when someone's eye color is light — such as blue or light gray. Red-eye occurs more often with these eye colors than with brown eyes, again because the light color allows more of the light from the flash to bounce off the back of the eye.

There are various techniques for minimizing or eliminating red-eye. Some cameras use one or more "preflashes," which cause the iris to contract prior to the main flash going off. Some people tend to blink after the first flash, so you end up catching them with their eyes closed. This *does* eliminate red-eye, but I hear that some people don't care much for pictures of people with their eyes closed. They have something against showing a little eyelid for some reason. Prudes.

 Note

Figures 8-8, 8-9, and 8-10 can be viewed *in color* on the Web by going to **http://homepage.mac.com/tackyshirt** and selecting the iPhoto Book link located at the top of the page.

Another technique is to increase the ambient light. This also causes the iris to contract and does help, but increasing the ambient light enough is not always possible.

The best solution is moving the flash away from the camera lens. Some high-end cameras have an attachment to which you can mount a flash with a cable, enabling you to move the flash a foot or more away from the lens. This technique does work very well, but is not an option for most point-and-shoot digital (or film) cameras.

So what do you do if you end up with subjects that look like they are possessed? iPhoto provides a darn handy solution: the Red-eye tool. Although it isn't perfect, it does improve any red-eye-infected picture.

Selecting just the portion of the photo that contains the eyes is the first step (you can even work with one eye at a time). Then simply click the Red-eye tool (see Figure 8-9).

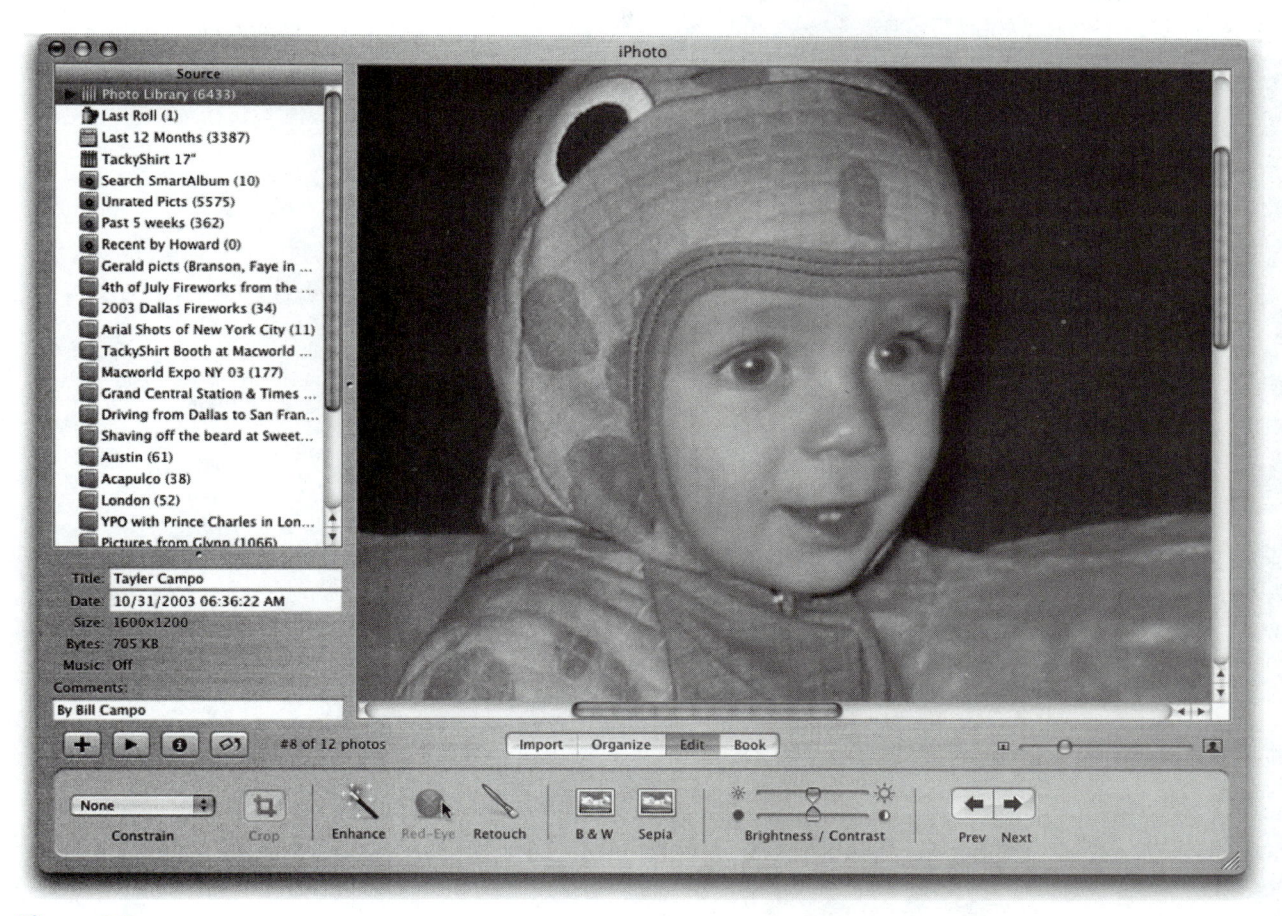

Figure 8-9
Using iPhoto's Red-eye tool fixes red-eye

WHEN EYE DROPS WON'T GET THE RED OUT

Red-eye is either tragic or hilarious. I mean face it: What Halloween costume wouldn't look better with a pair of glowing, demonic peepers staring back at you, such as those in Figure 8-10?

The Red-eye tool either works perfectly or totally botches the job, depending on the quality of your picture. If the resolution is low, the focus is soft, or the subject is just too small in the frame, then the tool tends to wipe out the whole eyeball and occasionally a good chunk of the face. You'll get your best results with this tool when you have good contrast between the iris and the red pupil. If it's hard to see where the red stops and where the baby-blues start, then odds are you're looking for trouble.

If you have a picture that won't work with the Red-eye tool and you have access to another photo-editing application, you may get better results by using a tool that can *desaturate* an area. Adobe calls theirs the Sponge tool. Make the brush a bit smaller than the pupil and suck out all the chroma (color) until the pupil has gone from red to gray. In most cases, that's just what you need.

Figure 8-10
Do not anger the evil Ian Campo Beast!!!

Using the Red-eye tool involves several issues. The first is that the red color is replaced with a dark gray. It doesn't matter what color the subject's eyes were before: They are now dark gray. The other issue is that iPhoto simply replaces particular shades of red with dark-gray in the selected area. If you don't select just the eyes and these shades of red appear in other areas (such as lipstick), those areas become dark gray as well. So you really need to select just the eyes before applying this tool.

DUPLICATE A PHOTO

On occasion, you may find that you need two copies of a photograph. For example, you may want to use a photo on the cover of a book as well as in the pages. Because of the way books work (see Chapter 16), you need two copies of a photo to pull off that little trick.

You may also need two copies of a photo if you want to crop one photo for printing and another to use in a slideshow. To duplicate a photo, either open the photo in the Edit Display pane or select the thumbnail in Organize mode. Then choose Photos ➡ Duplicate, or choose Duplicate from the context menu. Either way, a copy of the image is made. The title is the same as the original, but with "copy" stuck on the end of it. All other data (such as the date/time and additional photo information) is duplicated as well. If you are working in the photo library, the duplicate is added only to the photo library. If you are working in an album, the duplicate is added to the album in addition to the photo library. However, the copy is *not* added to any other albums that contain the original image.

ROTATE A PHOTO

Rotating a photo can be very handy in a number of situations. The most common is when you rotate the camera on its side to get a better composition when taking the picture. For example, it made sense to take the picture of the tall ship, Sir Francis Drake's *Golden Hind*, shown in Figure 8-11, by aligning the mast to the long axis of the picture — in other words, turning the camera 90 degrees.

However, after you have a picture such as this one in iPhoto, orienting it so that it isn't lying on its side is obviously going to make working with it a lot easier. If you are editing in the Display pane, click the Rotate button (located just below the Info pane) to rotate the image 90 degrees in the direction you specified in iPhoto preferences back in Chapter 2. To rotate the image in the opposite direction, hold down the Option key and click the Rotate button. If you need to rotate an image less than 90 degrees, you have to do it in an external image-editing program.

If you are editing in a separate window, click the Rotate button in the toolbar. As with the Display pane, holding down the Option key when clicking the Rotate button rotates the image in the opposite direction. You can also rotate the image by choosing Rotate Clockwise or Rotate Counter Clockwise from the context menu.

 Tip

Rotating an image can be useful if you scanned it in upside down. Simply rotate it twice to turn the image right side up.

 Note

Some cameras have an internal gravity sensor that tells the camera which way is up. If your camera has such a sensor, the picture will likely be saved in its correct orientation on the camera.

Figure 8-11
Some pictures end up lying on their sides

SWITCHING BETWEEN BEFORE AND AFTER

As you make changes to your photos, such as those discussed in the next few sections, you have the ability to switch back and forth between the current version of the photo and how it looked just prior to the last change. To do so, press the Control key to view the "before" image, and release the key to view the "after" image. For example, say you adjusted the brightness and contrast of a photo. Pressing the Control key shows you how the image looked just before you made the change. iPhoto does tend to be a little inconsistent with what the Control key pulls up, at least for me: Sometimes it pulls up what the picture looked like when I first came into Edit mode, even if I've performed several modifications since then. It may be a roll of the dice as to what you'll see, but pressing the Control key will always rewind to *somewhere*.

If you really want to see some funny stuff, get a picture with particularly bad red-eye. Use the Red-eye tool to fix the problem. Now start clicking the Control key repeatedly. Heh heh heh.

 Tip
If you decide you like the "before" image better, simply choose Edit ➜ Undo, or press ⌘+Z to reverse the change and return the image to the "before" version.

ONE-CLICK ENHANCE YOUR PHOTO

Unlike more powerful photo-editing programs, iPhoto doesn't give you the ability to make a lot of custom adjustments to a photograph. For example, although you can adjust the brightness and contrast of the entire photograph (see the next section), you can't adjust the brightness of only a portion of the photo, or increase the color saturation of only a small section of the image.

Instead, iPhoto offers the one-click enhance function. This function applies a variety of adjustments to your photo, primarily changing brightness, contrast, and color saturation. However, unlike the changes you can make yourself, the one-click enhance function analyzes the photo and tries to balance the brightness and contrast, adjusting these quantities by different amounts in different areas. The

function may increase the color saturation, which can have the effect of over-compensating on one color, resulting in a color cast. You can even apply the one-click enhance function multiple times, although more than two or three times is almost guaranteed to ruin a picture.

Remember that one-click enhance function is not a magic bullet. Sometimes it makes the picture better, sometimes it doesn't. All you can really do is try it and see whether you like the result. Figure 8-12 shows a great sunny day at the beach in Acapulco, but sometimes those one-time use,

Figure 8-12
Sunny Acapulco isn't looking so fun

waterproof cameras don't take the best pictures. As you can see in Figure 8-13, the Enhance button fixed the contrast and color balance so that the sky is appropriately blue and the whole outlook of the picture just feels warmer and more inviting.

 Note

Figures 8-12 through 8-15 can be viewed *in color* on the Web by going to **http://homepage.mac.com/tackyshirt** and selecting the iPhoto Book link located at the top of the page.

Figure 8-13
One click of Enhance and the beach brightens right up

MAGIC OF ENHANCE

Enhance performs a bit of magic based on elements that exist in your picture. Wherever you point your camera, odds are you'll have something in the frame that qualifies as white and something that qualifies as black. In Figure 8-14, the wave foam is white and the shady part of the back of Jeff's head is the blackest part of the picture. If the software is correct in assuming that those two spots are indeed white and black, then it can adjust the rest of the picture to the correct color and fix the contrast so that black actually does reach down to where black should be and white reaches up to the brightness where white should be. Photoshop's Auto Levels feature performs similar calculations, but to tell you the truth, on *this picture*, iPhoto's Enhance button produced better results than Photoshop. I'm not saying I'll be scrapping ol' PS or anything. I'm just saying, this time, iPhoto kicked its butt.

The exact formula for the Enhance button may also work for flesh tones and the like to ensure that people's skin is the correct hue. I'm pretty sure that only the software engineers at Apple know for sure, but I can say this: The Enhance button can easily be tricked. If the brightest part of your picture is a red colored light bulb in the background, or if the darkest part of your picture is actually a really dark blue instead of black, Enhance will probably make your picture go haywire (see Figure 8-15).

Figure 8-14
Without the right clues...

continues

Figure 8-15
...Enhance gets it wrong

This isn't very practical when you're on vacation, but on professional shoots, photographers often shoot a reference card that has white, black, 50 percent gray, and possibly several color samples so they can calibrate their pictures correctly later. If you find yourself in a situation where you're up against a big pink wall, it may be worth the trouble to work in something that actually *is* white so you can correct the image later if your camera's auto balancing thinks the wall is white.

▼ **Note**

Not seeing what's really going on in Figures 8-14 and 8-15? Visit **http://homepage.mac.com/tackyshirt** and click The iPhoto Book link at the top of the page to get the *full color* effect.

ADJUST BRIGHTNESS AND CONTRAST

The Brightness and Contrast sliders enable you to adjust the brightness and contrast for an entire photo. Adjusting the brightness makes the photo lighter or darker, and adjusting the contrast increases the difference between the lightest and darkest parts of the image. Figures 8-16 and 8-17 show the difference making a brightness and contrast adjustment can make.

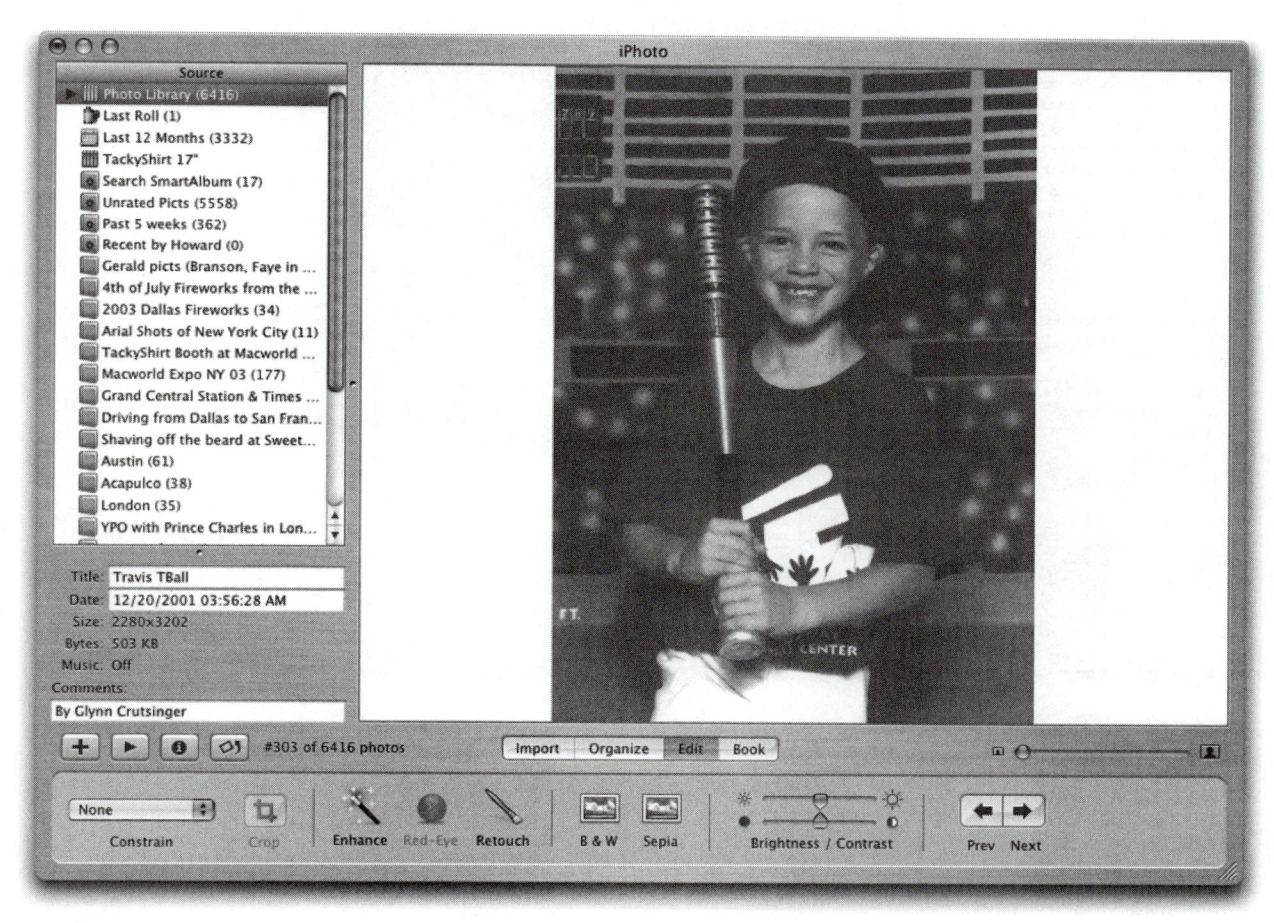

Figure 8-16
The original is dingy

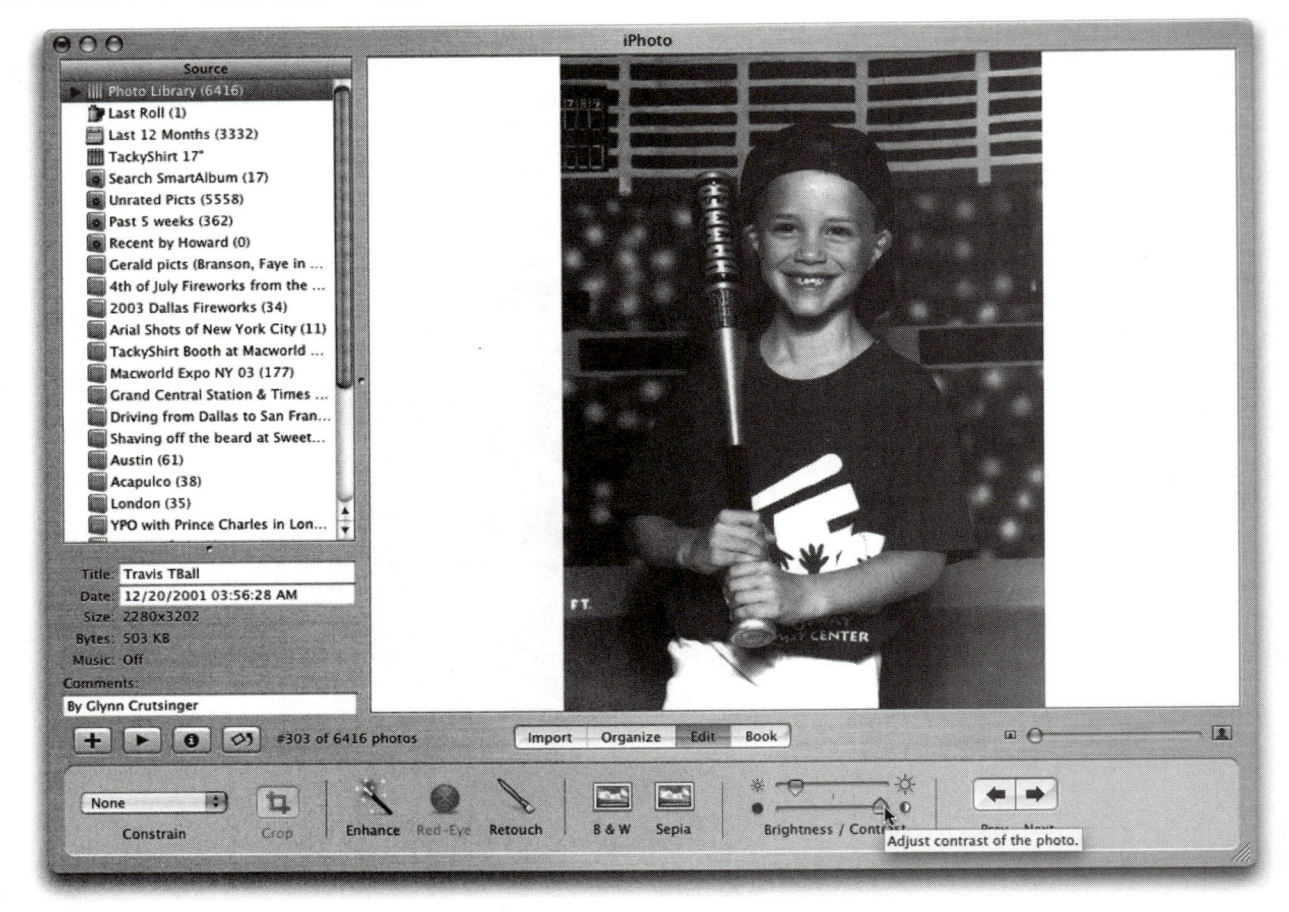

Figure 8-17
Adjusting the brightness and contrast makes it better

▼ Note

If you adjust the Brightness and Contrast sliders and then switch modes (for example, to Organize mode from Edit mode), that adjustment is applied to the image; if you switch back to Edit mode, the sliders are back in the centered position. You're now looking at the edited version of this picture, so don't leave Edit mode if you don't want your adjustments to stick. Of course you can always choose Undo (⌘+Z) or Revert to Original. On the bright side, if you'll pardon the pun, you *can* adjust the brightness or contrast all the way in one direction or the other, switch to Organize mode and back to Edit mode, then adjust it *even further* on the second pass if you just can't get the look you're after in one shot (Figure 8-18).

Figure 8-18

Five full cranks of the Contrast slider can look pretty sweet

The one-click enhance and the brightness/contrast controls work together to a certain extent. If you aren't getting quite the effect you want, you should try various combinations of these tools. For example, first adjust the brightness and contrast, then try one-click enhance. You can reverse the order of applying these tools to see if you get better results; don't be afraid to experiment. You can always undo the change, or even revert all the way back to the original. In addition, because the one-click enhance function uses all the picture information to try and fix the image, you can try cropping the image prior to applying the changes.

 Note

To see the full impact of the Contrast slider *in color,* visit **http://homepage.mac.com/tackyshirt** and click the iPhoto Book link at the top of the page.

RETOUCH A PHOTO

If a photograph has a small imperfection, such as a scratch, blemish, or wrinkle, you can often repair it with the Retouch tool. This tool works by blending information from surrounding areas and hiding the imperfection. For example, take a look at Figures 8-19 and 8-20. My nephew's got a little freckle on his cheek (er... well, he *had* a freckle on his cheek).

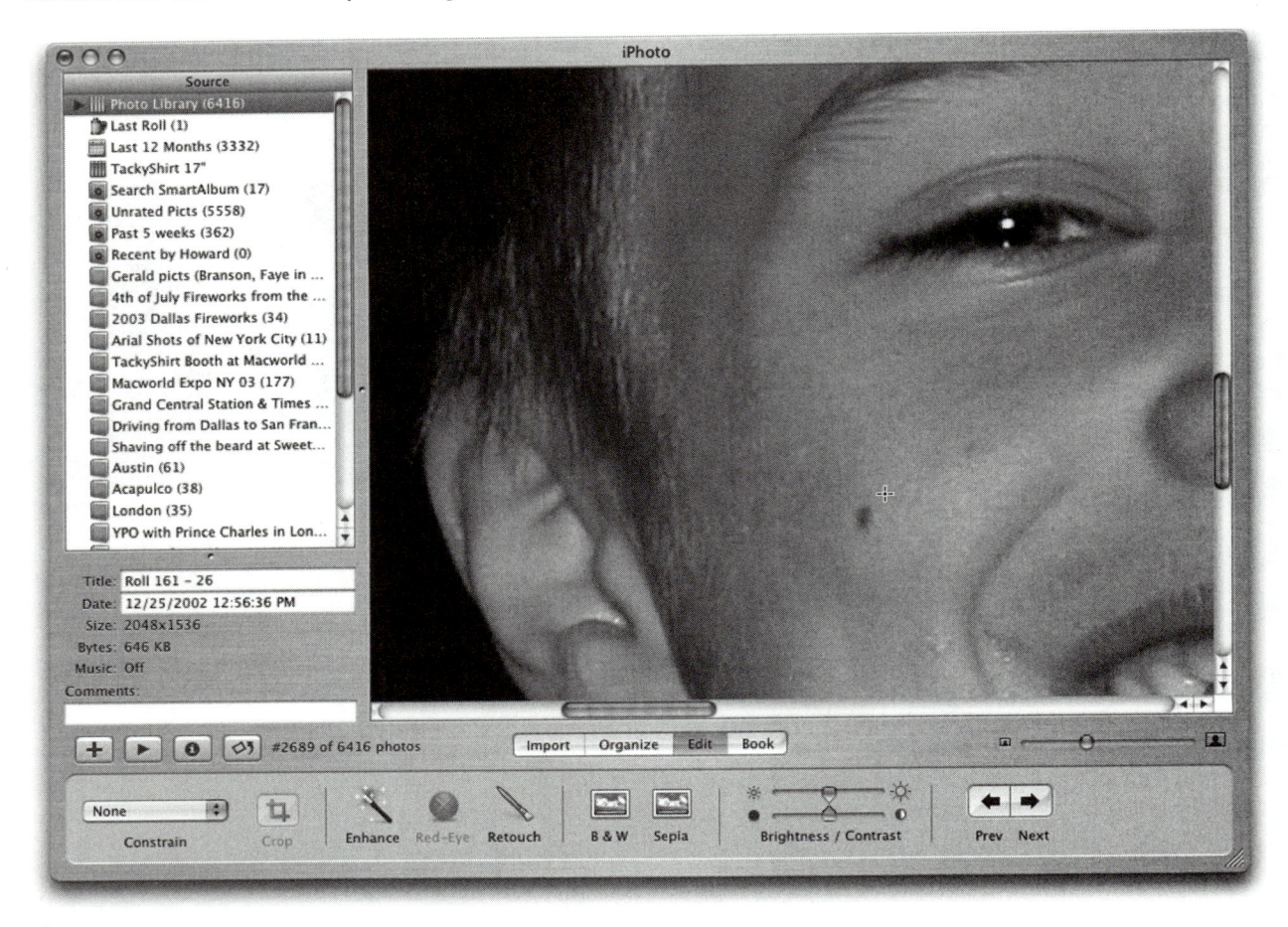

Figure 8-19

Before the Retouch tool...

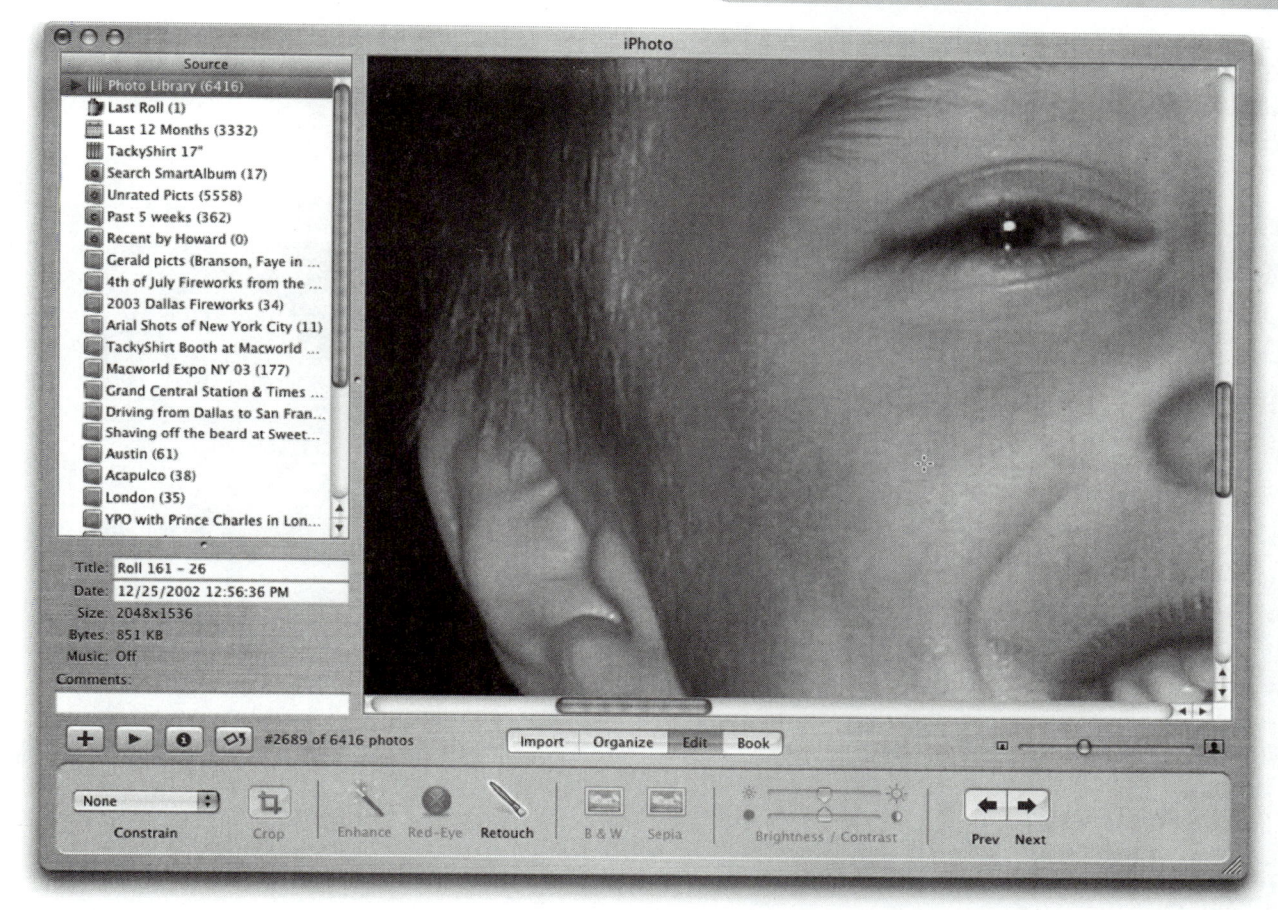

Figure 8-20
Retouch buffs out scratches, flecks, and even freckles

To use the Retouch tool, follow these steps:

1. **Click the Brush tool so that the mouse pointer becomes a crosshair.**

2. **Drag the brush across the blemish or scratch.**

3. **Continue to click and drag until the blemishes have disappeared (or you have utterly destroyed the picture).**

Here are some hints to help you use the Retouch too more effectively and with less stress:

- Drag from an area that looks like what you want the target area to be.

- Use small strokes.

- Do *not* drag across sharp breaks in color. This is because the tool works by smearing the image slightly, and this will show up markedly across sharp color edges.

Here's a picture of Aunt Faye on her 100th birthday (Figure 8-21). She's, well, um, look, she's over a ***hundred years old!*** You'll pick up a few wrinkles in your last 75 years or so too. Figure 8-22 shows the result of careful work around the eyes. Notice how the wrinkles are gone? Well, not ***all*** of them are gone, but she looks more like a spry 80-year old now.

Figure 8-21
Faye before her painless iPhoto facelift

Figure 8-22

Faye after — you have to look good at your 100th birthday party

REACH OUT AND RETOUCH SOMEONE

Sure, Retouch is a great tool for buffing out scratches and dirt flecks, but I dare you to try *not* to abuse this tool for your own amusement. The first thing I did when I played with it was to make my nephew's mouth disappear... then the eyes... then the nose. Of course, without a nose he just looked silly, so I backed up and undid the rhinoplasty (see Figure 8-23). Sure, it starts to look like a big uniform smear after you go too far, but you've got to admit, I've got one funny looking nephew, and having fun making family look like nightmares in a Stephen King story is what we all bought computers for, right?

Okay, maybe it's just me.

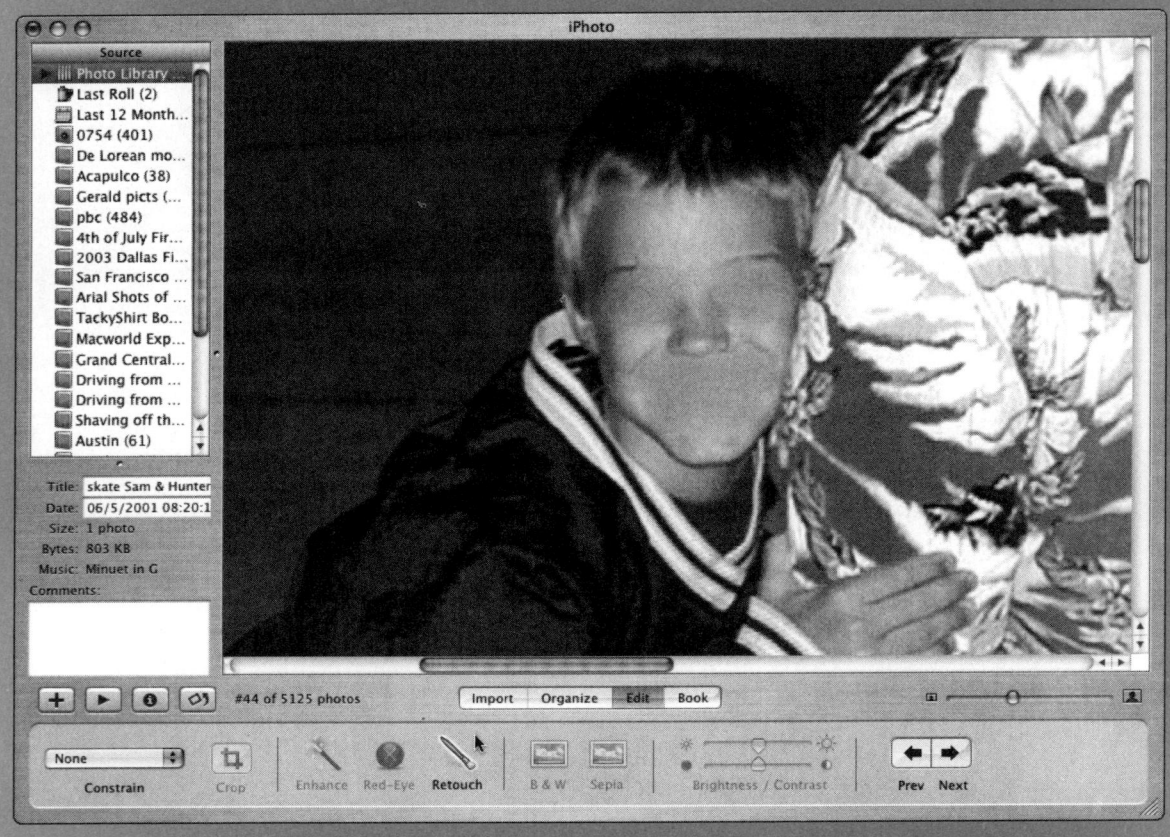

Figure 8-23
Bwahahah!! When Retouch goes overboard

CROP A PHOTO

When you shoot pictures quickly, getting the composition perfect isn't always possible. Your main subject may be well off to the side (not in a *good* way), or you may get tripped up by parallax — when your viewfinder doesn't accurately reflect what the finished picture will look like.

Fortunately, you can trim away the edges of a picture through a process called *cropping*. You can pick the portion of the picture you want to keep, and then discard the rest.

> ▼ **Note**
> Another reason to crop an image is to achieve the aspect ratio you need for either displaying a slideshow or printing.

Cropping is easy to do. To crop using an unconstrained rectangle, follow these steps:

1. **Click and drag a rectangle on the picture (Figure 8-24).** The unselected portions of the picture are dimmed out.

Figure 8-24
Select the part of the picture you want to keep...

2. **Click the Crop button or choose Crop from the context menu.**

3. **The dimmed-out area of the image is discarded, leaving only the selected rectangle (Figure 8-25).** iPhoto automatically zooms in on the cropped photo.

To use a constrained rectangle (such as a 4 x 6 rectangle) for cropping, follow these steps:

1. **Set the constraints by choosing a value from the Constrain pop-up list, typing values into the Custom fields in the toolbar, or using the predefined constraint buttons (also in the toolbar).**

Figure 8-25

...and click the Crop button to remove everything else

2. **Click and drag a rectangle on the picture.** The resulting rectangle maintains the dimensions of the selected constraint.

3. **Click the Crop button or choose Crop from the context menu.**

4. **The dimmed-out area of the image is discarded, leaving only the selected rectangle.**

One thing you need to be careful about is that cropping removes pixels from the picture. Pixels are the smallest colored dots that make up your picture. And although iPhoto tells you the pixel width and height in the Info pane, it does *not* tell you the resolution (pixels per inch) of the photo when you want to print it. The higher the resolution, the smaller the pixels, which gives you finer details. The only warning you'll get if there aren't enough pixels to print the picture is the yellow warning icon that appears when you try to print the image or use it in a book.

 Tip

Many other photo-editing programs (such as Adobe Photoshop Elements) *do* tell you the resolution of the photo. So one way to check the resolution after cropping in iPhoto is to reopen the image in an external photo editor that has this feature.

CHANGE PHOTOS TO BLACK AND WHITE

Converting a color photo to black and white is easy in iPhoto. You may want to do this to hide jarring color changes, or to produce the sort of images for which Ansel Adams was famous. To convert an image, simply open it in Edit mode and click the B & W button. After that you can tweak the brightness and contrast to improve the picture.

ALL THERE IN BLACK AND WHITE

Converting your pictures to black and white comes in handy if you're going to be printing out pictures on a non-color printer. A picture may suddenly take on an entirely different look when you strip away the color. For example, imagine a picture of a woman in a flowery blue dress in front of some pink flowers; it looks great in color, but when the picture is converted to black and white, the dress and the background blend into a single pattern. Suddenly a nice portrait turns into a woman's head poking out of a bush.

Another great reason to convert a picture to black and white is to fix an otherwise horrid picture. Let's face it, these camera phones are everywhere now, and 9.9 times out of 10 they take pretty bad pictures. Usually the colors are *way* off, and somehow different hues are off in different directions, which baffles me to no end. There's just no way to easily fix the hodgepodge of hues. Hitting the picture with a black and white conversion often takes a phone photo from *color spew* to a picture you can show off without apologizing.

Most pictures will need to have the contrast kicked up a bit to bring out details a little better.

CHANGE PHOTOS TO SEPIA

If you want the look of "old-time" pictures, you can convert your photographs to sepia (see Figure 8-26). Basically, a sepia photo uses shades of brown to display the image; think of it as "brown and white" instead of "black and white." To convert an image to sepia, open it in Edit mode and click the Sepia button.

Figure 8-26
Use sepia to give your photos an antique look

 Note

If you are wondering what sepia looks like *in color,* visit **http://homepage.mac.com/tackyshirt** and click on The iPhoto Book link at the top of the page.

UNDO AND REVERT TO THE ORIGINAL PHOTO

One of the really fun things to do with iPhoto is experimenting — playing with cropping, adjusting brightness and contrast, retouching, and perhaps even taking a few shots at one-click enhance. And of course, you *always* remember to make a duplicate of an image before you start experimenting, right? Yeah, right. Well, fortunately, even if you really mess up a picture, iPhoto can rescue you by enabling you to revert back to the original image and start over.

This is possible because the moment you make any change to an image in iPhoto, the program copies the original and makes the change to the copy. The original image is stored safe and hidden just in case you should need it. This even occurs if you decide to modify the image in an external photo editor, provided you open the external photo editor from within iPhoto (as described in Chapter 9).

▼ Note

To revert to the original version of the photo and start your changes over, choose Photos ➡ Revert to Original, or choose Revert to Original from the thumbnail context menu. After confirming that this is what you *really* want to do (there is no undo in this case), iPhoto discards the changed copy and replaces it with the original image.

If you modify a picture and then duplicate it, iPhoto still has your back. It duplicates the modified picture *as well as the original.* If you botch something on the copy, you can still revert to the original imported picture. What it won't do is take you back to where you duplicated the photo. Be careful when you revert to the original. Sometimes you may be better off making sure you can't get where you want to with an undo or two.

Heh, heh, heh.... Admit it. You're starting to have fun with this now. You're finally really getting your hands dirty and whipping those rowdy pixels into shape! Edit mode is where you really start to flex your artistic muscles. Like I mentioned, I'm partial to a bit of oddball cropping and going crazy on the other controls on occasion to go for a really *unnatural* look instead of always trying to make the picture look more realistic.

Go nuts! Really get in there and play with all the sliders and buttons and how they work with each other when you apply them in a different order. You may just end up with something really zany that you want to print out and put up on the wall. I've got to admit that I was pretty shocked at how cool Figure 8-18 turned out just by adjusting the contrast higher and higher. Hmmm... I might need to send that one off to get a print made.

Next up you'll have a gander at how iPhoto ties in with other photo-editing applications for when you need to bring out the big guns and teach those pixels who's really in charge here!

Editing Outside of iPhoto

In This Chapter

Understanding the limitations of iPhoto

Making edits in other applications...

iPhoto's *raison d'être* is to help you keep track of your photographs. In that department it's excellent. It's better than anything else I've had on my computer.

When it comes to sharing your photos with a minimum of fuss, I tend to hit walls occasionally with iPhoto where simplicity has eroded flexibility, so iPhoto's somewhere between good and great for sharing.

When it comes to editing pictures, my *television* has more picture control settings than what iPhoto gives you!

Brightness, contrast, cropping, B&W, sepia, red-eye, and the magic of Enhance can only get you so far. I hardly ever have iPhoto opened up and flying solo. iPhoto is like a Boeing C-17 troop transport; if you don't know what that is, think about a warehouse with wings. It's holding your army of photos and getting them where you need them. If I'm working with pictures, hardly any time at all passes before I have iPhoto send out for support from the B-1b Lancers. (That'd be the long-range, multi-role, heavy bomber in this disturbingly militaristic analogy, which is very uncharacteristic of a techno-hippy like me. I started with *flying solo* and ended up *bombing bad photos into the Stone Age.*)

At any rate, Apple knows you want to do more with your pictures than you can get done with iPhoto, so they integrate whatever application you want to use into the workflow.

GOING BEYOND IPHOTO

Although it would be nice to say that you can make all the changes to your photo within iPhoto, the truth is that iPhoto's edit tools are actually pretty simple. A considerable number of photo editors are on the market — from inexpensive shareware to high-end applications such as Adobe Photoshop — that enable you to make amazing changes to images. For example, I used Photoshop Elements to change an entire background, remove and add people and items from pictures, adjust color balance, sharpen and color-correct in limited areas of an image, and much, much more. I even used it to insert an image of myself (suitably dressed in a tux) into a 70-year-old photo of my great-grandparents, grandparents, and maternal aunts and uncles — including my mother as an infant. Heh, heh.

My point here is that unless you are either a very good photographer, or just aren't interested in making your photos the best they can be, you will eventually need an image editor that goes beyond the capabilities of iPhoto. Fortunately, plenty of choices are available, and although I use Photoshop Elements in the examples in the rest of this chapter, you can do many of these same tasks in other capable photo editors as well.

MAKE EDITS IN OTHER APPLICATIONS FROM IPHOTO

The best way to edit a photo in an external photo editor is to open the photo editor from within iPhoto. When you do this, iPhoto makes a copy of the image so that you can later revert back to the original *even if you made all the changes in the external photo editor.* In addition, after you save the image in the external photo editor and switch back to iPhoto, iPhoto updates the thumbnail in Organize mode to reflect the new changes.

If you need to set up iPhoto to use an external editor, you do that in the Preferences window. (Covered back in Chapter 2.) To open an external photo editor from within iPhoto, use one of these two methods:

- Configure iPhoto to open an external photo editor when you double-click an image in Organize mode, and a simple double-click of the thumbnail will pull up that picture in the other application.

- Choose Edit in External Editor from the thumbnail contextual menu in Organize mode.

Either way, the external editor opens and loads the image. Figure 9-1 shows the image open in Photoshop Elements.

After you make your changes in the external photo editor, you can simply save the image as you normally would. You do, however, need to make sure that the saved file is still in the original format in which you opened it. For example, if you open a JPEG image in Photoshop Elements (or Photoshop), add layers to it, and then go to save the file, the default file format will be PSD (Photoshop's native format, which preserves layers and other elements). Although the image saves fine in its new format, iPhoto doesn't know to look for that new file so it will just assume you made no changes since you never saved over the original JPEG.

ACCESSORIZING IPHOTO

iPhoto doesn't do it all. You're eventually going to want to do something that falls into the realm of *getting fancy*, like maybe rotating the picture some amount other than 90 degrees. Sheesh! Next thing you know you'll want to put text onto a picture! What? You already do? Well, odds are you'll have to crack the piggy bank at this point.

Lots of applications out there give you more control over your image editing, but some of them are a bit beyond the affordability of the beginning photographer.

The 700-pound gorilla of image manipulation is, of course, Adobe Photoshop.

[pause]

I'm sorry; I just had to stop and picture a 700-pound gorilla holding a graphics tablet and a Cinema Display flat panel, delicately adjusting the color balance of a picture of flowers. My Ritalin must be wearing off....

[pause]

Heh, heh, heh. It's funny because it's a gorilla. Heh, heh, heh. Oh, no, wait. What was I talking about? Oh yeah. Photoshop.

- **Adobe Photoshop** has been around since 1990 and it's gotten bigger and bigger. If it can be done, Photoshop can do it. On the down side, you have to spring the $550+ to put it in your toy box. It comes with ImageReady, which is specifically designed for making graphics for the Internet.

- **Macromedia's Fireworks** is another application along that same line, but at $300, it won't bleed you quite so much. It lets you do about anything you want to your picture and then some. It's loaded with tools that animate Web graphics, and other features.

- **RetouchPRO** is another high-end product, but if you think Photoshop is pricey.... Let's just say that this one falls into the category of "If you have to ask how much it is, it's probably not for you."

- **Adobe's Photoshop Elements** is Adobe's answer to the fact that most people don't need a fully loaded RV to run down to buy milk and bread. Photoshop Elements is a wonderful, streamlined application that gives you most of the tools you need, and it's priced to move. It's about $85, but you can find it for as little as $50 on occasion. If you don't have anything and you're just getting started, Photoshop Elements is a great place to start.

- **Graphic Converter** has been bundled with Macs for a while now. If we stick with the automotive analogies, it's like a muscle car engine in a dusty old car frame. The application has an amazing amount of features, but you may find the interface a bit hard to get through. The batch processing features of Graphic Converter are what I tend to use, but it falls a bit flat if you're trying to deal with just part of the picture instead of applying changes to the whole image.

Figure 9-1

Open an image in an external photo editor when you want to make more significant changes than you can in iPhoto

 Note

To see this figure and other figures from the book *in color,* visit **http://homepage.mac.com/ tackyshirt** and click the iPhoto Book link at the top of the page.

SAVING OUTSIDE IPHOTO

When you jut out to an external editor to make changes and save your picture, you may run into a few issues. First of all, if you've added layers to your image, like maybe adding text to the picture, JPEG has no way of coping with the layers. When you go to save the file, the program will most likely try to steer you in a direction other than JPEG. In the Save dialog box, you must save the file back in the same format as it was when iPhoto sent it out for editing. Usually that's JPEG, but whether your pictures are in TIFF or another format, the point is that *you have to save over the original file*. If you don't, iPhoto keeps looking at that original without any clue that you've got a better version sitting right next to it on your hard drive.

If you added layers, switching the format to JPEG in the Save dialog box flattens the image, which in turn discards the layers. The resulting image looks the same as the layered image, but you can't work on the separate layers any more (to move a bit of text a little to the left, for example, or to change a layer's drop shadow).

TIFFs have come a long way; they *can* preserve layers now. You may fall into trouble when you try to use a layered TIFF in some applications, but if you're shooting or scanning files into TIFF format, and you want to add on layers without losing the ability to make changes to them later, this is a fantastic option. I do recommend that you turn on LZW compression when you save, though; that's a lossless data compression feature that keeps your TIFFs from bloating out of control if you have several layers in the file. The important thing is to make sure you save over the file you are editing; don't save it as "Filename-rev2.tiff" or any other alternate name. If you're asked to pick a name, and you're not asked if you want to replace the file on disk, you made a booboo.

DRAGGING PHOTOS INTO OTHER APPLICATIONS

As mentioned in the last section, the best way to open and edit a photo in an external photo editor is to open the editor from iPhoto. But what if you want to open the photo in a different external editor, perhaps one that offers a special feature not found in your "default" external photo editor? You could, of course, reconfigure iPhoto to temporarily use the different external photo editor.

Another way to open the image in an external editor is to drag the image from iPhoto's Organize mode onto the application's icon in the Dock or in the Finder. The problem with doing this, as mentioned earlier, is that iPhoto is no longer "aware" that a change has been made. iPhoto does not make a copy of the image, and you therefore lose the ability to revert to the original if desired. It also does not update the thumbnail in Organize mode.

But there is a workaround for all this. Follow these steps:

1. **Make a change in iPhoto *before* opening the image in another photo editor.** If you do this, iPhoto makes a copy and preserves the original, enabling you to revert to the original if you need to.

2. **Make the changes you need to in the external photo editor.**

3. **Save the image in the external photo editor.**

4. **Make another change in iPhoto *after* saving the image in the external photo editor.**

▼ Tip

One easy change to make is to rotate the image all the way around *while in Edit mode* in iPhoto. Although this leaves your image right back where it started, iPhoto actually sees this as a change and makes a copy, preserving the original. Actually, if you want to save a couple of clicks, pressing ⌘+R and then ⌘+Option+R does just a quarter turn and then back again. This trick does not work in Organize mode; you have to be in Edit mode for iPhoto to back up the original. After making the change in the alternate external photo editor, you can repeat this technique, which causes iPhoto to again "see" a change and update the thumbnail.

IPhoto is good at what iPhoto is good at. Hard-core image fixin' isn't really what it's for. It's an organizer first and foremost. The cool thing is that the industry is all over the fact that digital photography has hit the masses and they recognize that there's a strong market for simple photography editing utilities. That's where Photoshop Elements came from. Most people don't really need to do much to their pictures, and that makes a full-featured, professional image-editing program a hard pill to swallow.

Then again, you could always do what my mom does. She picks out her select shots and sends them to me with a note saying something along the lines of "I'm your mother. You owe me. Make these pictures look better." Wait... I'm not saying that *you* should send *me* your pictures. You have to find your own indentured servant super-geek to do your dirty work! (No, not you Mom. You've still got an extensive line of geek credit.)

Actually, now that I think about it, if you're a single, millionaire, supermodel, super-genius, Mac-using massage therapist and you want to send me pictures of yourself, that would be perfectly fine. I reserve the right to keep the pictures though.

PART IV

Getting It Out There: Sharing Your Photos

10

Making a Slideshow

In This Chapter

Choosing images for a slideshow • Setting order and duration of the slides
Setting the transition between slides • Using controls during the slideshow
Adding music to your slideshow • Interrupting and restarting a slideshow

Say the word *slideshow,* and it brings back memories of sitting in the dark in the living room with a flimsy screen, or a bed sheet thumbtacked to the wall, more likely. The whir of the 35mm slide projector drones from the other side of the room. The picture shines up on the screen that's swaying slowly as the air conditioner kicks on. You look at the picture only to realize that it's been loaded backwards. *Kachinka.* The second one is in backwards too. *Kachinka.* Damn. "Heh heh. Um. Looks like I loaded 'em wrong. Gimme a sec. I gotta flip all these around real quick. This shouldn't take too long. Wait! Where are you going? No! Come back. They're really cute pictures!" ...and the fan drones on in solitude....

Okay, this is not that kind of slideshow. Well, it *is,* but it's better. First of all you don't plan out a full-blown event, trying to black out the windows, reserving the living room, and whatnot to put on this slideshow. This one's much easier to build. A slideshow is a great way to show your vacation photos to your hostages willing audience of friends. It's like the microwave brownies of presentations, except it doesn't take as long to cook. The slideshow setup lets you set the pace, pick a transition style, and then, to make sure nobody falls asleep watching your photos, you can pick some Hüsker Dü or Parliament P-Funk tune-ification to keep people squirming in their seats in a good, groovy way (instead of the less popular version of "squirming in their seats" that usually goes with slideshows). I'd much rather listen to some P-Funk than *Kachinka, Kachinka, Kachinka.*

ASSEMBLE A SLIDESHOW

A slideshow automatically builds an instant presentation out of whatever album or pictures you have selected. There's not really any assembly required. It's just a matter of *click, click,* and *click* then you're up and running a personal picture presto. All you have to do is:

1. **Switch to Organize mode.**

2. **Open the album containing the images you want to use.** At this point, you have two options:

   ■ To include all the images in an album, don't select any images before moving to the next step (Figure 10-1).

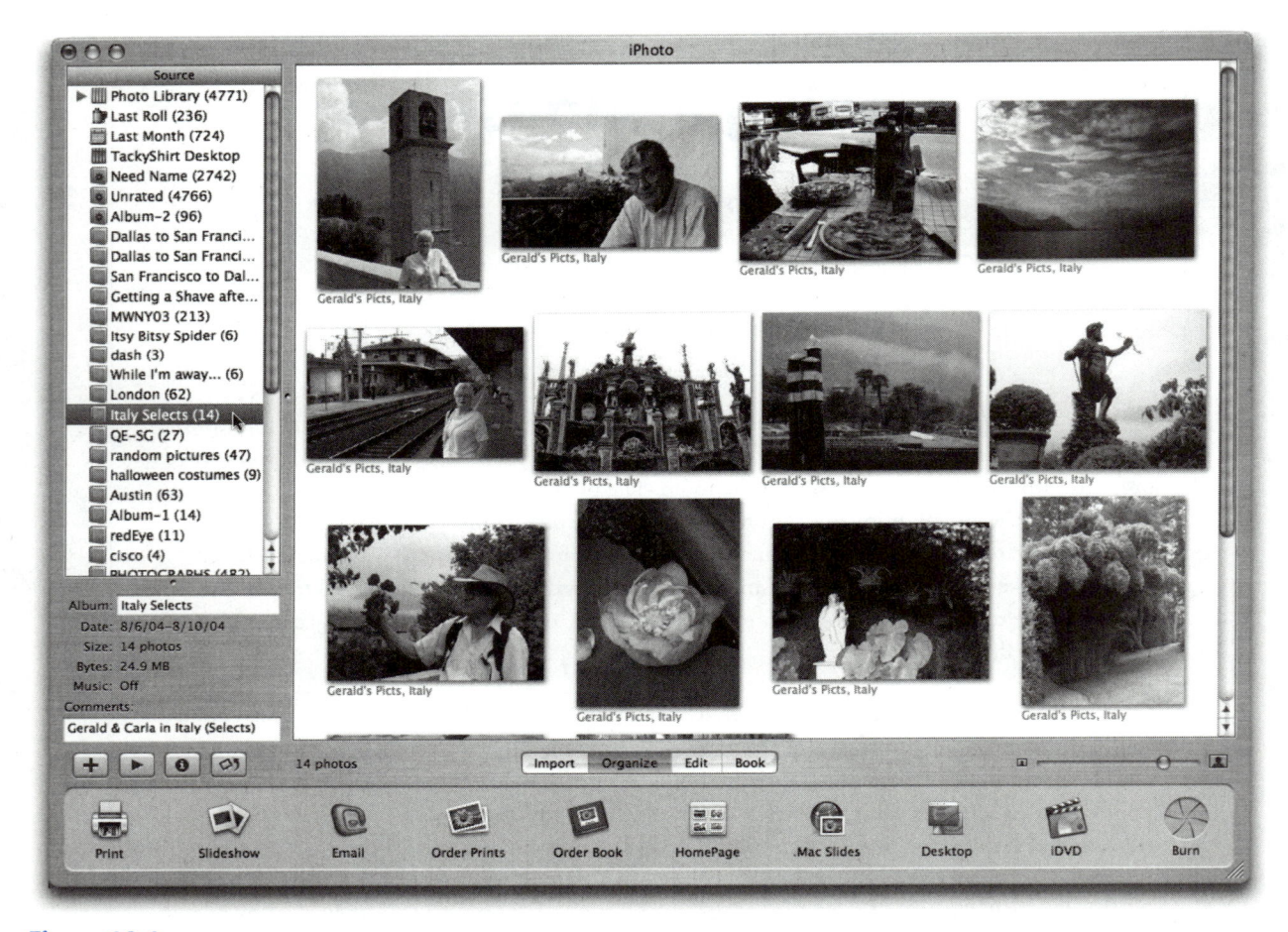

Figure 10-1
Select the album to use all the images in that album

■ To specify a subset of images for your slideshow, select the individual images in the album you want to include in the slideshow (Figure 10-2). Of course selecting *all* the images will do the same thing as just selecting the album. The slideshow always displays the images in the same order as they are shown in the album, so it doesn't matter

what order you select the images in. If you want to change the slideshow order, you'll have to change the image order in the album — either by rearranging the images in the album, or by duplicating the album and rearranging the images in the new album. You would then use the duplicate album for your slideshow.

Figure 10-2
Select individual images to make a slideshow of just those pictures

3. **Click the Slideshow button to open the Slideshow dialog box.**

4. **If you want to adjust the settings, click the Settings tab and specify the settings you want to use.** See the section "Specify the Slideshow Settings," later in this chapter.

5. **If you want to add music to your slideshow, click the Music tab in the Slideshow dialog box.**

6. **Specify the settings in the Music tab of the Slideshow dialog box.** See the section "Add Music to Your Slideshow," later in this chapter.

7. **Click Save Settings.** The window closes without playing the slideshow, but it will save all your settings for later. Another option is to click Play, which saves your settings, closes the dialog box, and plays the slideshow (that is a lot of stuff to accomplish with one mouse click!).

SPECIFY THE SLIDESHOW SETTINGS

Sure, you can just hit Slideshow and then hit return. That will jump you straight into a slideshow, but you probably want to change a few settings first just to make sure the show will put up what you want to see at the right pace and such. To specify the slideshow settings, click the Slideshow button to open the Slideshow dialog box. If necessary, click the Settings tab in the dialog box (see Figure 10-3).

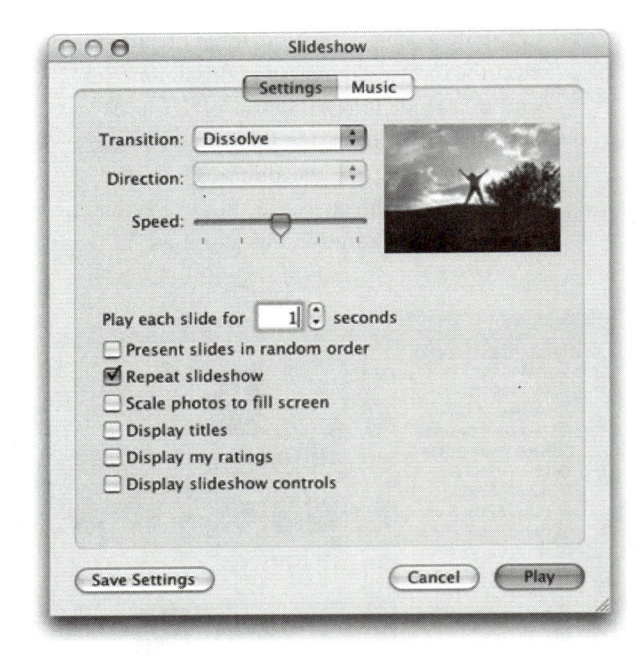

Figure 10-3
Use the Slideshow Settings dialog box to specify how you want your slideshow to play

The Settings tab of the dialog box enables you to configure the display options for the slideshow. The items you can set are

- **Transition.** The Transition pop-up list enables you to pick the type of transition you want to display as one slide "morphs" into another.

Note

Choose None from the Transition pop-up list if you don't want any transition between slides.

- **Transition Direction.** Some transitions (such as Wipe) also have a direction. Set the direction from the (can you guess?) Direction pop-up list. For example, if you choose the Wipe transition and the Left to Right direction, the new slide begins appearing at the left side and wipes to the right across the previous slide.

- **Transition Speed.** You can also choose the speed of the transition by dragging the Speed slider right (slower) or left (faster).

- **Slide Duration.** Use the "Play each slide for" field to set how long each slide is displayed on the screen. You can use the arrows to the right of the field to set any duration up to 60 seconds, or type a value into the field. Typically if you're showing people a sequence of pictures, you'll want something around 4–6 seconds. If you're picking a bunch of pictures to run a digital picture frame sort of thing, you might want to pick longer durations. Experiment a little to find a pace you like, but remember that more than 6 seconds per slide will get real boring if you're not talking them through every picture. Oddly, if you type a value higher than 60 seconds into the field, iPhoto makes the Play button in the Slideshow Settings dialog box unavailable so you can't run the slideshow directly

from the dialog box. But you *can* still click the Save Settings button to close the dialog box, and then run the slideshow from the Play button just below the Info pane. Go figure.

- **Display Order.** As mentioned earlier, the default order to display slideshow images is the album order. However, if you click the Present slides in random order checkbox, iPhoto mixes up the display order randomly for each pass through the images.

- **Repeat slideshow.** If you want the slideshow to repeat over and over (rather than just running through the images once before quitting), click the Repeat slideshow checkbox. To stop a slideshow that is repeating, click the mouse button or press any key except the Space bar.

- **Scale photos.** If your photos don't fit the screen exactly, you can click the Scale photos to fill screen checkbox. This expands the image to fill the screen in all dimensions. However, the two edges in the larger dimension are cut off because they extend past the edge of the screen. For example, Figure 10-4 shows a portrait mode image during a slideshow. The Scale photos to fill screen checkbox was not selected. The entire image is visible on the screen, but black bars appear to the left and right of the image. In contrast, Figure 10-5 shows the same image when the Scale photos to fill screen checkbox was selected. The image now fills the screen, but the top and bottom of the photo are not visible.

Figure 10-4

A portrait mode image doesn't fill the screen during a slideshow

 Tip

If you want to make your slideshow fill the entire display because you have some sort of letterbox phobia (Hmmm... I'll bet there's a "fear of black strips framing pictures" out there somewhere), you should crop your pictures to match your display aspect ratio. You remember: Edit mode, Constrain ➜ ? x ? (Display), draw rectangle, crop.

If you do that to all your pictures, they'll be wall to wall, floor to ceiling on your monitor. If you don't, you'll probably have black bars framing many of your pictures as iPhoto stuffs 10 pounds of picture into a 5-pound screen, so to speak. iPhoto fills the frame if you tell it to, but if the good bit isn't in the center, you won't like it.

Figure 10-5
Now the image fills the screen, but you've cut off the best part of the picture

- **Display Titles.** Click the Display titles checkbox to display the image title in the upper-left corner of the slide during the slideshow (see Figure 10-6). The titles are references in case someone is particularly impressed with an image and wants to ask you about it (or get a copy) later.

- **Display Slideshow Controls.** If you click the Display slideshow controls checkbox, a set of controls overlays the bottom of the slide during the slideshow (see Figure 10-7). If you want to see these controls and have forgotten to click this checkbox, just move the mouse pointer — the controls appear automatically.

Figure 10-6
Show the image title in the upper-left corner by clicking the Display titles checkbox

▼ Note

In iPhoto v4.0.2, the Display my ratings checkbox doesn't seem to have any function at first. There was a bug. Press Play and then press a number (1, 2, 3, 4, or 5) on the keyboard. That assigns that number of stars to that picture. iPhoto starts showing your ratings for all the pictures that follow as well as those in other slideshows, even after restarting the program. Bugs are weird critters. They fixed the bug in v4.0.3.

Figure 10-7
Use the slideshow controls to modify your images while the slideshow is running

As noted in Figure 10-7, you can click the individual controls in the slideshow control panel to do the following:

- Move to the next or previous slide.

- Play or pause the slideshow.

- Rotate the image clockwise or counterclockwise.

- Discard the image (click the Trash icon at the right end of the controls).

- Set or change the image ratings. To do so, click in the ratings area (to the left of the Trash icon) to set the number of stars.

ADD MUSIC TO YOUR SLIDESHOW

Here's a little experiment you can try yourself. Imagine watching 100 beautiful landscape pictures in a slideshow that plays in silence. Now imagine watching 100 boring pictures of some stranger's family in a slideshow that has a Beatles song or two playing throughout the show. You might be surprised at just how much more forgiving your audience will be if you entertain them with some good music even if your pictures are as exciting as watching grass grow. (Purely hypothetically speaking of course. I'm sure all of your pictures are wonderful.) Now if you have good pictures *and* good tunes accompanying them, that just takes everything to 11! iPhoto is neatly integrated with iTunes, so adding music to a slideshow is easy. The music starts automatically when you run the slideshow and plays until the slideshow ends, repeating as necessary.

 Note

Every album you create (as well as the photo library) has a default tune associated with it — "Minuet in G," which is built into iPhoto. The Info pane shows you what music is associated with the selected album or the photo library (see Figure 10-8).

To play music with a slideshow, click the Music tab in the Slideshow dialog box (see Figure 10-9), and click the Play music during slideshow checkbox.

Music associated with an album

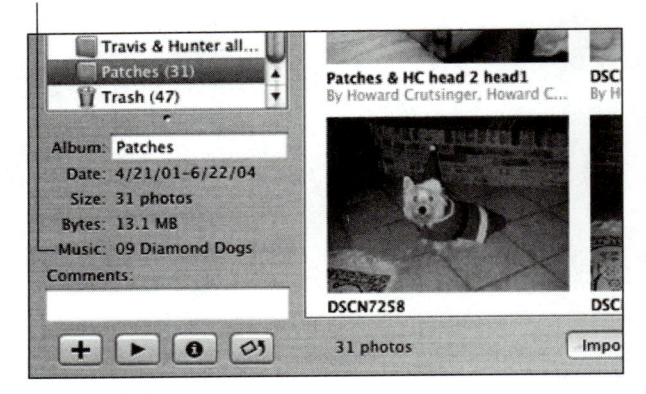

Figure 10-8
The music associated with an album is used for slideshows

Figure 10-9
Use the Music tab in the Slideshow dialog box to associate music with a slideshow

Tip

If you select your photo library and assign music to it in the Slideshow pane, that music becomes the default music assigned to each new photo album you create. If you want to kill the default music assignment, just uncheck the Play music during slideshow option and you're blessed with silence. When you first run iPhoto, "Minuet in G" is assigned as the default. Trust me. You'll eventually start to cringe at that first strum if you don't uncheck that box. It's a Pavlovian response thing.

The pop-up list just below the checkbox contains a set of playlists, including the iTunes Library option, which displays all the songs you imported into iTunes. To display the contents of a single playlist, select the playlist from the pop-up list (see Figure 10-10). The contents of that playlist are displayed in the table below the pop-up list.

You can also search according to song title by typing the word(s) you are looking for into the Search field. As you type, the list of songs narrows to just those that match the criteria. Unlike other Search fields in iPhoto, the song title must be an exact match to the characters you type, including spaces.

To associate a song with the album (and thus the slideshow), select the song and click Save Settings (to just save the settings) or Play (to save the settings and preview the slideshow). The Music tab displays the name of the playlist and the song near the bottom of the dialog box. To associate an entire playlist with the album (and thus the slideshow), select the playlist in the Source pop-up list but do not pick an individual song from the table; the Music tab displays the text *Entire Playlist:* followed by the name of the selected playlist.

Figure 10-10
Choose a playlist to use for slideshow music from the Source pop-up list

Tip

If you change your mind after having picked a song in the table and decide you want to use the entire playlist, reselect the playlist from the Source pop-up list.

TALK THEM THROUGH YOUR TABLEAUS

For a set of pictures over which you want to narrate, there's a little trick to give the slideshow its own narrator track.

First of all, pick how long you want your slides to be on-screen ahead of time so you'll know how long you can talk about each picture. We'll say 10 seconds, just to pick a number. Record an audio file where you talk about each picture for 10 seconds, and then pull that audio file into iTunes. The file is now available as a "music" track. If your timing is impeccable, it'll play back in sync with the picture changes, and you can hang back and relax while the Mac plays back your own personal commentary track.

You can record audio in any number of applications — iMovie for one. iMovie will create an audio file named Voice 01 in the Media folder that goes with the movie you created. That audio file is what you want to toss into iTunes.

This isn't really the *best* way to add a voiceover, as you'll see in Chapter 20 when we look at slideshows in iMovie. However, it is a neat little thing you can try "not because it's easy, but because it's hard," as JFK once said. Hey, sometimes you have to do something the hard way just so you can know *you got skillz*.

STEERING A SLIDESHOW

It won't take long for you to figure out that you just don't want to look at every picture for the same amount of time. You can take in a picture of a tree with puffy clouds in a couple of seconds, but other pictures might be more akin to a page out of a *Where's Waldo?* book. Just because you told the slideshow to show each picture for six seconds doesn't mean you can't fast-forward or pause the show.

There are manual controls that override the automatic playback. You can use keyboard commands or mouse around with the onscreen controls to direct a running slideshow (see Figure 10-11).

- **Move to the previous picture.** Press the Left Arrow key while the slideshow is not paused to move back to the previous slide. This also pauses the slideshow.

- **Pause a slideshow.** Press the Space bar to pause the slideshow on the current slide. Press the Space bar again to resume the slideshow. The music (if any) continues to play even while the slideshow is paused.

- **Move to the next picture.** Press the Right Arrow key while the slideshow is not paused to move to the next slide. This also pauses the slideshow.

- **Set your rating.** Pressing any of the number keys from 1–5 will assign that many stars to the current picture. Hitting zero (0) will remove all stars. You can use the numeric keypad as well as the regular number keys at the top of the keyboard.

- **Delete the current slide.** Press the Delete key to remove the current picture from the photo album you're watching. If you're watching a slideshow of the Photo Library, Last X Rolls, or Last X Months albums, the photo will be moved to the trash and every instance of that picture in any other albums will be removed. Delete is disabled if you're viewing a Smart Album.

- **Decrease the slide display time.** Press the Up Arrow key to decrease the slide display time by 1 second each time you press the key. The minimum display time is 1 second. (No on-screen equivalent.)

- **Increase the slide display time.** Press the Down Arrow key to increase the slide display time by 1 second each time you press the key. (No on-screen equivalent.)

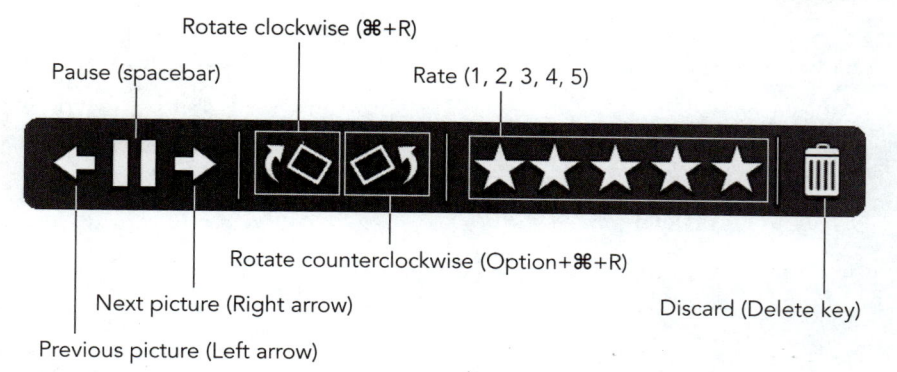

Pause (spacebar)

Rotate clockwise (⌘+R)

Rate (1, 2, 3, 4, 5)

Rotate counterclockwise (Option+⌘+R)

Next picture (Right arrow)

Discard (Delete key)

Previous picture (Left arrow)

Figure 10-11

On-screen controls and keyboard commands let you turn off the cruise control and drive the show yourself

- **End the slideshow.** Press any other key not listed above to end the slideshow. You can also click the mouse button anywhere outside the on-screen overlay to end the slideshow.

The one place that the slideshow might fall short is that communal experience of having several friends in the living room watching the big sheet, er, screen. There is something to be said for having a group of people all watching the show at the same time, especially if they're the sort to get in on the act themselves.

Usually desktop Mac's aren't sitting where half a dozen people can comfortably watch the show with their feet up on the coffee table. Laptops let you take the show to a more comfortable setting than a computer desk, but once you get past three people huddled around the laptop, you have to take turns leaning in for a look.

Laptops usually come with a handy video out adapter that will let you play the slideshow on the TV. Because most living rooms are centered on the television, this is probably the closest most people will get to the old slide presentation feel. Your TV has much lower picture quality than your computer though, so if things are looking a bit fuzzy and some of the colors are bleeding, it's supposed to look like that. Regular TV at it's *best* is actually a pretty bad picture, and most TV sets fall well short of even that low standard.

Of course if you have a video projector, you can pin up the ole bed sheet and round out the experience by saying *Kachinka* every time iPhoto switches to a new slide. Just make sure you clear the room of any small knickknacks. After your sixth *Kachinka*, you can expect to start dodging friendly fire, and those little Hummel figurines may look adorable, but they'll leave one heck of a whelp if you throw them hard enough. Maybe it's best to just let iPhoto show its pictures with its music and leave out the sound effects.

RATE PHOTOS ON THE FLY

Slideshows aren't just for showing off your pictures: A slideshow is the fastest way to assign ratings to your pictures. (See Chapter 4 for more info on ratings.) Want to add star ratings to all of your pictures in no time?

1. Create a Smart Album set to show pictures without ratings.

2. Select that Smart Album.

3. Click Slideshow.

4. Set the Transition to None.

5. Set the slide timer to 1 second.

6. Play the slideshow.

Now, while each picture is going by, all you have to do is press 1, 2, 3, 4, or 5 on the keyboard and that number of stars is applied to the picture!

This rips through 225 photos in 15 minutes. It should be 900 in that time, but when you set a rating, the show hesitates for a few seconds, which is a bit of a bummer for these purposes. Want to go faster? Place your left hand on the numbers and your right hand on the arrow keys. Now you can press a number to assign a rating, and then press the Right Arrow key to jump forward without waiting for the picture to auto-change. If you get ahead of yourself, you can always press the Left Arrow key to back up. Oh, and if you get a little twitchy like I do, you can press a number for your first impression, and then press another number right after that if you disagree with your impulse assessment. I sometimes end up pressing three or four numbers before switching to the next picture. Hey, sometimes a "bad picture" makes me laugh, so I end up giving it extra credit after the humor sinks in.

If it wasn't for this trick, I doubt I'd have many ratings in my collection. Assigning ratings is buried in the contextual menu on a submenu, or in the Photos menu under a submenu — not the easiest place to access quickly. Sure, there are keyboard shortcuts, but that option doesn't dawn on me most of the time. With a slideshow running, you won't get distracted from the task as easily because the pictures just keep on coming one after the other.

Paper and Ink: Using Your Basic Print Tools

In This Chapter

Setting up the features of your printer • Understanding your paper options
Previewing a photo • Understanding resolution
Understanding the basics of printing

iPhoto lets you make slideshows, Web pages, photo CDs and DVDs, among other fancy twenty-first-century tricks, but sometimes you still want to stick something in a frame and put it up on the wall. Not to worry. iPhoto has you covered there too. It's time to take a peek at printing pictures. Of course there's more to it than just hitting Print and watching exactly what you need come out of the printer. That just wouldn't be a very twenty-first-century way of doing things.

You've got to think about the size of the print, the aspect ratio, the resolution, the kind of paper you want to print on, the kind of printer you want to use.... Basically all the stuff we cover in this chapter! What are the odds?

Of course, if you just hit Print and let it ride, you'll probably get along just fine. It's when you have specific needs that you really want to fine-tune the process, and iPhoto tunes just fine.

UNDERSTAND PRINTER TYPES

Unless you've been hiding in a cave somewhere, you know that a variety of basic printer types are available. Laser printers are great for printing text quickly and cheaply. There are even color laser printers, though these, in general, don't do a good job printing photos.

To print decent photographs, you need either an inkjet printer or a dye-sublimation printer. Dye-sublimation printers actually melt special ink dyes onto special papers, creating images that are, in general, richly colored and long lasting. However, although dye sublimation printer prices have come down in recent years, both the printers and their supply packs are still fairly pricey, especially for printers that can produce prints larger than 4 x 6.

Inkjet printers, on the other hand, can be had for a whole range of prices; some cost less than $75. However, the better printers — those that use more colors and higher print resolutions to produce high-quality prints — start at about $150 and go up from there. These printers come with a whole range of features, including the ability to insert a digital camera memory card into the printer and print without using the computer at all. Some even come with small screens so you can see your images right on the printer. As neat as some of these features may seem, if you plan to catalog your prints in iPhoto and edit them on your Mac, you'll find most printer features somewhat gimmicky. To print quality photos, you should pay attention to the following features:

- **Number of ink colors.** Basic inkjet printers use four colors: black and three other colors. They mix (spray) these colors together on the paper to approximate the exact colors in the image. "Photo" inkjet printers use more ink colors. The Epson line of Stylus photo printers used six colors, and recently HP has come out with printers that use as many as eight ink colors. The basic rule is that more ink colors is better because the printer can do a better job of color matching when it has more colors to work with. My own personal experience is that six colors are sufficient (with the right paper) to produce a result virtually indistinguishable from a professionally printed photo.

- **Print speed.** If you plan to print a lot of photos, the printer speed may be important to you. The manufacturers publish print speeds for both color and non-color printing, but these numbers (especially the color print speeds) are laughable. No standard for measuring print speed exists, so printer manufacturers often clock their printers in "draft" mode (low quality) printing out images that don't have much color coverage. This is, of course, not anything like what you'll be printing. To compare print speeds, checking the results of independent testing is best, such as those published in magazines. Not surprisingly, higher-cost printers tend to be faster. In fact, for many years HP made a line of printers at several price points that all had the same characteristics and even used the same ink cartridges. The only difference: the print speed. Sometimes, you *do* get what you pay for.

- **Printer resolution.** Not to be confused with *image resolution,* printer resolution describes the number of dots of ink the printer can lay down in a given space. The more dots the printer can lay down, the better the approximation of the image details and color the printer produces. Printer resolution used to be a lot more important; today, virtually any printer that uses six colors for photo printing can produce resolutions that do a fine job producing prints. Your printer driver may allow you to set the resolution (some do, some don't), and as I said, higher resolutions are better, *up to a point*. Beyond a certain point (about 1400 dpi on my Epson Stylus Photo), the results don't get any better with higher resolutions — but the print times go way up. So experiment with your printer to find the point of diminishing returns on resolution settings.

WHAT PRINTER FOR PICTURES?

Several kinds of printers are out there, and when it comes time to buy a printer, digging in and doing your homework can be a bit daunting.

The **inkjet printer** is the runaway leader at this point and for the foreseeable future. The bad news is that they've been pretty much the worst technology at creating the most accurate photographic prints. The good news is that they're *really* cheap, and in recent years, the printer companies have raised the bar of what inkjet technology can do so much that you can pretty much ignore that bad news I was talking about. Inkjet printers use water-based ink, typically cyan, magenta, yellow, and black (CMYK). The problem is that a single drop of water on your printout makes everything in that area start to bleed together into a big mess.

Laser printers use *toner,* which is a fine powder that I suppose is somewhere in the plastic family. Laser printers melt that plastic onto the page with great precision, and after the stuff is fused onto the page, you couldn't smear it with a mop. These printouts are about as sharp as you can get, but the printers aren't down in the $100 range; they're more up in the $900–$3,000 neighborhood.

Solid-Ink printers are stunning. If you get a chance to print out a photo on a solid-ink printer, do it. These use... well, the closest thing you'd probably recognize is crayons. Yeah, I didn't believe it at first either. They use CMYK-colored wax sticks that are melted to the page. The resulting color will knock your socks off. These printers are a bit expensive though, at about $450 and up, and they run through color cartridges pretty quick, so they can be a bit expensive over the long haul. And they're not too good for printing text or material that has sharp edges.

Dye-sublimation printers have ink ribbons. The ink is heated up, which turns it into a vapor; then the ink is allowed to cool on the paper, turning back to a solid. When it comes to photographic printing, this is the cat's meow. Dye-sublimation printers produce fantastic colors. Because it actually dyes the paper, the image isn't prone to smearing and fading, and it's dry so the paper won't be all wet like an inkjet printout. The explosion of digital photography has made small-format dye-sublimation printers a hot new item. They are in the $150–$300 range, but they only print out 4-x-6-inch prints; printers that produce larger photos are closer to $1,000.

HOW TO CONFIGURE YOUR PRINTER

Today's photo printers are (in general) pretty good. Of course, the printer's capabilities depend on the printer make and model. But what exactly you can do with your printer also depends quite a bit on the printer driver. The *printer driver* is a piece of software that enables your computer to talk to the printer. In my case, because of the different drivers, the capabilities of my inkjet printer are different depending on whether I have it hooked up to my PC or to my PowerBook. The driver controls the quality of the print you can make (with settings like Draft, Normal, or Photo), available layouts, the amount of ink laid down, the type of paper you can use (more on that later in this chapter), and much more.

To explore the options you have for printing, choose File ➜ Print to open the Print dialog box (see Figure 11-1).

Figure 11-1
Use the Print dialog box as the first step in getting your image on paper

If you have more than one printer connected to your Mac, you can make a selection from the Printer pop-up list. You can configure your printer by clicking the Advanced Options button. This opens a dialog box that is unique to your printer. Figure 11-2 shows the version for my Epson Stylus C80 printer.

Note

Your version of this dialog box will look different, depending on your printer. To return to the standard options version of the Print dialog box (where you can specify the type of printing you want to do in iPhoto), click the Standard Options button.

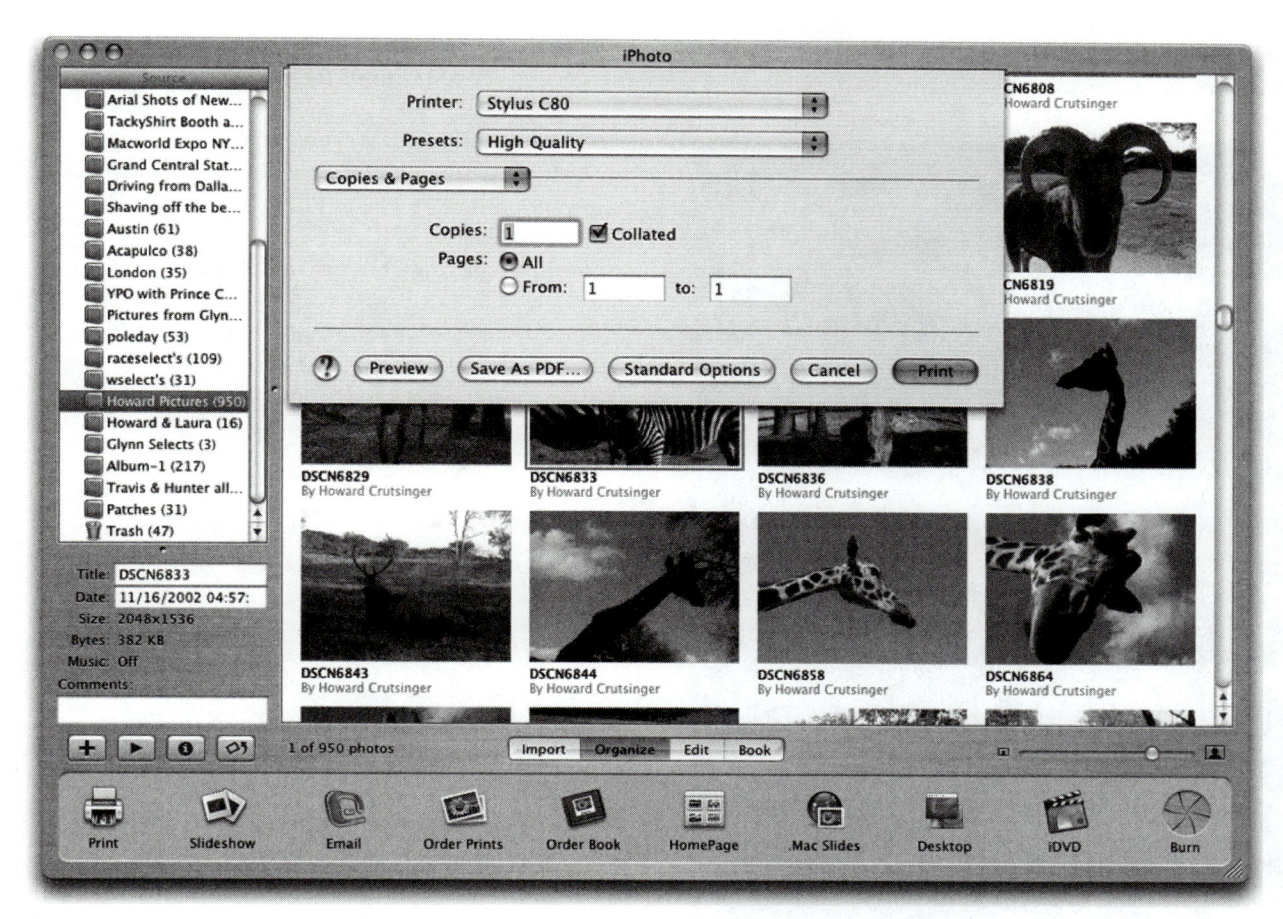

Figure 11-2

Use the Advanced Options version of the Print dialog box to configure your printer

UNDERSTAND THE DIFFERENT PAPER TYPES

The fact that inkjet printers are the king of the mountain right now makes the kind of paper you use that much more important. With inkjet printing, the difference between printing on top-quality photo paper and cheap bulk paper you stole from the office supply closet is like the difference between — well, I suppose between Windows 95 and Mac OS X.

Each printer manufacturer makes a range of papers, and most recommend that you pair their paper with their printers. Although this may sound like marketing hype, the truth is that following this advice often makes a huge difference to the print quality. For example, you can use a glossy photo paper from Staples or Office Depot with an Epson printer, but the print is not as bright and starts to fade much more quickly than if you used Epson paper. This is because the printer manufacturers design the papers to work best with their inks.

The Advanced Options version of the Print dialog box enables you to specify the type of paper you have loaded into your printer (see Figure 11-3).

Some drivers offer options such as "other photo paper," but many offer only papers made by the printer vendor. Picking the paper that you actually have loaded into the printer is very important; the "behind the scenes" settings that the printer uses to create the best print depend on correctly identifying the type of paper.

Several general types of paper are available, and sometimes various grades and weights (as you can see from the previous figure) of each type:

- **Plain paper.** This is just the type of cheap paper you buy for laser printers, copiers, fax machines, and the like. It usually sells for just a few dollars a ream, and isn't good for much except perhaps experimenting with photo layouts without wasting expensive paper. Using this paper, you cannot get a good idea of the quality of the final image. Super-cheapo discount paper *is* good for printing out test pages though. I usually print out a picture on the cheap stuff before I load up the expensive specialty paper just to make sure it's the right size and properly placed on the page as well as to spot when one of my print heads gets clogged, so the printer won't only lay down magenta, yellow, and black.

ACID-FREE PAPER

(Feel free to insert your own psychedelic hippy joke reference here.)

Acid-free paper is a wonderful answer to the ongoing attempt to salvage what we print out for future generations. The problem is that some papers use heavily acidic chemicals to turn two-by-fours into 8½-by-11-inch sheets. That acid remains in small amounts in the paper fibers, and this is what we call "a bad thing."

Do you have any paperback books or newspaper clippings from a couple of decades back? Take a look at what's happening there. The paper is getting yellow. The ink is fading. The pages are more and more brittle. Eventually, the paper eats itself along with the material stored on it and your memories are lost forever; but if you think *you* have it bad, try the Library of Congress. Millions of publications are rotting in the archives and there's not much we can do about it.

When it comes to printing pictures in iPhoto, if you're going to put the picture in a frame that may be sitting up on a shelf for decades, bringing back fond memories all the while, use the *good* paper. A nice cotton paper that says it's "acid-free" or "archival quality" should be used for any inkjet printing that you intend to look at for more than a year or so.

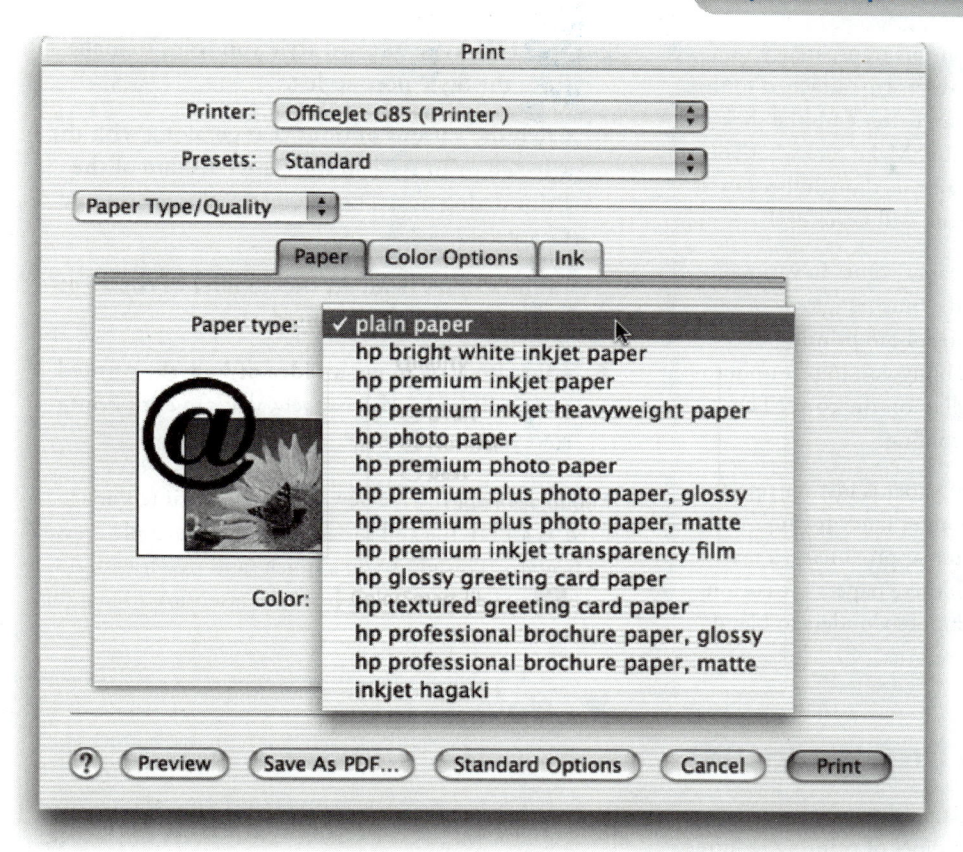

Figure 11-3
The list of papers for my HP inkjet printer includes only papers made by HP!

- **Inkjet paper.** This is a somewhat more expensive paper. It is usually a little heavier than plain paper, and has a special coating on one side designed to keep the ink from spreading when sprayed onto the paper. This paper is good for proofs, sampler sheets, and other prints where the quality is not too important.

- **Glossy photo paper.** This is the sort of heavyweight, glossy-finish paper that you get from commercial prints when you order a glossy finish. It tends to be pretty expensive, but produces very good quality.

Some vendors (HP is an example) make several grades and weights of this sort of paper.

- **Matte photo paper.** This is similar to glossy photo paper, but has a matte (non-shiny) finish.

- **Transparency film.** This paper is, well, not actually paper at all. It's a clear sheet of acetate. As it turns out, cellulose acetate actually *is* made from wood or cotton pulp, but it's plastic, not paper. Transparencies are used on overhead projectors or in artwork that uses layers like old cartoons. All your favorite classic cartoon characters were all painted on this transparency film. Often there will be a small paper strip attached to the leading edge so the printer can better grab the sheet and send it through the printer. Make sure what you use is specifically *for inkjet printing* though, because if it's not specially coated, the ink will never dry!

- **Greeting card paper.** This paper comes in various styles (quarter-fold, half-fold), finishes (glossy or matte), and may be coated for photo printing on either one or both sides, enabling you to print photographs inside the card as well as on the cover. The paper is pre-scored for easy folding.

- **Art papers.** This category of paper is just starting to become common. It incorporates fancy textures and finishes — one of my favorites approximates a textured canvas finish. Many of these papers use cotton instead of wood pulp, which does wonders to blend the inks and eliminate dot patterns.

THE BASICS OF PRINTING IN IPHOTO

To print photos from iPhoto, you need to take several basic steps. Some of the different types of printing require you to make more decisions, and I'll cover those in the next chapter. Basically, though, to print your photos, you need to do the following:

1. **Choose File → Print and make sure that the "standard options" version of the Print dialog box is displayed.** (This is shown in Figure 11-1 earlier in this chapter.)

2. **Select the printer from the Printer pop-up list and (if necessary) configure the printer using Advanced Options.** This is described in "How to Configure Your Printer," earlier in this chapter. Select at least the correct paper type and print quality. Then switch back to the standard options version of the Print dialog box.

3. **Select the type of print style you want to make from the Style pop-up list.**

4. **Click the various options that go along with the selected print style in the center section of the Print dialog box.** The specifics of this are covered in Chapter 12.

5. **In the Copies field, set the number of copies of each page you want printed.**

6. **Click Preview to get an idea of how the printed page will look.** Alternatively, you can click Print to start printing the page.

When you click the Preview button, the printed image is saved as a PDF file and then opened in the Apple Preview application. This gives you a quick (and tree-friendly) way to check your layout, paying special attention to margins and aspect ratios.

 Note

If you preview a print job that requires multiple pages, you can switch pages by clicking the thumbnail of the page you want to see from the list of thumbnails on the right side of the Preview application window. If the thumbnails are not visible, click the Drawer button located on the left of the toolbar at the top of the Preview window.

From the Print dialog box, you can also save the file as a PDF file so you can share the results with anyone who has the free Adobe Acrobat Reader. Mac OS X users can open it without Acrobat Reader.

Oh no. That's not it by a long shot. We're just getting started when it comes to printing. That was just a primer. I do want to drive home the axiom "Garbage in, garbage out." You need to start out with good material if you're going to want to get good prints. Now, I'm not talking so much about what you're taking pictures *of* so much as

MAKING SURE YOU HAVE ENOUGH RESOLUTION

If you take pictures with a low-resolution digital camera or heavily crop an image, you may find that you don't have enough pixels left to produce a good-quality image. Although iPhoto alerts you if you try to print a photo at a size that produces poor results, knowing what photo resolution produces a good-quality print is important. The basic rule is that you should have 300 dots for every inch of photo you want to print, although you can get away with less. But below about 200 dots per inch, the printed results start looking pretty ragged. Thus, to print a 4-x-6-inch snapshot, the image should measure at least 1200 x 1800 pixels. iPhoto provides the pixel size of the image in the Info pane. Use the information in Table 11-1 as a guideline for creating good-quality prints.

Table 11-1: Recommended Print Resolutions

Print size	Recommended resolution	Minimum resolution
wallet size	320 x 240	
4 x 6	1200 x 1800	800 x 1200
5 x 7	1500 x 2100	1000 x 1400
8 x 10	2400 x 3000	1600 x 2000

iPhoto warns you with a yellow warning icon in the upper right corner of the picture if a photo's resolution is too low to print well (Figure 11-4). You can go ahead and print the photo if you want, but it will come out looking blocky and you won't like the result. It's better to select a smaller size that better matches your image's resolution.

Figure 11-4
If you see the yellow warning icon, don't print the photo; you won't like the result

making sure your camera is recording in a high enough resolution for how you want to print your pictures. You can always *lower* the resolution of a picture, but increasing the resolution after you take the picture doesn't do anything to improve the printout.

When you see those guys in the three-letter crime shows like SVU, they always grab a low-resolution picture off the ATM security camera. Somebody like Richard Belzer brings the tape in to the boys in the lab. They load it into the computer and then Belzer says,

"Can you clean that up?"

"Let me boost the resolution with this matrix enhancement algorithm...." Up pops a sharp picture.

"Zoom in on that license plate on the Camaro."

"This one?"

"No, the one *way back* in the distance."

"Ah. Gotcha." {doot doot doot} Up pops a razor sharp license plate image.

"We GOT him! Fantastic! Print that out!"

"No can do, Detective."

"Why not?"

"Well, cuz I faked all that resolution boosting and zooming in stuff. I was just pulling your leg. You brought me a fuzzy low-resolution picture from an ATM camera you bonehead! That license plate was only SIX #$%&*@ PIXELS! Garbage in, garbage out. If it weren't for that nerd over there off-camera changing out the pictures up on this screen we wouldn't be seeing anything at all! This keyboard isn't even plugged in. See?"

Okay, well, maybe you haven't seen that episode. It might have been on the DVD outtakes now that I think about it. All I'm really saying here is that you need to have quality all the way through the process if you want it to look nice in the end. That means starting with a high-resolution picture and capping it off by using the good photo paper.

Using iPhoto to Print Your Pictures

In This Chapter

Previewing and printing standard photos
Printing contact sheets and sampler sheets
Printing multiple photos on a page

When you print out your pictures from iPhoto, you have a variety of preset configurations to choose from. You don't have to waste your time manually building pages that will be printed only once and then discarded. The presets can stick several different pictures or many of the same picture on a single page. Of course, you're welcome to just do a single picture on a single page, but what fun is that?

If only you could revisit your elementary school days with a sheet full of wallet-sized photos any time you want. You know you've been looking back at those photos for decades, secretly wishing you could recreate that look for a "then and now" thing. Your day has finally come!

PRE-PRINT PAGE SETUP

Before you actually print anything, it's usually a good idea to take a trip to the Page Setup sheet at least once to make sure everything in there is copacetic. Like every other Mac application, the Page Setup settings will be used for every job you print, unlike the settings you'll be using in the Print sheet. Those settings are for that single print job.

Select File ➜ Page Setup... to open the Page Setup sheet (Figure 12-1). The sheet drops down to show Page Attributes, but let's take a quick detour over to the custom paper sizes.

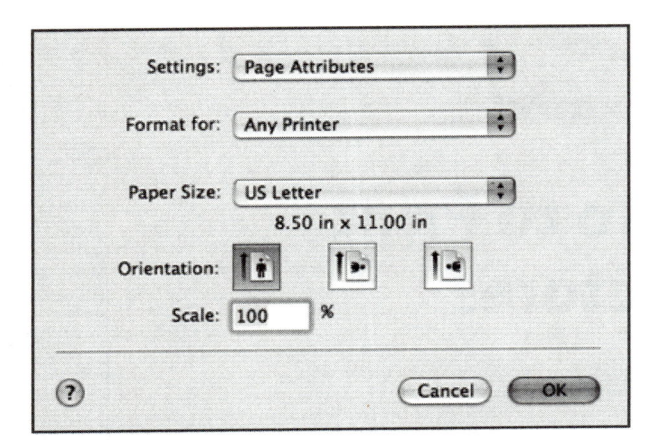

Figure 12-1
Use the Page Setup dialog box to specify default print settings

Click the Settings pop-up list and select Custom Paper Size. This is where you can input your own dimensions for any paper that is listed among the normal page sizes (see Figure 12-2). To add a new paper size, follow these steps:

1. **Click the New button create a new paper size.**

2. **Type in an appropriate name since Untitled isn't very helpful.**

3. **Enter the Height and Width of the paper.**

4. **If the printer can't print to the edge of the page, enter the amount of margin it requires on each side so you will be sure to always stay inside the printable area.**

5. **Click the Save button.**

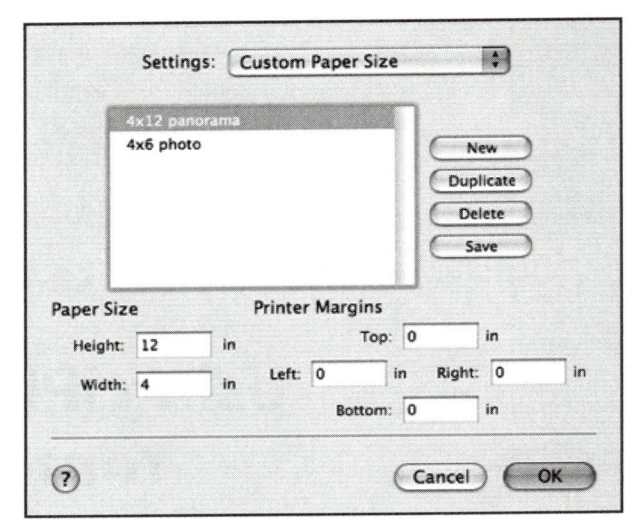

Figure 12-2
Set up custom paper sizes using the Page Setup dialog box as well

That new paper size will be listed at the bottom of the default paper sizes back in the Page Setup window. You can enter as many custom paper sizes as you like. Actually, if you want to, you can even enter "custom" paper sizes to match all the regular paper sizes but with more descriptive names. You may not know that "Legal" = 8.5" x 14", but if you see a custom paper named *8.5x14,* that's pretty easy to figure out. I mean, seriously, who knows the difference between A4 and B5 paper sizes without googling for an answer?

Some printers use a photo paper roll. This paper is 4" wide and you can print off a 6" length or a 16" length if you want to. This is perfect for printing out those panoramic pictures that some digital cameras can take. Simply create a custom paper size that's 4" wide and as tall as necessary to print out your particular panorama.

Click the Settings pop-up list and switch back to Page Attributes. Here's what you see in this window:

REMIND YOUR PRINTER ABOUT QUALITY

Most printers have a low-quality setting and that's where they spend most of their lives. We're usually perfectly happy to sacrifice quality if it gets our pages out of the printer faster. When you're printing out a page just so you can read it and then file it or trash it, the image quality isn't so important; but when you're printing out photos, quality is king.

You have to delve into the Advanced Options of the print sheet to get at the necessary settings. After you pull up that sheet, click on Copies & Pages and then select Print Settings if it's available. Different printers have different settings.

Print Settings is a custom preference pane tailored to your selected printer. Inkjet printers probably have all sorts of features you can turn on or off here. If you can tell your printer to take its time and print a quality printout, go ahead and do so. After that, go up to Presets, choose Save from that menu, and give the setting a name.

From now on, when you go to print, you can call up this setting under the Presets menu so you know you're getting the best your printer can give you.

Format for: This pop-up lets you select a particular printer to set up. Selecting "Any Printer" will apply the settings across the board. If you have more than one printer, you might have one printer set up for your 8.5" x 11" printing and another special photo printer that handles 4" x 6" prints. Just set each of them up in here and then you can pick the right printer for the job in the print sheet.

Paper Size: This pop-up is easy enough to figure out. Just pick the paper size that matches what you have loaded in the printer. This isn't necessarily the size of *picture* you plan on printing. It's the *paper* size we're looking at right now. Typically, even if you're printing an 8" x 10" photo, the actual paper you're printing onto is 8.5" x 11" (aka: Letter). If you created any custom paper sizes, they'll be listed at the bottom of this pop-up.

 Note

There are other settings in Page Setup that you can change, but iPhoto ignores them. Changing the Scale or hitting the Orientation buttons will have no effect whatsoever on your final printout. They're only in there because this is a standard Page Setup sheet that always looks like this in every Mac OS X application.

WHAT PICTURES TO PRINT

The next order of business when you're printing out pictures is to pick out what pictures you want to print. This is pretty straightforward. Whatever you have selected when you tell iPhoto to print is what will be included on that print job. The only tricky bit is if you select nothing. That prints everything. It sounds backwards but it actually makes sense.

- **Select one photo.** iPhoto will use that one photo in all of the printing styles we're about to go over.

- **Select more than one photo.** iPhoto will use every photo currently selected in the print job. This may result in several photos per page or multiple copies of each photo filling each page like those elementary school wallet pictures I was talking about. That depends on which print style you use.

- **Select nothing.** iPhoto will print *everything* in the currently displayed album.

- **Select more than one album.** If you have pictures you want to print in more than one album, you can ⌘+click on multiple albums to select them all at once. Like above, if you don't select anything out of the displayed pictures, iPhoto prints *everything* in *all* of the currently displayed albums.

Once you have your pictures selected, it's a simple matter of hitting ⌘+P to get the printing sheet to drop down just like pretty much every other application on your Mac. Of course the sheet itself is chock full of preferences that determine what your printer will be spitting out.

PRINT A STANDARD PHOTO

Use the Standard Prints option to print standard-sized photos, which include 2 x 3, 3 x 5, 4 x 6, 5 x 7, and 8 x 10 (Figure 12-3).

To print standard prints, follow these steps:

1. **Select the photos you want to print.** If you don't select any photos before choosing to print, iPhoto prints all the photos in the album.

2. **Choose File ➔ Print to start the printing process.** The print sheet will drop down from the top of the iPhoto window where you enter your print job settings.

3. **Select what printer you wish to use from the Printer pop-up menu.**

4. **Choose one of the configurations from the Presets pop-up menu if you have preference.**

5. **Choose Standard Prints from the Style pop-up menu.**

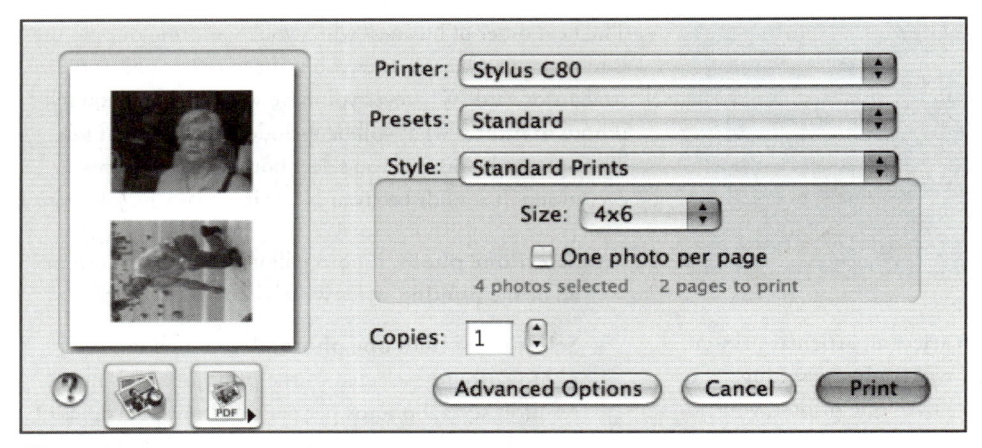

Figure 12-3
Use the Standard Prints style setting to print a standard-sized set of photographs

6. **Select the size of photograph you want to print from the Size pop-up list (see Figure 12-4).** If you are printing on letter-size paper (8.5 x 11 inches), iPhoto can fit two 3 x 5, 4 x 6, or 5 x 7 pictures on a page, or eight 2 x 3 (wallet size) photos on a page.

7. **Use the Copies field to specify the number of copies to print.**

8. **Click Print to print the picture.** If you click the PDF button, you can choose to preview your image. The preview creates a PDF file of the print job and then opens it in an application called Preview. You can print from there if everything looks right.

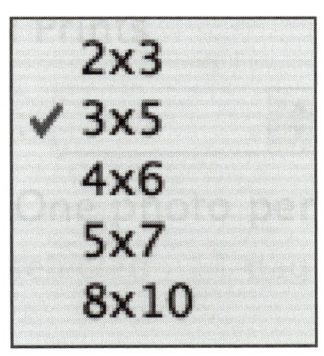

Figure 12-4
Standard Prints sizes

 Tip

Use Standard Prints when you are printing on large (such as letter-size) paper. If you want to (for example) print a 4 x 6 snapshot on 4 x 6 paper, use the Full Page setting instead, as discussed later in this chapter.

If you are printing more than one photo, the One photo per page checkbox controls how many different photographs get printed on a page. If you leave the checkbox deselected, iPhoto places as many pictures on the page as will fit, but prints only one copy of each picture. For example, if you are printing on 8.5 x 11 paper and choose the 5 x 7 size, you'll get two different pictures printed on that page, as illustrated by Figure 12-5. If you select the checkbox, iPhoto will place a single image on the page, which is kinda wasteful if you cut away all that extra paper, but it does have that artsy, matte frame look going for it. (see Figure 12-6)

Setting the aspect ratio (by cropping) of an image before printing is very important. If you don't match the aspect ratios, your photo will be the wrong shape. iPhoto shrinks the image to the photo size you selected, but it won't fill the whole area. Okay, that's a hard one to explain. Look at Figure 12-7. The top image *was* cropped, so the resulting print is larger and fills the standard photo size without leaving white borders. The bottom image was *not* cropped, so iPhoto shrank it. You won't actually see any white borders. I dimmed the rest of the page to make the extra space visible. If you were to cut out those two pictures (printed out at full size of course), the top one would be exactly 5" x 7". The bottom one would be 4.66" x 7" because it wasn't the right aspect to begin with. It was a 4 x 6 picture. If you were to put that lower picture in a picture frame, it would fill the hole vertically but have two holes on the sides. Is this getting clearer or am I just digging a deeper hole here? The moral is to crop your picture to match your photo print size. Remember that and you'll be fine.

Figure 12-5
With the One photo per page checkbox deselected, two different 5 x 7 photos are printed on a sheet of 8.5 x 11 paper

Figure 12-6
With the One photo per page checkbox selected, one 5 x 7 photo is printed on this sheet of 8.5 x 11 paper

Figure 12-7
Crop your images before printing to keep from printing pictures that won't fit your frames

PRINT A FULL-PAGE PHOTO

In the printing sheet, if you select the Full Page style, iPhoto reduces or enlarges the photo to fit the size of the paper you have loaded in your printer. This is the ideal setting to use when you want to print on 4 x 6 paper or roll paper (or any other special size). The Full Page style Print dialog box is shown in Figure 12-8. Depending on the printer, you may have some white left around the edges because most printers can't print all the way out to the edge of the page. Printers specifically designed for printing photo prints will fill the whole space (assuming you matched your aspect ratios, that is).

To print a full-page photo, simply follow the previous set of steps selecting the Full Page style instead of Standard Prints.

PRINT CONTACT SHEETS

A contact sheet is a printout that typically shows many photographs at a small size. Its name comes from traditional photography. Photographers lay down strips of negatives directly in contact with a sheet of photo paper and then a quick strobe exposes all of the images onto the page.

The images burned onto the contact sheet are positives, or I guess you could call them *double negatives* if you like grammar jokes. The contact sheet develops with dozens of little positive copies of all the images that you can abuse, mark up, and show around while the negatives are safely stored away. That's what you always see people looking at through that shot glass looking thing called a *loupe*. Whatever you do, don't actually use somebody's loupe for tequila shots. Photographers are very sensitive about people touching their gear, and I hear the rock salt tends to scratch the optics. Hey, I'm just looking out for you guys.

What were we talking about again? Oh, contact sheets. Basically, you're making an index or sampler page of everything you have selected. I like to print out a contact page after loading in a fat bunch of photos from a trip or a photo shoot because you can look at several sheets of paper all spread out at a glance. Your computer screen only shows you a few images at a time. Yeah, you can cram hundreds of pictures onto the screen, but then they're too small to really see any details. Take a look at Figure 12-9. It's a couple of contact sheets from a photo shoot I posed for to get a picture for a book. See? That's something you can put in front of your friends and say, "Pick your favorites. Here's a marker."

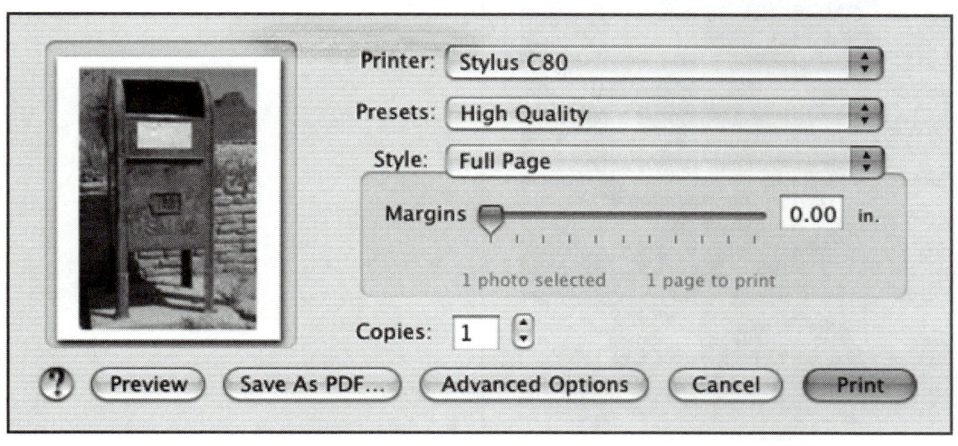

Figure 12-8
Print a single photo on a full page with the Full Page setting in the Print dialog box

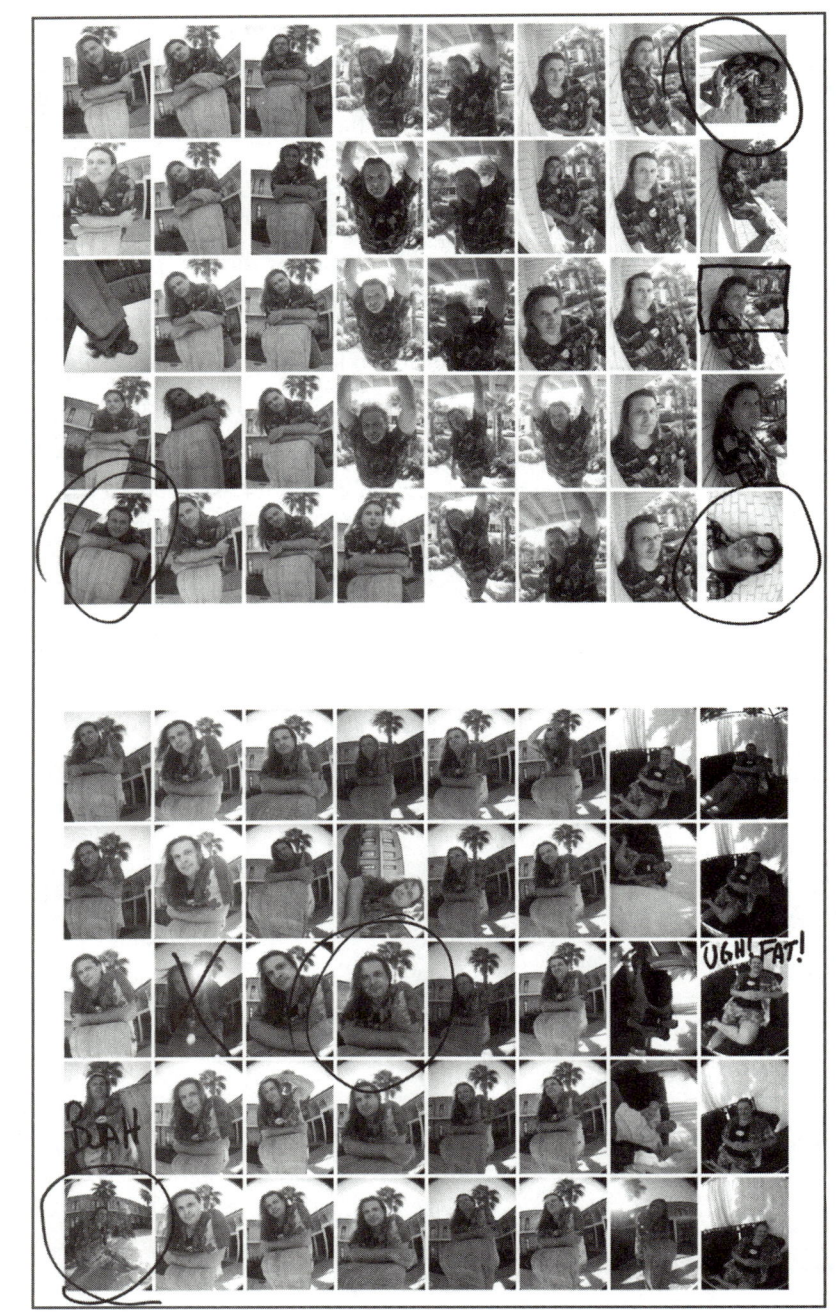

Figure 12-9
Contact sheets are great for picking out favorites

A PICTURE WITH-OUT A NAME IS NOT AS SWEET

The thing that iPhoto doesn't let you print is any of that text you've been so careful to add to all of your photos. The only thing the print button lets you print is the picture. You can't print out pictures with their associated titles, comments, key-words, or date information alongside the image.

Although external image editors *will* allow you to print out file names with photos, those applications are not tied into iPhoto's database, so unfortunately they won't know about all your comments and such.

Now if enough of you were to use that Provide iPhoto Feedback feature I was talking about back in Chapter 2 to tell them how cool it would be to be able to add titles to your contact sheets and such, the world just might be a better place in a later update of iPhoto. Tell 'em Big Sam sent ya!

To create a contact sheet, follow these steps:

1. **Select the photos you want to print.** Your options are described later in this section.

2. **Choose File ➜ Print to start the printing process.**

3. **Select Contact Sheet from the Style pop-up list in the Print sheet (see Figure 12-10).**

4. **Set the size of the images on the contact sheet by adjusting the Across slider.** This slider adjusts the number of columns of photographs. As the number of

columns increases (up to a maximum of 8), the size of each photograph shrinks, thus the number of rows increases as well (up to a maximum of 13). As a result, you can actually fit 104 pictures on a page if you want to.

5. **If you want to, click the Save paper checkbox to fit more images on the page.** This checkbox is only available if you are printing more than one photo. The Save paper option positions the photos closer together and automatically rotates vertical photos so that they fit into an evenly spaced grid.

6. **In the Copies field, choose the number of copies to print.**

7. **Click Print to print the picture or Preview to see how the printed page looks in the Preview application.**

Exactly what prints on the contact sheet depends on what you select before starting the printing process. Your options are

- **Select nothing.** The contact sheet contains the entire contents of the album. iPhoto uses as many pages as necessary.

- **Select one photo.** The contact sheet contains multiple copies of the single photo. If you adjust the number of columns to a small number (such as 3), you can create some very nice wallet-sized prints.

- **Select more than one photo.** The contact sheet contains one of each of the selected images. iPhoto automatically uses multiple pages if all the selected images won't fit on a single page.

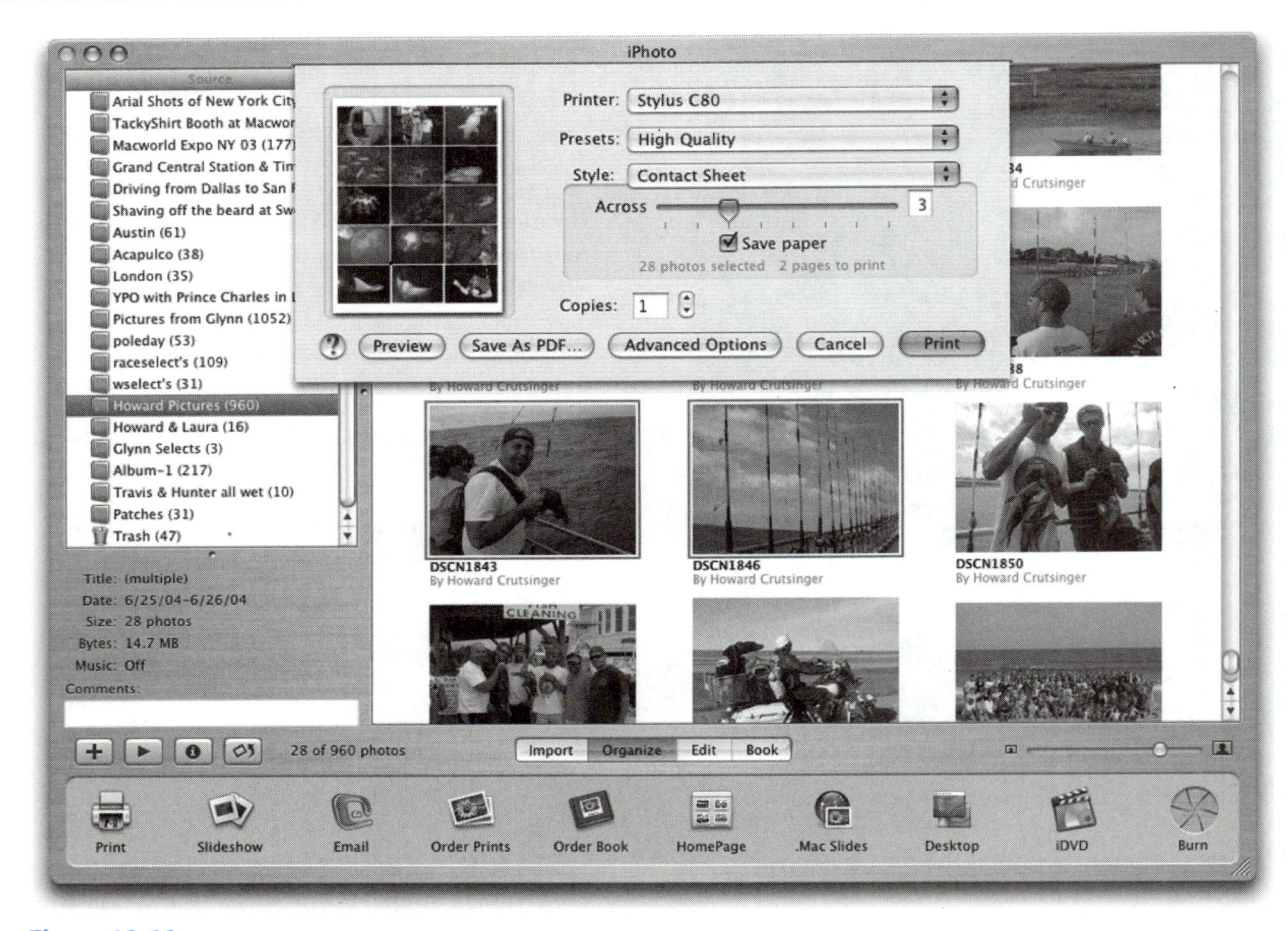

Figure 12-10
Print a large number of photos on a sheet using the Contact Sheet style

PRINT N-UP PHOTOS

If you choose the N-Up style, you can tell it to print 2, 4, 6, 9, or 16 photos on a single page. There's a checkbox where you can choose to print just one image per page that comes in handy. If you select 5 pictures and print a 4-Up with that checkbox active, it will print out 5 pages with 4 copies of picture 1 on the first page, 4 copies of picture 2 on the second page, and so forth (see Figure 12-12).

If you uncheck that One photo per page box, it turns into something very similar to the Contact Sheet style, with a different photo in each slot on the page, but you're limited to 2, 4, 6, 9, or 16 photos on each page. Use N-Up if you're printing just a few pictures. Contact Sheet is more suited for cramming *lots and lots* of pictures onto a page.

To print using the N-Up feature, follow these steps:

1. **Select the photos you want to print.**

2. **Choose File ➜ Print to start the printing process.**

3. **Select N-Up from the Style pop-up list in the Print sheet (Figure 12-13).**

4. **Use the Photos per page field to set the number of photographs to print: 2, 4, 6, 9, or 16.**

5. **Select the One photo per page checkbox if you only want a single image per page.** This option is only available if you selected more than one photo.

6. **In the Copies field, choose the number of copies to print.**

7. **Click Print to print the picture or Preview to see how the printed page looks in the Preview application.**

Figure 12-12
Print out multiple pictures on a sheet of paper (you get to decide how many and what size)

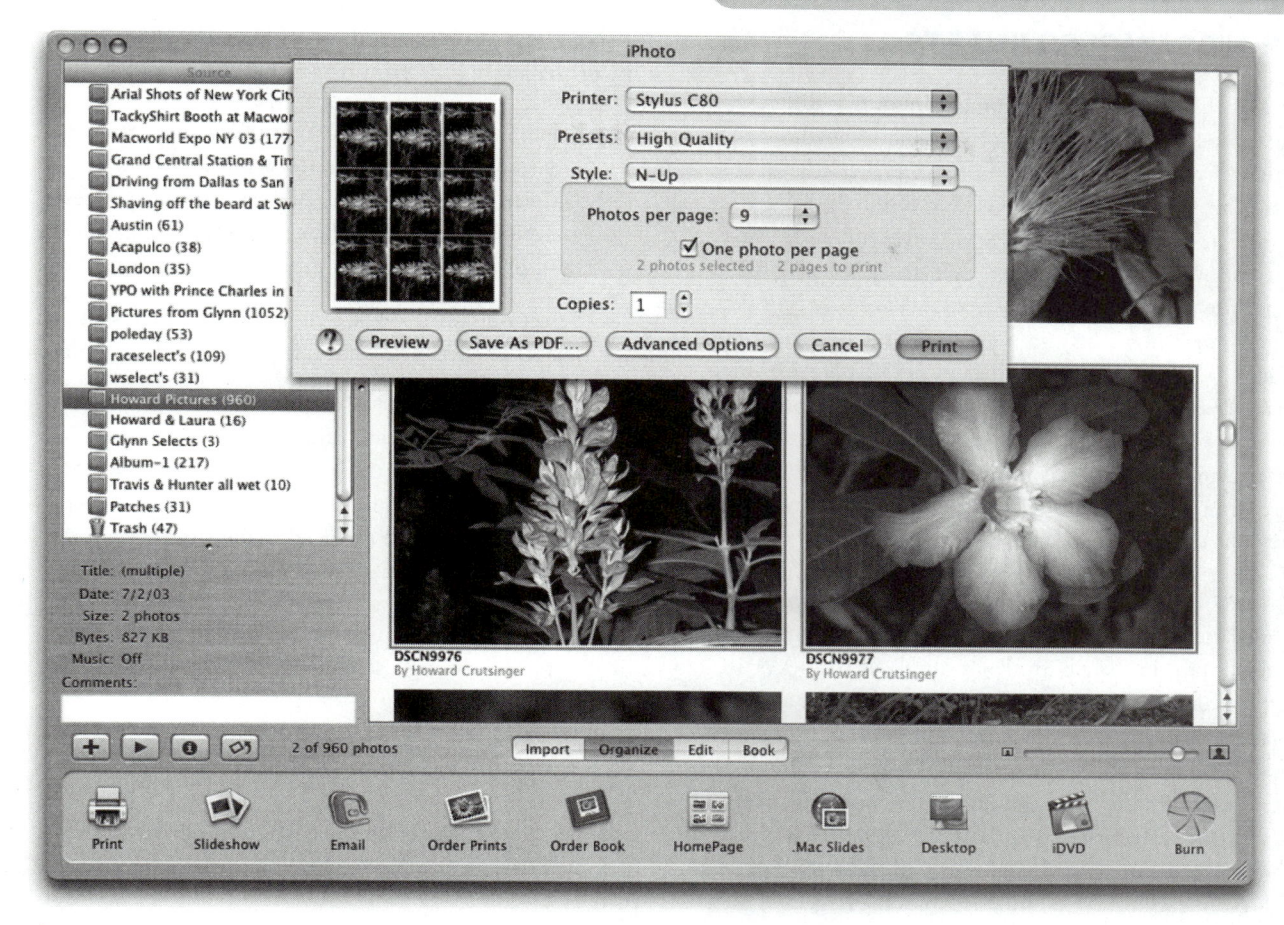

Figure 12-13
Pick the number of photos you want to print on a page with the N-Up printing option

PRINT SAMPLER SHEETS

A sampler sheet prints a grouping of photos at different sizes, depending on which photo template you choose. I guess if you like the look of that layout then this is for you. This method of printing is kind of silly if you ask me, because it just prints out a page with two different arbitrary print sizes and then crams everything it can on the page. You can't tell it to give you useful sizes like 5" x 7", 6" x 4", or 2" x 3". Instead it gives you one large picture that's 6.6" high and several smaller ones that are 3.3" high, or an 8" x 5.3" and a couple of 3.953" x 2.613" pictures. I suppose if the other printing options are just too boring for you and you feel like having different size pictures on the page just because it looks cool, then it's a lucky thing they put this in here for you.

You have no control over which photo prints in the large area of the template; this is strictly dependent on the order of the photos in the album. For example, if you select 18 pictures and use Template 1 (which has one large and two smaller image areas, as shown in Figure 12-14), iPhoto produces six pages. The first picture selected (in album order) occupies the large area on the first page; the next two pictures inhabit the smaller spaces along the bottom. The fourth picture is in the large area of the second page, and so on; each fourth picture occupies the large area on a page. Just study the thumbnails of the individual pages to the right of the Preview pane to see how your pictures will look on the page.

Exactly what prints depends on what photos you select before beginning the printing process:

- **Select nothing.** iPhoto uses as many pages as necessary to print the entire contents of the album. The sampler sheet uses the selected template and places each third photo (Template 1) or each seventh photo (Template 2) in the large area on the page.

- **Select one photo.** The sampler sheet contains all images of the single photo. Each area in the template contains a copy of the photo.

- **Select more than one photo.** The sampler sheet places the selected photos into the grid for the template. Each fourth photo (Template 1) or each seventh photo (Template 2) is placed in the large area on the page. iPhoto automatically uses multiple pages if all the selected images won't fit on a single page.

To print photos using a sampler sheet, follow these steps:

1. **Select the photos you want to print.**

2. **Choose File ➜ Print to start the printing process.**

3. **Select Sampler from the Style pop-up list in the Print sheet (see Figure 12-15).**

Figure 12-14
Print a sampler sheet that fits photos into the selected template (Template 1)

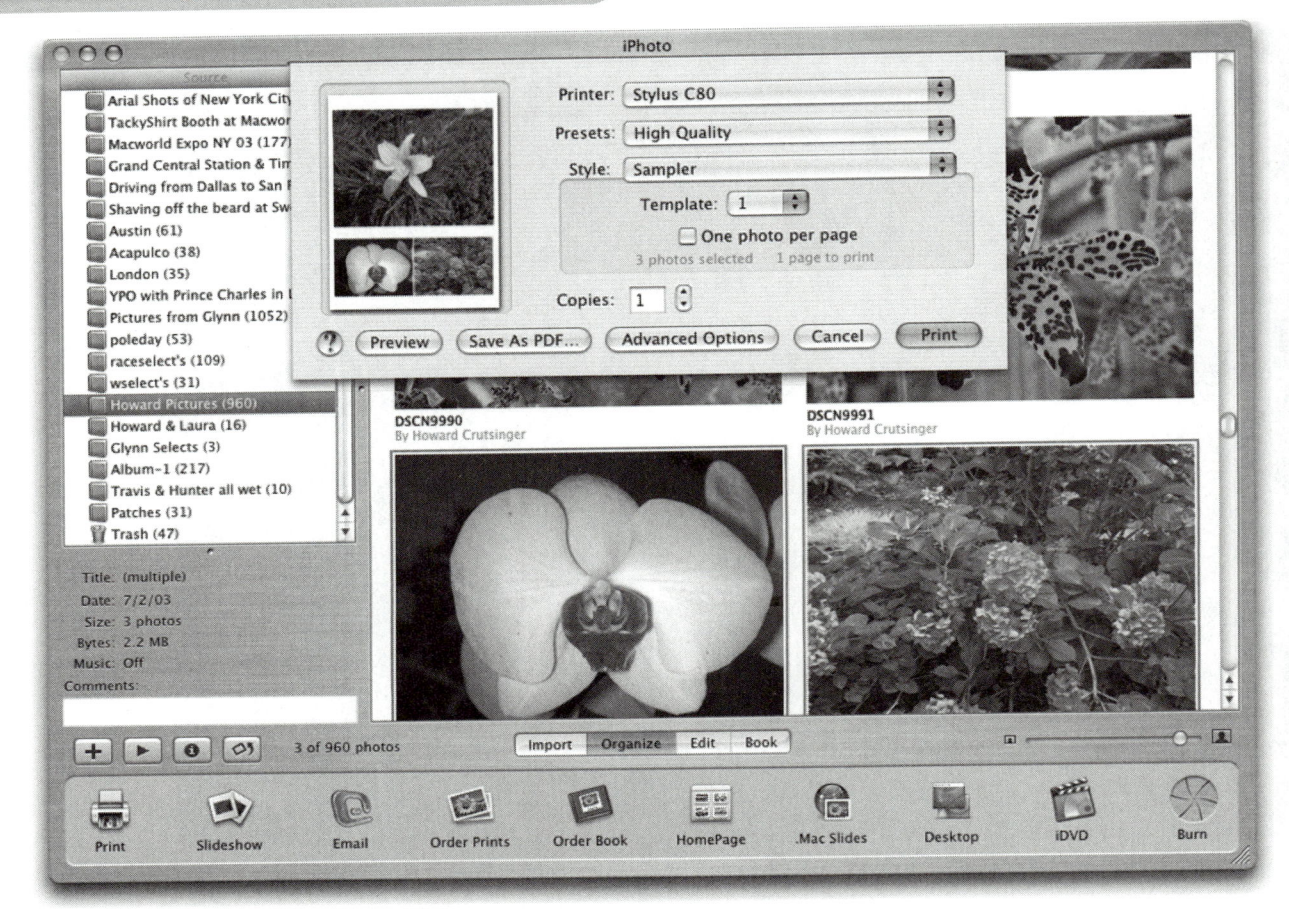

Figure 12-15
Specify a template and print multi-sized photos on a page with the Sampler printing option

4. **Pick the template you want to use from the Template pop-up list.** Figure 12-14 (shown earlier) shows photos in Template 1; Figure 12-16 illustrates the only other available template (Template 2).

5. **Select the One photo per page checkbox if you only want a single image per page.** This option is only available if you selected more than one photo. It's just like public school picture time again (see Figure 12-17).

6. **In the Copies field, choose the number of copies to print.**

7. **Click Print to print the picture or Preview to see how the printed page looks in the Preview application.**

Figure 12-16
Template 2 provides an alternate layout to Template 1

Figure 12-17
Click the One photo per page checkbox to print multiple sizes of a single photo on each page

PRINT GREETING CARDS

You can print in a greeting-card format using iPhoto — either single-fold or double-fold. Figure 12-18 shows a sample of a single-fold card. Single-fold prints the image on half the paper, and double-fold prints the image on a quarter of the paper (see Figure 12-19). Actually, folding the cards is up to you, as well as writing something in them; iPhoto does not allow you to print a sentiment, other graphics, or anything else for that matter. In addition, the results are pretty amateurish because iPhoto prints the image right up to the fold.

Figure 12-19
Double-fold cards print an image on one quarter of the paper so you can fold the card in quarters

Follow these steps to print a greeting card:

1. **Select the photos you want to print.**

2. **Choose File ➜ Print to start the printing process.**

3. **Select Greeting Card from the Style pop-up list in the Print sheet (see Figure 12-20).**

4. **Choose one of the Style options (Single-fold or Double-fold).**

Figure 12-18
Single-fold cards print an image on the front of the paper so you can fold the card in half

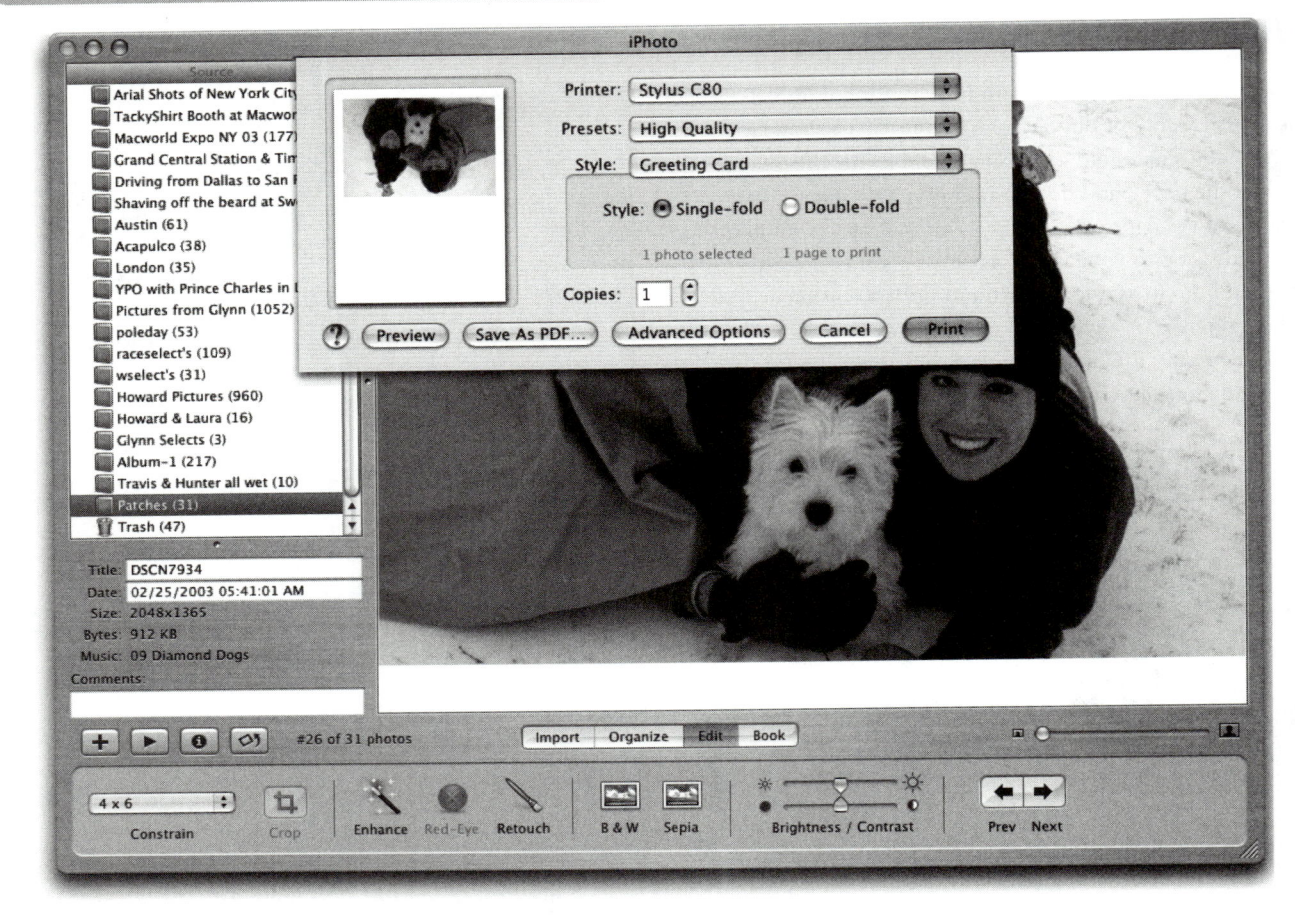

Figure 12-20
Select Greeting Card from the Style pop-up list to print greeting cards from iPhoto

5. From the Copies field, choose the number of copies to print.

6. Click Print to print the picture or Preview to see how the printed page looks in the Preview application.

 Tip

If you intend to print double-fold cards, you should crop the image you are using to a ratio of 8:5 for a better fit.

Note

If you select more than one photo before starting to print, iPhoto prints one card of each of the selected photos. If you also choose multiple copies (in the Copies field), you get the specified number of copies of each card.

Printing out your pictures somehow makes them feel a little more "real" all of a sudden. I mean, it's one thing to have 6,000 pictures in your computer, but holding a couple of your better photos in your hand just legitimizes the whole thing.

There are many printers that have started to roll out that are specially designed for printing digital photography. It's gotten to the point where many stores assign them to a whole new category called Photo Printers, aside from their regular Inkjet Printer cousins. It's pretty amazing what a measly $100 to $200 photo printer can do these days. In fact, as soon as I get my advance check, I think I may have to splurge on a new toy.

One thing that also comes in handy when printing photos is a nice paper cutter. The old scissors method gets the job done but it's just not nearly as fun as going *ShaaaKUNK, ShaaaKUNK, ShaaaKUNK, ShaaaKUNK!* Four lops with the old paper guillotine and you have the job all done with nice straight lines. Just make sure you keep the blade good and sharp because a dull blade will give you more of a tear than a clean snip. I think mine's due for a sharpening. It might have something to do with the fact that I just like to listen to it go *ShaaaKUNK, ShaaaKUNK, ShaaaKUNK,* even if I don't have any paper to actually cut. It's fun.

Why are you looking at me like that? I know I'm weird. *ShaaaKUNK!*

13

Printing Your Photos Professionally

In This Chapter

Getting prints made locally
Ordering prints over the Internet

Printing photos with your own printer is all good and well, but my $80 inkjet printer just can't hold a candle to a nice, professional printing facility cranking out my pictures. Most of the drugstore photo processors have gotten with the program now. You can bring in your digital snaps and they'll make them into yummy, glossy goodness for you. If you want, you can even send your pictures to many of these places over the Internet so they'll be ready when you pick them up. Of course, the iLife preferred method is that pretty little Order Prints button in Organize mode. That one sends the files over the Internet and the prints show up in the mail so you never have to deal with that scary outside place.

BENEFITS OF PROFESSIONAL PRINTING

One big reason to have your photos printed professionally is that you may not own a high-quality color printer. For many years I had only my faithful laser printer, which was great for printing text documents.

But even if you *do* have an inkjet printer, there are many good reasons to consider professional prints. Here are a few of them:

- **Quality.** Your inkjet printer may not be capable of producing very-high-quality prints. The $100,000 in equipment installed at your local drugstore or photofinishing shop is designed specifically for this purpose and is run by a trained technician. While this doesn't guarantee better quality than you can print yourself, you do have to consider that both the equipment and the technician are in the business of creating professional photographs.

- **Time.** Even if you have a high-quality inkjet printer, you may have to spend lots of time (and money for test prints) getting the settings right to produce an outstanding photograph. And there is no guarantee that the settings that work well with one photo will work as well with another, so you may have to do further experimentation. While some of the cheaper photo-processing outfits simply set the machine based on the first print of the roll, the higher-quality photo-processing companies analyze each individual print and adjust the machine to produce a good result for that print.

- **Longevity.** Professionally printed photos stand up well over time — today's prints can last 50 years or more without appreciable fading. Inkjet prints are usually not so hardy. Some start to fade in a matter of months. While following the printer vendor's recommendations carefully for combinations of inks and papers can lengthen this time to approach (or even exceed) the fade resistance of professional photos, these archival inks and papers can be very expensive.

- **Cost.** Make no mistake about it, printing photo-quality prints on an inkjet (or dye-sublimation) printer is *expensive*. Don't think so? Add up the cost of that heavy, glossy photo paper and the ink cartridges. Even if you ignore the waste (prints that come out crooked, smeared, too dark, or whatever), the cost to print a 4-x-6-inch photo is usually between 40 and 50 cents each. This is actually *more* than most photo-processing outfits in my neighborhood charge (and I live in one of the most expensive areas of the country), and with coupons and two-for-one sales, you can reduce the cost of professional printing even more. And most photo-processing companies will reprint a photo for free if you don't like the result.

- **Convenience.** If you still use a film camera, you're going to be at the store anyway, so it's not like you're going out of your way or anything. To get the film processed (turned into negatives), you still have to go to the drugstore. So why not have prints made right then and there? And the drugstore I go to even offers to digitize the negatives and provide them on a CD for a nominal charge. Furthermore, even if you shoot digital pictures, it's still more convenient to have them printed commercially if you have a lot of pictures. For example, I shot 480 digital pictures on my last vacation. Even after weeding through them, I still had over 200 good ones. So I burned them on a CD, took 'em down to the drugstore, and picked 'em up two days later.

GETTING PRINTS MADE LOCALLY

The key to getting professional prints made from digital images is to get the images to the photo processor. The processor may be a kiosk at the local supermarket, drugstore, or photo finisher.

The most obvious way to deliver your digital prints is to simply pull the memory card out of your digital camera and take it to the store. Many photofinishers have a machine that can read the images right from the memory card, storing them on a hard drive connected to the photofinishing machine. But you should check to make sure that your type of card is supported. Recent cameras from Olympus and Fuji use a memory card called *xD* that is not yet supported by many photofinishing card readers.

Tip

If you find that your photofinisher of choice doesn't support xD cards, you can get an inexpensive adapter that allows the card to be read just as if it were a CompactFlash card. All photofinishing card readers can handle those.

Another option is to load the images into your Mac and then burn a CD of the images or put them on a Zip disk, and then take the CD or Zip disk to the drugstore. Pretty much all drugstores and photofinishers support CDs, and most of them can read a Zip disk as well. Just be sure that you use the Finder to burn the CD. Don't use iPhoto to burn the CD, because when you burn a CD from iPhoto it is essentially making a backup, preserving the convoluted directory structure that iPhoto needs and including many files that will confuse the photofinisher. They'll be able to read it without iPhoto, but they'll just be digging around in the folders iPhoto put on the disk, and that might get Mr. Photoguy a bit miffed when he tries to "print them all" as you instructed only to realize that only half of the files on the CD were actually photos.

Don't forget to crop your images to the correct aspect ratio (such as 4 x 6 for snapshots) before burning them on the CD or placing them on the Zip disk. If you don't crop the images, the person running the photo machine will have to decide what to crop out of your picture, and that person has no idea what is important to you. This, by the way, is one reason *not* to simply pull the memory card out of your camera and take it to have the photos printed — unless you have one of the newest cameras that takes digital pictures in the correct aspect ratio for printing.

ORDER PRINTS ONLINE

With the advent of fast Internet connections, another option for getting prints made is to upload them to a photofinishing service, which will produce the prints for you and mail them back (for a fee, of course).

Why would you want to do that rather than take them down to the corner drugstore? Well, some of these services offer you space to store your images on their servers (so they will be safe in case something horrible happens to your computer and all your backups). Other services offer utilities for adjusting the pictures (much like what is available in iPhoto) and enable you to order a gift (coffee mug, apron, athletic bag, T-shirt, and so forth) with an image printed on it. With some services, you can even publish your photos on an Internet page and send emails to people inviting them to view the images and order their own prints. This last option is especially handy after a family reunion or other event, and it relieves you of the responsibility (and cost) of making many sets of prints and mailing them.

You also may be able to save some money. A number of online photofinishing services enable you to buy packages redeemable for a certain number of prints, often at a discount. I have seen print prices as low as 20 cents when you buy in bulk from some services.

USE THE ORDER PRINTS BUTTON

iPhoto makes it easy to order prints online. Essentially, Apple has signed a contract with Kodak that enables you to upload your images directly from iPhoto, specify how many and what size of each print you want, and then upload the images to, um, well, I'm not actually quite sure where they go to be honest. They just go up to some server and get printed with love and care, and then delivered to your mailbox by that nice person who brings you all your magazines and bills. I'm pretty sure there are either elves or photo pixies involved in the process at some point, but none of that really matters. It just happens.

To order prints online from iPhoto, you have to have an Apple ID. If you don't have one, the first time you click the Order Prints button, you'll need to click the Set Up Account button that appears in the lower-right corner of the Order Prints dialog box (see Figure 13-1). Go through the steps to set up an Apple ID. These steps involve setting up shipping addresses and billing information.

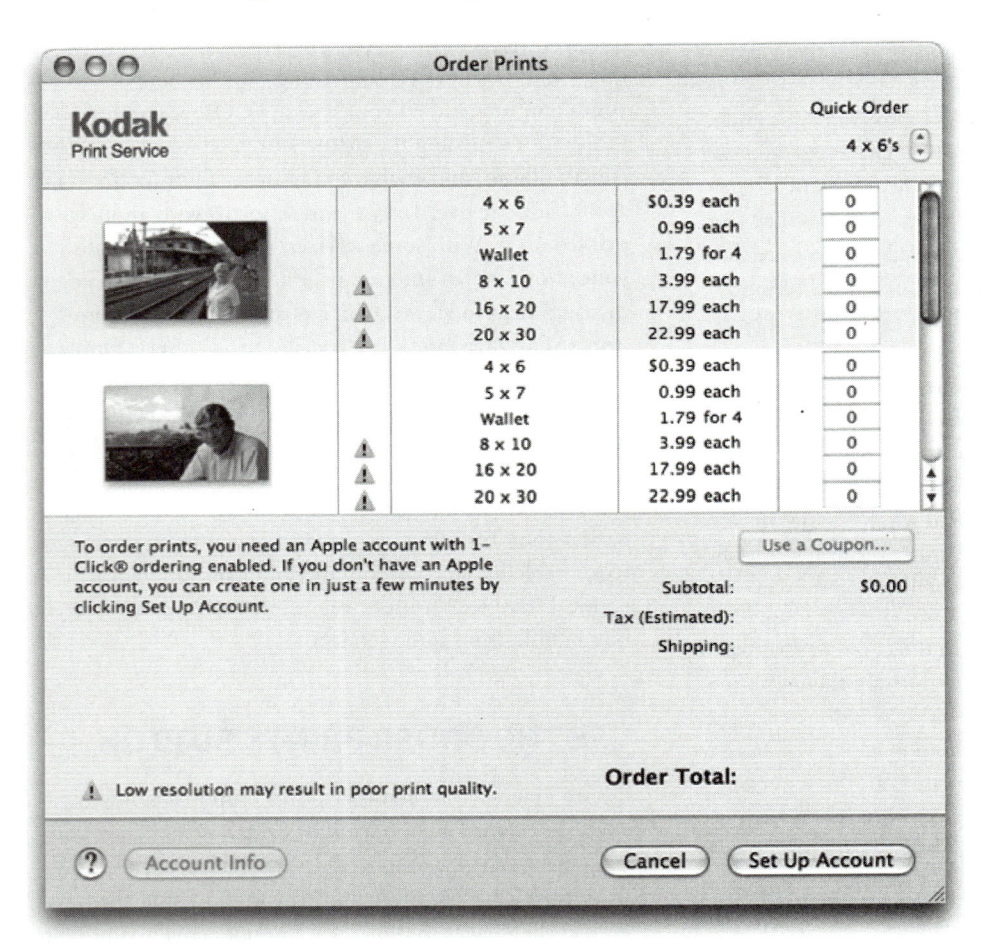

Figure 13-1
Set up your Apple ID account

APPLE ID

The Apple ID isn't just for ordering prints. This info comes into play elsewhere as well. When you registered your computer, or your copy of iLife '04 for that matter, you created an Apple ID. You can use that login and password when you order prints in iPhoto. If you buy music in the iTunes Music Store, you can use it there as well. That same ID is what you use to authorize other computers to play back music you buy in the music store. Oh, and when shopping at the Apple Store online, you guessed it. Same thing. It comes in handy, but only if you remember what email it's attached to, so make sure you email the info to yourself or do whatever you have to do to remember it. (I'm a bit of an email drifter. I've had 17 email addresses since I first logged on in 1995, and as a result I'm still trying to get my original Yahoo ID back. It's tied to a long since dead email because I forgot to update the address before I forgot the password. DOH!)

The system keeps your credit card on file so you can order prints without having to re-enter your info each time. It's a good idea to keep your Apple ID to yourself so you don't end up with a card statement full of 20-x-30-inch poster prints and several musical choices way outside of anything you'd ever pick. Kids will be kids, but parents have to pay their bills.

To order prints online, use the following steps:

1. **In Organize mode, select the images you want printed.**

2. **Make sure you are connected to the Internet, and click the Order Prints button.**

3. **After a few moments, the Order Prints dialog box opens (see Figure 13-2).**

▼ **Tip**

Occasionally, the Order Prints dialog box will appear with the Set Up Account button instead of the Buy Now button even if you have already set up an Apple ID. If that happens, simply click the Set Up Account button and sign in to your account in the Account Info dialog box that follows.

GATHER 'ROUND THE GLOW OF THE MACINTOSH

Here's a fun little thing that comes in handy at the holidays or whenever you get the clan together and take several pictures. One of the great things about digital cameras is that they make it a cinch to take just one holiday group picture and then email it to everybody instead of doing the camera shuffle. "Hold on a sec. We have five more cameras here. Keep smiling. Travis! Stop squirming!"

Of course, there are people on the planet who, believe it or not, still don't have email, or even computers for that matter! [shudder] Don't leave them out of the holiday fun. Right there on the spot, import the pictures from your camera to iPhoto, and have them pick out any images they want for themselves. Crop them accordingly real quick, and then order them a set of prints with their home address as the shipping address. They'll be delivered straight to Grandma's house and suddenly you, my friend, have just become her favorite grandkid.

Prints ordered through Order Prints take about four days to arrive. I put in my last order at 12:36 p.m. on Sunday; my prints arrived on Thursday at 10:27 a.m. Not bad.

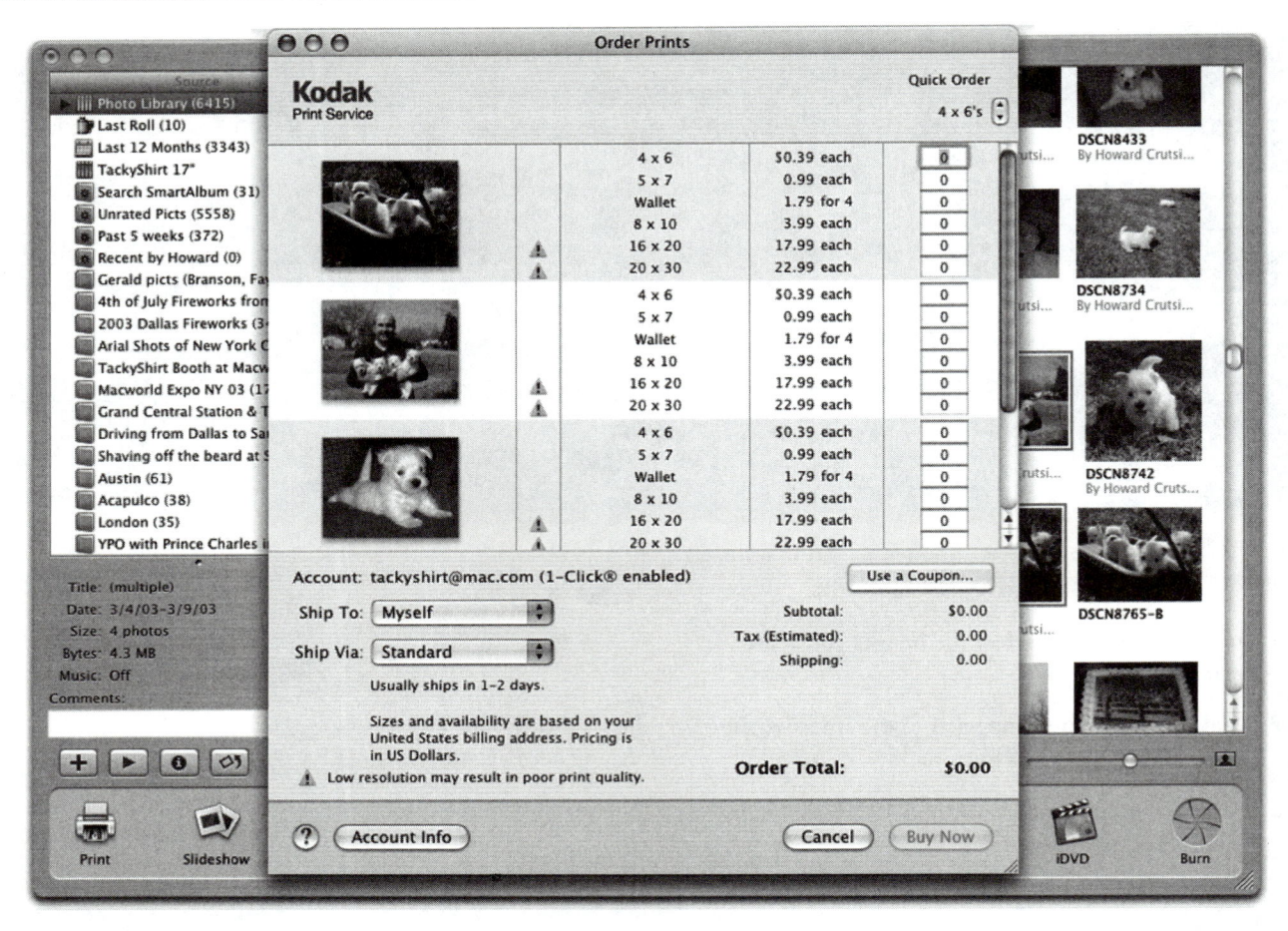

Figure 13-2
Use the Order Prints dialog box to order and pay for your prints

4. **For each selected image, type in the number of each size print you want.** As you do so, the price in the lower-right corner is updated automatically. The Buy Now button is not available until you select at least one print.

 **Tip**

To quickly order 4 x 6 prints of all the images, use the Quick Order arrows in the upper-right corner to add to (click the up arrow) or subtract from (click the down arrow) the number of 4 x 6 snapshots of each print. You can also manually override the results of using the arrows by typing a different number of 4 x 6 prints for any of the images.

5. **Choose the address where the prints are to be shipped from the Ship To pop-up list.** You can also select Add New Address from this list. You will be asked to log in. After you prove to them that you're you, enter in all the address info (see Figure 13-3).

6. **Choose a shipping method from the Ship Via pop-up list.** There are only two choices — Standard and Express. Express is more expensive, and your prints should arrive faster, but I can't say for sure.

7. **Click Buy Now.** Your photos are uploaded to Kodak and a dialog box appears that confirms the order and gives you an order number. You'll also get an email confirming the order. The prints should arrive in a few days.

As with printing images on your own printer, the low resolution of some images may result in poor quality if reproduced at larger sizes. Yellow warning icons will appear in the Order Prints dialog box next to any sizes of prints for which you will get poor results (see Figure 13-4).

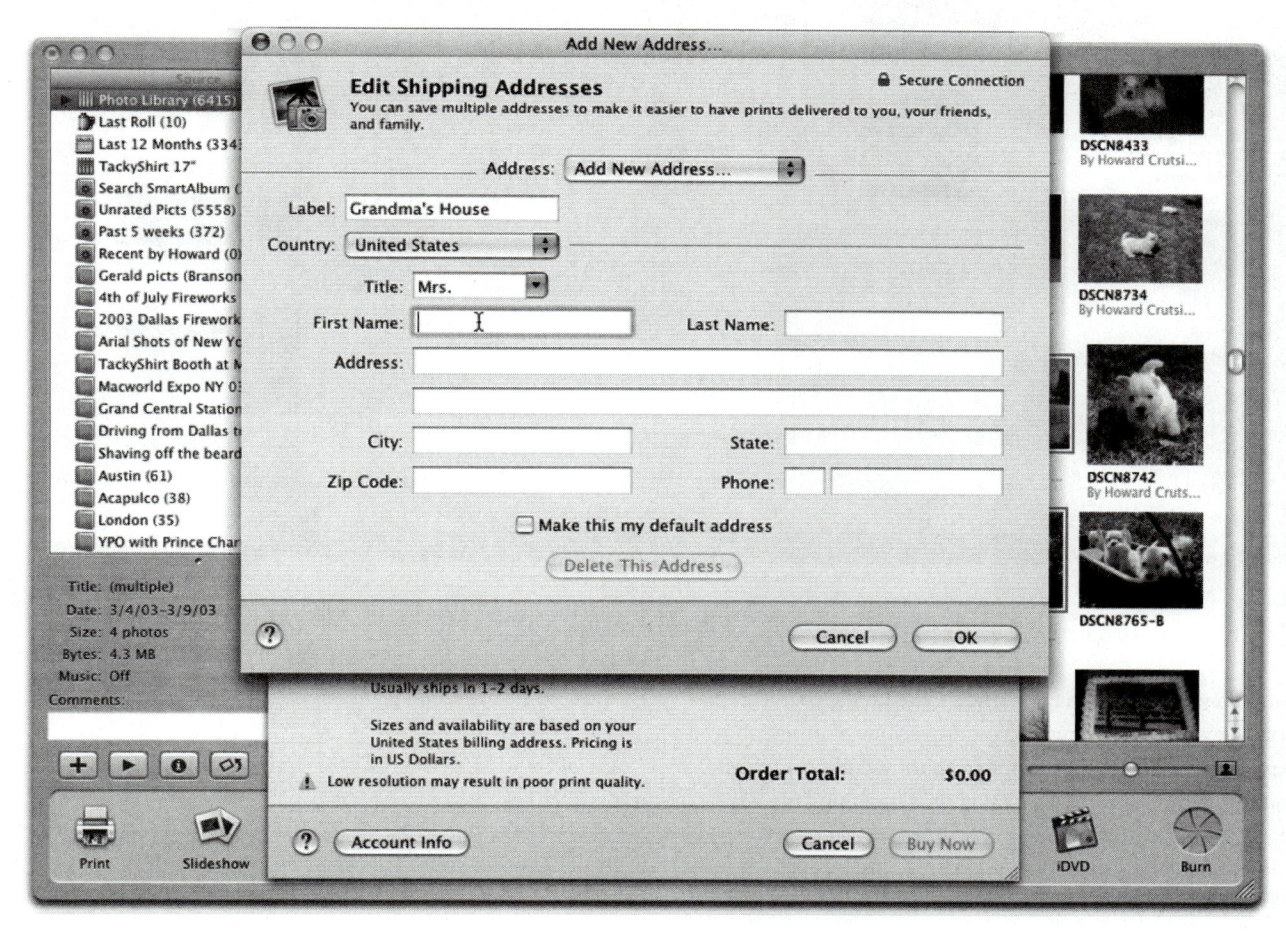

Figure 13-3
Add a new shipping address so you can send your prints to a new recipient

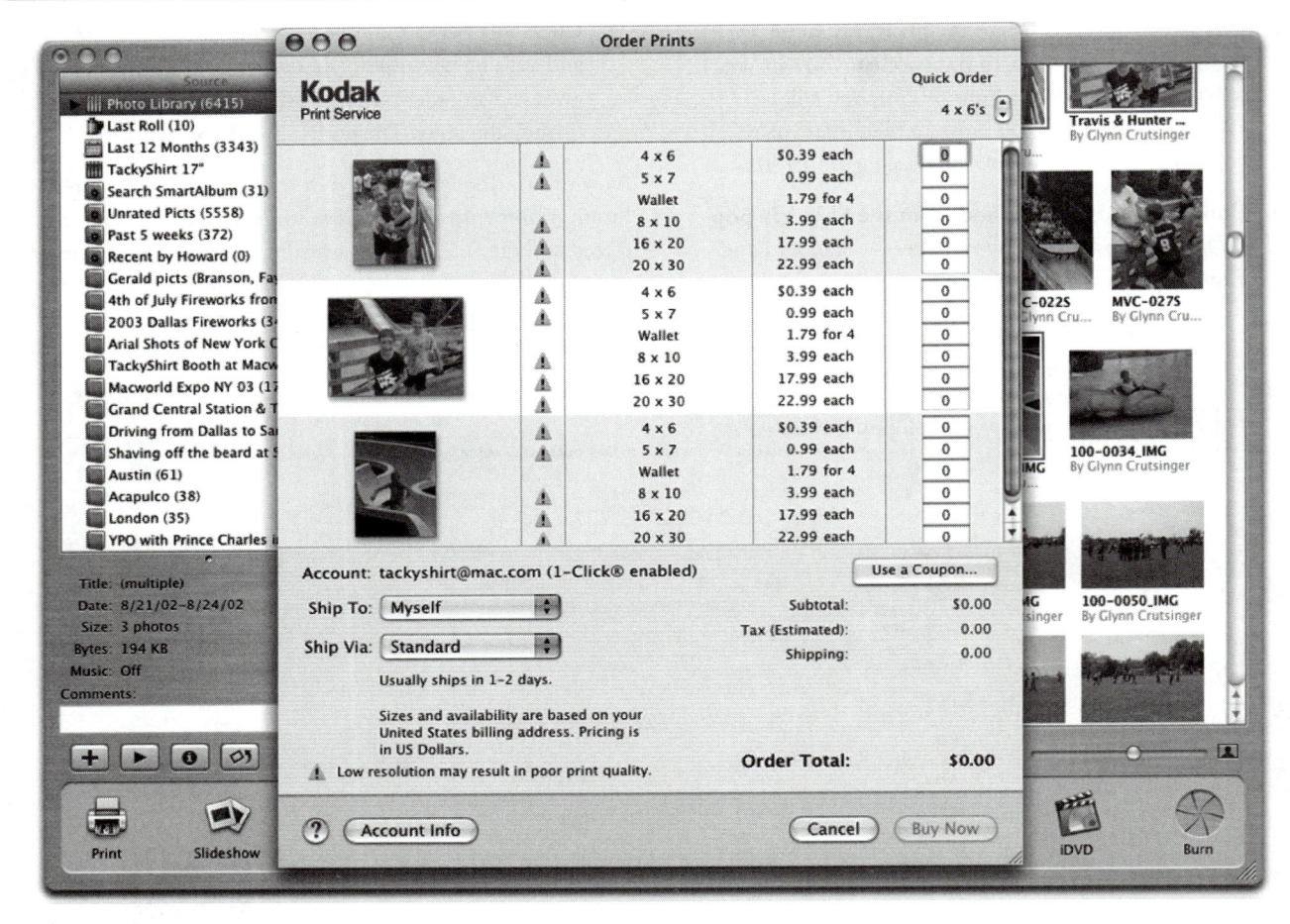

Figure 13-4

Don't try to print images at sizes that show the yellow warning icon

You know in the last chapter when I was saying that printing your pictures really legitimizes your photography experience? Well, getting prints from the lab almost makes you feel like you must be cheating or something because this is just *almost too cool*. I mean come on. You have the little Kodak logo seal all over the back of the prints. Well, sure, you *could* have printed them yourself, but you

didn't. You had *the lab* print them out for you! It just seems so decadent!

I haven't felt this way since the first time I ordered a Papa's Special with pepperoni, sausage, bacon, onions, and extra cheese from their Web site and within the hour it was in my belly! That's right. It's *extra-cheese* cool!

RESOLUTION CUTOFFS

When you're buying prints online, it's handy to have actual numbers so you can know *why* your computer is saying you can't make an 8 x 10 print out of your picture instead of just seeing a little yellow triangle that sits there insulting you for no good reason.

Table 13-1 is a chart of the file sizes you have to exceed to keep the yellow triangle of mockery at bay. When you're taking pictures, make sure that they are at or bigger than these numbers for best results. My camera tops out at 2048 x 1536, which means I'm a bit short of the cutoff for 16 x 20 prints.

One other thing that's good to know is that while having plenty of excess resolution may seem like a good thing, the quality of your pictures won't improve much if you send in a super high-res file. I tried. I ordered two 8 x 10 prints, one shot at 1500 x 1200 and the other at 1918 x 1534. I printed the resolution in the photograph so I'd know which was which. I can't see any difference whatsoever.

Table 13-1: File Sizes Availability

Print size	Crop selection	Minimum pixel size	Resulting resolution
4 x 6	4 x 6 (Postcard)	900 x 600	150 dpi
5 x 7	5 x 7 (L, 2L)	1050 x 750	150 dpi
Wallet (2 x 3)	2 x 3	450 x 300	150 dpi
8 x 10	8 x 10	1500 x 1200	150 dpi
16 x 20	16 x 20	2000 x 1600	100 dpi
20 x 30	20 x 30 (Poster)	2400 x 1600	80 dpi

The lab doesn't let you choose different types of paper though, which is probably just as well. That should probably be reserved for when you're at the photo store and you can point to some samples and say, "I want them like that." Most people have no clue about what kind of paper they want their prints on if you ask them, but they definitely have an opinion if you put samples in their hands. You can't do that sort of tactile selection through a computer screen.

Hmmm... maybe when I'm rich and famous I'll find some way to link iPhoto to my fan club database of addresses and then I can just scan in one big autographed photo of me and have the photo pixies send it out to all of my... *THUD!* Oh dang. My head got too big and I toppled over. Owie! Help! I can't get up!

[You have no girlfriend. You dress funny. Your car is missing a hubcap. –ed]

Gee, thanks Editor. No, really. I'm feeling deflated now.

Sharing Your Photos Electronically

In the previous chapter you learned how to print your photos and send them out for professional prints. Now it's time to save a tree and get all twenty-first century on your friends. Digital is where it's at now, and iPhoto has you hooked up in so many ways it's hard to decide which way is more fun.

It couldn't be easier to email a couple of pictures to someone. You can even make a compact QuickTime movie of several photos all strung together, with nice little dissolves between the shots and music added in the background. If you just want to admire your own work all day long, you can make a Desktop background or screen saver out of selected photos. Of course, iPhoto just wouldn't be complete without a simple way to back up your pictures to CD or DVD. After all, I'm talking about a visual record of your life here. The last thing you want is a drive crash robbing you of your pictures!

iPhoto also lets you get your pictures to the people on this new fangled thing called the World Wide Web in other ways, but that's for the next chapter.

EMAIL YOUR PHOTOS

iPhoto makes packaging up and sending your photographs by email easy. iPhoto even shrinks the size of your photos if you want so that they don't take too long for the recipient to download. You can also include the title and any comments with the email.

To send your photos by email, follow these steps:

1. **Select the photos you want to send.** Unlike many other ways of sharing photos with iPhoto, you must specify the photos to include; you can't just specify an entire album. If you don't specify any photos, iPhoto simply displays a dialog box instructing you to choose some photographs.

2. **Click the Email icon below the Display pane to display the Mail Photo dialog box (see Figure 14-1).**

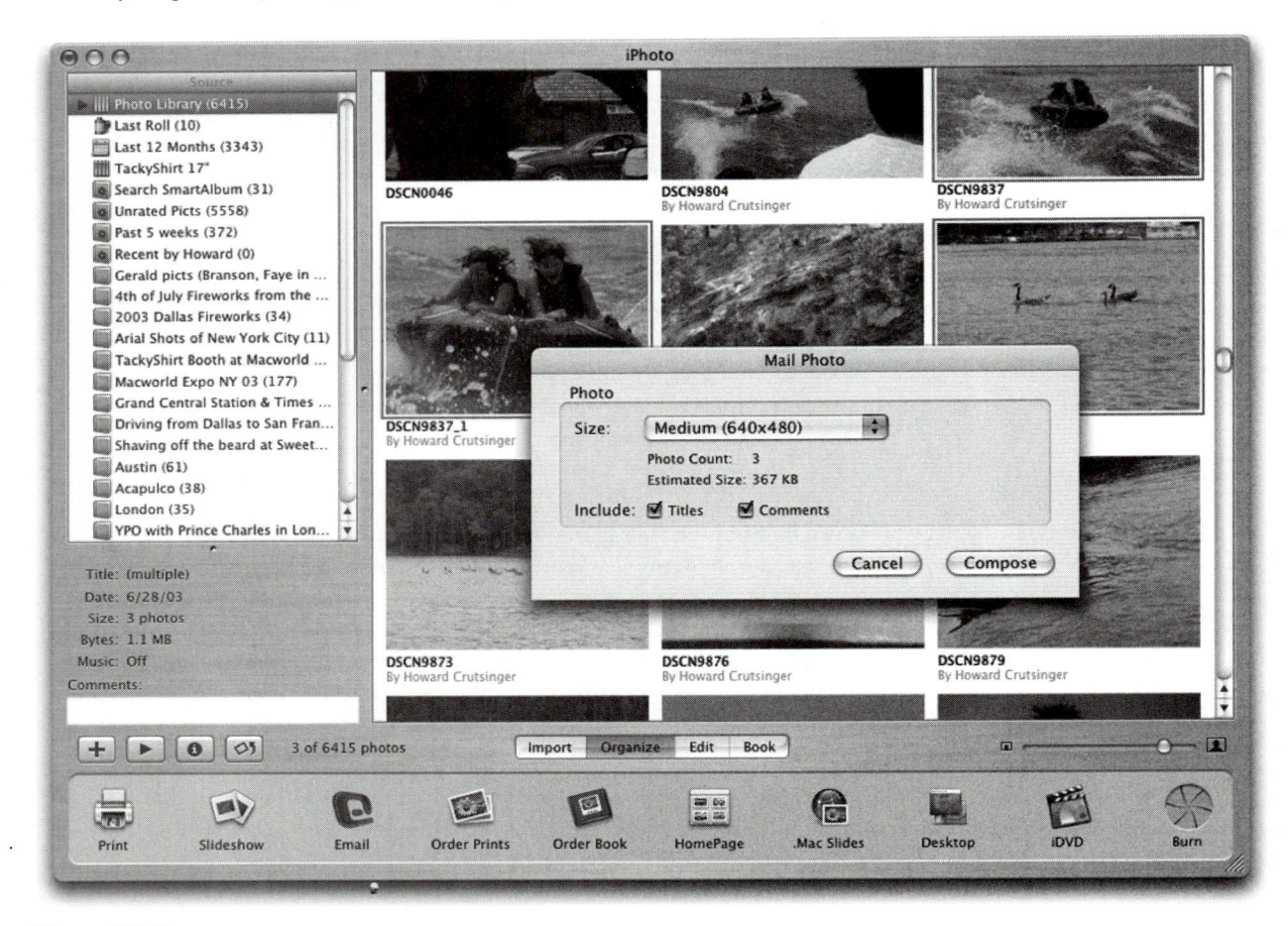

Figure 14-1
Configure your photos for emailing to friends and family

3. **Set the maximum size of the images using the Size pop-up list.** There are various sizes to choose from (Large, Medium, and Small), as well as an option to send the images full size.

4. **To include the titles attached to each photo in the email, click the Titles checkbox in the Mail Photo dialog box.**

5. **Click the Comments checkbox in the Mail Photo dialog box.** This includes the comments attached to each photo in the email.

6. **Click the Compose button to create the email.** The email program you have selected in the iPhoto preferences opens and creates a new email message with the photos attached (see Figure 14-2). Your computer

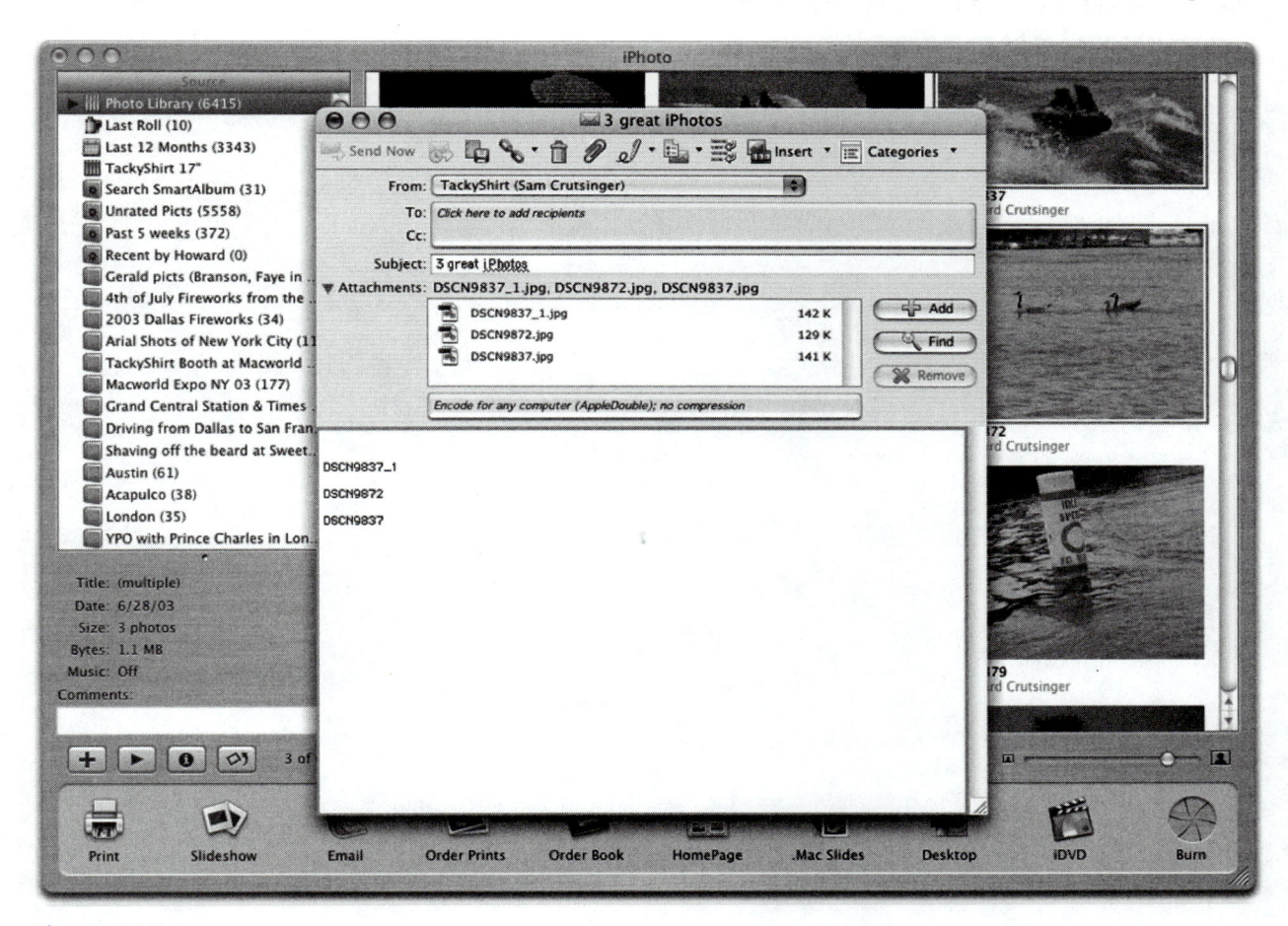

Figure 14-2
Your photos are attached to an email and ready to send out

may look different than this screen shot depending on what email program you use. If you only use a Web mail account, you're kinda left out in the cold here. This feature requires you to use an email application.

7. **Address the email, change the default subject, and add your own text message.**

8. **Send the email to share it with all your friends (or people who used to be your friends).**

▼ Note

Whether the images appear "in-line" in the email (as they do in the previous figure) or as attachments depends on the email program you use. With Apple's Mail program (the one I use), the images appear in-line. This works out well for small images, but can be unwieldy for very large images because the email message gets very long.

WHEN EMAILING IMAGES, DON'T BE *THAT* GUY

Emailing is the first method people think about when they have a picture they want to show someone. Depending on how you get the job done, this can be a good or a bad thing. Luckily, iPhoto has some safeguards to keep you from falling for some of the most common mistakes.

I can't tell you how many times I've had people tell me they sent me some pictures but the email bounced back. Almost every time the reason was that they sent me like 30 pictures at 1.5MB each, which adds up to 45MB just for one email. My email box only allows me to have 30MB of mail on the server at any given moment, so BOING! Also keep in mind that lots of people may not have Internet access that works as fast as yours. A single 1MB file takes about three minutes to download over a modem. After you get used to your cable modem, you don't think twice about sending a 15MB file; but if you send it to a modem user, you just choked up their connection for 45 minutes, at least.

There's a little thing called *netiquette.* Like regular etiquette, netiquette is a set of guidelines that keeps people from hating your guts for behavior that may seem innocent enough to you, but to everybody who knows the rules, you behavior may be the equivalent of holding a screaming baby and eating stinky cheese while talking on a cellphone in a movie theater on a Friday night.

When emailing pictures to people, you *have* to be considerate of their space. Some people are lucky enough to have virtually unlimited email space, but most people don't. Most people don't even know how much they have available, but there's almost always a limit. The polite thing is to keep the email small. iPhoto helps you out here by making you pick what size you want to send. At the Small setting, your pictures are about 50KB each; Medium makes them around 150KB each; and Large is around 500KB to 1MB each. The final setting, Full-Size, sends the picture at its current height and width.

No matter what setting you choose, the file you email is converted to a JPEG file (if it's not a JPEG already), which is nice because everybody can open that file format. Sending your PC-using cousin a Photoshop document will probably get you a confused reply. Actually, if they have QuickTime installed, they should be able to view it but it might not come out right if it's a complicated image file.

The gist is that you probably shouldn't send more than five photos in an email, and even then, keep the photos small. If you have more than that to show off, check out how to make a Web page in the next chapter.

CREATE A QUICKTIME MOVIE

Because pretty much everyone has access to a QuickTime movie player, you can share your wonderful images by packaging them and sending a slideshow as a QuickTime movie. This is by far the best way to view pictures, and is the electronic equivalent of your Uncle Carl pulling out that old, dusty Bell and Howell slide projector and showing slides on a tattered screen in the basement family room. (With this method, however, the chance of you burning your pinkie on a smoldering projector is nil.) Showing your pictures in sequence, and with a musical soundtrack, adds an entirely new (often emotional) dynamic to the story you're telling, and all your recipient has to do it sit back and enjoy!

QuickTime movies from iPhoto are nice because they're self-contained and very portable. I just cranked out a 63-image QT movie (without a music track mind you) and it was only 2.7MB for the whole caboodle. In my book, anything under 4MB is fair game for email as long as you tell the recipient it's coming.

To create a QuickTime movie from your images, follow these steps, which allow you to select images from either the Library or a single album:

1. **Select the album or individual images.**

2. **Choose File → Export.**

3. **Click the QuickTime tab to display the controls for creating a QuickTime movie (see Figure 14-3).**

4. **In the Images section, select the maximum width and height by typing a value into the appropriate fields.**

5. **Set the slide duration by typing a value into the Display image for field.**

6. **In the Background section, you can choose either a color to use for the background (if the image doesn't fill the entire frame) or a background image.**

   - To change the color, click the color box and pick the color from the color tool.

   - To specify a background image to use, click the Image option, and then either type in the path to the image or click the Set button to pick the image from the Open dialog box.

7. **To add the album's music to the movie, click the Add currently selected music to movie checkbox.**

8. **To create the QuickTime movie, click the Export button in the Export Photos dialog box.**

9. **Choose a title for your new QuickTime movie, choose the folder to store the .mov file in, and click OK.**

Unfortunately, if you are selecting multiple albums for the QuickTime movie, the soundtrack you get is the default "Minuet in G." To pick images from different albums and use a different tune, follow these steps:

1. **Create a new album.**

2. **Add the images to the album.**

3. **Create a slideshow from the album as described in Chapter 10, associating the album with the music you want to use.**

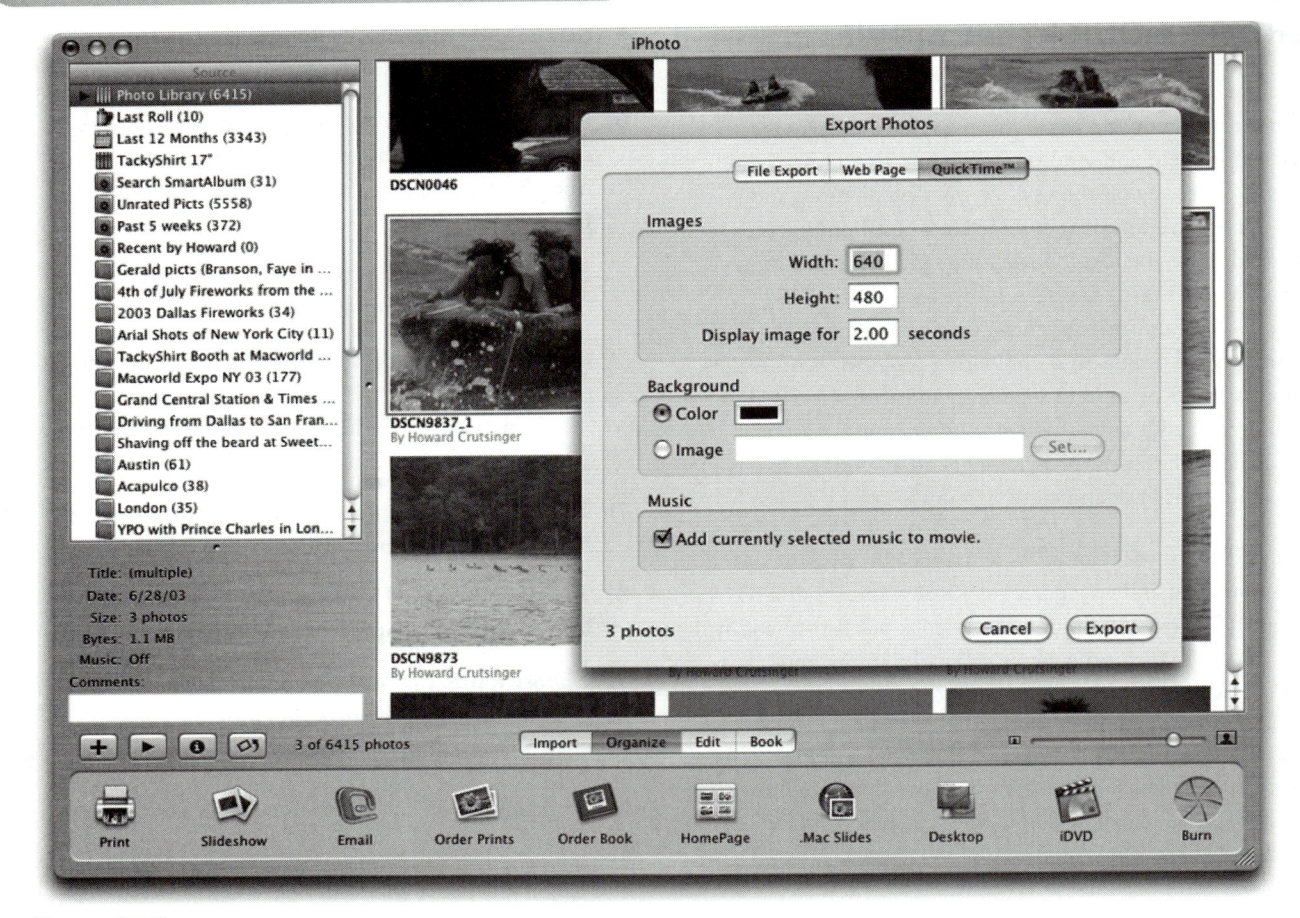

Figure 14-3

Use the Export Photos dialog box to create a QuickTime movie

4. **Build a QuickTime movie from the album as described in the previous set of steps, and click the Add currently selected music to movie checkbox.**

To play the movie, navigate to the folder containing the movie and double-click the file. The QuickTime movie player opens and plays the movie (see Figure 14-4).

Figure 14-4

Your images are now in a QuickTime movie for everyone to see

WHAT THAT QUICKTIME MOVIE REALLY IS

A QuickTime movie may not be what you think it is. It's not actually a video of your pictures: What you have is a file containing all of the still images, with instructions about how to get from one picture to the next. That's why the pictures look so amazingly clear and why they don't take up much hard drive space. Whether you set each picture to play for five seconds or five minutes, the file size is the same. Of course, if you have music playing with the picture, that's going to make the file larger.

Because of this special sort of movie file, users have to download the whole file before they can start to view the presentation.

CREATE A FAST START MOVIE

A Fast Start movie begins to play as soon as enough of the file has downloaded that the computer thinks it will have it all by the time you get to the end of the movie playback. The upgrade to QuickTime (Pro) has a way to make the movie into a Fast Start movie, but you'll sacrifice file size and image quality in the process. This only works for normal, video movies though, so you'll have to convert the slideshow movie into a video movie after you open it in QuickTime Player. Here's how:

1. **From QuickTime Player, choose File ➜ Export to open the Save exported file as dialog box.**

2. **Click the Options button to open the Movie Settings dialog box (see Figure 14-5).**

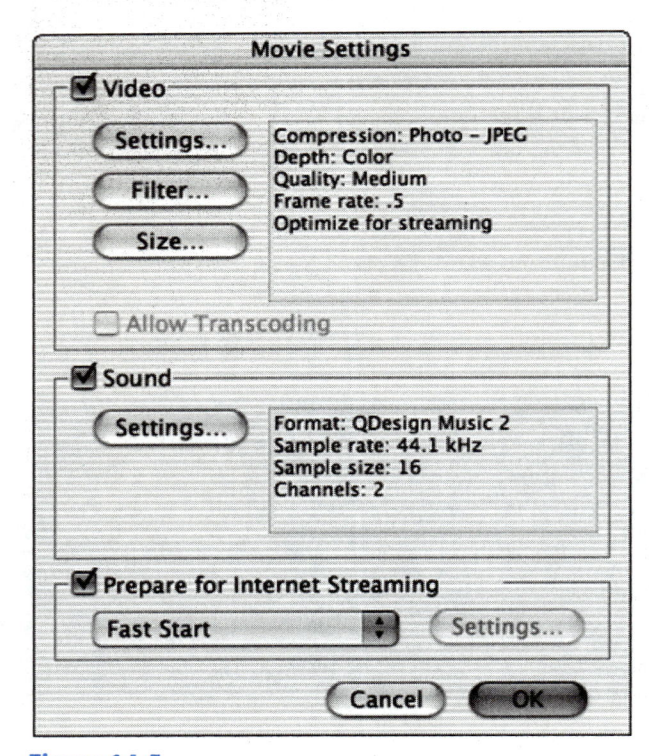

Figure 14-5
Set the movie parameters in this dialog box to create a Fast Start QuickTime movie

3. **Click Settings in the Video section to open the Compression Settings dialog box as shown in Figure 14-6.**

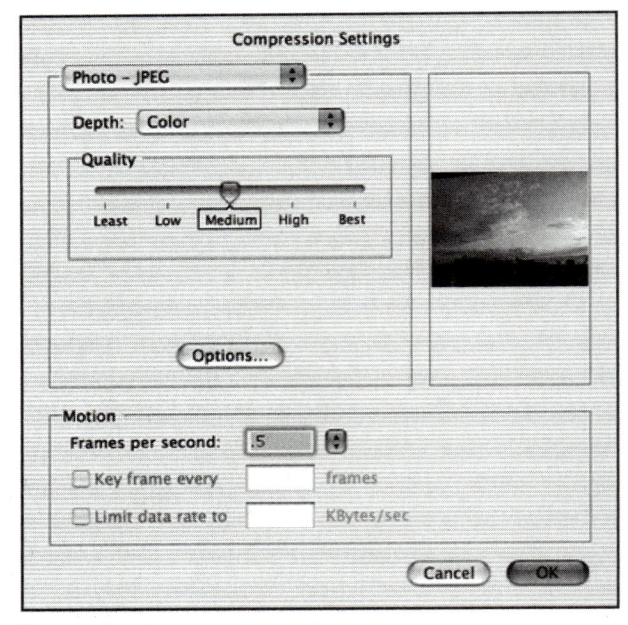

Figure 14-6
Set the video quality and number of frames (slides) per second

4. **Choose Photo ➜ JPEG from the pop-up menu at the top of the dialog box, and set the Quality to Medium or High.**

5. **In the Motion section of the Compression Settings dialog box, type a value in the Frames per second field that corresponds to how long you set each slide to appear in iPhoto.** For example, I set my slides to appear for 2 seconds, so I set the Frames per second to .5. Then click OK to return to the Movie Settings dialog box.

6. **Click the Settings button in the Sound section to open a new version of the Movie Settings dialog box.**

7. **Choose QDesign Music 2 from the pop-up list (see Figure 14-7).** You can also select Mono to reduce the size of the music portion of the file even more. Click OK to return to the main version of the Movie Settings dialog box.

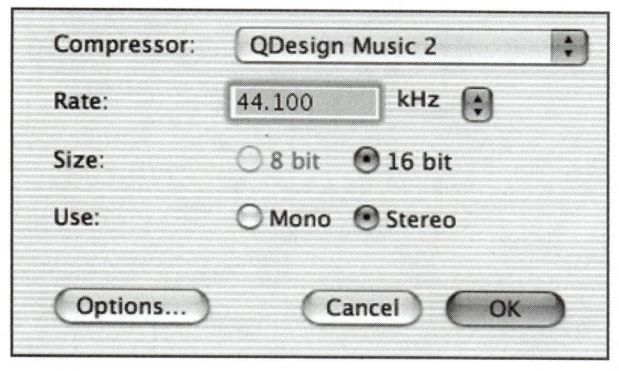

Compressor:	QDesign Music 2
Rate:	44.100 kHz
Size:	○ 8 bit ● 16 bit
Use:	○ Mono ● Stereo
Options...	Cancel OK

Figure 14-7
Compress the sound so it doesn't take too long to download

8. **Click the Prepare for Internet Streaming checkbox and select Fast Start from the pop-up list.**

9. **Click OK to close the Movie Settings dialog box.**

10. **Give your movie a name and a location on your hard drive, and then click Save.**

11. **After exporting a few moments, the movie is ready to use — either on your computer or on your Web site.**

This movie is simply a series of pictures with cuts between images instead of dissolves. This movie will also likely be about triple the file size of the slideshow movie you started with; although it takes longer to download, it starts to play back sooner, so the user isn't waiting so long.

CREATE A DESKTOP IMAGE

The background image on your Mac Desktop doesn't have to be that blue swoosh, although I do like the swoosh. You can set up one or more of your iPhoto images as your Desktop image. To set a single image as your Desktop image, follow these steps:

1. **Switch to Organize mode.** (Click Organize in the four-button bar below the main window.)

2. **Click the thumbnail of the image.**

3. **Click the Desktop icon below the Display pane.** The Desktop switches immediately to the selected image (see Figure 14-8).

You can also choose a set of images to use as your background; your Mac rotates through your selections at regular intervals. To do so, follow these steps:

1. **Switch to Organize mode.**

2. **Select several pictures in the Display pane.** Alternatively, you can pick the entire album by clicking the album in the Source pane and not clicking any of the thumbnails in the Display pane.

3. **Click the Desktop icon.** iPhoto displays the Desktop & Screen Saver preference pane (see Figure 14-9). If you find yourself on the Screen Saver pane, just click on the Desktop to flip to the displayed pane.

Figure 14-8
With just a few clicks, you can make an iPhoto image into your Desktop background

4. **To rotate through the pictures, click the Change picture checkbox and pick the duration from the pop-up list.** If you want the desktop images to change in random order, click the Random order checkbox.

5. **Close the Desktop & Screen Saver preference pane.**

 Note

If you want to stop using iPhoto images for your Desktop, select another option (such as Apple Background Images) from the Source pane to the left of the Desktop & Screen Saver preference pane. To switch to a different set of iPhoto images, simply repeat the process of picking the Desktop images. The old set of images is replaced with the new set you choose.

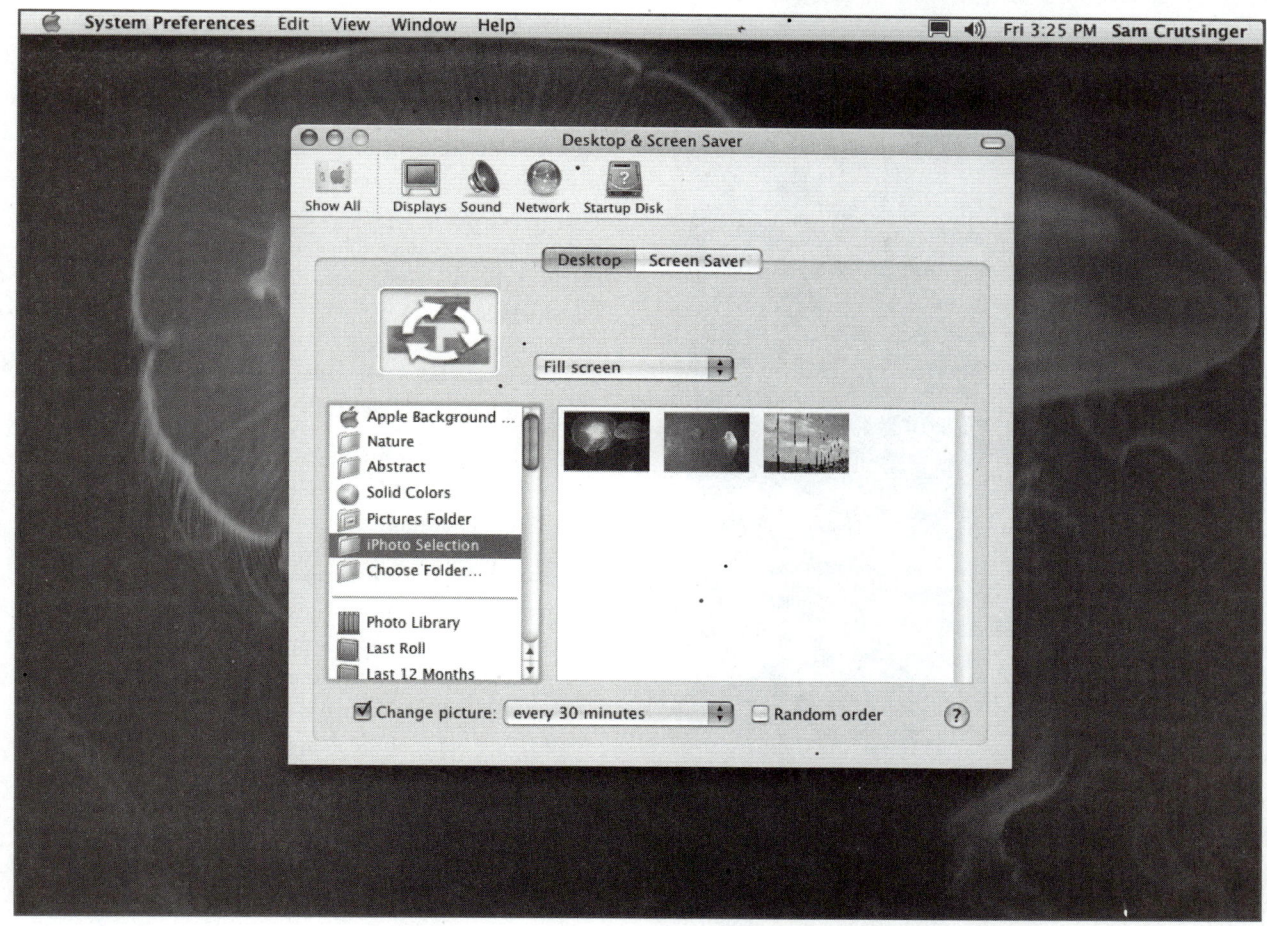

Figure 14-9
Choosing multiple images for your Desktop displays the Desktop & Screen Saver preference pane

CRUEL DESKTOP ABUSE PRANK

If anybody asks you, you didn't get this from me.

Okay, here's a cruel stunt you can use to really stick it to somebody. You can take snapshots of the computer screen by pressing Command+Shift+3. If you bring that picture into iPhoto, crop off the top menu bar, and then make *that* image the person's desktop background. It will drive even the most expert Mac guru absolutely bonkers trying to figure out why they can't close the windows or why they can't select the icons on the Desktop. Make sure you hide the Dock before you take the picture or that will be a dead giveaway.

For an advanced prank, take several pictures and create a changing Desktop background out of them but with a long change time. Make the first picture look like their normal Desktop if you need time to leave town before they figure out what you've done.

Like I said, you didn't get this from me.

CONFIGURE A SCREEN SAVER

If you pick multiple images or entire albums for your Desktop, the selections are also automatically used as your screen saver. On the down side, you have to select several pictures and then click the Desktop button to get that selection of photos for use in a screen saver regardless of whether you wanted to make one of your desktop image or not. Well, actually you could make a new album with your screen saver selection images and then choose that in the following procedure. I think they just added "iPhoto Selection" to both of the sources for Desktop and for Screen Saver but neglected to put in a way to change that iPhoto Selection without resorting to *Desktop*. To configure your screen saver, click the Screen Saver preferences button in the Desktop & Screens Saver preference pane. This opens

the Desktop & Screen Saver preference pane in System Preferences (see Figure 14-10).

The Preview area on the right shows you a preview of the screen saver rotating through the images.

Click the Options button to open the Display Options sheet so that you can enable and disable the various effects used for displaying the images (also shown in Figure 14-10). These include

- **Cross-fade between slides.** One image starts to fade as another image becomes visible.

- **Zoom back and forth.** Zooms in on one image while it is displayed, and then zooms out on the next image. This cycle repeats.

- **Crop slides to fit on screen.** If the image is smaller than the screen, the image is stretched to fill the screen. Two edges are cropped off so that the entire screen is filled with the image. If you deselect this checkbox and the image is smaller than the screen, you'll see black borders on the two edges where the image doesn't fit the screen.

- **Keep slides centered.** Keeps the slides centered on the screen. You can't turn this option off if you deselect the Crop slides to fit on screen checkbox.

- **Present slides in random order.** If you deselect this checkbox, the images in the screen saver are presented in the same order they appear in the album. Clicking this checkbox presents the images in random order.

You're not stuck with that iPhoto selection as your only source for screen saver content. If you scroll down in the Screen Savers listing to the left, you'll see all your iPhoto albums listed. You can choose any album you want, including Smart Albums, and that will be your screen saver source now.

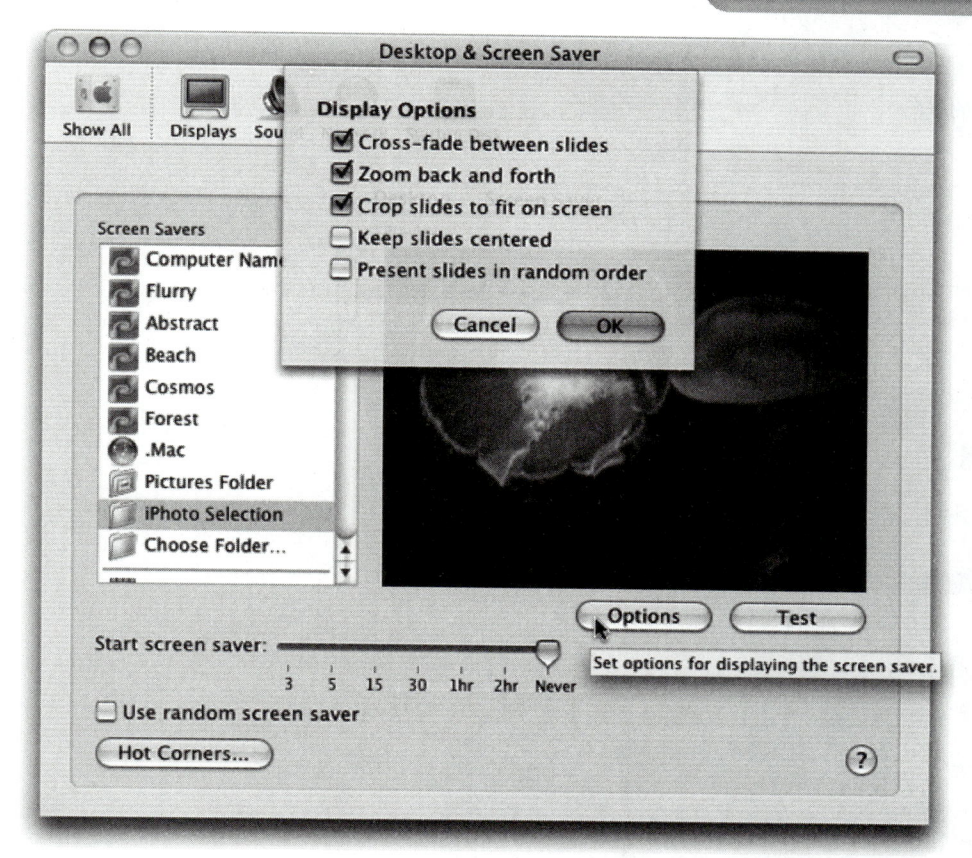

Figure 14-10
Configure your screen saver in the Desktop & Screen Saver preferences pane

SCREEN SAVER ACTIVATION AND SECURITY

The screen saver will switch on after you fail to move or click the mouse or type on the keyboard for the amount of time you specify on the "Start screen saver" slider in the Screen Saver preferences pane (see Figure 14-11). Additionally, you can set the screen saver to come on when you park your cursor in one of the four corners of your display. This is set up using the Hot Corners button (see Figure 14-12). Your options for each corner are

- **Start Screen Saver.** This immediately activates the screen saver.

- **Disable Screen Saver.** This will prevent the screen saver from activating even after the timer would normally activate it.

- **– (dash).** This disables that corner so it has no effect.

There are other settings in there for Exposé, but that feature is getting a bit off the iPhoto path again.

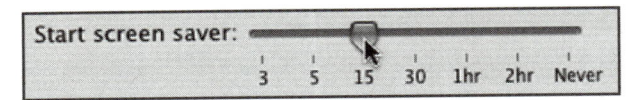

Figure 14-11
Start screen saver when I've been idle for this long

The screen saver can be set as a timed lockout feature. Basically it makes you type in your login name and password to get back into the computer once the screen saver has kicked in. This lets you leave the office for a lunch break and you know that if you're away long enough for the screen saver to activate, then people won't be able to walk in and use your computer without authorization.

1. **Pull up System Preferences again.** They are available from the Apple Menu.

2. **Choose Security from the Personal row.** This shows you several security settings for your computer.

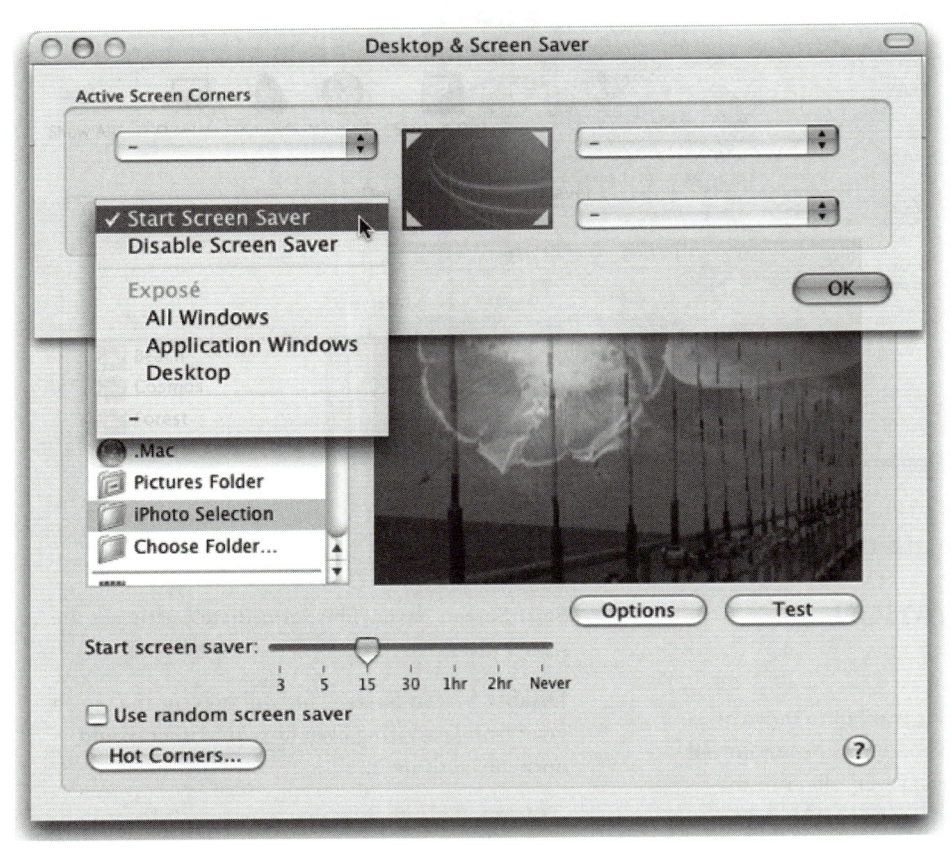

Figure 14-12
Set up the corner controls on the screen with the Hot Corners sheet

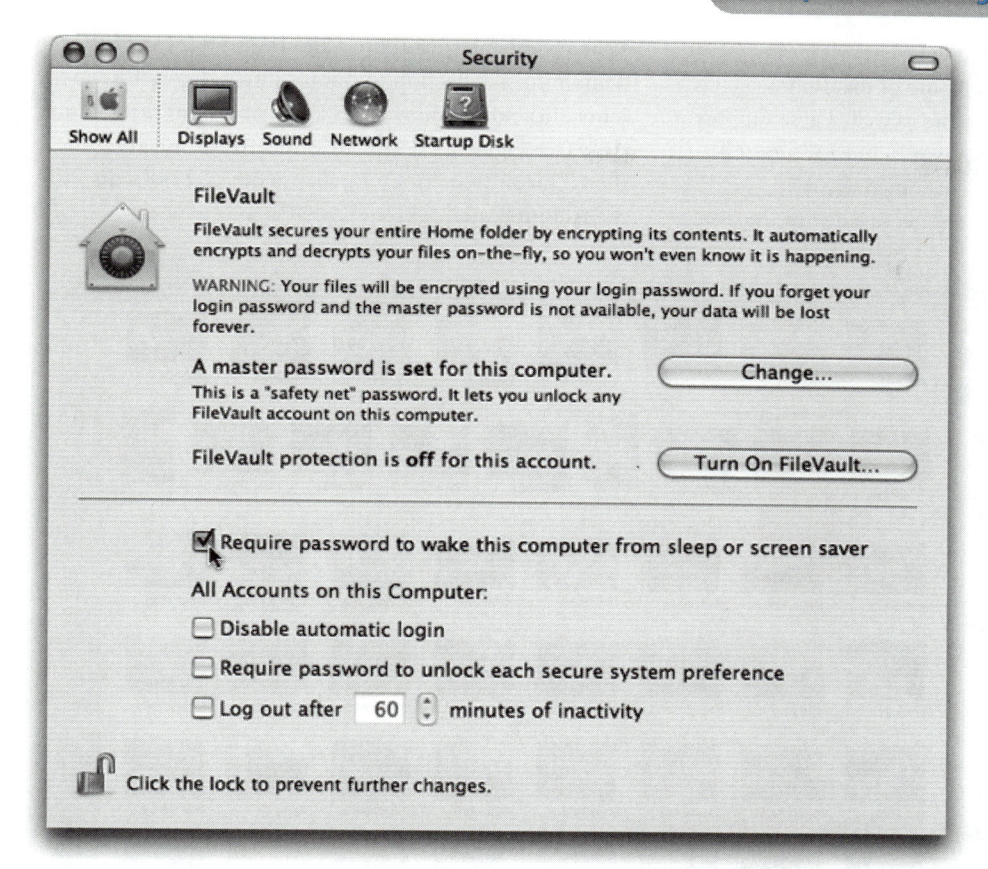

Figure 14-13

Use the Security System Preference to determine whether or not to require a password

3. **Check "Require password to wake this computer from sleep or screen saver" to activate the timed lockout (see Figure 14-13).** Now when the computer goes to sleep or the screen saver activates, you will have to know the password before you can wake it up or dismiss the screen saver. Nobody will be able to see that you left the Victoria Secret Online Web site up on your screen when you dashed off to pick up a submarine sandwich.

BACK UP AND SHARE PHOTOS ON AN IPHOTO DISC

Right. Enough of that System Preferences hullabaloo. Let's get back into iPhoto. Let's talk about backing up all those photos you have in iPhoto and very possibly nowhere else. Guess what! Right now it would take a bolt of lightning striking within several miles of your computer *[snap]* that long to totally wipe out your entire picture collection. You can easily burn a batch of photos onto a CD or DVD to put safely on a shelf or to share with anyone else who uses iPhoto. The disc preserves the structure of the iPhoto library. It includes all the support files as well. These support files include albums, titles, and keywords, but *not* film rolls: Your "roll 17" isn't the same thing as someone else's "roll 17," so that information doesn't get saved with the disc.

When someone runs iPhoto and inserts a CD or DVD containing a collection of photos into a drive, the contents of the drive show up as a sub-library in the Album pane (see Figure 14-14). Click the arrowhead alongside the CD icon to expand or collapse the CD contents in the Album pane.

Figure 14-14

The contents of a CD-ROM show up in the Album pane as a separate library

You can edit and organize the albums and images on the disc much as you would with your regular images; you can even order prints using the methods described in Chapter 13. Of course, you can't modify the images while they're still on the disc, because it is read-only media. To make changes to the images, you have to import them into your photo library. To do so, follow these steps:

1. **In the Album pane, select one or more of the albums on the CD or DVD.**

2. **In Organize mode's Display pane, choose the pictures you want to import.**

3. **Click and drag the images to one of the following destinations in the Source pane:**

    - The photo library

    - A blank area in the Source pane (to create a new album)

    - One of the existing albums in your Album pane that is *not* on the CD or DVD

If you want to import a whole album from a CD, *just drag the album* from under the CD name to a white space in your Source column. iPhoto imports all the pictures in the album and creates a new album, keeping the album title from the CD. If you drag the *whole CD* icon instead of individual albums listed on that CD, any album layout is lost. Even if the disc has five albums on it, dragging the disc to an open space in the Source column lumps all the albums into a new album with the name taken from the disc title. If you want to keep the albums intact, select all of the individual albums listed on the disc and drag *those* to an open space. This will import them into their own respective albums.

▼ **Tip**

To eject the CD or DVD, Control+click the disc in the Album pane and choose Eject from the contextual menu.

To create your own iPhoto disc, follow these steps:

1. **Click the Burn button.** This will open the iris. (It all kinda looks like its nuclear powered or something, don't it?)

2. **Insert a blank disc when prompted.**

▼ **Tip**

After you insert the blank disc, the dialog box disappears on its own if you just wait a few seconds.

3. **Select the film rolls (in the photo library) or the albums to include on the disc.** As you select film rolls or albums to place on the disc, iPhoto displays the disc name, the number of photos, the amount of space the selected albums will occupy, and the amount of free space left on the disc in the Info pane. You can edit the disc name, although the name appears only in iPhoto; on the Desktop, the disc appears simply as "iPhoto Disc." The little capacity gauge icon fills up as you add more photos to burn. If it's green (not full), then you still have room if you want to add more. If it's red, you've exceeded the number of pictures you can get on that disc and you need to select fewer pictures (Figure 14-15).

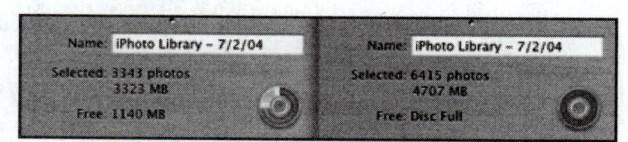

Figure 14-15
The green gauge (it's green, trust me) tells you when everything fits. A full gauge (red) means you've gone too far

▼ **Note**

If you have the Info pane turned off (not displaying), you won't get any warning that the disk is full because the warning indicator appears in the Info pane. If the Info pane is not visible, click the *i* button to display it.

4. **Enter a name for the disc in the Name field below the Source list.**

5. **Click the yellow and black pulsing Burn button.** The missiles launch from the thermonuclear port on your... oh like that's not what that button looks like it should do! Fine then, the Burn Disc dialog box will come up.

6. **Click the Burn button.** iPhoto burns your selections to the disc as a complete iPhoto library (see Figure 14-16).

▼ **Note**

If you change your mind and decide *not* to burn the disc by clicking Cancel in the Burn Disc dialog box, you have a bit of a problem. The blank disc does not show up on the Desktop, so you can't eject it! To work around this, quit iPhoto. The Finder then displays a dialog box that enables you to eject the blank disc. An even better idea is to click the Eject button in the Burn Disc dialog box (which ejects the disc) and *then* click Cancel.

Wow! This chapter felt like Around the World in 80 Days, er, pages, or whatever. I'm pooped from just switching back and forth so much to all those System Preferences! Yeah, fine. I'm not in quite as good shape as I was back in high school. When mousing gets you winded, that is a pretty bad indicator that it might be time for a few sit-ups. Maybe tomorrow.

SOME THOUGHTS ON BACKING UP YOUR PHOTOGRAPHS

Your photographs are probably among your most prized possessions; so don't leave their fate to chance. You should back them up to something more permanent than your computer's hard drive. Why?

- **Because hard drives fail.** Hard drives are complex devices with many moving parts. Hard drives are very reliable, but as with many other mechanical devices, they do stop working — and everything on them may go bye-bye. There are companies that can recover data from dead hard drives, but their services are often quite expensive and, as I can tell you from experience, when the heads gouge a deep groove in the drive platters, you don't get much at all back (if anything at all), but you *do* still get the wonderful bill to pay for them trying.

- **Because computers get stolen.** This is especially true if you have a PowerBook or iBook; thieves just love these pretty (and powerful) machines.

- **Because backups are easy to share.** If the people you want to share your photos with have iPhoto, you can duplicate a backup CD or DVD and sent it to them. All they need to do is insert the disc and they can start viewing and using your photos. If the people you want to share your photos with are folks who *don't* have iPhoto, you can still use the Finder to burn a CD whose content a Mac or PC user can access.

Figure 14-16

Confirm in the Burn Disc dialog box that you want to burn a disc

Probably the most important thing in this chapter is the *backup* bit. Your pictures are irreplaceable. You can't hop into the DeLorean, take it up to 88 MPH and have Michael J. Fox help you take your pictures again. Oh and just a quick, totally irrelevant commentary if I may, 88 MPH? Raise your hand if you think going a wussy 88 MPH in a racer like that DeLorean should cause the fabric of time to shatter. I hit that on an average trip down the

tollway. It should have been 188 MPH at least. Sorry, had to say it.

Back up your stuff! When your drive takes a dirt nap you want to be able to stroll past the computer store and get a new drive. You don't want the nervous sweating and gut wrenching dry heaves that accompany realizing that everything you've worked on for the past three years just went *click click click... whirr... grind... click... • poof •*.

15

Sharing Your Photos on the Internet

In This Chapter

Publish .Mac Slides • Publish photos with HomePage
Publish photos to your personal Web site

I have this friend. We'll call her Debi. Debi recently bought a new 12" PowerBook and she has a digital camera but she had no .Mac account. One evening we were iChatting away and I sent her a link to one of my HomePages that I'd uploaded with iPhoto (Figure 15-1). She instant messaged (IM) me back with "look at your little thumbtacks!" I told her about how easy it was to make and upload and how I had all this space up there for stuff like that. I won't bore you with all the details of the chat, but it involved:

- Her looking at several of my HomePages.

- Her telling me that I looked like Charles Manson when I had my beard, only scarier.

- Three instances of "LOL."

- Her saying, "I can only get several pages on my ISP. It sucks. I have to take something down to put something up. Of course I could pay for more space if I wanted to."

- Her finally sending me her new .Mac address.

Elapsed time, 45 minutes. Amount of time estimated before she beats the snuff out of me for talking about her in my book? Thirteen minutes, 24 seconds after she reads this. She lives pretty far away but those Miatas can really zip you where you need to be when you've got snuff to beat out of someone. Heh heh, I think I'll IM her and tell her she's become an anecdote.

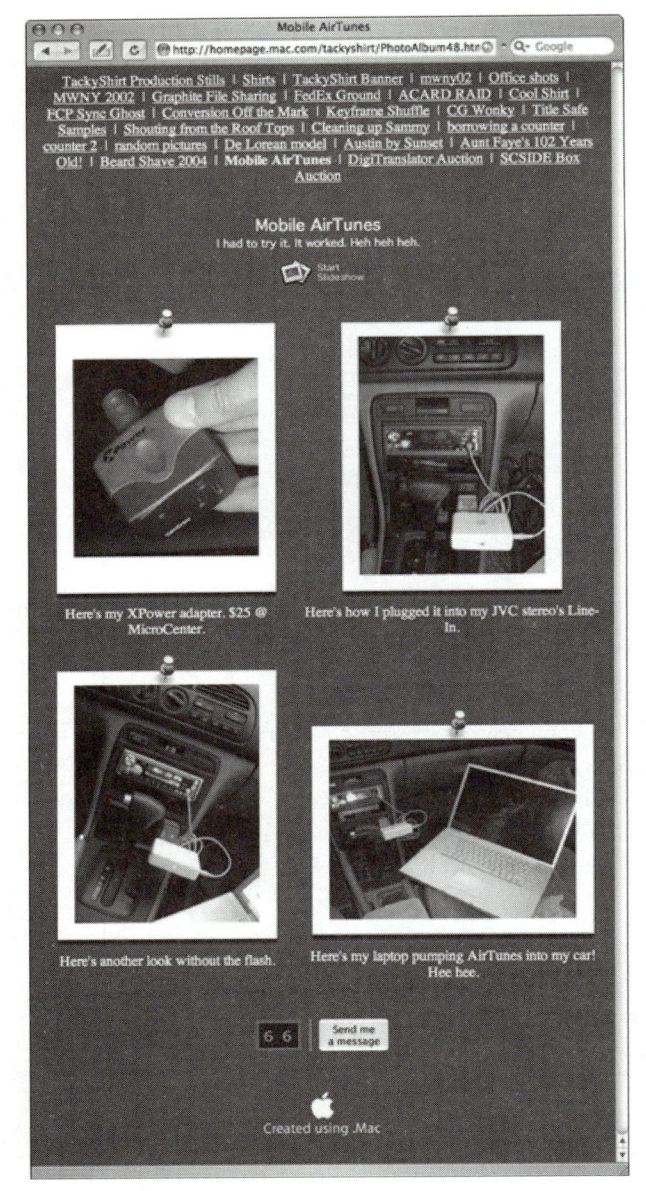

Figure 15-1
Simple little HomePage that sold another .Mac account

iPhoto jacks straight into a .Mac account. That Figure 15-1 Web page took me exactly five clicks and one line of text typing to build from an album. I could have gotten the job done in two clicks, but I decided to get fancy with it. After that fifth click, iPhoto uploaded the Web page to a server along with all the graphics, code, links, and other assorted *stuff* that most people don't want to have to learn about. The only way to make it any easier would be to get someone else to click the buttons for you. There's also a lesser-known way to publish pictures involving a .Mac account, iPhoto, any Mac running 10.2 or later, and a ham and cheese sandwich (okay, just kidding about the ham and cheese).

Even if you don't have a .Mac account, you can still make fancy Web pages, but you'll probably have to double or triple the number of clicks it takes to get the job done.

PUBLISH .MAC SLIDES

When you see the .Mac Slides button down there in Organize mode, it's hard to guess what that might do. My first guess was way off the mark. It's much cooler than what I was thinking.

If you have a .Mac account, you can publish a set of slides that anyone running OS X 10.2 or later can use as a screen saver. In other words, if the user is set up to watch your .Mac Slides, you control what the screen saver shows. Of course, "the other user" might also be "you" but on another computer. To publish your .Mac Slides, follow these steps:

1. **Connect to the Internet.**

2. **Switch to Organize mode.**

3. **Select the images you want to use.**

4. **Click the .Mac Slides button.** After a moment, iPhoto displays a confirmation dialog box (Figure 15-3).

5. **Click Publish to proceed.**

IDISK: HARD DISK OR WEB SERVER?

When you get a .Mac account from Apple, one of the services they give you is called iDisk. Essentially what it is is storage *space*. What's special about it is how well that space is integrated into your Macintosh. The storage space is actually a small piece of a hard drive on a server bolted into a rack in a very cold room out in a building about 50 miles southeast of San Francisco, CA. It's a happy place. Lots of trees.

Let me back up a little. If you don't have a .Mac account and have never had an account, head over to System Preferences and pull up the .Mac pane. In the bottom-right corner is a button to get you a free 60-day trial. Of course, you have to know where to look to get the free trial. That button takes you to a Web page. See under the Join Now button that says "or click here to learn more" in fine print (Figure 15-2)? Click *that*. From there it's easy to find.

Once you have your account activated, you put your .Mac Member Name and Password into this same preference pane which allows your computer to access your iDisk over the Internet.

Once you're configured, you can go into the Finder, and in the menu bar choose Go ➜ iDisk ➜ My iDisk. That will mount your iDisk and now you can just copy files to and from there just like it was any other disk, so in that respect it acts like a hard disk, but the folder inside your iDisk named Sites is actually shared by a Web server. You can put a picture file in that folder and then access it from anywhere in the world with any Web browser. Just send your browser to http://homepage.mac.com/*member_name*/*picture*.jpg, where "*member_name*" is your .Mac member name and "*picture*.jpg" is the name of the file you put in the Sites folder. For instance, I'm sticking a file called shameless-plug.jpg in my folder right now. You can hit http://homepage.mac.com/tackyshirt/shameless-plug.jpg and you'll pull up the picture off of my iDisk.

In iPhoto, when you use .Mac Slides or HomePage, you're uploading pictures to that disk space so they can be accessed by anybody who knows what address to put in. Only very specific folders in your iDisk are open to the public though, so don't worry about people going through your Documents folder or anything. Check out http://www.mac.com/ for more info.

(So that's a plug for me, one for Apple.... Let's go for three.) Be Original! Be you! Dr. Pepper.

Figure 15-2
Secret lair of the elusive free .Mac trial account

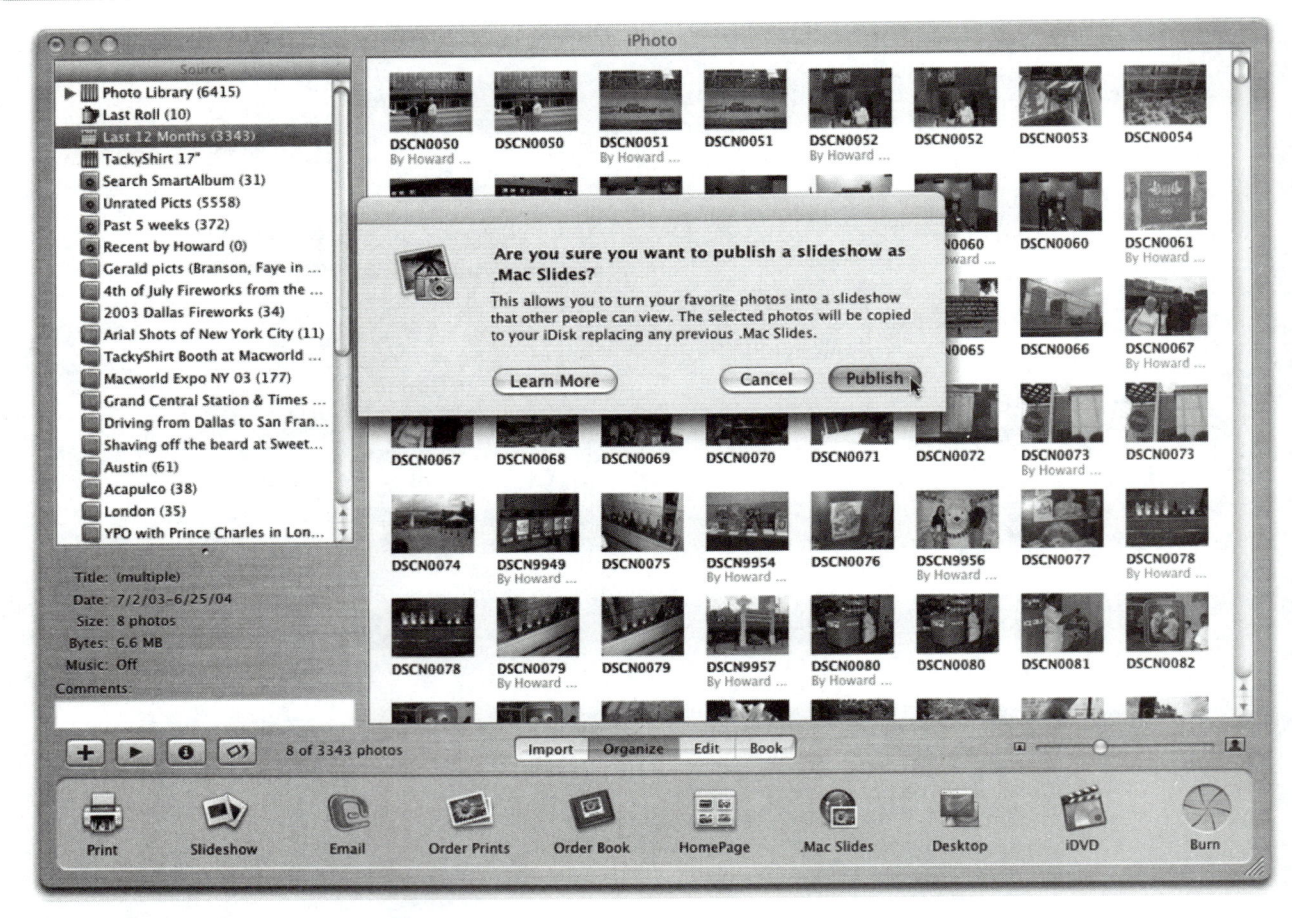

Figure 15-3
Confirm that you want to publish your new .Mac Slides, replacing your old ones

▼ Note

Each time you publish a set of .Mac Slides, the new set replaces the previous set. That is, you can only have one set of .Mac Slides at a time. The slides are stored on your *iDisk* in the Pictures/Slide Shows/ Public directory. If your iDisk is not visible on your Desktop, run the iDisk Utility (in the Applications/ Utilities folder).

Once you click Publish, iPhoto compresses and shrinks the size of the photos and uploads them to your iDisk. When the upload is complete, a dialog box appears telling you how to access your own .Mac slideshow. (The instructions depend on whether you are using OS X 10.2 or OS X 10.3.) You can then click the Announce Slideshow button in the dialog box to create an email message. This message announces the availability of the slideshow and gives the recipient the necessary instructions on how to subscribe to the slideshow (Figure 15-4).

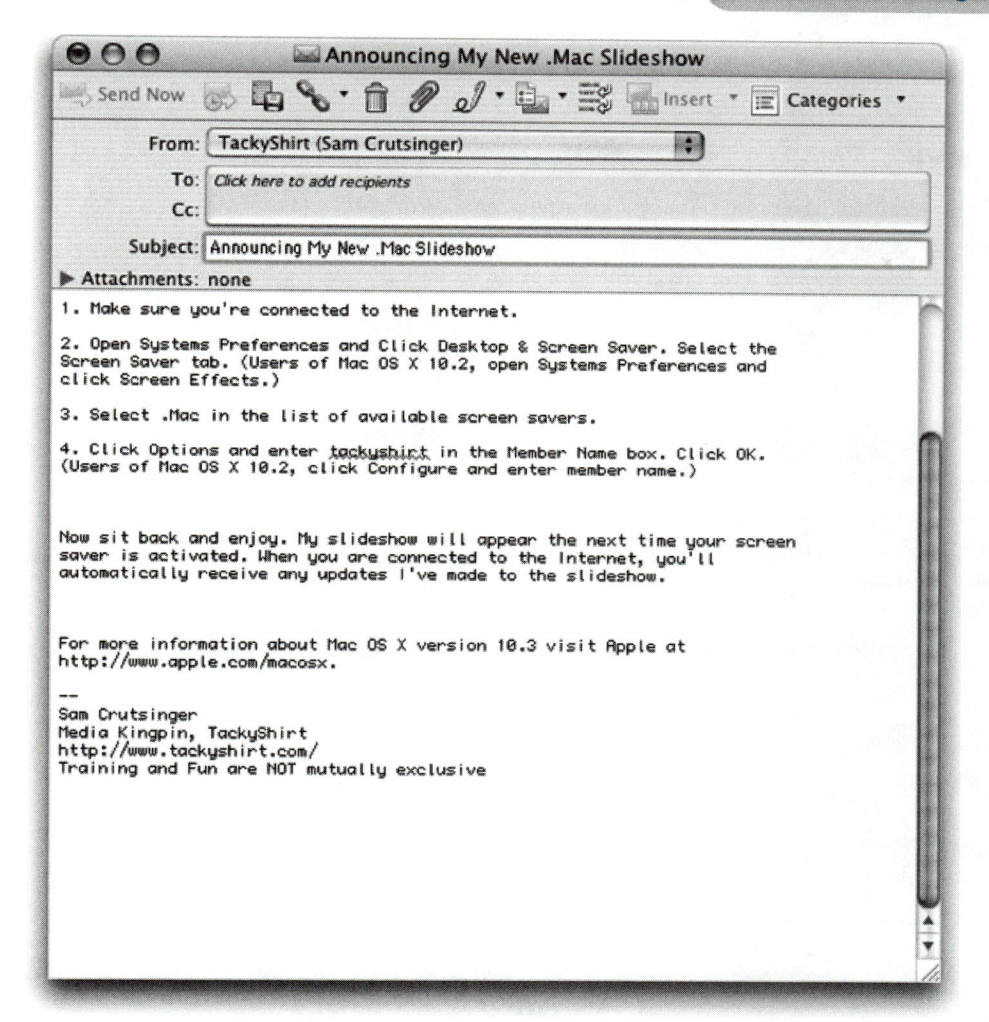

Figure 15-4
Send an email telling people how to get your new .Mac slideshow

For someone else (the subscriber) to obtain and use your .Mac slideshow using OS X 10.3 (Panther), the subscriber should use the following instructions:

1. **Choose System Preferences from the Apple Menu in the upper-left corner of your screen and click the Desktop & Screen Saver icon.**

> ### ▼ Note
> Users of OS X 10.2 (Jaguar) should open System Preferences and click Screen Effects.

2. **Click .Mac in the Screen Savers list.**

3. **Click the Options button to display the Subscriptions and Display Options sheet** (Figure 15-5).

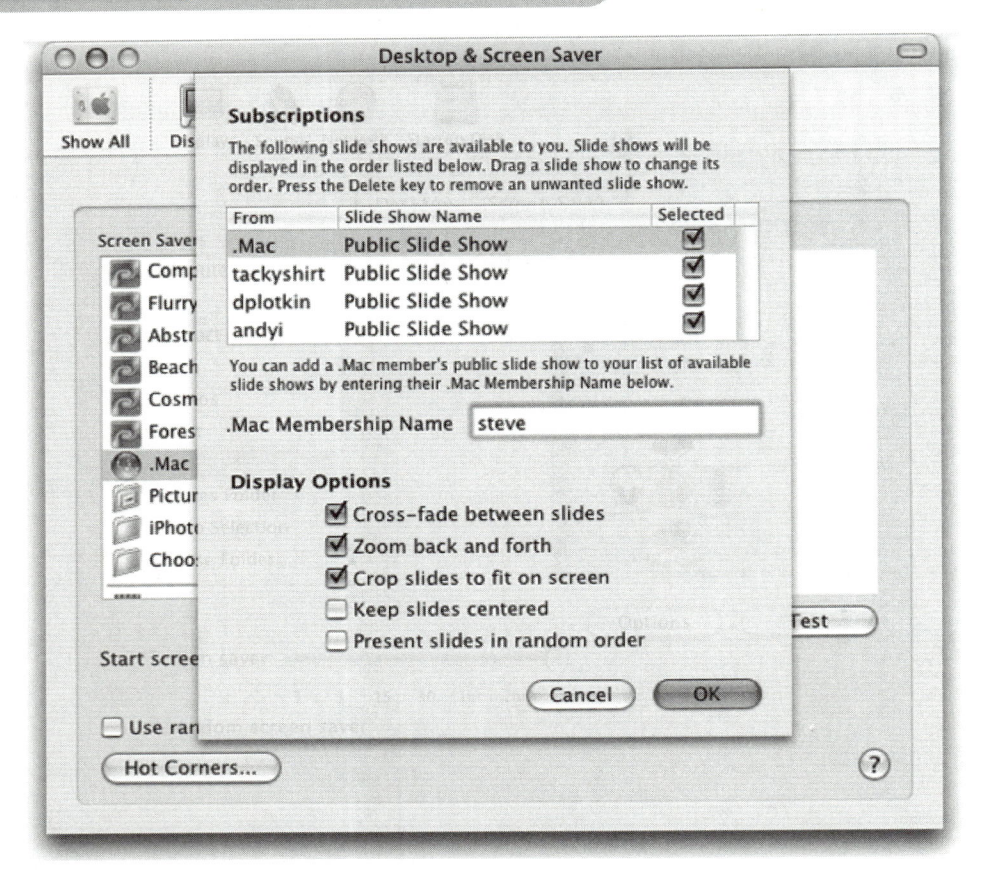

Figure 15-5
Specify the .Mac Slides to use and choose your display options

4. **Enter your .Mac member name in the .Mac Membership Name field.**

5. **Click OK.** iPhoto adds the member name to the list of subscriptions and closes the sheet.

6. **Click Options to reopen the sheet.** Make sure the checkbox next to the .Mac member's name is selected in the subscription list.

 Note

The subscribers can select the checkboxes for multiple .Mac Membership Names. If they do, the slides are shown in the same order as the names are listed in the subscription list. To change the order of the .Mac Membership Names, click and drag the names up or down in the subscription list. Selecting "Present slides in random order" will shuffle all the pictures from all the .Mac accounts together. To delete a .Mac Membership Name, select the name and press Delete.

.MAC SLIDE HUNTING

It's unfortunate that more people don't know about .Mac Slides. I think it's fun to just check out people's slides whenever I see someone has a .Mac account, but almost everybody I've ever tried is empty. Probably the most famous .Mac account of all is Apple CEO Steve Jobs, who snagged the name steve before the masses took all the good names. As I'm typing this, steve has no .Mac Slides. Personally I think it's a nice little Easter egg to have *something* up there in case people like me come looking. I keep my .Mac Slides stocked up for visitors.

7. **Configure the Display Options using the checkboxes at the bottom of the sheet.** These options have the same meanings as they do with any other Screen Effects.

8. **Click OK to close the sheet.**

9. **Quit Screen Preferences.**

The subscriber's computer downloads the .Mac Slides in the background the next time he or she connects to the Internet. Subscribers (and you) must be patient, however, and wait for the slides to download.

PUBLISH PHOTOS WITH HOMEPAGE

HomePage is one of the best reasons to get a .Mac account. The fact that you can build such a slick looking Web page to show off your pictures, with just a few clicks in most cases, is sweeeeet.

The HomePage button lets people with .Mac accounts publish Web pages using the images from iPhoto. Anyone with a Web browser can view these pages (and the photos).

To publish your photos using the HomePage feature, make sure you are connected to the Internet and use the following steps:

1. **Switch to Organize mode and select the photos you want to publish to your .Mac Web site.**

2. **Click the HomePage button.** iPhoto opens the Publish HomePage dialog box (Figure 15-6). The top of the dialog box shows a preview of your Web page. The bottom of the dialog box provides a set of controls for customizing the look of the Web page. A list of themes you can use for your Web page appears on the right side of the dialog box.

 Note

If you find the list of themes distracting, click the Hide Themes button in the lower-left corner of the Publish HomePage dialog box to hide the list.

3. **Select and edit the title text.** The title text is located at the top of the page. The title is set by default to the name of the album.

 Note

The contextual menu you get from Control clicking on any of the text blocks has all sorts of stuff in there about Bold, Italic, and Fonts. PSYCHE! They don't work. The font that first comes up is all you get, so don't bother wishing for anything else. You will eat vanilla and you will like it. You *can* turn on spell checking from that menu though, which is nice.

4. **Select and edit the description.** Just below the title is a text block in a smaller font, which is perfect for a description. As with the title, you can select the default text and change it.

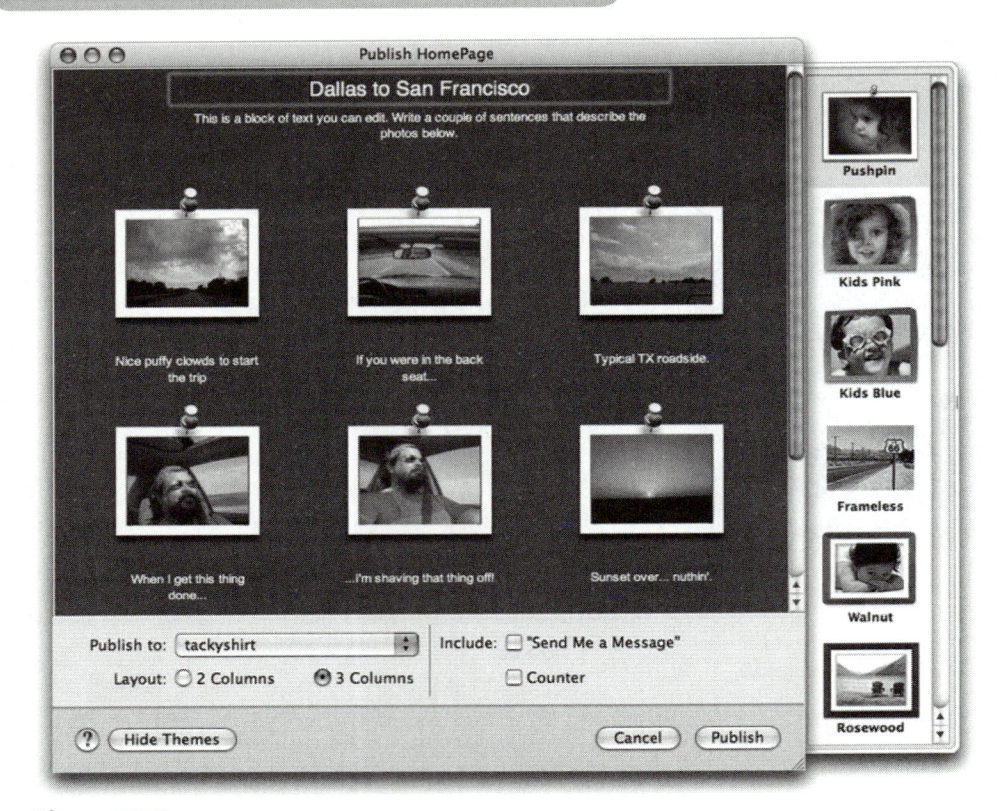

Figure 15-6
The Publish HomePage dialog box gives you a preview of your finished Web page

---

▼ **Tip**

Be sure to remove the description text if you are not going to use it. Otherwise, the default text appears on the Web page!

---

5. **Select and edit the image titles.** Just below each image on the page is text containing the image title from iPhoto. You can select this text and edit it to make it more appropriate for display on the Web. For example, my picture titles are often just the file name. I changed this text and substituted a brief description of each photo for the HomePage.

▼ **Note**

Any changes you make to the image captions on the HomePage do *not* affect the image titles in iPhoto.

---

6. **Select a theme.** If the theme side panel isn't showing, just click the Show Themes button to bring it out. You can select from several different theme styles by clicking the button for the style you want in the scrolling pane poking out of the side of the window. The themes set the border style and background and font for the Web page. Hit Hide Themes if you want to put away that panel (Figure 15-7).

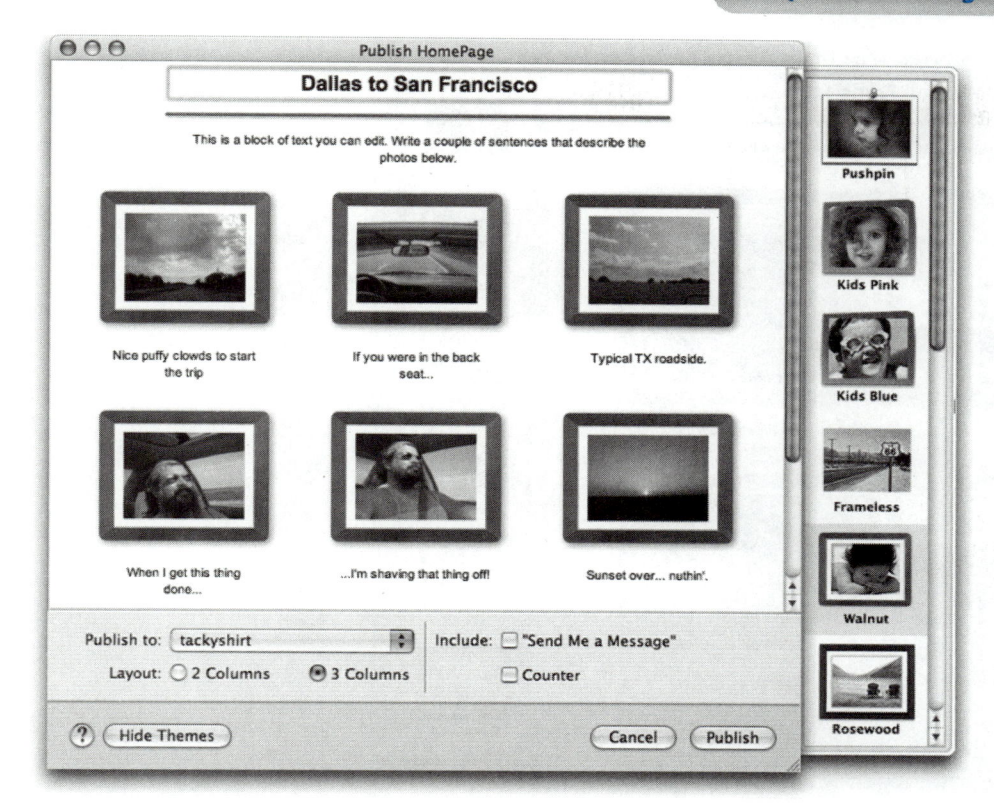

Figure 15-7
Selecting a different theme changes the background, frames, and font

▼ Note

The theme side panel can be either on the left or right side of the window. If you want to make it switch to the left, move the window so that the panel is off the right edge of the screen. Click Hide Themes and then Show Themes. The panel will slide out of the left side because now there's not enough room on the right to show it. Simply flop those directions to move it to the right. (Personally I'm not too fond of this behavior. I think it should pick a side and stay there. I've got the same beef with Apple's Mail application.)

7. **Select the number of columns.** Choose whether to display the images in two columns or three columns by choosing either the 2 Columns option or the 3 Columns option from the Layout options. The 2 Columns option shows the images in a larger size (Figure 15-8).

8. **Add an email button.** If you want someone viewing your Web page to be able to easily send you an email, click the Send Me a Message option. Selecting this checkbox adds a button to the Web page that the viewer can click to compose an email message to you. The email is delivered to your .Mac email account and can include an image from your HomePage.

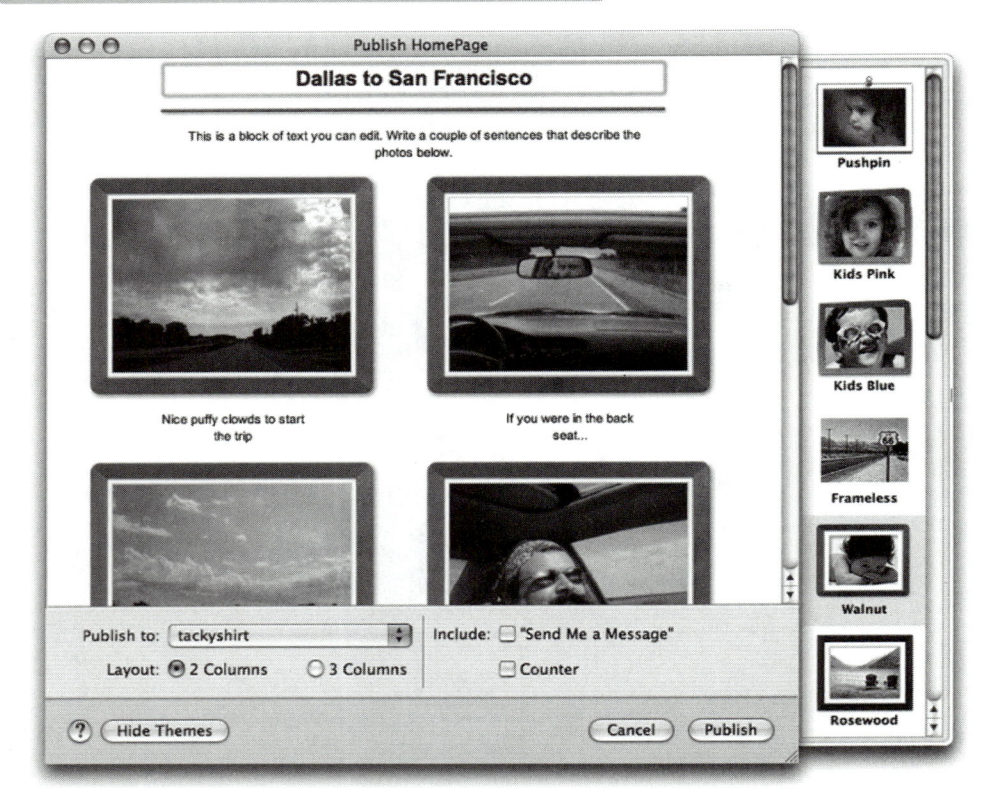

Figure 15-8
The 2 Columns option displays the images in a larger size than the 3 Columns option

9. **Add a counter.** If you want a numeric counter on the bottom of the page to keep track of how many times the page has been viewed, click the Counter checkbox.

10. **Arrange your layout.** You can rearrange the images on the Web page by clicking and dragging the photos in the Publish HomePage dialog box. Simply click and drag one image on top of another image and they switch places on the page.

11. **When you are done specifying how your page will look, click Publish.** iPhoto compresses the images to 800 x 600 and uploads the images and the Web page to your .Mac Web site. When the operation is complete, a dialog box appears that provides the URL of the new page (Figure 15-9).

 Note

If you want to edit your page, click the Edit Page button in the dialog box. This enables you to log in to your .Mac account and use the tools to change your HomePage as described in "Editing Your Homepage," later in this chapter.

Your HomePage has been published.

You can reach your page by entering the following URL into any web browser:

http://homepage.mac.com/tackyshirt/PhotoAlbum45.html

Edit Page | Visit Page Now | OK

Figure 15-9
This dialog box confirms that you have successfully published your new Web page

HOMEPAGE SHORTCOMINGS

When using HomePage to build your Web site, one of the things that might annoy you is that every page you build has that header on it with links to all of your other pages. That's all good and well when you have half a dozen pages you're showing off, but if you create loads of HomePages, those header links can get out of hand. I've started to call mine the *link wad*. You can modify the page on your iDisk to remove the links, but as soon as you add or delete another HomePage, the .Mac system goes through and "fixes" all of them. It's just easier to use the Export feature explained at the end of this chapter for pages you don't want linked up on every other HomePage.

Another limitation is that you're only allowed to have 48 pictures in any one HomePage. If you have more than 48 photos, again, head for Export where you don't have to deal with those limitations.

Of course, there are the little things such as picking more than just two or three columns. Export has much more control in that area.

The last limitation I'd mention is privacy. Sometimes you put up photo pages for just some of your friends. Let's say, for example, that you're a student down at State University. You've got lots of party pics from a recent kegger, but you're not all that keen on Mom and Dad seeing that your leftover tuition money is really being used to fund your research for finding out which hooch produces the worst hangover. This would be something you probably *don't* want to publish on HomePage.

On a related note, publishing the *appropriate* HomePage content might be a good way to build an elaborate façade full of good, clean living and a disturbingly high number of pictures taken from inside the school library. They might send you more money with a note that says, "You're working too hard. Go out and have a good time for a change!"

Procuring research grant money can be a very nefarious business!

Note

The Web pages are stored in the Sites folder on your iDisk, but the images are placed over in the Pictures folder in such a way that it breaks all the relative links in the HTML code if you open the Web pages directly from your iDisk in the Finder. The pictures won't show up. It works fine via the HTTP URL though. If you like hacking into HTML, you understand what I'm saying. If you have a blank look on your face right now, just say, "Silly geeks" and ignore this note.

If you want to view the page right away, click Visit Page Now. Your browser opens, displaying the page you just built. If you have built other HomePages, their titles (references) are visible across the top of the browser (Figure 15-10). You can view any of these pages by clicking their reference in the browser.

The images on the HomePage are actually thumbnails, which are links to larger versions of the images. To view a larger version of an image, simply click the thumbnail in the browser. The larger version opens in its own window

(Figure 15-11). You can use the arrow buttons at the bottom right of the window to step through the large images. You can also click the Start Slideshow button to open the larger version of the first image in the window.

Note

People viewing the images on your .Mac Web site won't be able to print the images at any reasonable size because the resolution is too low. As mentioned earlier, you need at least 150 dots for every inch of photograph, commonly seen as dpi. Thus, the 800 x 600 photos can (at most) be printed at a size of 4 x 3 (inches). If you want to put higher resolution originals on the Web so that people can print at larger sizes, you'll need to publish the images and associated Web pages without using the HomePage facility. This is because you can't adjust the default size of the published images in HomePage — they are fixed at 800 x 600. To publish a Web page without using HomePage, see the section "Publish Photos to Your Own Web Site," later in this chapter.

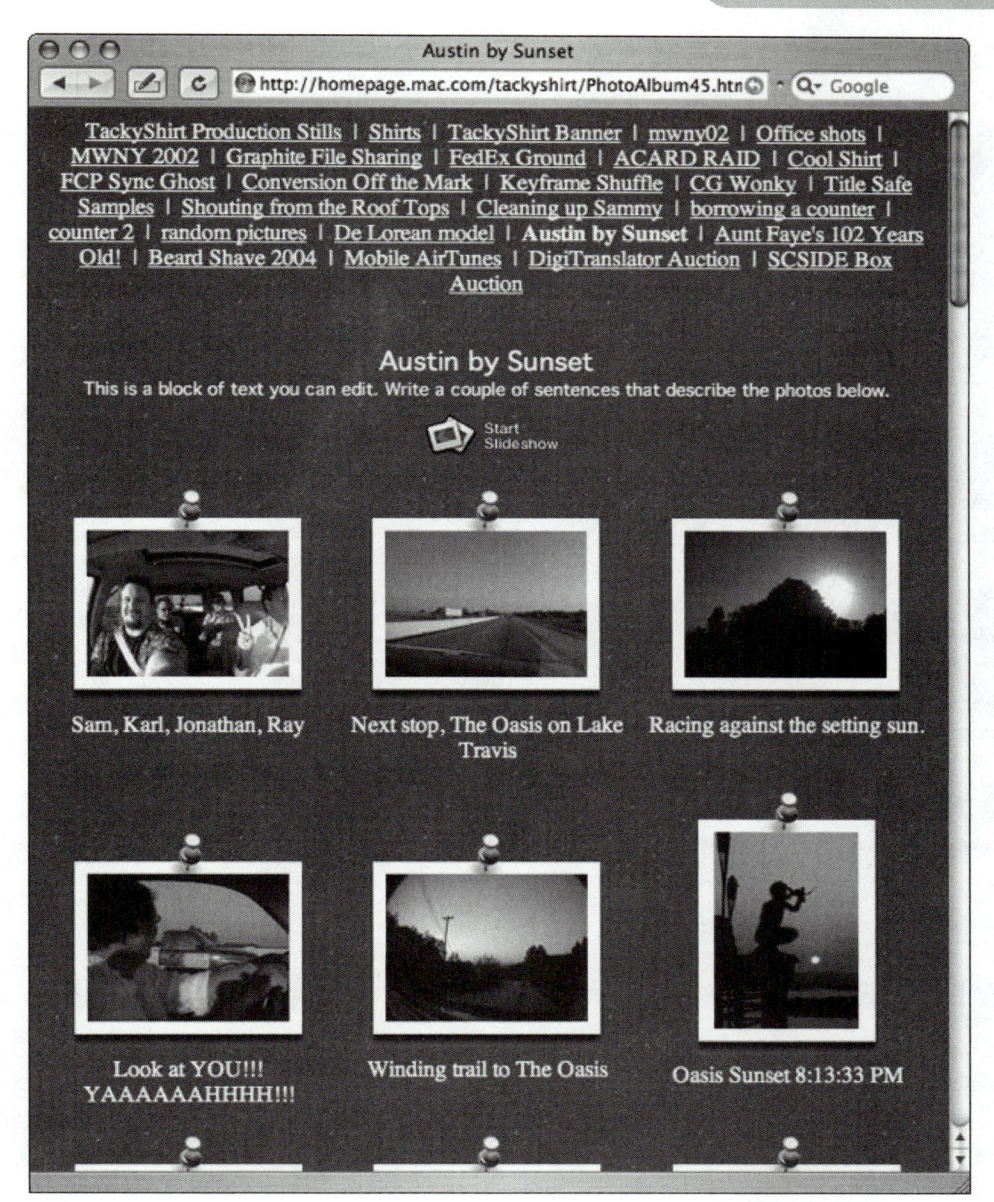

Figure 15-10
View your new HomePage in your browser

Sam, Karl, Jonathan, Ray

Figure 15-11
View the larger versions of the images in their own window

EDITING YOUR HOMEPAGE

Once you've published your HomePages on your .Mac site, you can edit them directly on the site — and you have more options than you did when you created the pages originally in iPhoto. To edit your HomePage, use the following steps:

1. **Go to http://www.mac.com/ in your Web browser.** This takes you to the .Mac main page shown in Figure 15-12.

Figure 15-12
.Mac front page (www.mac.com/)

2. **Click the HomePage button on the left side of the screen.** A list of your HomePages appears (see Figure 15-13).

3. **Select the HomePage you want to work with and click the Edit button below the list.** A version of that selected Web page will come up with editable fields, shown in Figure 15-14.

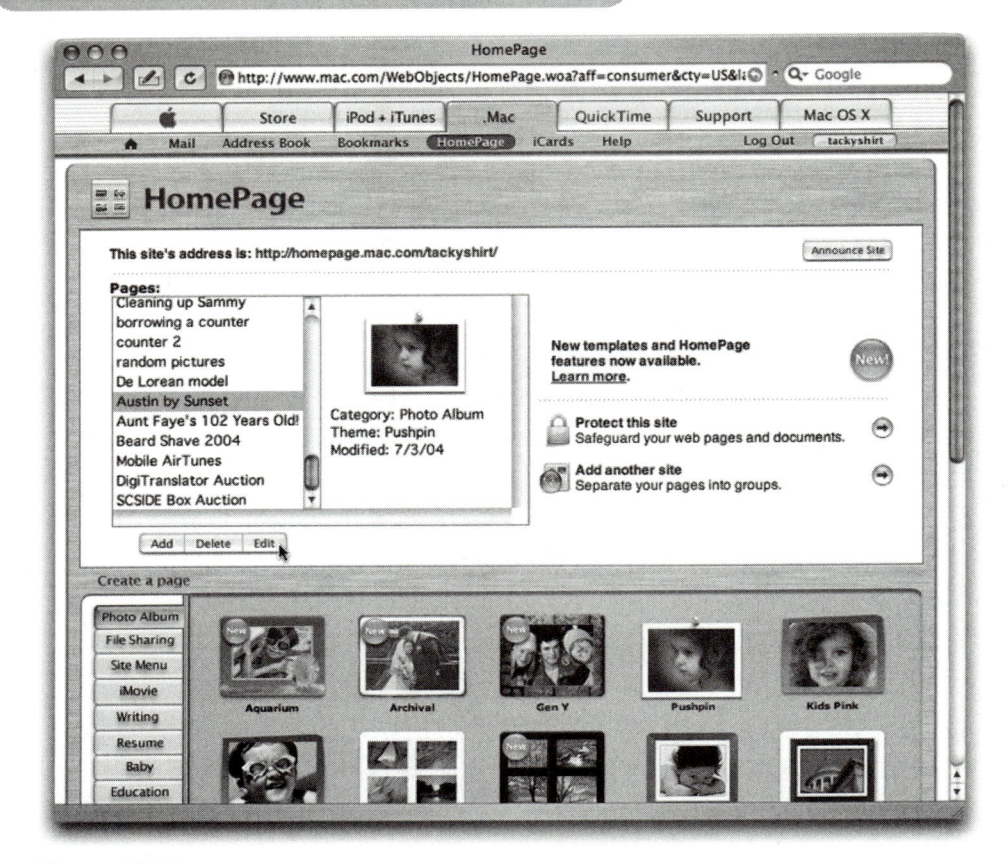

Figure 15-13
The HomePage Web page displays a list of your HomePages

4. **Make the changes you want.** These include the following:

   ▫ **Change the number of columns.** Choose either the 2 Columns option or the 3 Columns option in the Select layout section at the top of the page.

   ▫ **Change the page reference.** When viewed in a Web browser, each HomePage has a reference you can click to navigate to that page. The default text is the page title, but you can modify the reference text by selecting the text and editing it.

   ▫ **Change the page title.** Click the page title and edit the text of the title.

   ▫ **Change the page description.** Click the page description and edit the text of the description.

   ▫ **Change the image position.** Click and drag an image on top of another image to swap the positions of the two images.

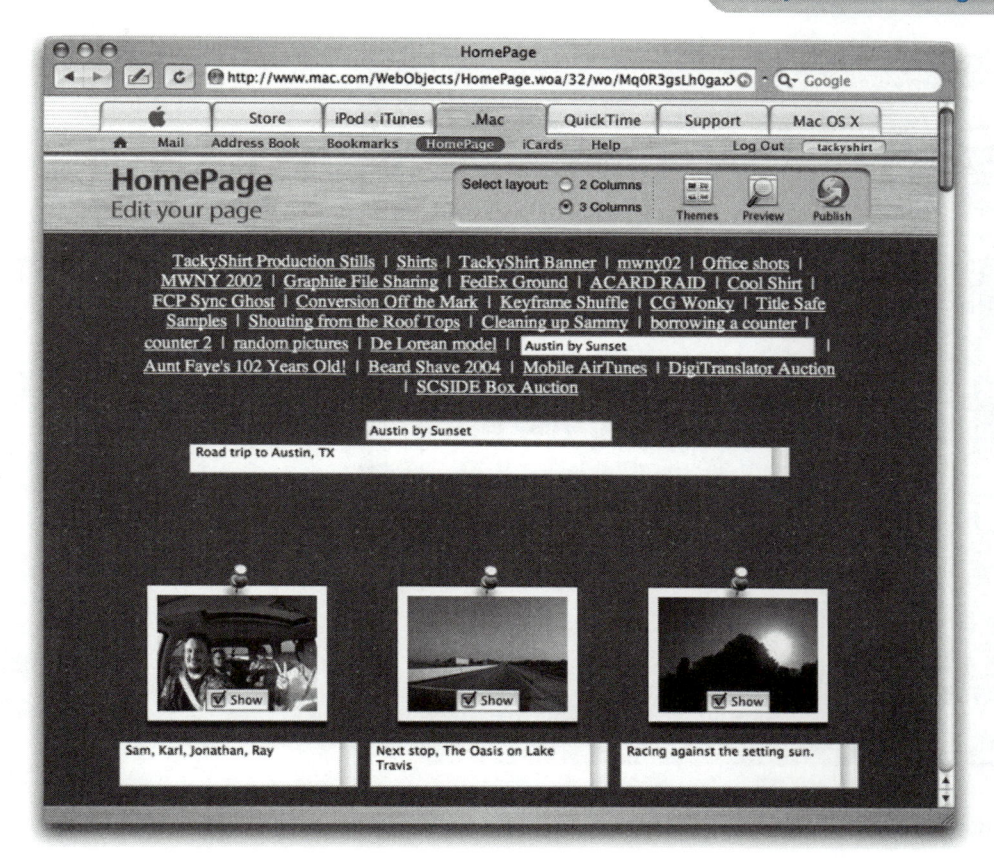

Figure 15-14
Edit a HomePage using your browser

- **Show or hide an image.** Deselect the Show checkbox on any image you don't want visible on the HomePage. Select the Show checkbox on an image to make the image visible.

- **Show or hide the Send Me a Message button.** Deselect the Show checkbox on the Send Me a Message button to hide the button. Select the checkbox to redisplay the button.

- **Show or hide the counter.** Deselect the Show checkbox on the Counter to hide the counter. Select the checkbox to redisplay the counter.

- **Change the theme.** Click the Themes button near the top of the screen to open the Change your theme dialog box (see Figure 15-15), then click the theme you want to use. Notice that there are a few more themes available here than there were in iPhoto.

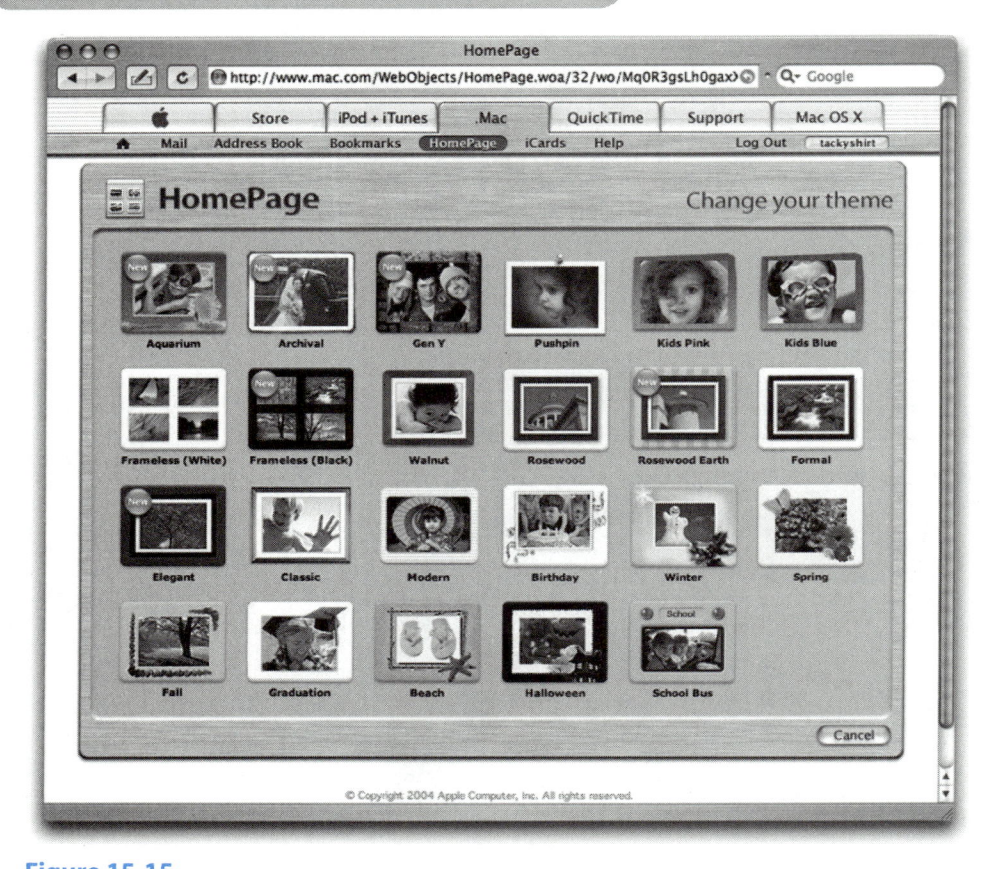

Figure 15-15

Pick a new theme to dress up your photo HomePage

> ▼ **Note**
>
> Once you choose a new theme, you are in Preview mode. To switch back to Edit mode, click the Edit button, which replaced the Preview button.

5. **Click Publish to publish your changes to your .Mac Web site.**

Figure 15-16 shows what the Birthday theme looks like. Isn't Aunt Faye a cutie? You should look so good at 102!

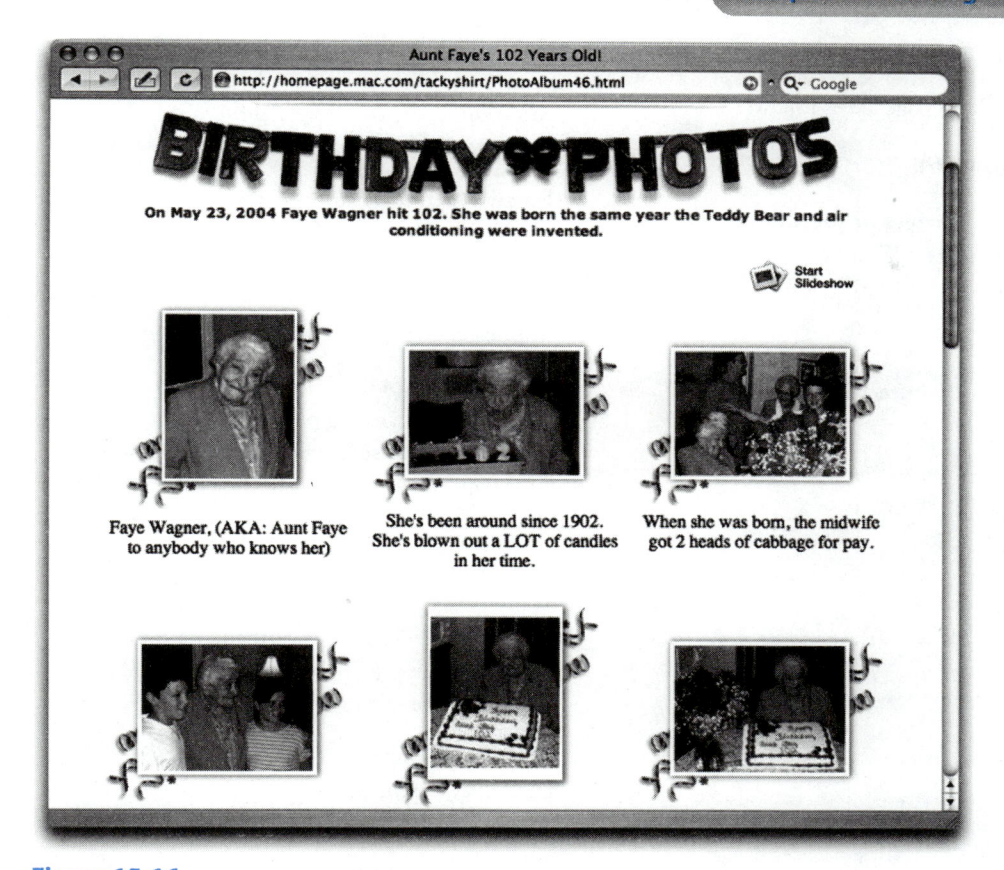

Figure 15-16
A new theme can really make a difference in how a page looks

PUBLISH PHOTOS TO YOUR OWN WEB SITE

HomePage is neato and all, but it's for .Mac members only. That doesn't mean you're left out in the cold if you don't subscribe though. You can have iPhoto build a Web site using the Export feature that doesn't require an annual subscription fee. This method also isn't limited to only 49 pictures, and you have more control over the size and layout of your pictures. On the down side, it doesn't have all the pretty frames and themes of a .Mac HomePage. It's more generic looking, but every bit as functional though. Also, pages that are built with Export don't have the link wad at the top of the page, which is a good or bad thing depending on your opinion of the wad. (They're cute when they're small, but they grow up so fast!)

Exporting a Web page

The basic steps for exporting a Web page are as follows:

1. **Switch to Organize mode.**

2. **Select either the individual images or the album from which you want to create a Web page.**

3. **Choose File → Export.** This opens the Export Photos dialog box.

4. **Click the Web Page tab (see Figure 15-17).**

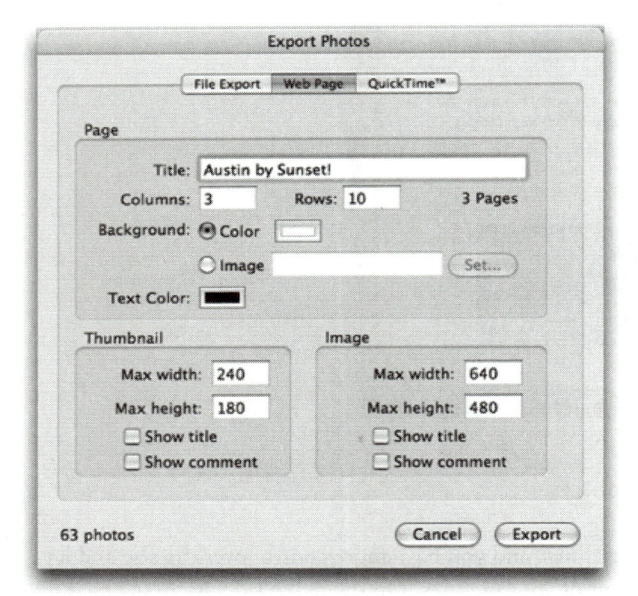

Figure 15-17
Set up your photos to create a Web page with the Web Page tab

5. **Set the parameters described below.** From the Web Page tab of the Export Photos dialog box, you can set the following parameters for your Web page:

   - **Title.** Type the title you want to appear at the top of your Web page. The default title is the name of the current album.

   - **Columns.** The thumbnails are laid out on the page in columns and rows. Type the number of columns you want in the Columns field. iPhoto automatically sizes the thumbnails to fit.

   - **Rows.** Type the number of rows of thumbnails you want in the Rows field. iPhoto will automatically size the thumbnails to fit. Just to the right of the Rows field, iPhoto lets you know how many pages will be generated to fit all the selected images.

   - **Background color.** To set the background color for the generated Web pages, click the Color option, click the rectangle just to the right of the Color option, and then pick the background color from the Colors dialog box.

   - **Background image.** If you'd rather use an image as the background of your Web page, click the Image option. Either type the full path to the image or click the Set button and pick the image from the Open dialog box.

   - **Text Color.** The text on the page consists of the page title, the titles and comments for the thumbnails (if you choose to display them), and the titles and comments for the larger images (if you choose to display them). All text has the same color in the generated page(s). To choose the color, click the Text Color rectangle and pick the color from the Colors dialog box.

 Tip

Make sure the background color and text color are sharply contrasting colors. Otherwise, it's difficult to read the text against the background. Also, if you decide to use an image for the page background, make sure the image is not too complex or busy. A complex image not only makes it hard to read the text, but also increases the time it takes for the page to load because the background image must be loaded in addition to your pictures.

- **Thumbnail maximum width and height.** Type the maximum width and height for the thumbnails in the Max width and Max height fields in the Thumbnail section of the dialog box. This sets the maximum size of the thumbnail even if the number of columns and rows you entered would have allowed the thumbnails to be bigger. As with almost everything else on the Internet, the size is a trade-off: Larger thumbnails show more detail, but take longer to load. Setting either the maximum width or the maximum height automatically sets the other quantity.

- **Show thumbnail title.** If you want the title associated with the image to be shown on the Web page along with the thumbnails, click the Show title option in the Thumbnail section of the dialog box.

- **Show thumbnail comment.** If you want the comment associated with the image to be shown on the Web page along with the thumbnails, click the Show comment option in the Thumbnail section of the dialog box.

- **Image maximum width and height.** Type the maximum width and height for the large-size images in the Max width and Max height fields in the Image section of the dialog box. This limits the ultimate size of the images so that they don't take too long to load from the Internet. Setting either the maximum width or the maximum height automatically sets the other quantity.

- **Show image title.** If you want the title associated with the image to be shown on the Web page with the larger-size image, click the Show title option in the Image section of the dialog box.

- **Show image comment.** If you want the comment associated with the image to be shown on the Web page with the larger-size image, click the Show comment option in the Image section of the dialog box.

6. **Click Export.** When you do so, you must specify where you want to store the files for the exported Web page(s). iPhoto automatically chooses the Sites directory in the user's home directory, but you can navigate to another location, as shown in Figure 15-18.

▼ **Note**

iPhoto borrows the name of the folder you're saving into for the name of the HTML page and supporting folders. Make sure you don't export your files into the Sites folder or Desktop folder because then your files will be named Sites or Desktop as the case may be (see Figure 15-19). It's best to create a new folder with an HTML-friendly name to save into. (See the "HTML Naming Issues" sidebar, later in this chapter.) You can create a new folder from the Save sheet by hitting the aptly named button in the bottom left corner of the sheet.

7. **Select the location where you want the Web page(s) to be located.**

8. **To name the HTML page and all the folders that go with it, type the name in the Go To field.**

9. **Click OK.** This exports all the files necessary to generate the Web page(s).

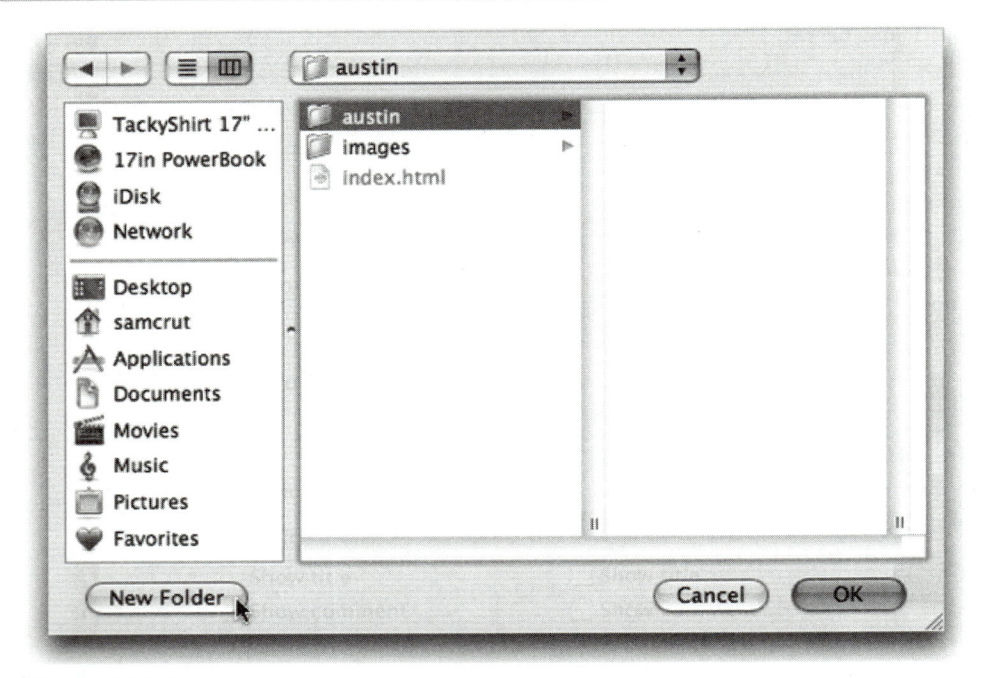

Figure 15-18
Choose where to save the Web page(s) and assorted files

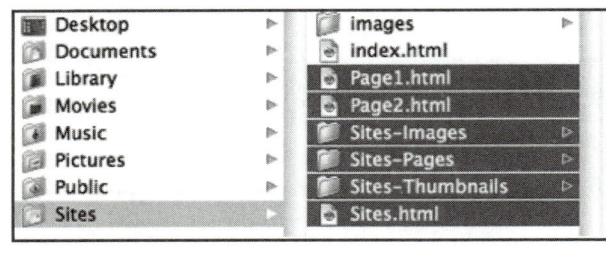

Figure 15-19
Take care where you save; that tells iPhoto what to name the files, and "Sites" has nothing to do with this photo album

Viewing your Exported Web Page

To view the Web page(s) you created, in the Finder, navigate to the location where you just exported the Web page(s). In my case, I built a new folder inside the Sites directory called Austin. In Figure 15-20 you can see the files and folders.

To view the page you built, double-click the HTML file. It opens in your Web browser (see Figure 15-21).

HTML NAMING ISSUES

When you're making folders and files you plan on uploading to a Web server, you have to remember that while you may think that "This" and "this" are the same, many Web servers treat capitalization very strictly. The general rule is that if it's capitalized, it may or may not work when not capitalized, but if it's lowercase, it's golden. Steer clear of the Shift key when you're making folders for your Web pages.

Another thing is the dreaded Space bar. If you put your files into a folder named birthday party, then the link will have to be .../birthday%20party/index.html because most Web servers don't do spaces. %20 is the ASCII code for a space, which is a whole different story a bit off the topic of iPhoto. Suffice to say it's good to skip the Space bar in file and folder names.

Other things to avoid are / \ : , . % and, well, it's easier if you just stick to basic letters and numbers than memorize what is off limits. About the only things that I use outside of abc's or 123's are dash (-) and underscore (_). Those are fine. Anything else is a potential headache.

And now, because I've taught so many people this lesson, I'll just go ahead and tell you now where you're going to mess up. People always remember to avoid symbols but repeatedly forget the other part. Let's get the scolding out of the way preemptively.

BAD USER! *Stop putting spaces in your HTML names!* You were warned! Now go sit in the corner and read quietly.

To see one of the images at a larger size, click the thumbnail and the larger version will come up (see Figure 15-22).

To navigate from the page with the large-size image, you can use the browser's Back button or the following controls on the Web page:

- **Previous.** Moves to the previous large-size image (the image associated with the previous thumbnail).

- **Up.** Moves back up to the thumbnails page.

- **Next.** Moves to the next large-size image (the image associated with the next thumbnail).

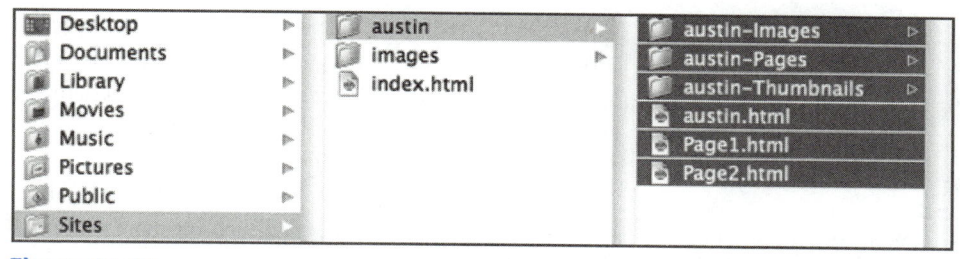

Figure 15-20
Use the Finder to view the files and folders you generated when you built your Web page

Figure 15-21
Open the Web page you built by double-clicking on the HTML file you created when you exported the images

Putting your pictures up on the Web with swanky backgrounds and easy-to-use navigation buttons with just a few simple clicks is pretty much why I have a .Mac account. It's no secret that there are lots of places out there on the Net to get free Web space. Odds are your ISP gives you a slice of storage with your ADSL or Cable Modem account that you may or may not even realize is out there waiting for you. Spots like that are great places to put your Export pages. How to upload them is a bit off *The iPhoto 4 Book* story line because the procedure varies among ISPs, but

Figure 15-22
Click the thumbnail to view the image in its large size

the abbreviated version is: You need to get the addressing info from your ISP, get hold of an FTP program like Transmit or Fetch, and then upload the whole folder to your Web space.

If you haven't tried out a .Mac account, there's no harm in giving it a try. The free trial has a dinky 20MB of disk space, but if you do like the way it's working and you decide to buy the service, your account will just jump up to 100MB just as soon as your credit card clears.

I make HomePage Web pages for about anything from vacation pictures, to eBay auction photos, to just plain silly photos of me shaving off my beard in stages. I put them up. I take them down. You know what it's like? Go to any university dormitory and have a look at the doors. Unless they have stodgy rules against artistic expression, you're going to find almost every door covered in clippings, cartoons, pictures, posters, and other assorted junk. Mine was wrapped with a cut-up hammock net that made a cool

COLLEGE APOLOGY

I'd like to take this public opportunity to apologize to Chris who lived next door to my dorm room. Sorry for renaming you "Stu" just because there were far too many Chris' in the dorm. Also, to anybody who lived on floors 10 through 14 in the general vicinity of my room during the '87–'88 school year: Sorry about blaring AC/DC's *Back in Black* so loud that complaints were made from two floors down. Sometimes you just gotta jam though, I hope you can understand.

web-looking pattern all over the door back when I lived in the dorms at the University of Texas in Austin.

Oh, well, it's like that. It's a public display of your personality, travels, and a few of your favorite things. It's where you express yourself. Expect people to go digging around in those pages and let them know what kind of person you are, or at the very least what kind of person you wont them to *think* you are.

PART V

Working with the iPhoto Book Feature

16

Creating an iPhoto Book Design

In This Chapter

Switch into Book mode • Understand the book-building tools
Choose the type of book you want • Create a new book

When you're ready to turn iPhoto all the way up to 11, you're talking about Book mode. iPhoto has tools that allow you to lay out pictures and text in various templates, and then once your layout is done, you click a few more buttons and the whole bundle gets shipped off to the North Pole where elves spend the off-season turning what you send them into a hardback book, custom printed and bound just for you! I may be off on the elf part, but the woman who delivers my mail is pretty short and she's the last person who handles the book before I get it. Other than that, I never see any other people or machines. You hit the button and a few days later you're published in hardback. If that's not elfin magic, I don't know what is!

I'm going to spend the next, *flipflipflipfilp,* oh wow, four chapters looking at all the nooks and crannies of making books with iPhoto. Trust me. This is a lot easier than spending four years getting one of those fancy degrees most people think you need to get your work printed in a book. Take a look at what all you have to do to make this happen. The first step is to understand the Book mode tools and to create the new book, which is the topic of this chapter.

SWITCH IN AND OUT OF BOOK MODE

To switch into Book mode, select an album and click the Book button at the bottom of the Display panel. Book mode displays a row of thumbnails of the book pages, as well as a larger version of the currently selected page in the Display pane (see Figure 16-1).

Large version of currently selected page

Book page thumbnails

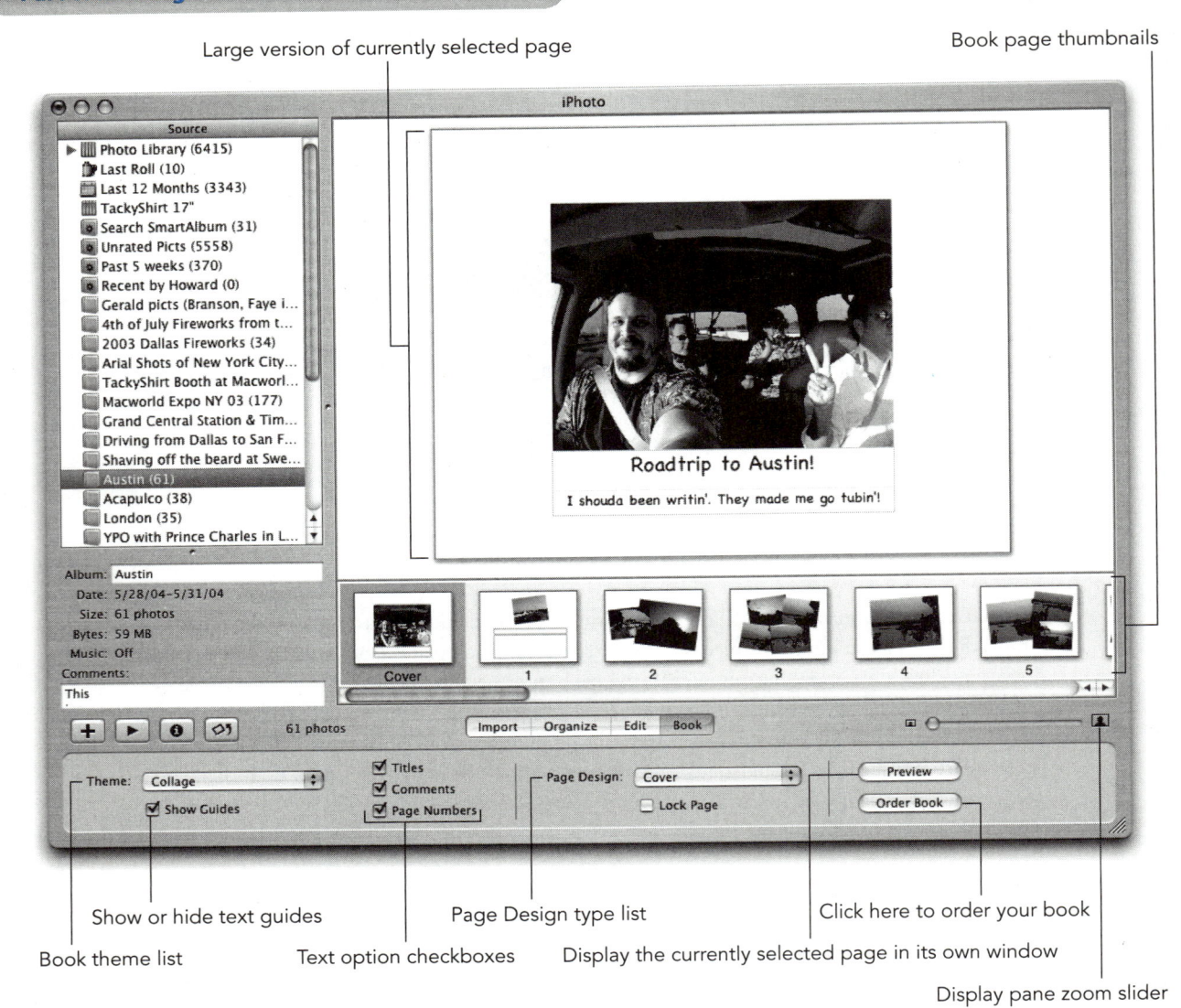

Show or hide text guides

Book theme list

Text option checkboxes

Page Design type list

Display the currently selected page in its own window

Click here to order your book

Display pane zoom slider

Figure 16-1

Use Book mode to build and order a commercially printed book of your photographs

As you build a book, you may need to switch into other modes to perform various tasks. For example, although you can rearrange photos while in Book mode (the book displays the photos in the same order as in the album), it is often easier to do large-scale rearranging in Organize mode. To switch to Organize mode, click the Organize button. Once you have everything in the order you want, switch back to Book mode by clicking the Book button.

 Note

While you can select more than one album for several other features, like printing, for example, that's not the case for making a book. If you select more than one album, the Book button will be grayed out. It's strictly 1 album = 1 book.

You may also need to switch into Edit mode to correct brightness or contrast, crop an image, remove red-eye, and so forth. To edit an image in Edit mode, either select the image in the Display pane (a colored border appears around the image) and click the Edit button, or double-click the image in the Display pane. Once you're done making your edits, simply click the Book button to switch back to Book mode.

UNDERSTANDING HOW TO BUILD A BOOK

As with all the other modes, Book mode has its own set of tools you use to build the book, preview it, and get it ready for printing. You'll want to spend quality time building your book, because the finished product costs $3 per page, with a minimum charge of $30. Because these things ain't cheap, make sure it's right!

All of the Book mode tools are visible in Figure 16-1. To build a book, you'll use the following steps (which are discussed in more detail later in this chapter and in the following three chapters):

BOOK IDEAS ABOUND!

The Book feature of iPhoto has a wonderful charm simply for archiving your highlights through Europe, but the Book has many other uses. A friend of mine was having his 40th birthday and a covert email went out to all of us graphic types to send pictures of Jim for an album they were going to give to him on the big day. They specifically said that sticking his head on someone else's body was exactly the sort of thing they were looking for. (Jim works in television, so most of his friends are wacky, creative types.) The book was a resounding success. Everybody sent in pictures. Some were real and some were, well, disturbingly good fakes that left some people wondering just what kind of clothes he liked to wear when nobody was looking. It was a total riot, and people were fighting over who would get their hands on the book next.

The part that got me snickering was that everybody kept asking where the book was done because it was just too damn cool. I call that a successful party decoration!

1. **Design the basic book theme.** There are a number of these themes, and they control the available page layouts and whether you can display text on a page. I discuss this stuff in this chapter.

2. **Lay out the pages in the book, choosing how many pictures you want on each page and setting the order of the images.** Your selections may be impacted by the resolution of the images — some pages have large images on them and photos placed there may not have enough resolution to print well. I cover this information in Chapter 17.

3. **Enter and edit text in the book.** In some themes you have the picture title available, in others you have the

title and comment field available, and in one (Picture Book) there is no text. You can change some characteristics of the font and color, but not others. You should also make sure to use the spell-checker so your spelling errors are not enshrined forever. This is all outlined in Chapter 18.

4. **Preview the finished book carefully, and then place your order online.** You can also print a copy on your own printer. I explain this printing stuff in Chapter 19.

VIEW BOOK EXAMPLES

There are seven basic book themes built into iPhoto. Each has a purpose for which it works best. You should look at all of them before you try to decide which one will work best for your book project.

The Catalog theme is best for, well, catalogs (see Figure 16-2). It provides room for up to eight images on each page, and allows you to display both the title and the

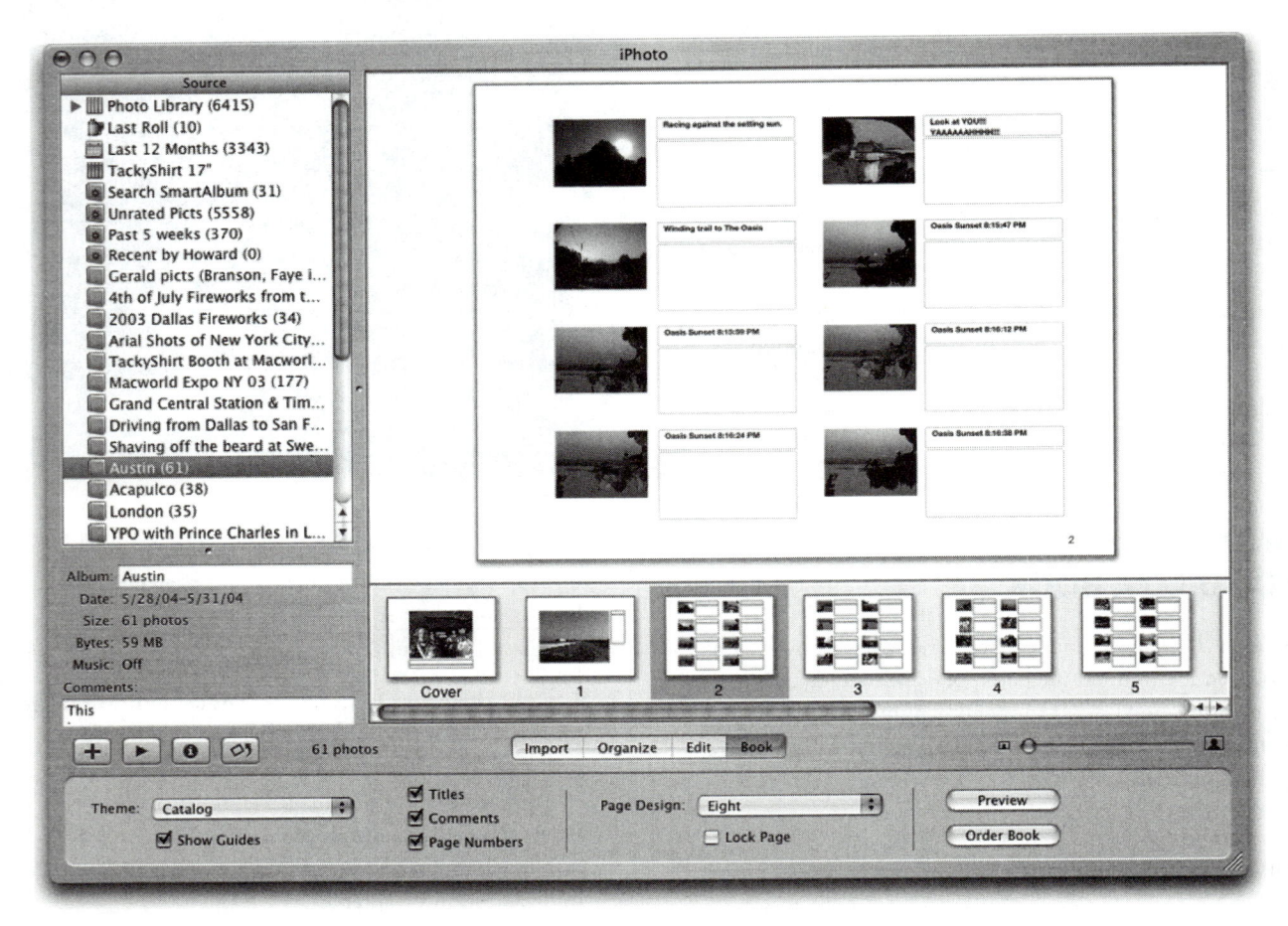

Figure 16-2
Use small images paired with two text fields to describe multiple items on a page in the Catalog theme

comment fields to the right of each image. This theme allows you to use a title page, introduction page, and layouts with one, four, and eight photos.

The Classic theme places images on the page with any text shown below the images (see Figure 16-3). This is useful for vacations or family outings, and is the closest of the

themes to a standard photo album. You can add a title page, introduction page, and pages containing one, two, three, or four photos. The layout of the photo pages changes depending on whether images are in a landscape or portrait position, so you may want to experiment with rearranging the photos in your album to see the different ways iPhoto presents them on the page.

Figure 16-3
Use the Classic theme to place text below images

The Picture Book theme is for pictures (see Figure 16-4). Period. You have no opportunity to add text to any page, so you'll probably want to add an introduction-style page (as described in Chapter 18) to explain what the pictures represent. In addition to the title page and introduction page, you can create pages containing one, two, three, or four photos. This layout uses more of the page for photos than any other layout.

Note

Although you can turn off the Titles, Comments, and Page Numbers text field options, this does not make the text space available for the pictures. It simply leaves empty space on the page where the text would have been.

Figure 16-4
The Picture Book theme gives you lots of pictures, but no text

The Portfolio theme is for people who need a portfolio of their work (see Figure 16-5). In addition to the cover and introduction pages, you can use photo layout pages that show one, two, three, or four photos each. This theme shows the pictures at the largest size possible, but also includes text fields (both picture title and comment) down the left side of the page.

▼ **Note**

Unfortunately, the Portfolio theme allows the least amount of space for the picture title. If the title is too long to fit in the text box, iPhoto displays the triangular yellow warning icon, which is visible in Figure 16-5. If this icon appears, you'll have to shorten the title. See Chapter 18 for more information.

Figure 16-5

The Portfolio theme shows your pictures big and bold, but also provides text fields for describing them

The Story Book theme is the most informal of the book themes. The photos can appear at crazy angles and even overlap each other (see Figure 16-6). The placement of the photos can change radically with the photo size and orientation (landscape or portrait).

You have no control over the angle or overlap, so you'll need to preview the results of this theme very carefully to ensure that important parts of a picture are not covered by an overlap. Your only option if something important is hidden is to rearrange the pictures or choose a different page layout and hope for the best. In addition to the title page, this theme includes a special Introduction page (see Figure 16-7) with three photos and two text blocks. The Introduction page of most other themes only allows text.

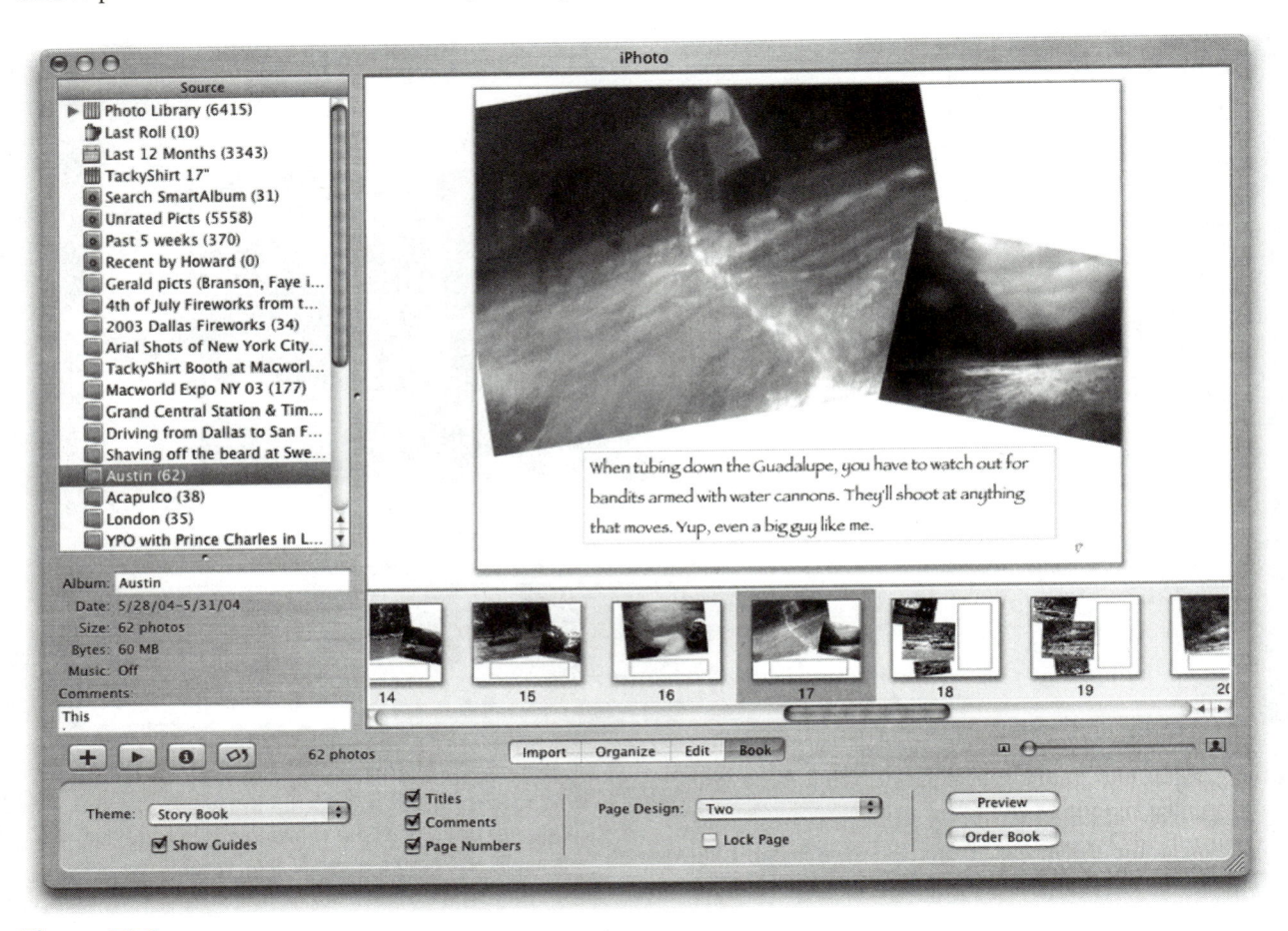

Figure 16-6
The Story Book theme is a crazy quilt of images, but it can be really fun to use

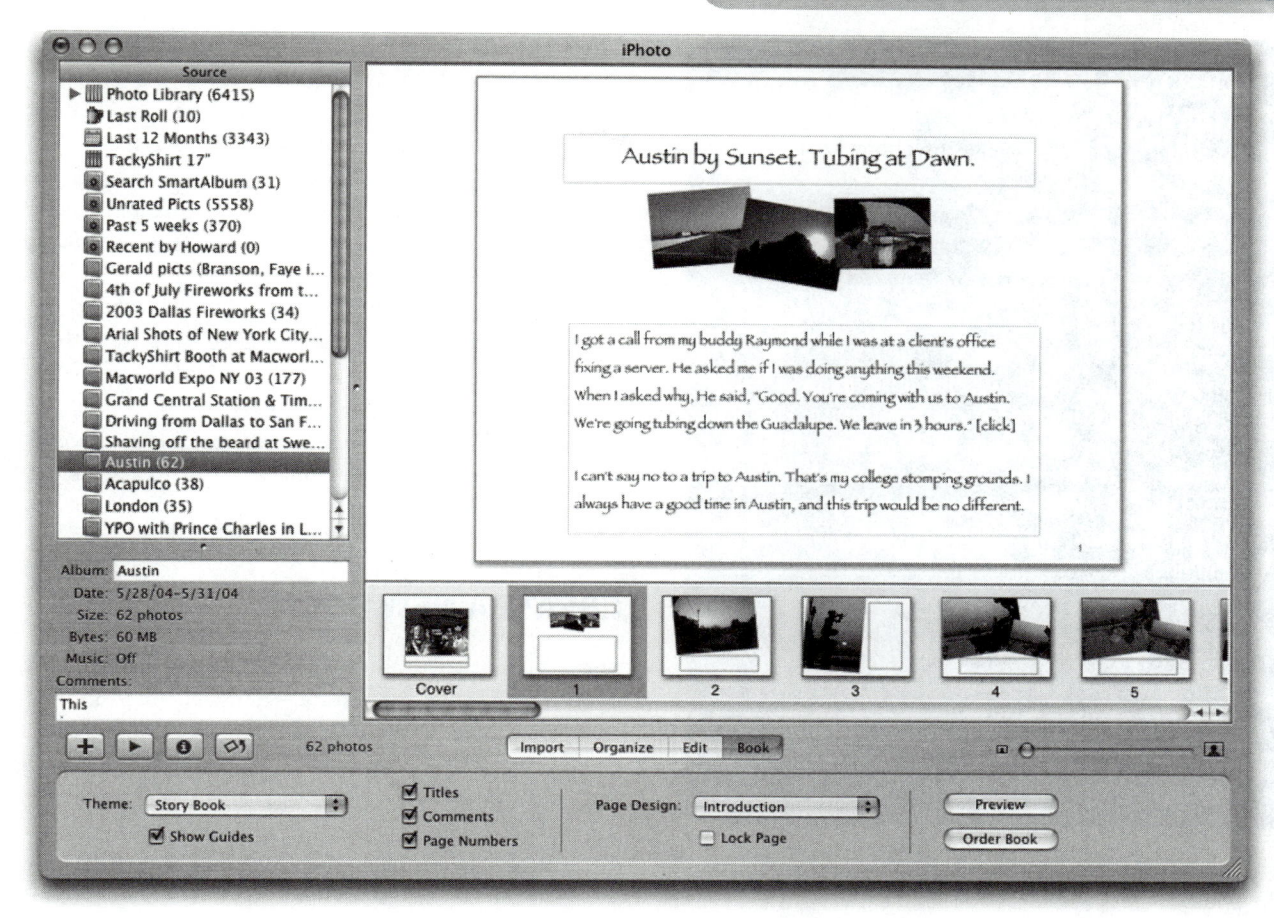

Figure 16-7
The Introduction page provides a place to show a cross section of your photos, as well as plenty of text to describe the book

PERSONALIZED FAIRY TALE

Want to be crowned the best parent ever? Here's what you do.
Take your kid's favorite fairytale and start looking for pictures that fit the story. Make sure you get some pictures of your daughter all dolled up as the Princess or your son flexing his muscles for a nice Prince Charming. Just whatever you do, *don't tell him or her what you're doing!* Got a poodle? A nice close-up makes him the Big Bad Wolf. Headed to Grandma's house? Put in a picture of Grandma's real house. Get creative with it. Go ahead and rewrite the story to work in their favorite stuff. Maybe the wicked stepmother took away his GameBoy, or it's Spiderman who saves Little Red Riding Hood. The thing here is to make it just for them.

I guarantee that it will be their favorite bedtime storybook *ever!*

Of course, if the story takes our hero to Grandma's house, you might have to have two books made so Grandma can have one for herself.

The photo layout pages can contain one, two, or three images. This theme also includes a special End page that can contain up to three photos. Each of the photo layout pages and the End page has a single large text block. The placement of this text block depends on the picture layout and is set by iPhoto.

▼ Tip

Try to set up the End page so that it includes at least two photos; three is even better. If the End page contains only a single photo, you are spending $3 to print a mostly empty page. To add photos to the End page, you'll need to either reduce the number of photos on an earlier page or add more photos to the end of your album.

The Year Book theme offers a grid of photographs much like the Catalog theme (see Figure 16-8). You can place 1, 2, 4, 6, 8, 12, 18, 20, or 32 images on a page, and each image has both the title and comments field available either to the right or beneath the image, depending on the layout. As with the other themes, you can also add a Title and Introduction page.

The Collage theme is similar to the Story Book theme in that the pictures are at crazy angles (see Figure 16-9). In addition to the Title page and Introduction page, which contains a cockeyed photograph as well as two text blocks, you can create pages with one, two, three, four, or six photos. You can also create a one-image page with a text block to the right of the image.

CREATE A NEW BOOK

Once you've readied your library and reviewed your layout options, you are ready to create your own book. And, creating a new book is very simple. Use the following steps:

1. **Select the album containing the images you want to use.** Consider creating a new album just for the book because you'll probably want to change the order of the images to appear the way you want in the book. You may also want to choose just a subset of the photographs, perhaps adding photos to and removing photos from the album to improve the book layout. Both of these tasks are easier with a custom album, and using a custom album offers you the freedom to experiment without affecting the base album.

2. **Organize your pictures using Organize mode.** You will have the opportunity to change the order of the pictures while you're in Book mode, but doing the overall layout is easier in Organize mode where you can see thumbnails of a large number of pictures at once.

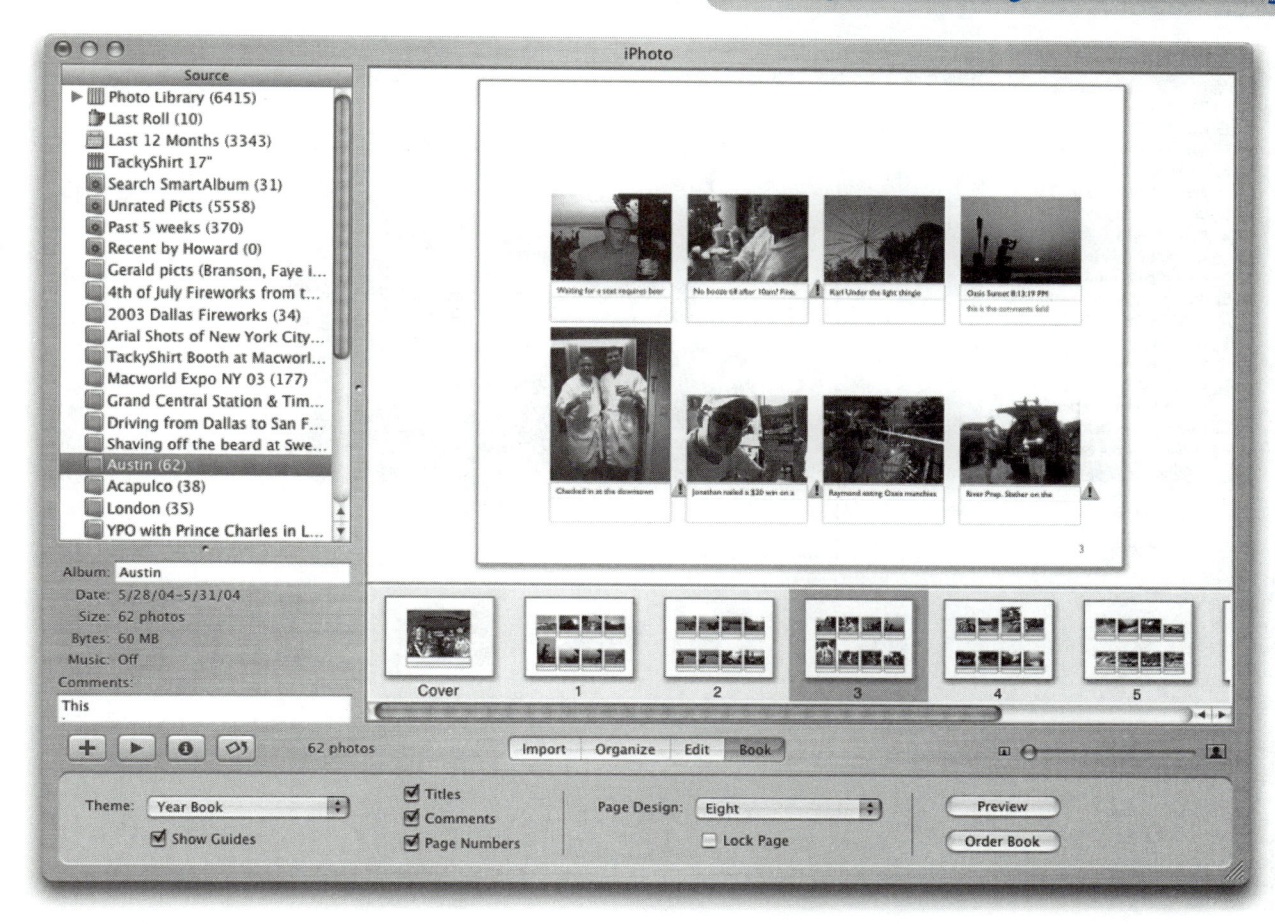

Figure 16-8
The Year Book theme places your images on a regular grid

3. **Click the Book button to switch back to Book mode.** This basically just dumps everything into a book template, using different page styles throughout. Now it's time to get into the design-decision phase.

DESIGN THE OVERALL BOOK

Once you are in Book mode, choose the theme from the Theme pop-up list. Give some thought to which theme you want to use, because although you can change themes after you start laying out the book, all custom text (such as the text on the Title page or Introduction page) is lost when you change themes.

Figure 16-9
The Collage theme is an informal set of photos at wild angles

▼ Tip

If you really feel the need to experiment with a different theme, duplicate the album (select the album and choose Duplicate from the contextual menu) first. That way, if you decide that you like the new layout better, you can at least copy and paste text from the original book into the new design. And if you decide you *don't* like the new layout better, you can just discard the new album and you haven't lost anything.

The next decision you have to make is which text fields you want available on the pages. Click the Titles, Comments, and Page Numbers options to turn the text fields on and off. Some themes (such as the Picture Book theme) don't show the text fields even if you select these checkboxes. The spaces for the available text fields are shown on the page using light blue lines. These are called *guides,* and they don't print. If you find them distracting, deselect the Show Guides checkbox. However, you may have trouble figuring out where the text fields go if the guides aren't there as a reference.

The different kinds of books you can crank out of iPhoto can be used for all sorts of things, and just to show you I mean it, I'm going to grab five random words out of the dictionary and show you how to use them in a book. Anybody care to lay odds on me picking *swimsuit*?

Okay, here goes...

[several minutes pass]

Okay, minor snag. I can't for the life of me find a dictionary anywhere in my house. That's fine. I've got something better. I'll be making my selections from my autographed copy of Douglas Adams' *Life, the Universe and Everything*. Here goes...

Interrupted, ground, smacked, squatted, and (wait, odd, I got *smacked* twice...[poke]) *was.* (was?!?)

(At least I didn't pick *the!*)

Let me brainstorm a bit... things that interrupt, cellphones, panhandlers, sales people, electricity, oooh.

- **Interrupted** — A comical photo exposé showing several different ways to keep occupied when the power goes out. I'm seeing lots of flash photographs, startled looks, candles, maybe some looting depending on what city you live in.

- **Ground** — Easy. White sands of New Mexico, red dirt of Hawaii, black sand beaches also of Hawaii. It's scenic landscapes of all sorts of interesting geology.

- **Smacked** — Easy again. Action shots of a boxing punch, a woman slapping a man, anything that has

somebody caught in the moment of bodily contact that makes their face distort in priceless ways.

- **Squatted** — Oh, like you could do that one without mentioning poop? Beautiful pets and the messes they leave behind? I guess you could do an urban social commentary book showing squatters living in abandoned buildings. Maybe a book of beautiful people in really uncomfortable poses. Hey, I didn't say your books had to be for *everybody*.

- **Was** — Before and after shots of vintage cars. Show one picture of a rusted-out old Chevy and then get a picture of a pristine restoration of that model car. Frame them identically, from the same angle for matching shots. Frankenstein the cars together in Photoshop. It's an expression on the ravages of age on the world around you.

The best bit about these books is that if you want to make them, you can just go shoot the stuff and make them and the best part is that it'll probably be cheaper than most of the coffee table books out there. Then there's that little bit of having your own coffee table book on your coffee table. If that doesn't spark some conversation, check for a pulse.

At this point you've just been looking at the broad strokes. Now you're going to get into some finer detail of working on the individual pages that will make up your book.

Oh, wait.

- **The** — Pictures of dozens of outdoor signs cropped down on just the word ***the.*** Neon, colors, lots of fonts, textures, rusty beat up metal, wood, painted on the sides of old brick buildings from the 20s... that's just crazy enough to work!

Laying Out Pages of the Book

In This Chapter

Choosing a page layout • Designing pages in the book
Rearranging the page order • Arranging photos in the book

When you have your theme picked out, it's time to lay this stuff out on the pages. Each theme has several page templates to choose from. Variety is the spice of life, so I suggest you use several different page layouts if for no other reason than to make it look like you did *even more* work on the book.

Don't worry. I won't tell them how easy it was to make the book if you don't want me to.

DESIGN PAGES IN THE BOOK

Now comes the fun part: laying out the individual pages of the book. You can see a scrolling list of thumbnails of all the book pages across the bottom of the Display pane. If you click on a page thumbnail, a larger version of the page appears in the Display pane. To control the magnification of the page in the Display pane, click and drag the Zoom slider.

 Tip

Need to edit one of the pictures on the page in the Display pane? It's easy: Just double-click the picture. iPhoto automatically switches into Edit mode and opens the picture. (iPhoto opens the picture in your external editing application if you defined one). Make any changes you need and click the Book button to switch back into Book mode.

You can also preview a page in a separate window (see Figure 17-1) by either double-clicking a page thumbnail or selecting the thumbnail and clicking the Preview button. The controls in the separate window work as follows:

- To change the size of the preview page window (and the page it displays), simply click and drag the lower-right corner of the window.

- To move through the pages, use the left and right arrow buttons or type a page number into the field in the upper-left corner of the window. You can also use the Left and Right arrow keys.

- To turn the text guides on and off, click or unclick the Show Guides checkbox. As described in Chapter 18, adding and editing text in the Preview window rather than the Display pane has its advantages.

The first page of the album is the Cover page (see Figure 17-2) and you can't change that — all templates have a Cover page. The Cover page is a good place for a general photograph that characterizes the album; the Cover page also includes two large text fields. I discuss how to type in and customize those fields in Chapter 18.

Figure 17-1
Preview a page in a separate window to view it bigger than the Display pane allows

Figure 17-2
The Cover page is always the first page in a book — and every book must have a Cover page

 **Tip**

If you want the Cover page image to appear elsewhere in the album, you'll need to duplicate the image in Organize mode.

You may decide to include an optional Introduction page (see Figure 17-3). Except for the Story Book and Collage themes, an Introduction page does not include any images, but it does include several text blocks you can use to describe the book.

 Tip

You are not limited to just one Introduction page; you can use as many as you want, using them to split up different sections of the book.

To configure a page, click a page thumbnail and select one of the page styles from the Page Design pop-up list. You can experiment with different page styles; the photos rearrange automatically as you pick styles that display more or fewer pictures. iPhoto reflows the images on the pages

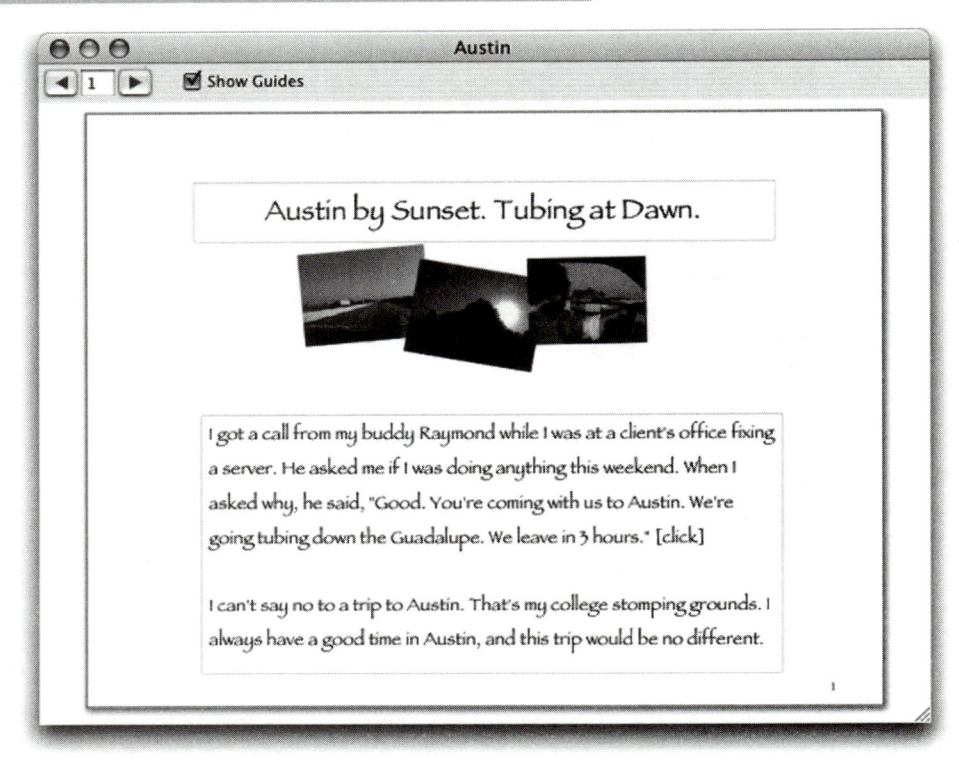

Figure 17-3
Put text on the Introduction page to describe your book

WHEN PICTURES BLEED

In publishing, *bleed* is a term used for when the picture sits a little bit over the edge of the printed page so the image is perfect when the edges are trimmed away. When your picture is right up to the edge of the page, like you see in the Picture Book, Portfolio, and Story Book layouts, the picture actually prints past the edge of the page, and then a paper cutter slices away the excess. This insures that you'll have no unsightly thin white strip along the edge of the page distracting you from your pictures. Odds are you probably would never have noticed anything was missing, but just in case you spot that $\frac{1}{16}$ of an inch was missing from the cutting edge, they're not shortchanging you: That's the way printing has been done for ages.

Oh, and if you hear someone saying the term *full-bleed*, that means the image uses every bit of the page, all the way to the edges without any empty margins. The Picture Book theme is an example of what full-bleed pages look like. By contrast, odds are your inkjet printer always leaves some sort of white border.

to the right of the current page as you make these changes, which brings up a very important point: You should work on your album *from left to right*. That way, as you get each page looking the way you want, you won't jeopardize the layout of that page by making changes in pages to its left. If you always work from left to right, you won't get any nasty surprises when you pick a different page layout.

 Tip

> If you want to apply the new page style to the currently selected page as well as all pages to its right, hold down the Option key when you apply the page design.

 Note

> iPhoto assumes the pictures have a 4" x 3" aspect ratio for the purposes of laying out the pages. If the picture has a different aspect ratio, you'll probably end up with more white space on the page than you'd like.

ARRANGE THE PHOTOS ON THE BOOK PAGES

The photos in a book are displayed in the same order as they appear in the album. The reverse of that also stands true. Changing the order of the pictures in the album will rearrange the pictures in the book layout. Changing the order of the pictures in the book layout will rearrange the pictures in the album. If you have any reason to want the album to stay in it's current order, duplicate it before you start juggling pictures in the book.

If a page contains multiple images, you can rearrange the images on the page by clicking and dragging an image from one "slot" to another (see Figure 17-4), which rearranges the other photos on the page. You can drag images between the slots on the currently displayed page, but you can't drag images from one page to another page, *which is a bit of a drag*. (Oh man, I have to be punished for that one.)

MAKE IT TELL A STORY

When you're arranging your photos in the book, try to make somewhat of a story line out of it. That doesn't mean you have to show all of your pictures in the order they were shot. Just try to make them have some sort of order that makes sense. If you're making a book from a weekend trip, you may toss in a driving picture that says "The next day we drove down to the river to go tubing." The picture can be *any* driving picture, even if it's from day one and you went tubing on day three. The point is to make a nice "story" that people will want to keep flipping through. Nobody will really hold it against you if you rearrange history a little in the pursuit of a better story.

 Note

> To rearrange images between pages, you'll need to switch to Organize mode and drag and drop the thumbnails.

 Tip

> As you begin to drag an image, the border of the source image turns yellow, and as your cursor moves over the other image slots, the current target area turns magenta. Nothing happens on a single-photo page. It takes two to... tango... or something like that.

You can drag entire page thumbnails left and right to move that whole page sooner or later in the book. You can also rearrange the pages in the album by clicking and dragging the page thumbnails below the Display pane. As with clicking and dragging the images on a page, this rearranges the images on the album. It's kinda like moving icons around in the Mac OS X Dock.

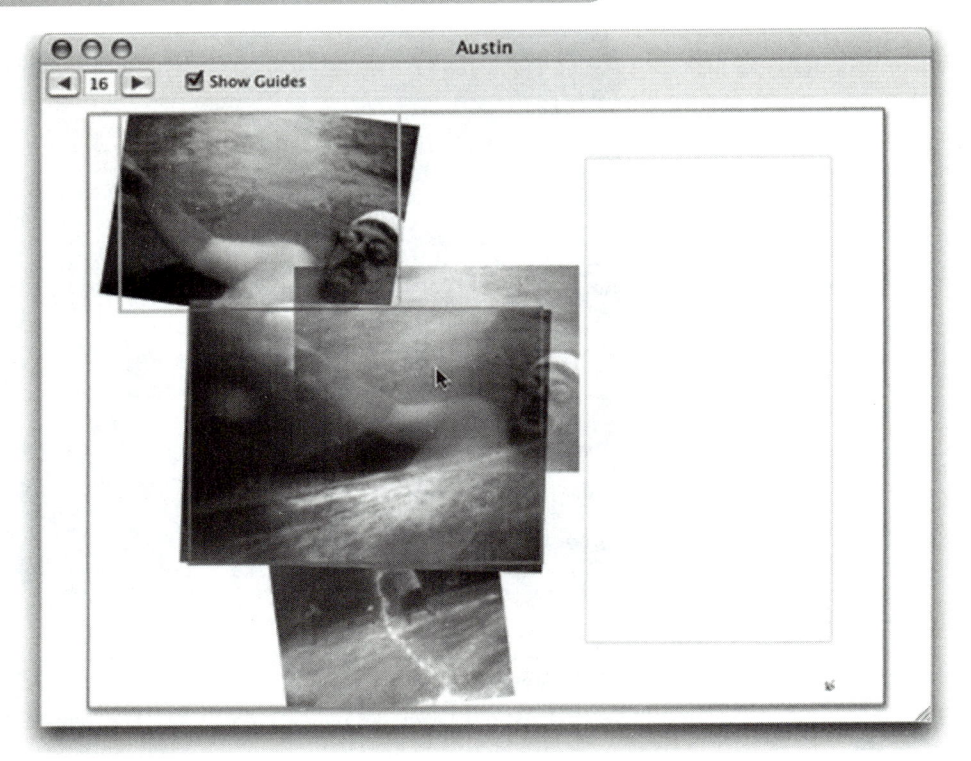

Figure 17-4

Drag and drop an image from one slot on the page to another to rearrange the images on the page (and in the album)

You can lock the design of a page by clicking the Lock Page checkbox. This means that the images on that page won't move around even if you rearrange images in Organize mode or change the design of a page to the left of the locked page. After a page is locked, you can't change the page design of that page, nor can you drag and drop images from one spot to another on the page. You can move the whole locked page.

You need to be *really* careful about unlocking the page. Basically, a locked page is holding the order of the images despite the album "thinking" the order should be different.

Heck, you can even delete pictures from the album in Organize mode and they'll stay on the locked page. If you unlock the page, that page *and all the pages to its right* rearrange themselves to match the album order. This can create quite a mess. It's a fun little experiment to try out and see what happens, but if you're going to use the lock, and you decide to unlock that page later, you might cause a photo explosion, or more like a picture avalanche I guess.

And really, you shouldn't need to lock pages if you just design the pages from left to right as I advised earlier.

HANDLE WARNINGS WHILE BUILDING A BOOK

As with printing, you may find that a picture has too low a resolution to print in the page slot where you put it. If the picture resolution is too low, you get the yellow triangular icon warning, as you can see in the rightmost image in Figure 17-5.

Figure 17-5
If you don't have enough pixels to print at the selected size, iPhoto warns you

If this happens while you are building a book, you must move the image into a smaller slot. The three ways you can achieve this are to drag the image to a smaller slot on the same page; move the image to a smaller slot on a different page (by rearranging the order of images in Organize mode); and choose a different page design that displays more photos so that the image is in a smaller slot.

Another alternative is to add a matte to the picture. To do that, follow these steps:

1. **Open the image in another image editor (such as Photoshop Elements).**

2. **Add a border to the image.**

3. **Resave the image.** The overall size of the image (which now includes the original image and a border) is larger.

The original image is still there and it still prints small in the book, but the added border keeps the image from printing too large and thus appearing pixilated.

▼ Note

I don't recommend using a Smart Album as the basis for a book. For one thing, the contents of a Smart Album can change without warning, which can foul up your layout and your book. In addition, because you can't rearrange the images in a Smart Album manually in Organize mode, you don't have much control over the order of images in the book. And under the heading of "It's Probably a Bug," if you rearrange the pages of a book based on a Smart Album (or move the photos around on a page), you'll find that the images in the Smart Album are now sorted in an unfathomable way in Organize mode. Specifically, if you choose View ➡ Arrange Photos, you'll find that the Manually option is now checked but grayed out.

These book pages really give you a chance to look at how your pictures work together. I was tinkering with some pictures of a trip to London. I had a picture of me looking out the window, a picture of scenery blurring past, and a picture of the inside of a train car that was totally empty except for me of course. Individually they were just okay, but together on the page, you can see that I was alone on the train ride looking out the window at a rather cold and dreary day in England. Separately the pictures weren't nearly as emotional as they were when I saw them together on the page (see Figure 17-6).

Figure 17-6
Strength in numbers: Put pictures together that complement each other

Page layout is more than just dropping stuff into the slots. Look at your pictures as little groups and try to arrange them where they work together in creative ways. In that train picture, I'm looking out the window and the scenery shot is to the right of my picture so it's along my eye line. It sort of feels like I'm looking out through the window in the next picture over. Oooor maybe it's 2:30 in the morning right now and I'm just tired and getting a bit overly emotional about the whole thing. Naaaah!

So, in the previous chapter I covered the setup for the whole book. This chapter was the setup for the individual pages. Next up you zoom in on the individual captions that go with each picture. You're halfway done now.

Adding Text to Dress Up Your Book

In This Chapter

Entering text to describe your photographs • Editing the text
Setting the text format (font and style) • Setting the text color
Checking your spelling

I'm perfectly secure enough to admit that when I was a kid, I tended to lean towards the books with the most pictures come book report time; but *some* words had to be in there or the teacher would have been on to my cunning — and what I thought was original — ploy. iPhoto makes the kind of books I was always looking for back then. The Themes give you various text fields for you to create the captions and story that go along with your pictures. It's not usually too big of a writing project, so don't worry if you're the sort to panic on the essay test. (All right! Fine! I was *that kid* too.)

Depending on what theme you select, half the work may be done already: Some of the themes bring over the picture titles, and some of the themes start from scratch.

The text you put in your book gives readers the context so they know what they're flipping through; think about not only what people can see in the picture, but also what they can't, such as "...and we were freezing our tails off!" or "These flowers smelled just like butterscotch." You get a chance to paint the rest of the picture with the words you use here.

ENTER AND EDIT TEXT IN THE BOOK

You can enter and edit text to add titles and explanations to your book. In general, adding and modifying text works much like it does in a word processor (including copy and paste), but some limits exist because iPhoto is not a full-fledged text application.

To enter or edit text in a text field, simply click in the field and type, or select the text and make your edits. If you edit the text fields in the Display pane, iPhoto has a disconcerting habit of zooming the view to 100%, and then zooming back out when you are done editing. I find this annoying and not entirely reliable: The zoom level that iPhoto returns to is not always the one I had set prior to starting my text edit. Thus, doing your text edits in the Preview window is much better (double-click the page thumbnail to open the page in the Preview window).

The Cover and Introduction page styles provide text blocks you can type in. The Cover page style provides a title and subtitle, and the Introduction page style provides a title (which can be different from the Cover page title) and a large text field for explanatory text.

All the book styles except for the Picture Book provide text fields for the individual picture title, comment, or both. These are the same fields you see in Organize mode (in the Info pane). You can edit these fields in Book mode, but realize the changes are reflected in Organize mode as well. As I said, the fields are the same, so changing them in Book mode changes them everywhere else. If the text you type won't fit, you'll get the triangular yellow warning icon alongside the text field (see Figure 18-1). The amount of text you can use varies wildly depending on which theme your book is using, what font, and what page design. You have to edit the text to shorten it, and because the text box doesn't scroll, you'll be editing blind.

ADDING A LITTLE #"•%! TO YOUR TEXT

If you are going to spend money to print your book professionally, you want to make sure your text is as good as it can be. That means using real bullets instead of asterisks and other little touches. Here is how you can get iPhoto to display and print the special characters you'll need:

- **Use true quotation marks.** Rather than using straight quotes ("), use true "curly" quotation marks. To create the left quote, press Option+[. To create the right quote, press Shift+Option+[.

- **Use true apostrophes.** Like straight quotes, straight apostrophes look amateurish. To create a left apostrophe, press Option+]. To create the right apostrophe, press Shift+Option+].

- **Use an em dash.** An em dash is a single dash that is approximately double the length of a standard dash (it looks like —). An em dash is often used to set off a comment from the rest of the sentence. To create an em dash, press Option+Shift+- (dash).

- **Copyright your work.** If you want to place a copyright notification on your book, you can create the copyright symbol ((c)) by pressing Option+G.

- **Use real bullets.** If you need a bulleted list, don't use asterisks. Instead press Option+8 to create a real bullet (•).

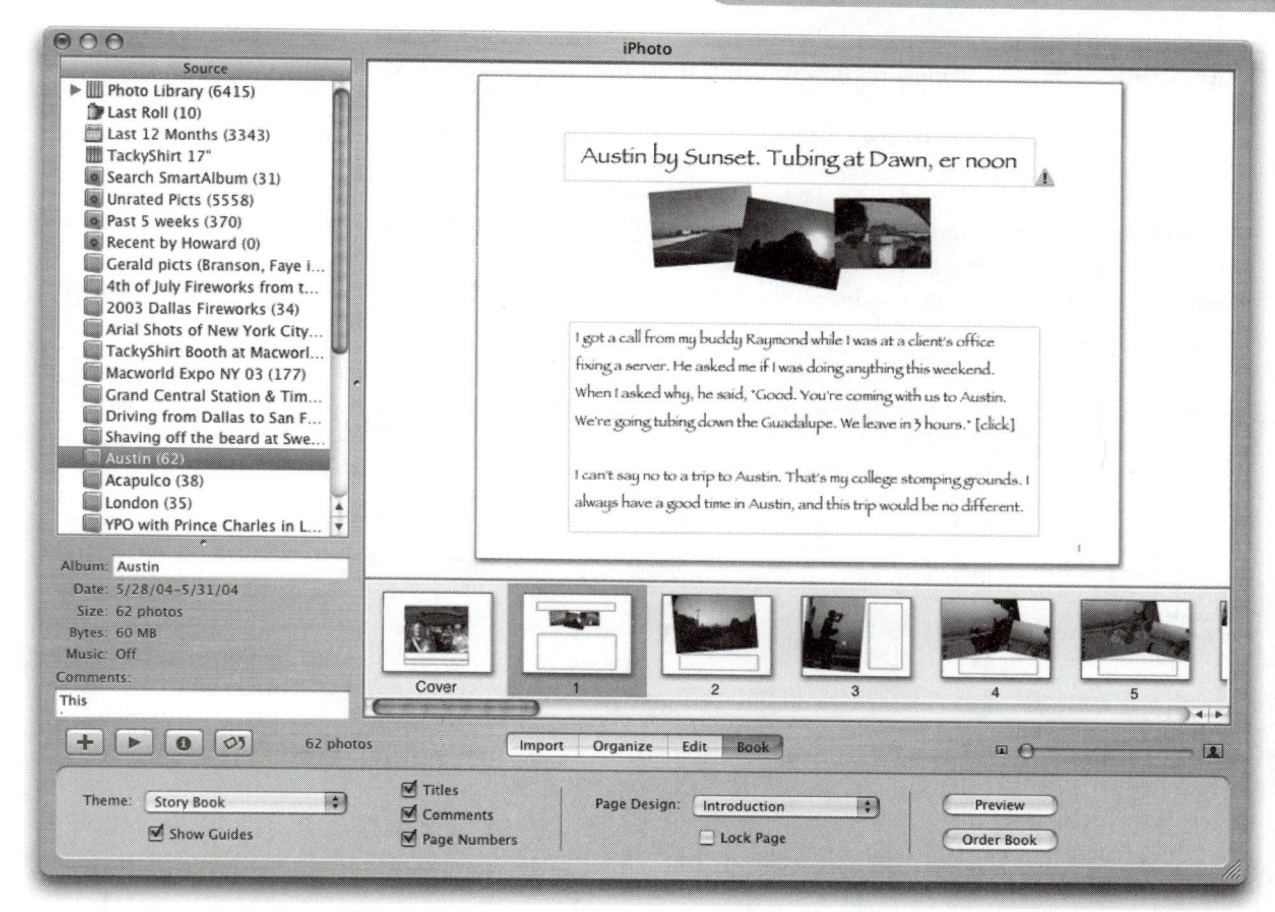

Figure 18-1

When there is too much text, you'll get the warning icon

CHANGE THE TEXT FONT AND STYLE

The font used for your captions and descriptions is a major character in this whole show. It can help change the whole tone of a book. I've been dealing with fonts in one capacity or other for about as long as there's been a Macintosh line of computers. I came through the evil later half of the 80s when everywhere you looked you would see amateurs using eight different fonts on a single page flier. We all

learned a good lesson in those days. Simple is good. Fortunately, iPhoto protects you from font deliria because you can only use a very few fonts. You can't make every caption a different type style. The settings are for *all* of the captions in the book or *all* of the descriptions. You'll never be able to subject readers to more than two fonts on a page and four fonts for the entire book. At times this may seem like a drag, but this limitation falls into the same category as child-resistant pill bottles. It keeps people who don't know any better from doing something horribly wrong.

You can change the text family and typeface for text in a book. To do so, follow these steps:

1. **Choose Edit → Font → Show Fonts, or right-click on the text field and choose Font → Show Fonts from the contextual menu.** iPhoto displays the Font dialog box (see Figure 18-2).

2. **Select the text field you want to change.** You can select a title field on the Cover page or Introduction page, subtitle on the Cover page, the large text block on the Introduction page, or an image title or comment field.

3. **Choose a font family and typeface (Regular, Bold, Italic, and so on) from the Font dialog box.** Don't bother choosing a size because you can't change the size of the text. The font window is a standardized

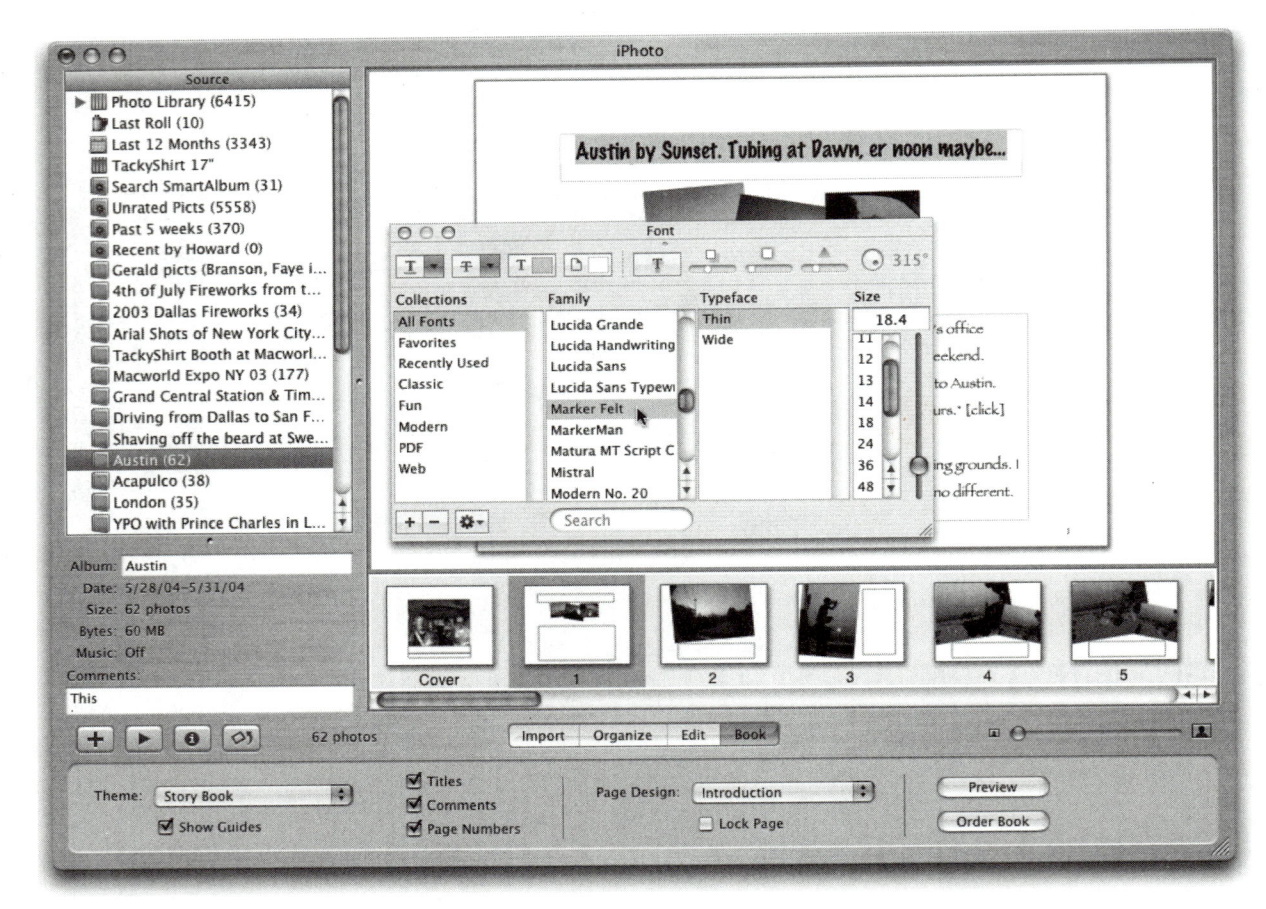

Figure 18-2

Use the Font dialog box to change how your text looks

Mac OS X element that's used throughout the system. I guess they never put in a bit of programming to let applications gray out the traits that aren't currently available. iPhoto changes all the text in the selected field — and in every other field like it — to the selected family and typeface.

The ramifications in Step 3 are fairly far-reaching. In general, you can't just select some text and change the family

and typeface for the selected text. For example, if you select some of the Cover page subtitle text and change the font, *all* the text in the subtitle field changes. Figure 18-3 shows what happened when I selected just the first word in the Introduction page text block (which was Regular typeface) and made it the Bold Italic typeface. As you can see, all the text changed, not just the selected word!

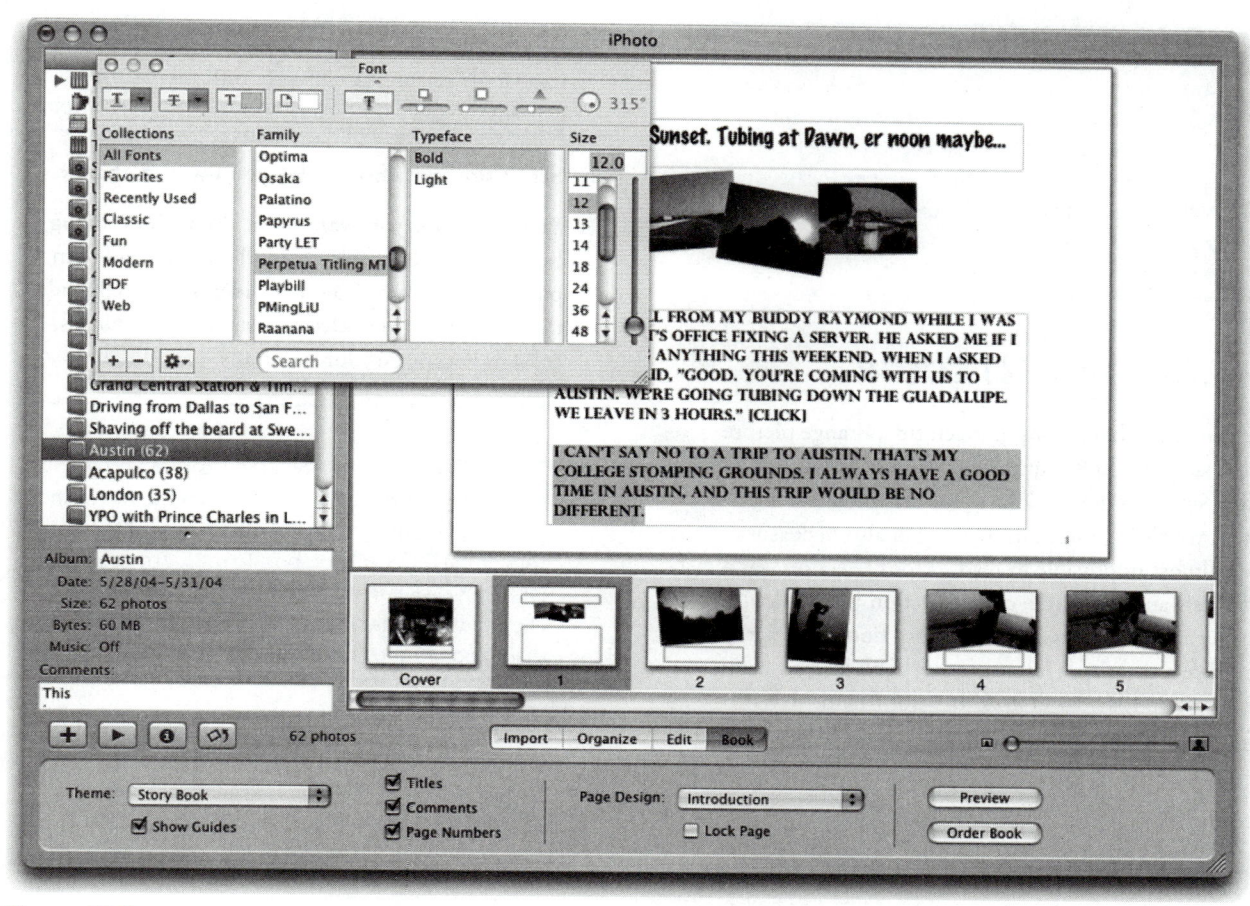

Figure 18-3
You can select only a portion of the text, but it all changes

The other major ramification of Step 3 is that if you change the family and typeface in an image title or comment, the family and typeface in *all* the other titles (or comments) throughout the whole book change as well.

 Note

The only exception to the "everything changes" rule is that if you select some text and choose the Underline style from the text contextual menu, only the selected text is underlined.

 Tip

You can copy a family and typeface from one text field to another. To do so, select some text and choose Edit ➜ Font ➜ Copy Font. Then select the target text and choose Edit ➜ Font ➜ Paste Font. As with using the Font dialog box, changing the font (even by using Paste Font) changes all the text in the text field and in all the fields like it.

CHANGE THE TEXT COLOR

Your book can have a bright green title, orange picture captions, and purple comments if you really want it to. Again, simple is good. Color can draw your attention to certain words for emphasis. Color can also make something almost impossible to read. If font selection was a child-resistant pill bottle, color selection is a bottle of Patron tequila with its easy-open cork bottle. In fact, you can make every single letter in your book its own color, but if you do that, I will *never* be your friend.

You can change the color of selected text easily. To do so, follow these steps:

1. **From the text contextual menu Choose Font ➜ Show Colors, or select Colors from the Extras pop-up list at the bottom of the Font dialog box.** iPhoto opens the Colors dialog box (see Figure 18-4).

 Note

There are actually five different tools you can use to choose a color, selectable from the buttons across the top of the Colors dialog box. You can use any of the tools you are comfortable with, but I'll just talk about the default color wheel (the leftmost button).

2. **Select the text whose color you want to change.**

3. **Pick the color you want from the Colors dialog box.** Pick the base color from the wheel, and then pick the brightness from the slider on the right side of the dialog box. The selected text actually changes color as you make your selections.

 Tip

To save a custom color for later use, click and drag the swatch from the color bar (across the top of the Colors dialog box) to one of the squares at the bottom of the Colors dialog box. To reuse that color later, just click it in the Colors dialog box. You can click and drag the bottom-right corner of the Colors dialog box to show more custom color boxes.

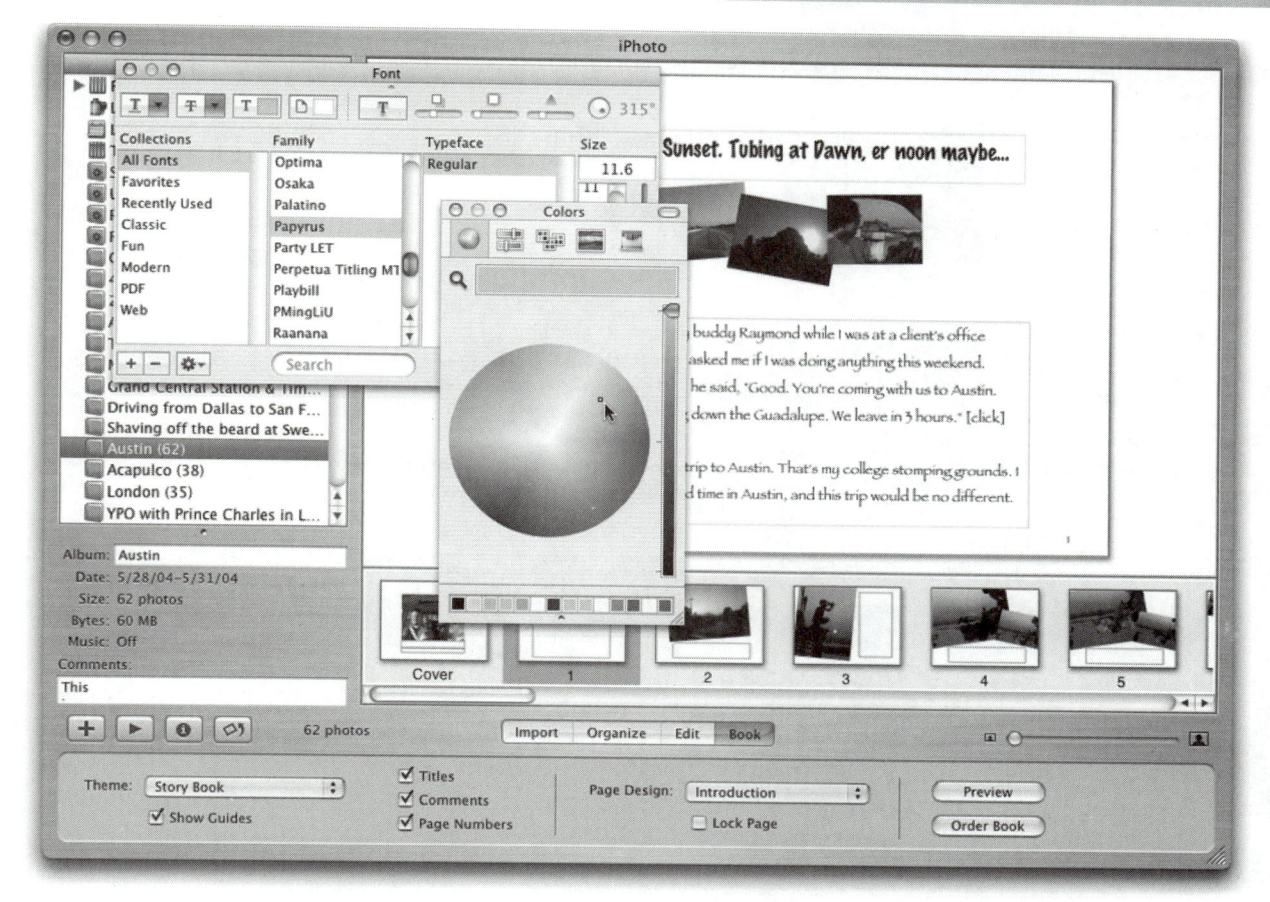

CHECK YOUR SPELLING

Nothing says "amateur" like mispeeelled words in your professionally printed book! To avoid looking silly (and providing amusement to the recipients of your book), use the built-in spell checker.

Using the Spelling dialog box is the first way to check your spelling. Right-click inside a text field and choose Edit ➜ Spelling ➜ Spelling, or choose Spelling ➜ Spelling from

the text contextual menu. iPhoto opens the Spelling dialog box (see Figure 18-5).

The first misspelled word is underlined in red. If the Spelling dialog box has any suggestions for correcting the misspelled word, the list of potential replacement spellings is presented in the scrolling Guess list. The Spelling dialog box provides you with the following options:

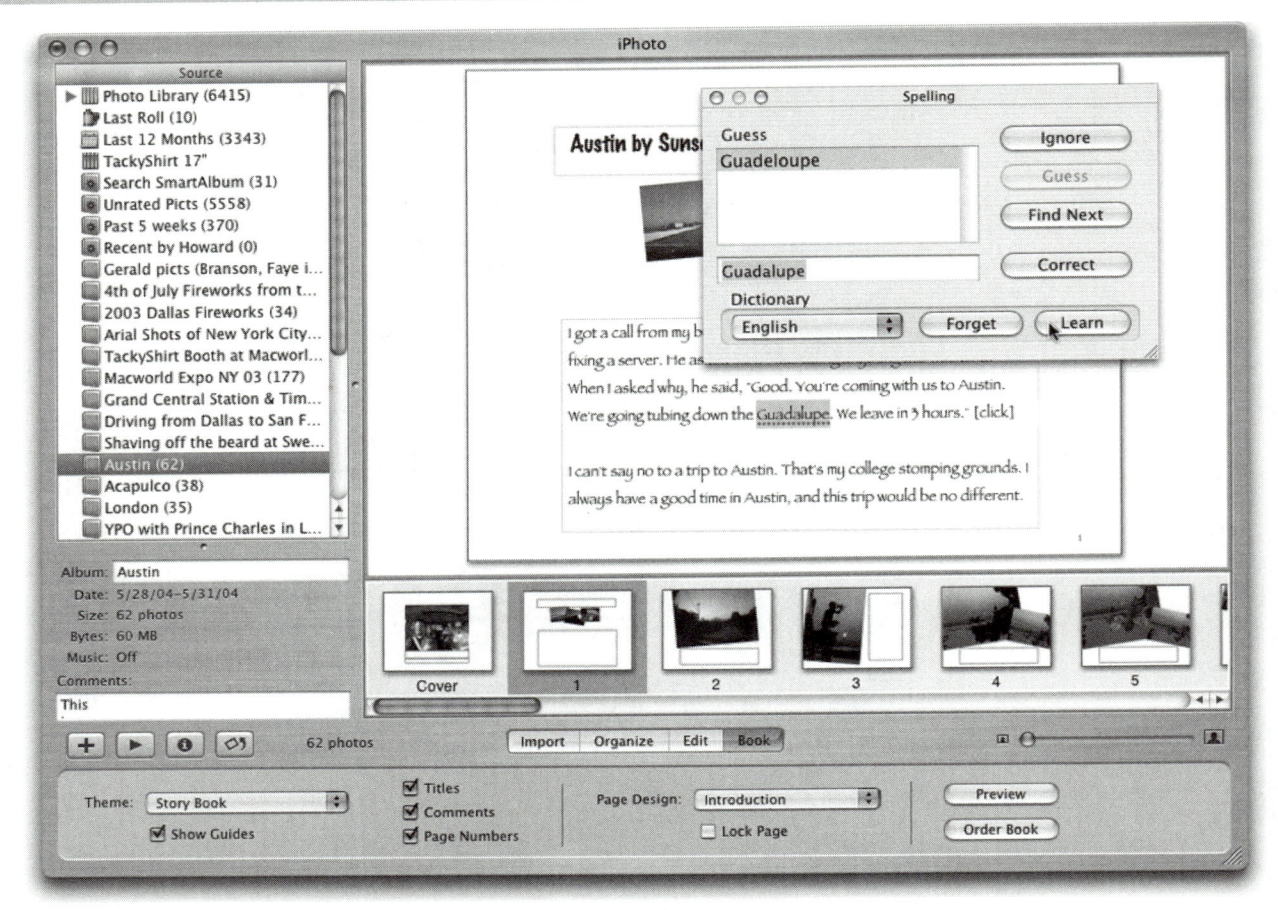

Figure 18-5
Step through spelling errors with the Spelling dialog box

- **Ignore.** This option ignores the misspelling and won't flag it as a misspelling if it encounters the word again. Unfortunately, this option is almost useless because the spell checker ignores the misspelling only until you switch to the next text box. If it finds the same misspelling in another text box, you have to choose Ignore again.

- **Find Next.** This option skips the currently selected misspelled word and moves to the next misspelling.

- **Correct.** If the Guess list contains the spelling you want to use, click the word and then click the Correct button to replace the misspelled word. You can also type the correct spelling into the text field just to the left of the Correct button and then click the Correct button. Finally, you can simply double-click the word in the Guess list to replace the misspelled word.

- **Learn.** The spell checker flags any word that is not in the dictionary. Thus, it may flag words that are not actually misspelled, such as Guadalupe in Figure 18-5. To add a word to the dictionary so it won't be flagged as a misspelling in the future, click the Learn button.

The second way to check spelling is to right-click in a text field and choose Edit ➜ Spelling ➜ Check Spelling, or choose Spelling ➜ Check Spelling from the text contextual menu. The first misspelled word is underlined in red. Control+click the misspelled word to open the contextual menu for that word (see Figure 18-6).

Make one of the following choices from the contextual menu:

- **Choose a suggested correction.** The first few entries in the contextual menu show any suggestions that the spell checker has for correcting the misspelled word. If one of these suggestions works for you, simply click it to replace the word.

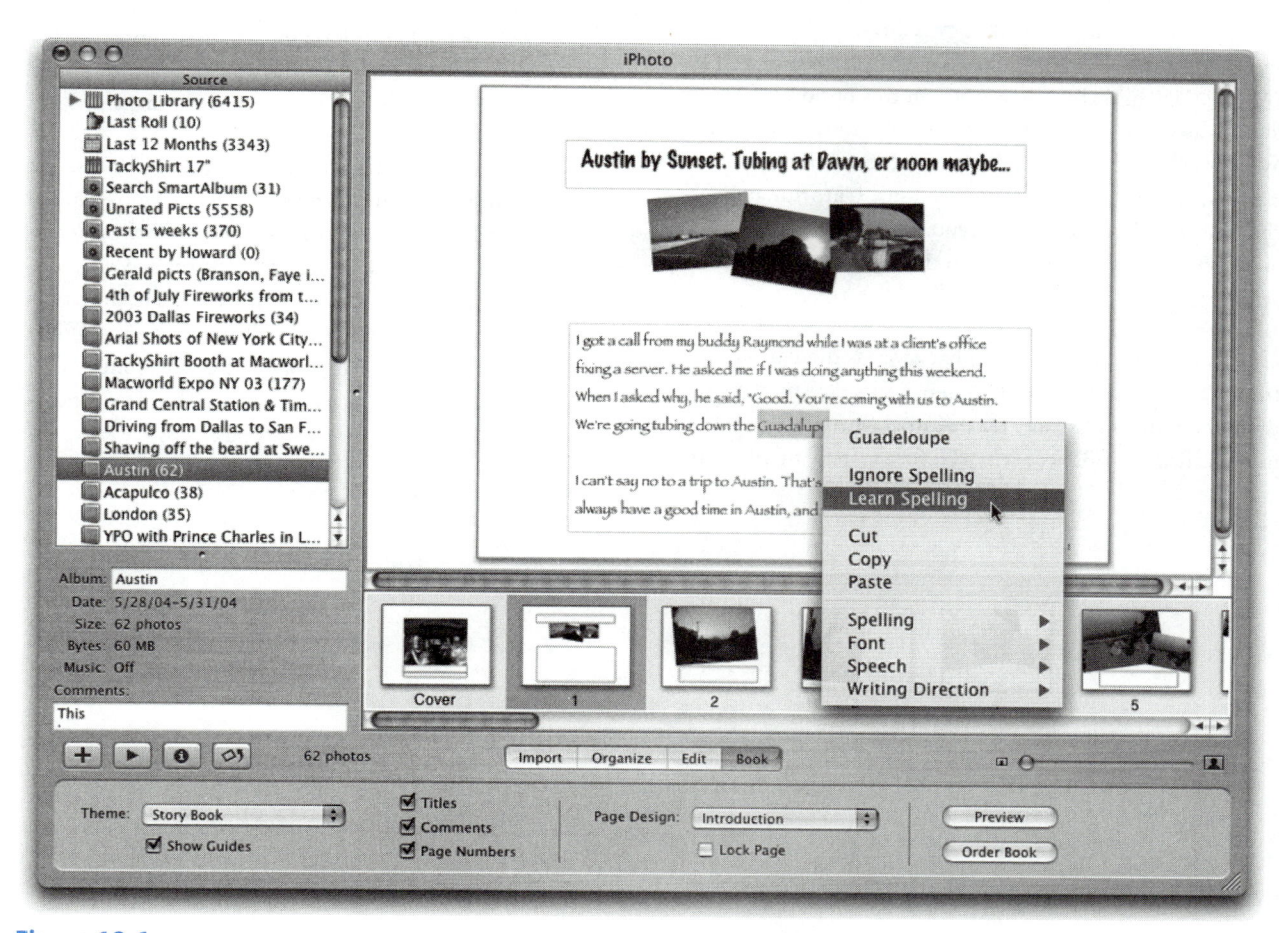

Figure 18-6
Make a selection from the text contextual menu to correct a misspelling

- **Ignore Spelling.** This option ignores the misspelling and won't flag it as a misspelling if the spell checker encounters the word again in the same text box. Unfortunately, this option only ignores the misspelling until you switch to the next text box.

- **Learn Spelling.** This option adds the word to the dictionary so the word won't be flagged as a misspelling again in the future.

The final way to check spelling is to right-click in a text field and choose Edit ➜ Spelling ➜ Check Spelling as you type, or choose Spelling ➜ Check Spelling as you type from the text contextual menu. When this option is selected, as you type, iPhoto immediately underlines in red any misspelled words. Use the text contextual menu as described earlier to make any corrections. Unfortunately, iPhoto keeps Check Spelling as you type active only until you move to the next text field, so this option is of limited usefulness.

Fonts and styles and colors — what more is there to say? Hmmm.... Oh, there's one. Different fonts take up very different amounts of space. One of my favorite caption fonts is called Carl Barks Script. Unfortunately, that font is enormous. It has a very cool comic book dialog look that's really easy to read, but I can only get about 15 characters in any title box. Arial Narrow on the other hand is a skinny little fella. Condensed fonts let you cram more text in a space, but on the down side, they tend to be a bit more difficult to read.

Don't underestimate the simple elegance of your basic Arial or Helvetica. The point of a font is foremost to be read. There are hundreds of fonts out there that are very cute, but utterly illegible. Sure a nice, scripty font is good for a wedding picture book, but look for one that's not all style over substance. If you can't read the text without straining your eyes or your brain, then move on to another font.

There are various Web sites out there dedicated to fonts. These days there are many, many free fonts to choose from if you dig around on the Internet a bit. Some of them you have to pay for, but are only barely worth the price; however, some others are quite nice. Just remember the lessons of the late '80s and don't get too caught up in silly novelty fonts. While that might work for a title page, if you use those fonts on your photo captions, you won't get arrested, but I can't guarantee that someone won't throw the book at you.

19

Previewing and Printing Your Book

In This Chapter

Previewing your book • Printing the book on your printer
Ordering a book online • Creating your own book designs

You've picked your theme. You've laid out your pictures. You've added text. Now it's time to double-check your work and shoot it off to the printer elves so they can make it into a book you'll cherish until you're old and gray, or grayer for those of you... well, you know who you are.

You're about to drop at least $30 on this thing, so have a look at some ways to preview your book before you commit to spending that money. I'm sure there's nothing worse than having everybody say, "Um, now when you say here that you '...headed off to conquer the misty' um, who's this Misty?"

"Misty *mountain!* I meant 'misty mountain,' but a word got cut off because I didn't check my work (sigh)."

You can see where that may get annoying many years later when your grandkids are flipping through your old picture books.

Of course when you're looking over your proof, you may come to the conclusion that the theme pages haven't given you just what you're looking for. If that's the case, in this chapter I'll show you how to make custom theme pages of your own; but before you get too excited, let me warn you that to do this you'll be exiting the light and fluffy world of the iApps and entering the spooky realm of the Developer Tools. You can do some cool stuff in there, but if you're not careful where you step, you may find yourself deleting iPhoto and reinstalling it so you can get back to a happier place.

I'm going to be perfectly upfront about that Developer Tool business. It's so utterly removed from the pleasant mood of the rest of this book that I'm recommending that my mother skip over it. She's never going to try any of the material in that section and there's no point in her going cross-eyed while I go on about things that make her cross-eyed. Mom, I'll tell you when to jump ahead. Okay?

PREVIEW THE FINISHED BOOK

As I mentioned in the previous chapter, you can preview any page by selecting the page thumbnail and clicking the Preview button or simply double-clicking the page thumbnail. You can also preview the "finished" book — and you should, before spending a lot of money on printing. This print preview is very similar to the Preview button experience, but it takes the book outside of iPhoto to the Preview application. The two are very similar looking, except that the iPhoto preview shows you the warning triangles while the Preview application doesn't.

To preview the book, follow these steps:

1. **Make sure you are in Book mode.**

2. **Choose File ➡ Print to open the Print dialog box.**

3. **Click the Preview button.**

iPhoto creates a preview of what the finished book will look like and displays the result in the Preview program (Figure 19-1). This process can take a few minutes, so be patient while the preview is generated.

After you finish reviewing your pages and close the Preview application, the preview of the book is lost. If you'd like to preserve the preview of the book, you can create an Adobe Acrobat (PDF) file. To do so, follow these steps:

1. **Choose File ➡ Print to open the Print dialog box.**

2. **Click the Save as PDF button.**

3. **Type in the file name and click Save.**

iPhoto creates the PDF file that you can view using either the Preview program or Adobe Reader.

 Note

You can get Adobe Reader for free from www.adobe.com/acrobat/. There's a button on the page that says "Get Adobe Reader". Click it. It'll be fun.

IPHOTO BOOK TO GO

When you click that Save as PDF button, you get a nice compact icon on your hard drive. The icon is compact looking, but the file is *huge*. It's certainly not something you'd want to email to somebody.

If you have a PowerBook, showing people your book while you're on the road is great. The book fits nicely on a CD if you want to snail mail it to someone or take it to the office to show your co-workers. I'm warning you, though: Showing co-workers something like this is probably going to bring on a flood of "Ooh!" and "Aaahh!" followed by you being grilled about how you managed to create something like that.

After that, you'll end up in a Mac-versus-PC discussion, and those tend to end badly. Nip it before things get that far: Just tell them you used iPhoto, and maybe that you really love what you can do with it. Don't ever say your Mac is *better* than their PC. It's not our superiority that makes them hate us, but that Mac users are always flaunting it.

Austin by Sunset. Tubing at Dawn.

They forced me to go to Austin! Well, maybe not forced...

Figure 19-1
Preview the book to make sure it looks exactly the way you want

PRINT THE BOOK ON YOUR PRINTER

You can print either a portion of the book or the entire book on your printer. Although you don't get the professional binding and nice cover, the quality of the photographs may actually be better than when you order a book online — if you have a really, *really*, **really** good printer that is. Mostly, it's just cheaper and faster than sending it

out. Some books might demand professional, hard-backed pampering, while other books may only really need an inkjet printout and four staples down the side of the page. I'm thinking that little Timmy's book of close-up macro shots of the inside of his nose might fall into the staple worthy camp. Maybe just one staple... or a reusable paperclip.

To print the book or any part of it on your printer, follow these steps:

1. **Switch to Book mode.**

2. **Choose File → Print to open the Print dialog box.**

3. **Click the Advanced Options button to set the properties of your printer (such as the type of paper and print quality).** The Advanced Options version of the Print dialog box also enables you to choose the range of pages to print by choosing Copies & Pages from the pop-up list (Figure 19-2). Since that figure is already *showing* the advanced properties, the button you see says Standard Options, which will take you back to the standard sheet.

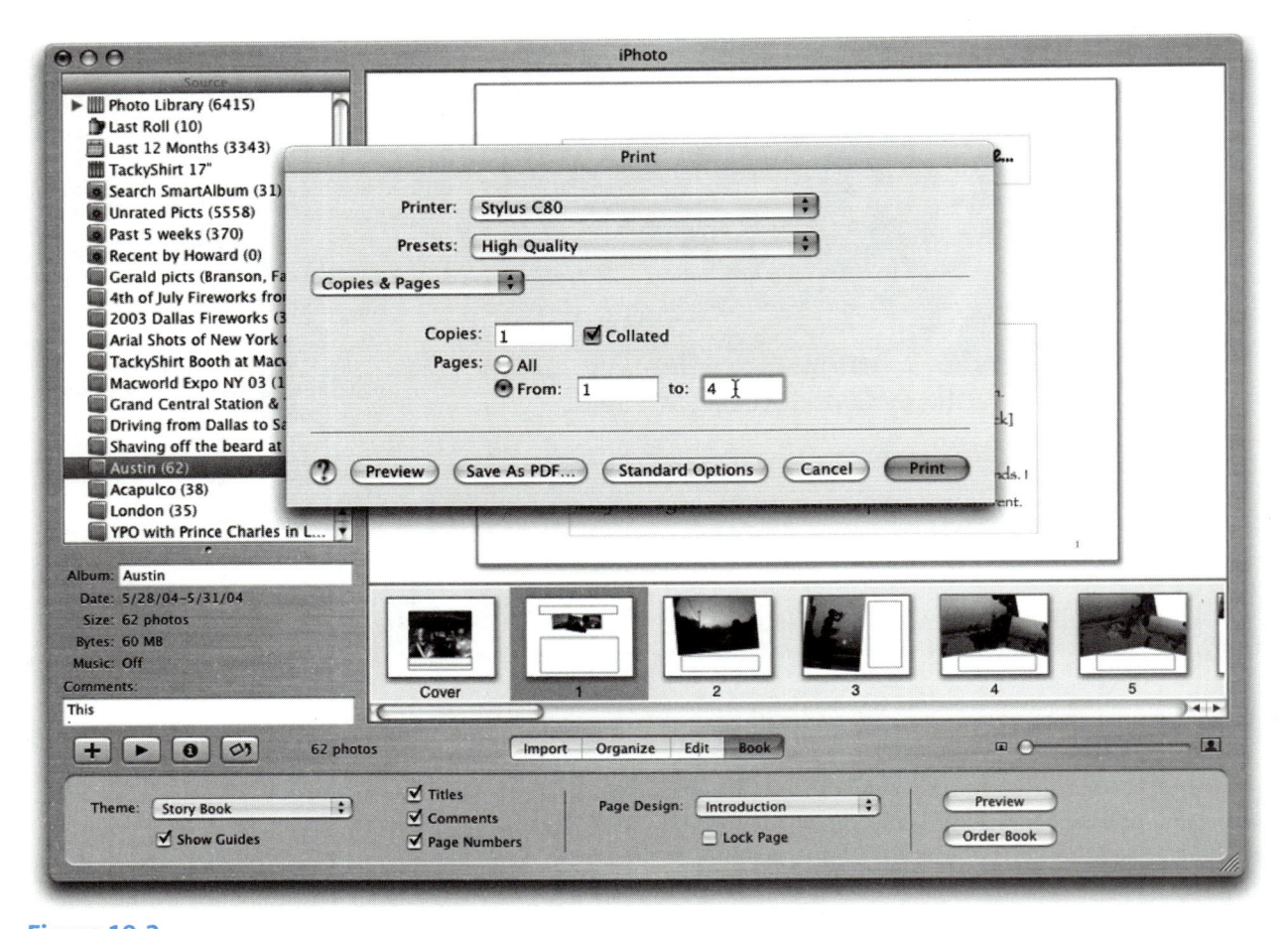

Figure 19-2

Choose the number of copies and which pages to print from the Print dialog box

Note

When specifying the pages to print, remember to add one to the page numbers in the book. For example, if you want to print book pages 1 through 5, specify pages 2 through 6 in the Print dialog box. The page numbers in the book *don't* count the Cover page, but your printer treats the Cover page as the first page for printing.

ORDER A BOOK ONLINE

You've shot, cropped, enhanced, organized, named, commented, laid out, arranged, captioned, proofed, and previewed *(gasping for air)* your book project and now it's time to push the red button! Um, technically it's not a *red button*. That's just an expression. All really important buttons seem to be big and red in the, oh never mind. It's time to click the little blue button with the tiny sunflower on it. I guess it's not the size and color of the button, but the result that counts.

To order your book, make sure you are connected to the Internet, and follow these steps:

1. **Click the Order Book button in Book mode or Organize mode.** After iPhoto spends a few minutes assembling the book and getting it ready to transmit, the Order Book dialog box opens (Figure 19-3).

2. **Choose a shipping address from the Ship To pop-up list.**

3. **Choose a shipping method from the Ship Via pop-up list.** The choices are Standard or Express, but they make no mention of guaranteeing when you'll get it. It just says that it usually ships in three to four days.

 Note

To order a book, you have to set up an Apple ID. If you don't have one yet, you are prompted to set one up when you try to order a book. You can also make changes to your account (such as adding a new shipping address) by clicking the Account Info button.

4. **Choose the color of the cover from the Cover Color pop-up list.** Your choices are limited to Black, Burgundy, Light Gray, or Navy.

5. **Use the Quantity field to choose how many books you want to buy.** The Order Book dialog box updates the price as you change the quantity.

6. **Click the Buy Now button to make your purchase.**

 Note

Remember, the minimum book size is ten pages. If you try to order a book that contains less than ten pages, you'll be warned that you are going to have blank pages (which you pay for) in your book.

(Okay, Mom. You can skip to the end of the chapter now.)

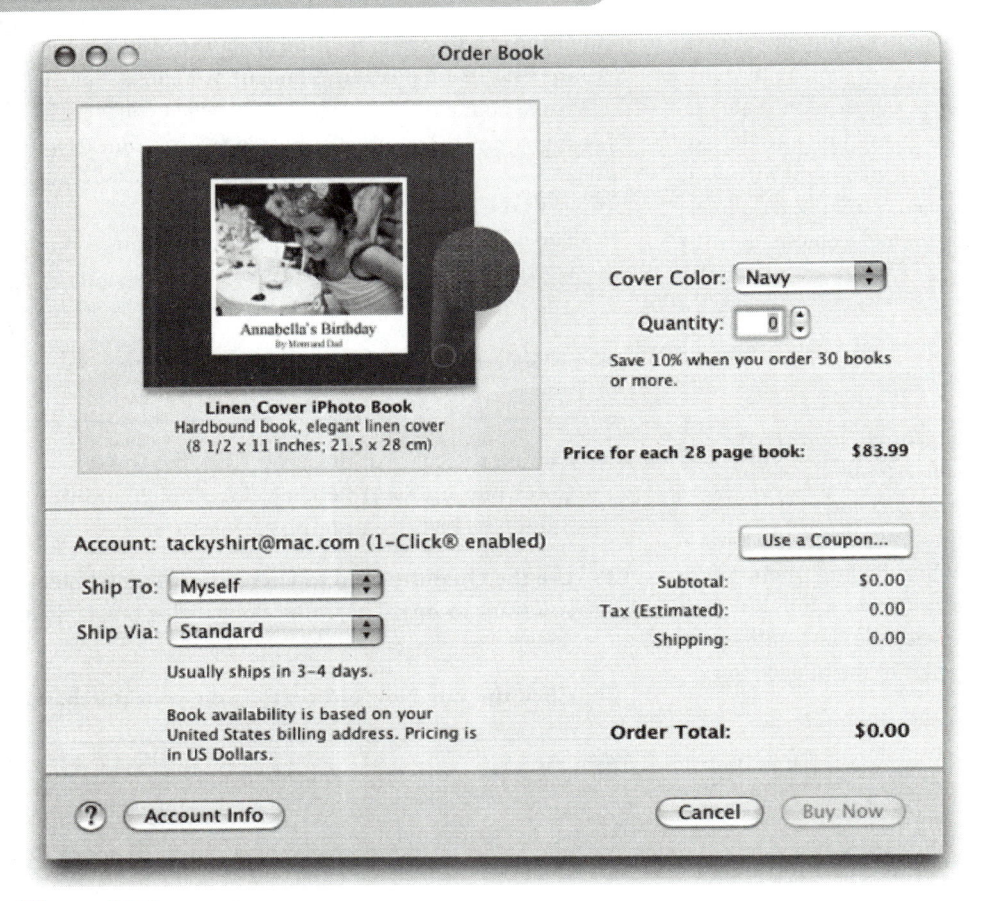

Choose a shipping address and method in the Order Book dialog box

CREATE YOUR OWN BOOK DESIGNS

iPhoto only provides a few simple themes for you to use when building a book. If you are willing to invest some time and effort, you can build your own book themes by modifying the themes provided by Apple. To do so, you'll need access to Apple's Developer Tools. If you bought a Mac with OS X installed, you'll find a folder called Developer Tools inside the Installers folder of the Applications folder. Open the Developer Tools folder and open the Packages folder. Then double-click the Developer.mpkg

icon to install the programming tools. After the install is complete, a new Developer folder appears on your hard drive.

To build your own book themes, follow these steps:

1. **Control+click the iPhoto program icon in the Applications folder.**

2. **Choose Show Package contents from the context menu.**

3. **Double-click the Contents folder, and then double-click the Resources folder to display a long list of contents.**

4. **Scroll down to the English.lproj folder and double-click to open it.** Inside is yet another folder: the Books folder. Inside the Books folder is a set of folders, one for each of the Book themes. The names should look familiar: Classic, Picture Book, Story Book, and so on.

5. **Duplicate the folder of the book theme you want to use as your starting point (one way is to choose Duplicate from the folder's context menu).**

6. **Rename the copied folder (I called mine Classic Updated) and open it.**

The contents of the folder have names like Page-Classic00Cover.nib, Page-Classic1.nib, Classic1P.nib, Classic2.nib, Classic2LP.nib, and so on (Figure 19-4).

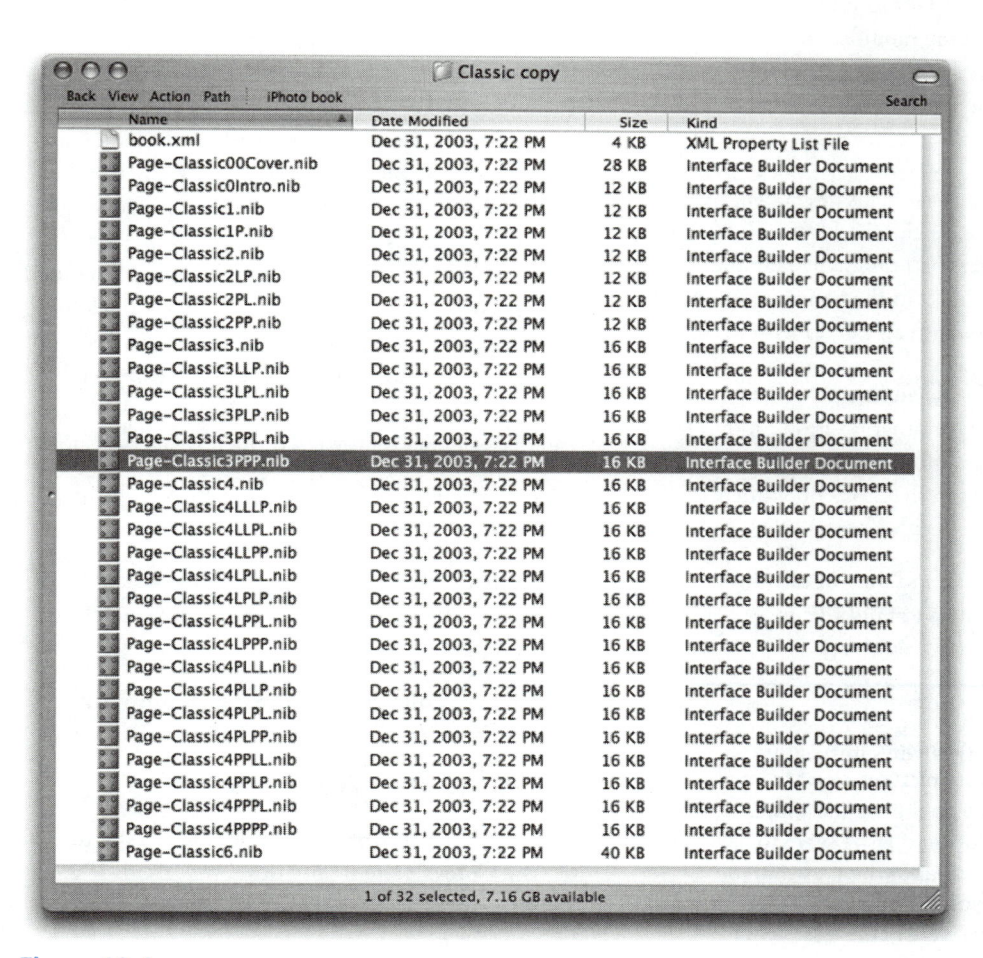

Name	Date Modified	Size	Kind
book.xml	Dec 31, 2003, 7:22 PM	4 KB	XML Property List File
Page-Classic00Cover.nib	Dec 31, 2003, 7:22 PM	28 KB	Interface Builder Document
Page-Classic0Intro.nib	Dec 31, 2003, 7:22 PM	12 KB	Interface Builder Document
Page-Classic1.nib	Dec 31, 2003, 7:22 PM	12 KB	Interface Builder Document
Page-Classic1P.nib	Dec 31, 2003, 7:22 PM	12 KB	Interface Builder Document
Page-Classic2.nib	Dec 31, 2003, 7:22 PM	12 KB	Interface Builder Document
Page-Classic2LP.nib	Dec 31, 2003, 7:22 PM	12 KB	Interface Builder Document
Page-Classic2PL.nib	Dec 31, 2003, 7:22 PM	12 KB	Interface Builder Document
Page-Classic2PP.nib	Dec 31, 2003, 7:22 PM	12 KB	Interface Builder Document
Page-Classic3.nib	Dec 31, 2003, 7:22 PM	16 KB	Interface Builder Document
Page-Classic3LLP.nib	Dec 31, 2003, 7:22 PM	16 KB	Interface Builder Document
Page-Classic3LPL.nib	Dec 31, 2003, 7:22 PM	16 KB	Interface Builder Document
Page-Classic3PLP.nib	Dec 31, 2003, 7:22 PM	16 KB	Interface Builder Document
Page-Classic3PPL.nib	Dec 31, 2003, 7:22 PM	16 KB	Interface Builder Document
Page-Classic3PPP.nib	Dec 31, 2003, 7:22 PM	16 KB	Interface Builder Document
Page-Classic4.nib	Dec 31, 2003, 7:22 PM	16 KB	Interface Builder Document
Page-Classic4LLLP.nib	Dec 31, 2003, 7:22 PM	16 KB	Interface Builder Document
Page-Classic4LLPL.nib	Dec 31, 2003, 7:22 PM	16 KB	Interface Builder Document
Page-Classic4LLPP.nib	Dec 31, 2003, 7:22 PM	16 KB	Interface Builder Document
Page-Classic4LPLL.nib	Dec 31, 2003, 7:22 PM	16 KB	Interface Builder Document
Page-Classic4LPLP.nib	Dec 31, 2003, 7:22 PM	16 KB	Interface Builder Document
Page-Classic4LPPL.nib	Dec 31, 2003, 7:22 PM	16 KB	Interface Builder Document
Page-Classic4LPPP.nib	Dec 31, 2003, 7:22 PM	16 KB	Interface Builder Document
Page-Classic4PLLL.nib	Dec 31, 2003, 7:22 PM	16 KB	Interface Builder Document
Page-Classic4PLLP.nib	Dec 31, 2003, 7:22 PM	16 KB	Interface Builder Document
Page-Classic4PLPL.nib	Dec 31, 2003, 7:22 PM	16 KB	Interface Builder Document
Page-Classic4PLPP.nib	Dec 31, 2003, 7:22 PM	16 KB	Interface Builder Document
Page-Classic4PPLL.nib	Dec 31, 2003, 7:22 PM	16 KB	Interface Builder Document
Page-Classic4PPLP.nib	Dec 31, 2003, 7:22 PM	16 KB	Interface Builder Document
Page-Classic4PPPL.nib	Dec 31, 2003, 7:22 PM	16 KB	Interface Builder Document
Page-Classic4PPPP.nib	Dec 31, 2003, 7:22 PM	16 KB	Interface Builder Document
Page-Classic6.nib	Dec 31, 2003, 7:22 PM	40 KB	Interface Builder Document

1 of 32 selected, 7.16 GB available

Figure 19-4
The objects in the theme folder represent various page layouts

As you can probably imagine, Page-Classic00Cover.nib is the Cover page, Page-Classic1.nib is the page with a single (landscape) photo, and Classic1P.nib is the page with a single portrait photo. An uppercase *L* in the page name indicates a picture in landscape mode, and an uppercase *P* indicates a picture in portrait mode. Thus, the file Page-Classic3LPL.nib is a page containing three pictures in a landscape-portrait-landscape arrangement.

After you understand what you're looking at inside the theme folder, it's time to make some modifications. Double-click the page you want to modify to open it in the Interface Builder (one of the Developer Tools). The results are shown in Figure 19-5.

Interface Builder is an application that helps developers layout windows, buttons, menus, text fields, and so forth. It's what you use to *build* an *interface* for a program. The Interface Builder is a fairly complex tool, but the basics aren't hard to master. Here is some of what you can do with it:

- **Move image slots.** Click inside an image slot and drag it to relocate the slot to another position on the page. You can even locate the slots so that they overlap each other (the page designs in the Story Book theme already overlap).

- **Resize the image slots.** Click and drag one of the sizing handles (the little blue dots around the image slot's border) to resize the image slot.

▼ **Tip**

Be careful about resizing the image slots. If you change the aspect ratio, your pictures won't fit into the slots as well as they did on the original page. Unfortunately, Interface Builder doesn't seem to have a function to lock the aspect ratio when resizing the rectangles, which means you're just going to have to eyeball it. Did I mention we were in the less friendly part of your Mac right now?

- **Change the stacking order of the image slots.** If you overlap image slots, you can change the stacking order to determine which slot is on top. To change the stacking order, click an image slot rectangle and choose either Bring to Front or Send to Back from the Layout menu.

- **Move and resize the text boxes.** You can click and drag the text fields and resize them, using exactly the same techniques as used to move the image slots.

- **Change the text box fonts.** Choose Format ➜ Font ➜ Show Fonts to display the Fonts dialog box. Using this dialog box, you can select a text box and set the Family, Typeface, and Size for the text field. Remember that when you set the text properties of a field while creating a book, the text properties of all other similar fields change as well. However, when using the Interface Builder, setting the properties of one text field (such as the title text box for the leftmost image) does *not* change the text properties for the other title fields. You therefore have considerably more freedom to customize the text properties in the Interface Builder than you do when creating a book.

- **Change the font color.** To change the font color, follow these steps:

  1. **Control+click on the text box you want to modify.** This brings up the NSTextView Info pane.

  2. **Choose Color from the Extras pop-up list in the Fonts pane.**

  3. **Pick the color you want to use.**

  4. **Drag the color from the color box at the top of the Colors pane to any other text fields if you want them to have that same font color.**

Image slot

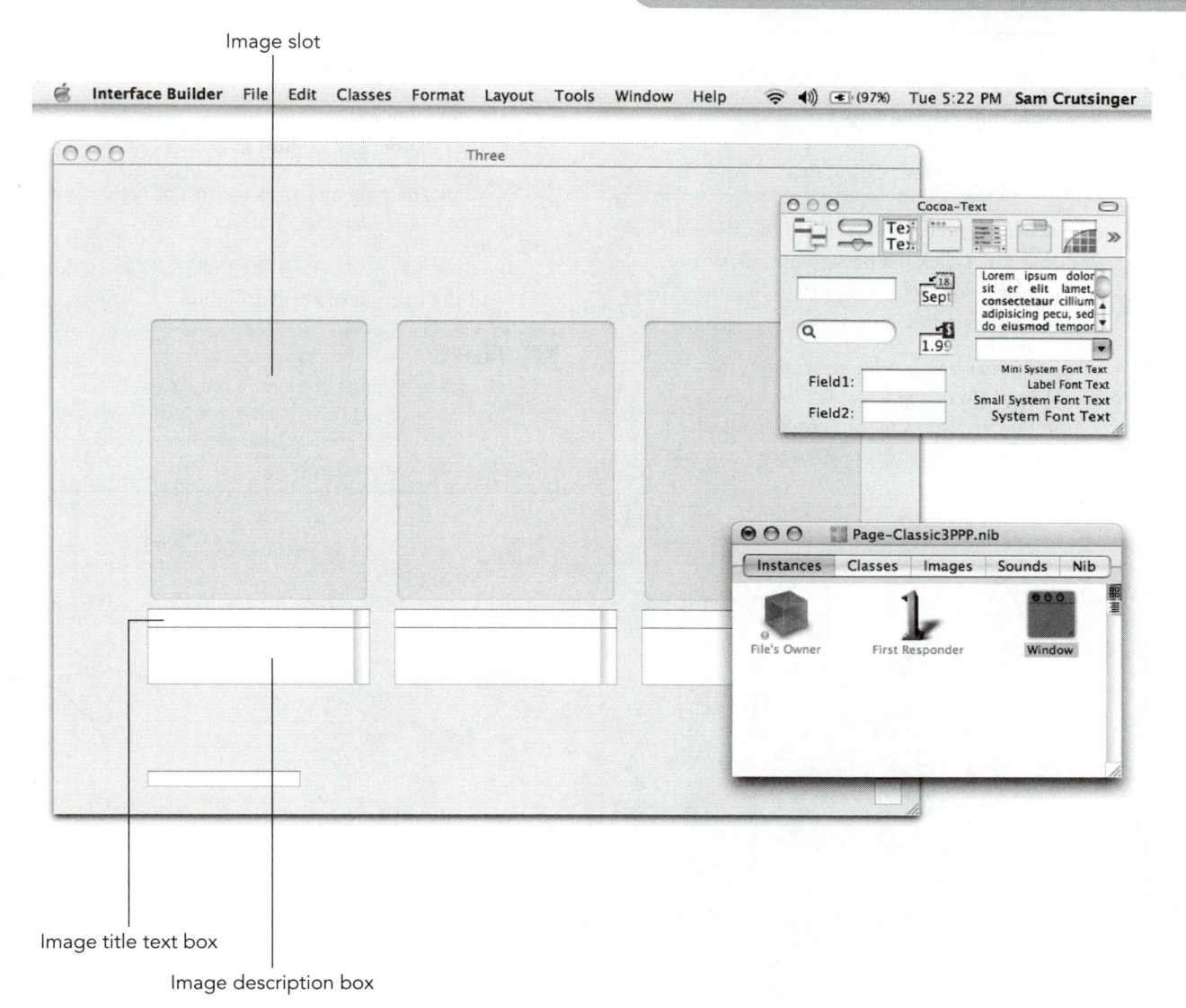

Image title text box

Image description box

Figure 19-5
Use the Interface Builder to change the page layout of a book theme

▼ **Note**

You *must* Control+click the text field. Even if you have a two-button mouse, right clicking does not open the NSScrollView Info dialog box (or any of the other dialog boxes described in this section).

● **Change the background color.** From the NSTextView Info dialog pane, click the Background Color box and when the color tool opens, pick a color from the color tool as shown in Figure 19-6.

● **Change the text box border style.** From the NSTextView Info dialog box, pick the border style from the Border section in the center of the dialog box. Try out the different choices to see them applied to the selected box.

● **Change the image slot border style.** To change the image slot border style, follow these steps:

1. **Control+click an image slot to open the NSBox Info dialog box (Figure 19-7).**

2. **Click the pop-up list at the top of the dialog box and choose Attributes.**

3. **Click an option from the Border Type section at the bottom of the dialog box.**

▼ **Note**

Occasionally (and I don't know why), Control+clicking an image slot doesn't open the NSBox Info dialog box. In that case, choose Tools ➔ Show Info to open the NSBox Info dialog box.

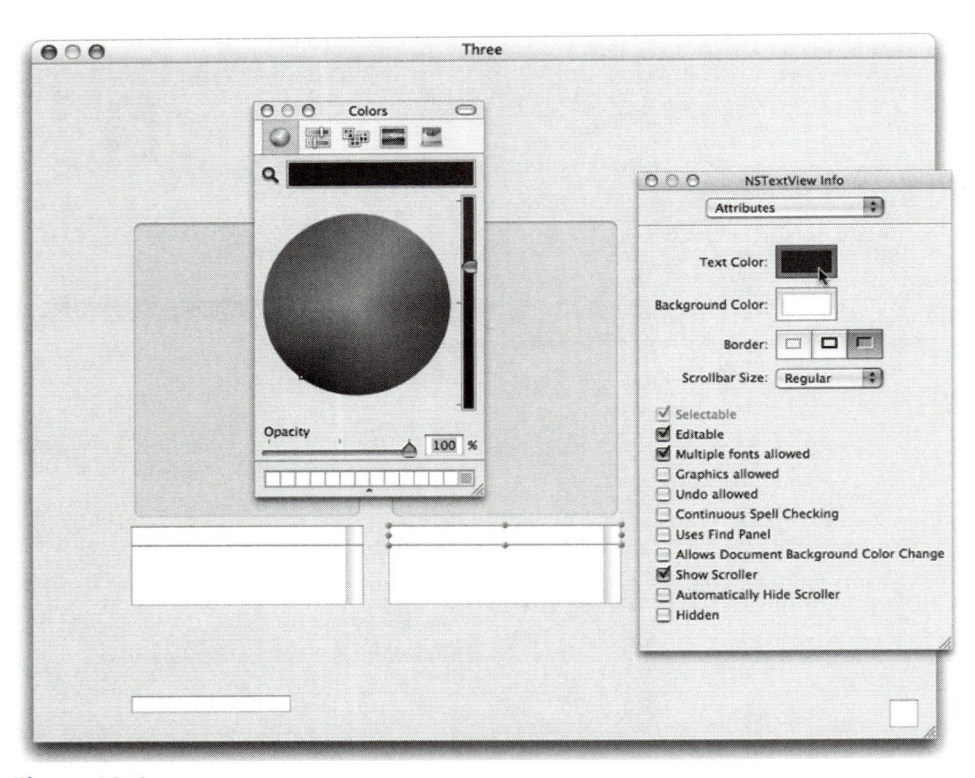

Figure 19-6

Use the NSTextView Info dialog box to change the text color, background, and border style

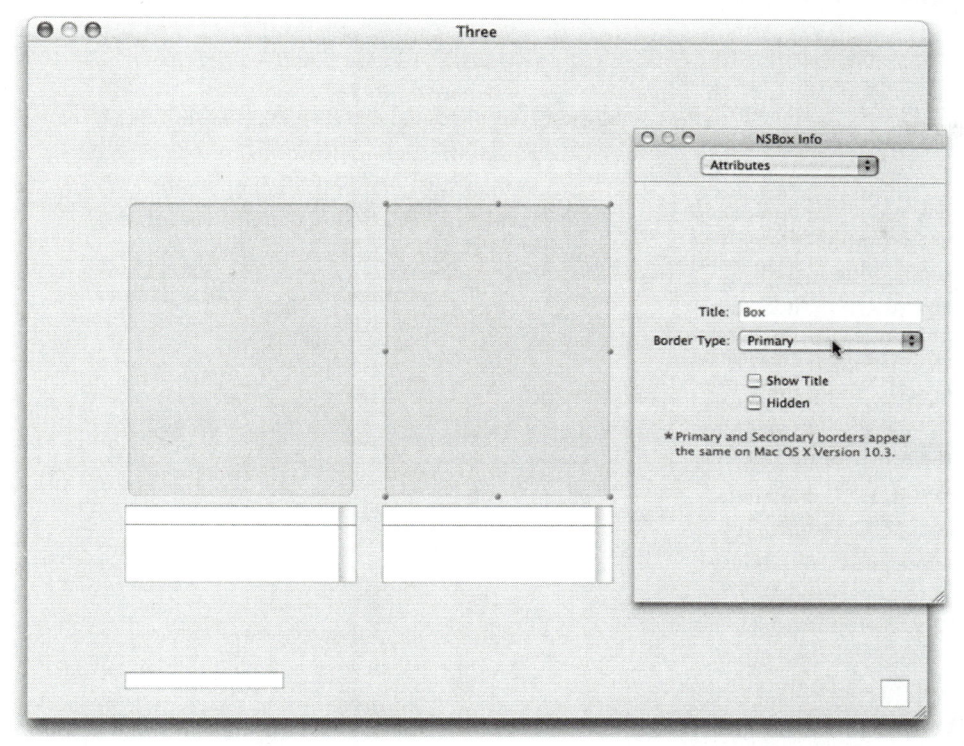

Figure 19-7
Use the NSBox Info dialog box to change the border style of an image slot

After making changes to the various elements of your custom layout, choose File ➔ Save to save the file and exit the Interface Builder.

 Note

Unless you really know what you are doing, you should limit your changes to those noted above. I know it's tempting to add another image slot to a page, but do you know how to hook it up so an image appears there? If not, it's best not to mess with the other tools in the Interface Builder.

What you need to do now is to add your new theme to the list of themes in iPhoto. Follow these steps:

1. In Developers/Applications/Utilities/ you will find the Property List Editor program. Launch that application.

2. Choose File ➔ Open and navigate to the Applications/iPhoto/Contents/Resources/English.lproj/Books folder.

3. Open the folder for your new theme (Classic Updated in our example) and open the book.xml file inside the folder (click the book.xml file and then click the Open button in the Open dialog box).

4. Click the triangle next to the word Root to produce a list of items in the file (Figure 19-8).

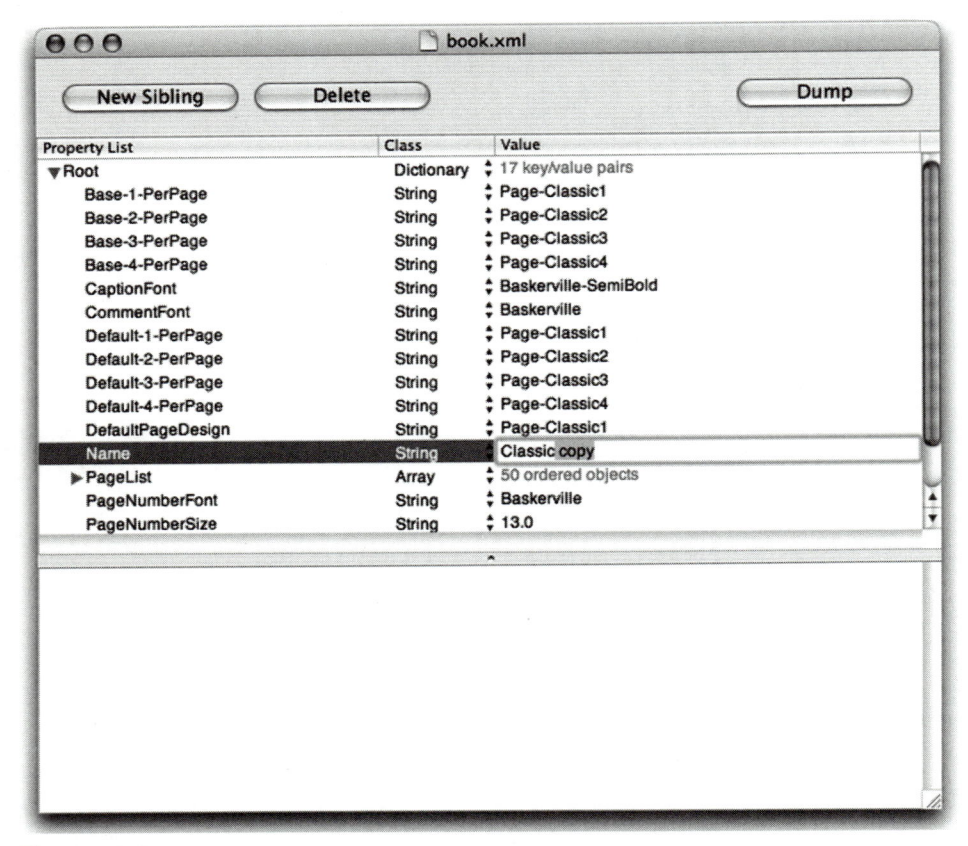

Figure 19-8
Modify the layout name in the book.xml file using the Property List Editor

5. **Scroll down the list until you see a line with the word *Name*.** Double-click the old theme name in the Value column to make it editable and type the new name.

6. **Choose File ➜ Save to save your changes and quit the Property List Editor.**

7. **Finally, navigate to your user's Library/Caches folder and discard the iPhoto Cache folder.**

The next time you open iPhoto, your new book theme appears in the pop-up list; if you select that theme, you'll see the changes you made to the page layouts.

Whaddaya say you come back out to a happier place? They made me do it. I was saying that this is an iApp book for people like my mom who just recently switched from having her secretary hand her printed-out emails so she could read them, to having an actual laptop in her office so she could read and reply to her own emails without replying on a yellow pad with a pen and handing that back to her secretary to type in. How I got the geek gene when she's a borderline Luddite (one who is opposed to technological change) is a complete mystery. I remember her saying once, "What does my little school need with a computer?" She's come a long way since then and brings up that quote on occasion and laughs.

PART VI

Using Other iLife Applications to Present Your Work

Creating an iMovie Slideshow

In This Chapter

Choosing the photos to show • Controlling the slide duration
Adding a narrative and music • Specifying slide titles and effects
Panning and zooming your slides

Back in Chapter 10, you took a look at the slideshow you can make from inside iPhoto. That was the fast-food version of a slideshow, something like a Jack in the Box I would estimate. Now it's time to see how to make the Chili's version of a slideshow, a very festive atmosphere slideshow, yet quite reasonable. To do this, you step away from iPhoto and head over to its brother, iMovie. Of course, iMovie is a whole book unto itself, but let's take a look at just the bits you need to cover to make a tasty bacon-burger slideshow smothered in cheddar.

I think, just maybe, I forgot to eat lunch today.

iMovie enables you to break out from the limits you had in iPhoto: You're not stuck with one duration for every slide. You can use just part of a song instead of the whole thing. You can add a voiceover, titles, transitions... aw, heck, you may just get lost in all the possibilities that have opened up here. I think you're really going to like this stuff. Actually, you don't even need to run iPhoto at all in this chapter, so you can quit it if you like.

Fire up iMovie (it's in your Applications folder) and let's get this party started!

SETTING UP THE PHOTOS

The first step in building a slideshow with iMovie is choosing the photographs you want to show. Click the Photos button to display the Photos pane shown in Figure 20-1. To limit the selection of photos to a particular album, select the album from the iPhoto pop-up menu just above the Photos pane.

To add images to the slideshow, click and drag the thumbnails from the Photos pane to the timeline area across the bottom of the iMovie window. This is easier to do when iMovie is in *Clip Viewer* mode, in which the thumbnails fill the entire timeline area. You can drag the thumbnail either to the end of the list (adding it to the end) or into the middle of the list, adding it between two existing clips as indicated by the arrow in Figure 20-2. If you do add the image between two existing clips, the existing clips move out of your way. You can also remove a clip from the timeline area by clicking that clip and pressing the Delete key (or choosing Edit ➜ Clear). To rearrange the order of the images, click and drag the clips within the timeline area.

You can also select an image in the Photos pane and click the Apply button next to the preview monitor to add that image to the end of the timeline.

Click any of the thumbnails in the timeline to view the images in the *iMovie monitor,* that thing that takes up the whole top-left hunk of the window. The blue line below it is called the *scrubber bar.* That's a term from the analog audio/video world. Scrubbing is grabbing onto the big fat reel to reels and twisting them back and forth to find a precise spot in the project. (I kinda miss the reels sometimes. Sure we have it great now, but working with a mouse and working with a 2-foot steel reel are two very different tactile experiences.) So you do the same thing with the scrubber bar, but instead of grabbing the reel to reels, you grab the play head and drag *that* back and forth to find a certain spot in the timeline. The number on the scrubber bar shows how far along you are in the current timeline.

PREVIEW YOUR SLIDESHOW

You can preview your slideshow at any time using the three buttons below the iMovie monitor. Just click the button with the double left-arrow to "rewind" the slideshow to the beginning. The large round Play button in the middle runs the preview in the iMovie monitor; the rightmost of the three buttons shows the preview in Full-screen mode. When running the preview in the iMovie monitor, clicking the Play Movie button a second time stops the preview; when running the preview in Full-screen mode, clicking the mouse button stops the preview and returns you to iMovie.

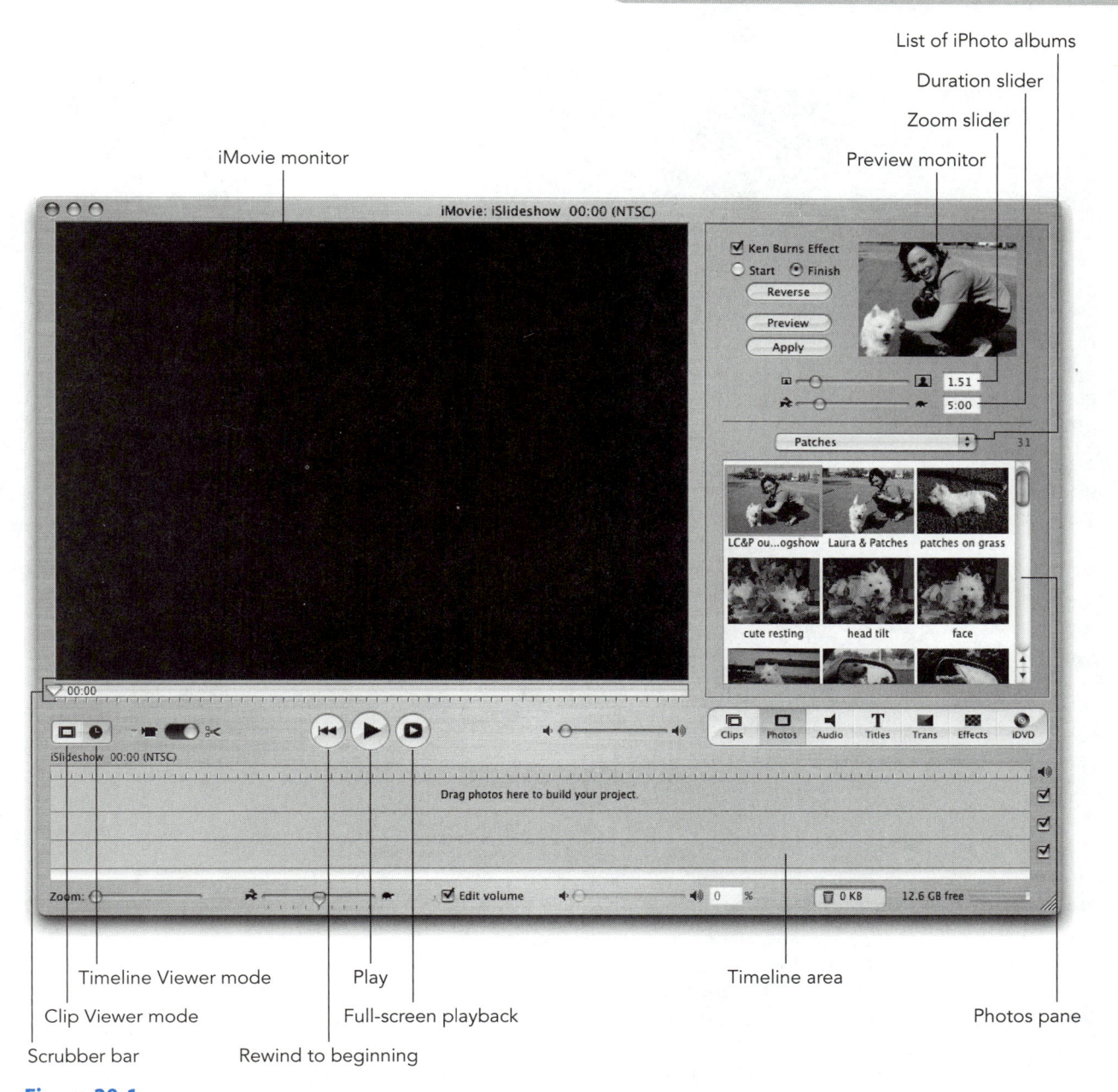

List of iPhoto albums

Duration slider

Zoom slider

Preview monitor

iMovie monitor

Timeline Viewer mode

Play

Timeline area

Clip Viewer mode

Full-screen playback

Photos pane

Scrubber bar

Rewind to beginning

Figure 20-1
Pick photos to create a slideshow with iMovie

Current time

Figure 20-2

Drag the photos into the timeline to build your slideshow in iMovie

iMovie graphically displays the progress of the slideshow during the preview. In Clip Viewer mode, a red vertical line progresses across the thumbnails in the timeline to show where you are (Figure 20-3). Granted, that picture over there is a bit lacking in the *red department,* but you can see the line jutting up above the word *door* in the

second thumbnail. In Timeline Viewer mode, a downward-facing arrowhead (known as the *playhead*) with a vertical line progresses through the thumbnails to show your progress (Figure 20-4). Oh, and don't worry on that one. The playhead is *gray* with a long *black* line so that picture is pretty much spot-on colorwise.

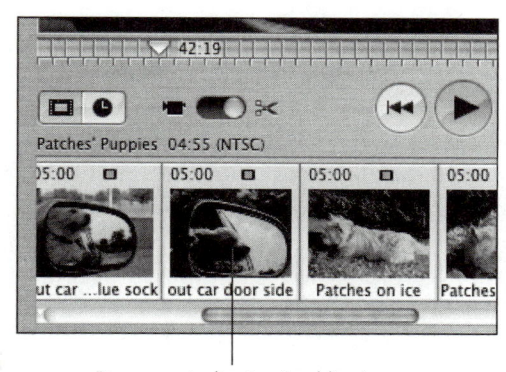

Progress indicator (red line)

Figure 20-3
Watch the progress of the slideshow preview in Clip Viewer mode (the red vertical line)

Progress indicator (playhead)

Figure 20-4
Watch the progress of the slideshow preview in Timeline Viewer mode (the playhead)

You don't have to start the slideshow from the beginning if you don't want to. In either mode you can click on a slide(s) and press the Play button to play that selection. This feature is nice for when you want to watch two to three clips in their entirety but *just* those clips. When you

select a clip, the playhead jumps to the head of that clip so if you click in an empty space (or the brushed metal areas of the iMovie window) to select *nothing,* now when you press Play, it won't stop until you tell it to. In Timeline Viewer mode, you can drag the playhead to any point in the timeline and then click the Play button to start the preview. Then again, at any time you can click anywhere in the scrubber bar or drag *that other* playhead to jump to that point in the movie.

SET THE DURATION AND NAME OF EACH SLIDE

You can set the duration of each slide of the iMovie slideshow. You can see the current slide duration just to the right of the cute wittle bunny wabbit/turtle slider (Figure 20-5) off to the right (3.03 seconds in my case). We'll just call it the *duration slider* from now on. If you want to put a picture on the timeline for a specific duration you can:

1. **Click on an image thumbnail from the available photos displayed in the Photos pane.**

2. **Adjust the duration slider or type in a specific duration in seconds.** The speed slider will choose from 0.03 seconds to 30.00 seconds. You can type in any number you want in the field to the right between 0.03 and 60.00 seconds.

3. **Press the Apply button to add the clip to the end of the timeline or drag the clip from the Photos pane to the timeline.**

Figure 20-5
Use the duration slider to extend or shorten clips

Note

0.03 seconds is a single whole frame of video, 1/30th of a second. In other words, there are 30 frames in one second of video. *Technically* it's actually 29.97 frames per second, but come on. Leave that attention to detail to the professionals. If you type in 03:15, the slide is displayed for 3.5 seconds.

The duration of each clip can be changed if you need a clip to be onscreen longer or shorter. From Clip Viewer mode, follow these steps:

1. **Select the Photos button if it's not highlighted.**

2. **Select one or more clips in the timeline area.** Selecting multiple clips at once will let you change them all at once.

3. **Adjust the duration slider or type a new duration in the field to the right of that slider.** If you're changing more than one clip, they will each become the duration you enter.

4. **Click Apply to make the settings take effect.**

An alternate way to get the job done is to follow these other steps:

1. **Double-click on a clip in the timeline area.** A Clip Info window opens as shown in Figure 20-6.

2. **Type in a new duration in the Duration field.**

3. **Click Set.**

Those two tricks I just mentioned work in either Timeline or Clip Viewer modes, but you can get really nice control over clip duration in Timeline mode by grabbing the edge of the clip and dragging it to increase/decrease the duration as shown in Figure 20-7.

 Tip

Want to change the duration of the entire slide show? Click the first thumbnail, Shift+click the last thumbnail to select all the images in the slideshow, and then use the speed slider to adjust the duration of all the slides.

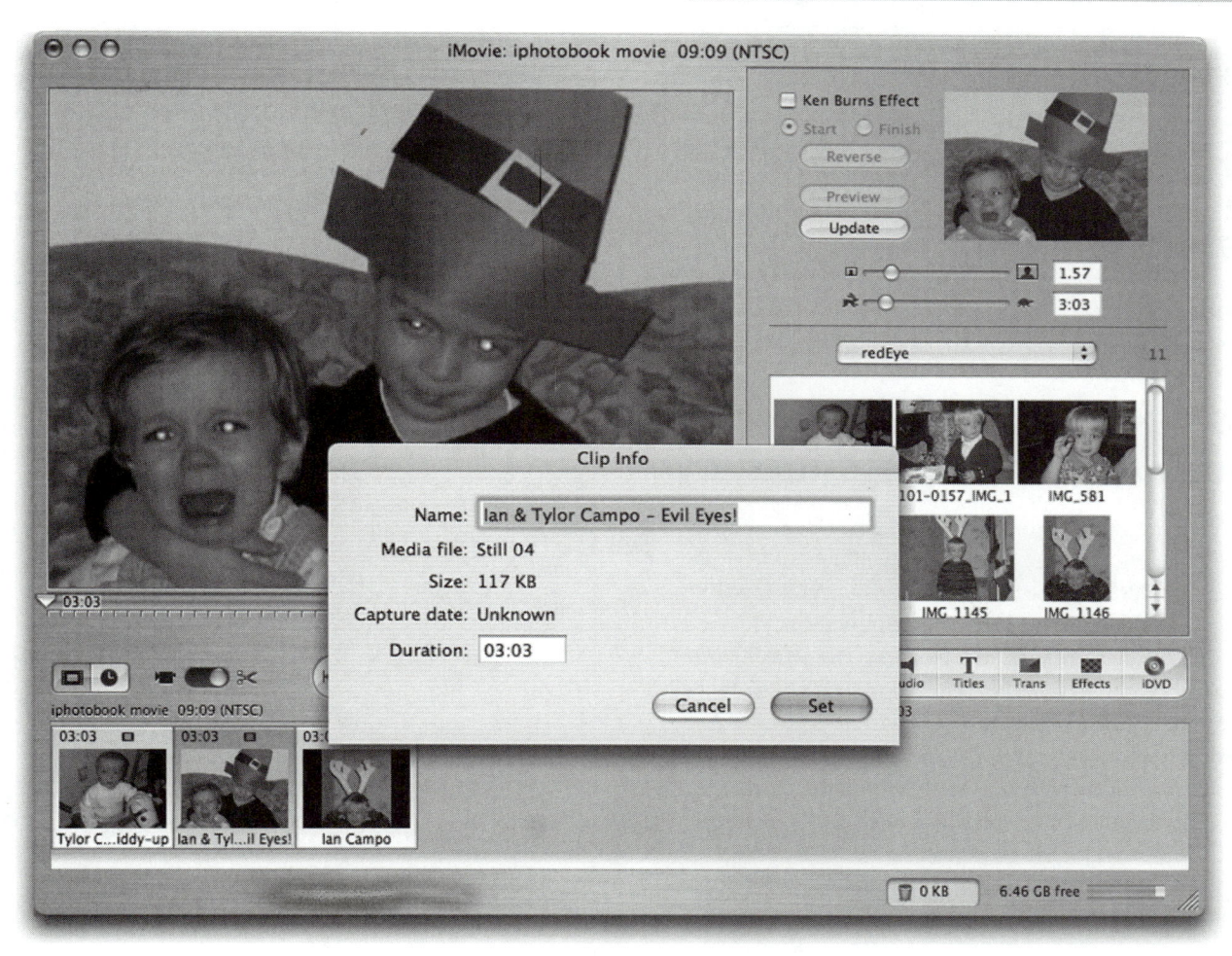

Figure 20-6
Change the slide duration and name in the Clip Info dialog box

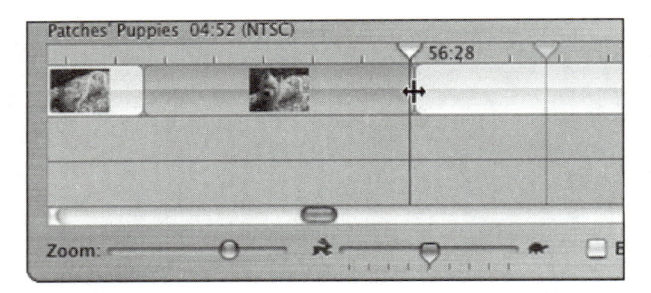

Figure 20-7
Change the slide duration in Timeline view; just grab an edge and drag

ADD NARRATIVE TO THE SLIDESHOW

While I'm sure all your pictures are just so immensely riveting that the audience would quite willingly sit in stunned silence at the awesome beauty that is your Aaaart, you might consider putting on a commentary so they're not so completely overwhelmed that they miss the actual point you're trying to make. The technical term for disembodied voice that speaks over video is, of course, a *voiceover*. And recording voiceovers takes a voice and a microphone. See the sidebar called *Where do I talk?* later in the chapter if you're wondering about the whole microphone thing.

In the meantime, here are some steps to help you add a voiceover to your slideshow:

1. **Click the Audio button.** The Audio pane comes up with a list of music from iTunes at the top of the pane. At the bottom of this pane is the Microphone recording control (see Figure 20-8). If you have a microphone attached or a built-in microphone, which is the case for most Macs today, the input meter should react to your voice.

2. **In the timeline, click the thumbnail of the image for which you want to record a voiceover.**

Figure 20-8
The Audio button makes your iTunes library and Microphone control available

3. **Click the round record button (just right of the audio meter) and record your voiceover.** You want the level to be in the yellow most of the time for best quality (see Figure 20-9). Yeah, the picture is all gray, but those lighter bars are the sweet spot. Unlike preview playback, iMovie will not stop when it reaches the end of the selected clip while you're recording a voiceover. If you talk past the slide change, that's fine. You can make the slide fit your story.

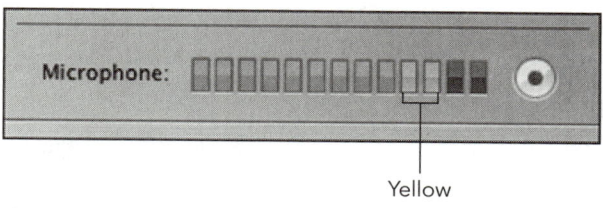

Microphone:

Yellow

Figure 20-9
Green is low; red is too loud; yellow is just right (yellow is the lighter gray)

4. **Click the record button again to end the recording.** Try to be concise. You don't want to go on and on and bore them to tears. It's a common enough problem among first-timers.

5. **Align the voiceover to the slide.** iMovie displays the voiceover as an audio segment in the Timeline Viewer below the thumbnails (see Figure 20-10). To align the transition to the next slide with the end of the slide's voiceover, click and drag the right-hand border of the slide's thumbnail to increase or decrease the duration of the slide to match the voiceover. To move the whole voiceover in the timeline, click and drag the voiceover to another location.

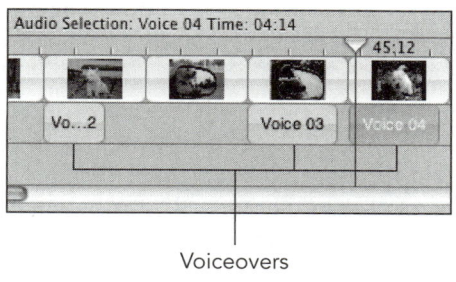

Voiceovers

Figure 20-10
Voiceovers appear below the thumbnails in the audio portion of the timeline

WHERE DO I TALK?

Every Macintosh model in the current lineup, with the exception of the towers, has a built-in microphone. If you have an iMac or eMac, look for a little hole or slot in the display bezel at the bottom on the Flat-Panel iMacs and at the top on the older CRT iMacs. PowerBooks have the microphone in the left speaker grill.

If you have an older model Macintosh and don't know if you have a microphone built-in, just hit record and start snapping your fingers. If you see the audio level hop to the snaps, you're getting sound in there somewhere. Start tapping on things. When you find the mic, the meter will peak out.

If you don't have a built-in mic, you'll need to buy one. Regular microphones that you can plug into your audio-in port are available, as are USB microphones that work nicely for systems without an audio input port.

If you have a digital video camcorder, plugging it into the computer via Firewire will allow you to use the camera's microphone in most cases. This depends on the camera.

▼ Tip

To remove a voiceover, click the voiceover and press Delete or choose Edit ➜ Clear. Removing a voiceover does *not* move subsequent voiceovers to fill in the gap. The subsequent voiceovers remain where they are.

ADD MUSIC TO THE SLIDESHOW

You've got breathtaking photographs and an absolutely *riveting* voiceover on the slideshow. Now it's time to knock it out of the park. Cue the band, 'cuz it's soundtrack time. This is possibly the most important decision you'll make in the quest to capture your audience's attention for anything more than about a minute. The truth is, if you put a good song over your less-than-stellar presentation, people will keep watching just to listen to the song.

Music is brought in from the Audio pane. You can preview any music track by double-clicking on it or selecting it and pressing the playhead below the song list. There's a search field. Please tell me you don't need my help for that one. Here's a hint. You type stuff in it.

Oh, one more thing. See the time limit for each song? Usually, that's not so important when you're just jamming, but now you can look at the 2 minute and 44 second slideshow you're working on, sort your music by time, and see that you've got several music cuts that are *exactly* that length.

Hip, Neck & Thigh	Big Audio Dynamite	2:44
The Long Day Is Over	Norah Jones	2:44
Having a blast	Green Day	2:44
Of These, Hope - Reprise	Peter Gabriel	2:44
The World Isn't Fair	Randy Newman	2:44
Never There	Cake	2:44
Good + Bad Times	INXS	2:44

Track 18	Michael Floreale	2:44
Auctioneer (Another Engine)	R.E.M.	2:44
With A Little Help From My Friends	Beatles, The	2:44

No. You're not supposed to have *those* music cuts in your list unless you've bought those albums. You don't get The Beatles' Sgt. Pepper included with your Mac OS X installer.

Here's how you pull tunes into your presentation:

1. **Click the Audio button.** Your whole iTunes music collection will be listed. The pop-up list above the music list has all your iTunes playlists if you want to select one of those to narrow down the listed music to those songs.

2. **Position the playhead in the timeline where you want the music to start.**

3. **Choose a music cut and click the Place at Playhead button.** Alternatively, you can drag a song from the list and position it in the timeline, releasing the mouse button at the point where you want the music to start. iMovie imports the song and adds it to the timeline (see Figure 20-11). I was going to say that you have to be in Timeline view to work with adding music to your timeline, but those crazy Apple folks kind of made that a moot point. As soon as you start to drag an audio file from the Audio pane, *Shazam,* it switches automatically, so never mind.

Figure 20-11
You can play music during your iMovie slideshow

4. **To adjust the start point for the music, click and drag the left edge of the song's timeline.**

5. **To adjust the endpoint for the music, click and drag the right edge of the song's timeline.** Figure 20-12 shows the end of the music aligned to the end of the slideshow.

Figure 20-12
Align the end of the music to the end of the slideshow and adjust the zoom level to see the result

 **Note**

You *should* adjust the endpoint of the music to correspond to the end of the slideshow. If you don't, the song continues to play after the slideshow has ended, but people viewing the slideshow see only a blank screen after the last slide has been displayed. Actually... it might be fun to see how long they sit there before they finally say "Is it over yet?"

Tip

You can add multiple songs to a slideshow by adding the second song to the timeline following the previous set of steps. Then adjust the start and endpoints of the two (or more) songs so that they start and end where you want them.

KEN BURNS EFFECT

Good old Kenny B. Yup. Ken Burns is a documentary filmmaker. Near as I can tell, some of his work on the old West and the Civil War relied heavily on still photos that he would drift through the frame and zoom in and on so it wasn't a bunch of still shots one after the other which would have been a tad dull. This is all pretty much guesswork on my part since I've never actually seen any of his documentaries.

I think it went down like this:

"I was watching PBS last night and got an idea. Let's make it so you can pan and zoom over your pictures in iMovie. I'm thinking something like what that Ken Burns guy was doing in that documentary last night. It was all photographs and it was so totally *not boring!*"

"Sure, we can do that. You came up with the idea so you get to come up with the secret code name."

"Well duh! Ken Burns!"

"Right, we'll get right on *Operation Ken Burns* for the next release."

I'm guessing the name kind of grew on everybody from then on. So today the Ken Burns Effect is a drifting and zooming technique you can apply to photos so the show will have a bit more pep.

By default, your slideshow has Ken Burns Effect enabled. Essentially, you pick a zoom level and a placement for the Start and Finish of your clip, and iMovie drifts the picture from point A to B. This can really add a great deal of energy to your show. This can also make people want to strangle you if you aren't careful.

 Note

You must add the Ken Burns Effect prior to adding titles because you cannot attach a Ken Burns Effect to a titled slide; that is, the title slide hides the original slide to which you can attach the Ken Burns Effect. But if you attach a Ken Burns Effect to a slide and *then* add a title effect, everything works. To adjust the Ken Burns Effect on a titled slide, you have to delete the title first, adjust the Ken Burns Effect, and then replace the title. We'll be covering titles here shortly.

To display a slide using the Ken Burns Effect, follow these steps:

1. **Click the Photos button if necessary.**

2. **Click the slide thumbnail in the timeline to which you want to apply the effect.**

3. **Click the Ken Burns Effect checkbox near the upper-right corner of the iMovie window (see Figure 20-13).**

4. **Configure the Ken Burns Effect to move or zoom the image.**

   - To pan (move) the image, click and drag it to a new position in the preview rectangle (just below the Ken Burns Effect checkbox).

   - To change the zoom level, use the Zoom slider to increase the zoom (you can't reduce the zoom level below 1.00).

Figure 20-13
Use a Ken Burns Effect to pan and zoom your slide

5. **Click the Preview button to see a preview of your effect.** To reverse the effect you created, click the Reverse button.

6. **When you are happy with the result, click the Update button.** Applying the effect to the slide can take a few moments, so be patient. If you look closely at the thumbnail in Clip Viewer mode, you can see a scroll bar updating along the bottom of the thumbnail, as shown in Figure 20-14.

To remove the Ken Burns Effect, discard the slide and replace it in the slideshow.

AVOIDING KEN BURNS-OUT

This effect can be very sexy and draw focus just where you want it, but it can also be the most monotonous, grinding thing you've ever seen if you don't customize your movements. To make your slide moves as pleasing as possible, you need to make sure you don't have every slide making the
same move,
same move,
same move, which they do when you first put your slides in the timeline.

Click on each slide in your show and adjust the Start and Finish positions. The closer these two positions are to each other, the slower the move will be.

While you're at it, adjust the Start and Finish zoom levels as well. Have some slides zoom in and some zoom out. Occasionally, you may *not* zoom and instead just pan across the countryside.

I've been forced to endure far too many iMovie slideshows where every single picture drifts left at exactly the same angle and exactly the same pace. What's worse is when the subject of the picture is standing near the left edge, because then the picture pans off of what you're supposed to be looking at and into a boring blue sky.

Please don't make me watch another one of those shows. Use your Ken Burns Effect wisely.

Figure 20-14
A bar below the thumbnail indicates the update is taking place

SET UP THE TITLES

Titles are text elements that you can use to dress up your iMovie slideshow. You can attach titles and other text to each slide if you choose. You can control text content, the effect used to draw the text, and the typeface, size, and color. You can also adjust the timing so that the text appears with just a single slide or stretched across multiple slides.

There are *lots* of title effects. This is where I have to pull back on the reigns and bring up that *this* is an *iPhoto book*. There are whole other books for iMovie, and going through all the different ways to get text across the screen will likely be a whole chapter unto itself. Think of it this way. You've got something to look forward to when you finish this book — a whole other book!

Until then, just play. Play is how kids learn. We forget that after we break our teens. Well, I mean we the people. I play all the time. That's why I get to write silly books about geeky things. I press *all of the buttons!* (...and then I get to figure out how to fix everything I break.)

To play with titles, do this:

1. **Click the Titles button.** The Titles pane appears (see Figure 20-15).

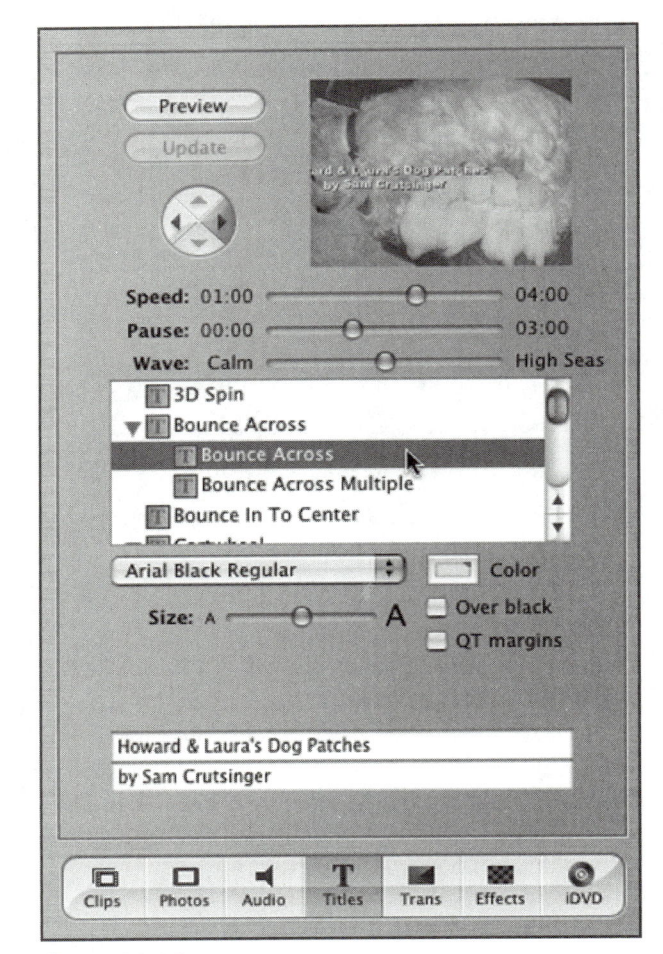

Figure 20-15
Click the Titles button to configure the slide titles you want to use

2. **Pick the basic text effect from the scrolling list.**

3. **If necessary, specify a direction for the text effect.** For example, the Bounce Across effect enables you to pick a direction to flow the text onto the slide (choose left or right from the circle with the four arrows in it).

4. **Set the Speed parameter, which controls how quickly the text appears.**

5. **Set the Pause parameter (not available for all effects).** The Pause parameter controls how long the text remains visible after the effect has completed.

▼ **Note**
As you adjust the Speed and Pause parameters, the overall length of the title effect changes. The total length is displayed at the bottom of the small preview rectangle in the upper-right corner of the iMovie window. If you want titles on only a single slide, make a note of this time in order to match the title duration to the slide duration. If you want the text to disappear before the next slide appears, make sure the title duration is shorter than the slide duration. And if you want the title to play over multiple slides, match the title duration to the combined duration of the slides.

6. **Set the Wave parameter (not available for all effects).** The Wave parameter controls the magnitude of the wave motion that the text follows as it moves over the slide. The left end of the slider (Calm) uses very small waves; the right end of the slider (High Seas) uses large waves.

7. **Add more lines of text (not available for all effects).** The Bounce Across effect allows only two lines of text (which you can see in Figure 20-15); however, other effects may allow for more lines of text. For example, the Bounce Across Multiple effect enables you to initially use four lines of text, but you can add more lines (two at a time) by clicking the plus sign button (+). You can remove lines of text (two at a

time) by clicking the minus sign button (-). Both of these controls are located at the bottom of the Titles pane, as shown in Figure 20-16.

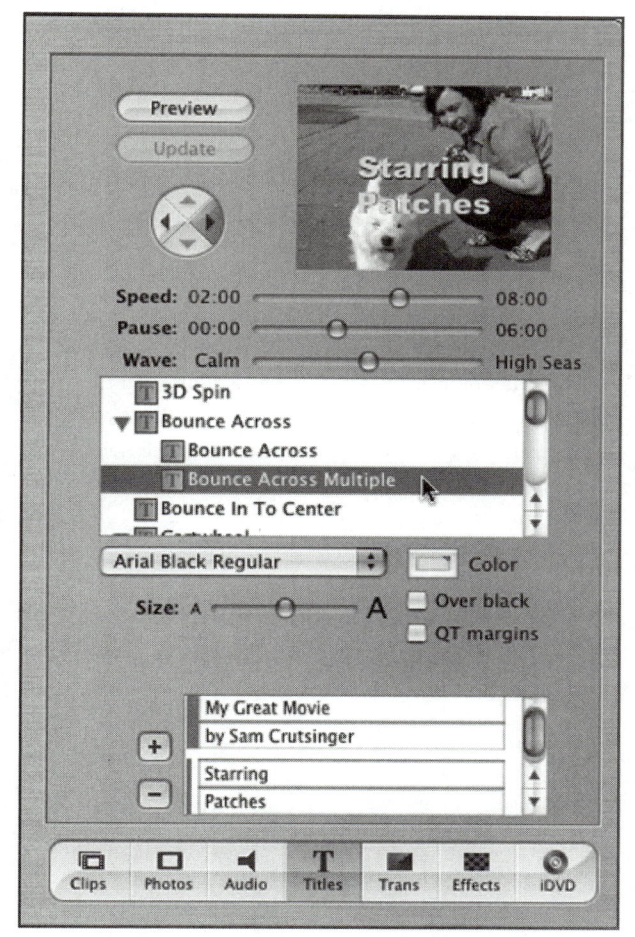

Figure 20-16
Add and remove lines of text for certain effects using the + and – buttons

8. After you've chosen and configured the effect you want to use, type the text in the provided fields.

9. Select the typeface from the pop-up list and use the font size slider (immediately below the typeface

pop-up list) to increase or decrease the size of the font. You can also change the font color by clicking the Color button and choosing the color from the Colors dialog box.

▼ **Note**

The typeface, size, and color are applied to all the text in the title; you cannot apply these parameters to just a selected portion of the text (or just one line).

10. After you've got everything configured just the way you want it, add the title to a slide by clicking the title effect and dragging it on top of the slide thumbnail. This is actually easier to do in Clip Viewer mode, where the thumbnails are larger. After you've completed this operation, the thumbnail changes to indicate that the slide has titles attached to it (see Figure 20-17); you can see the title text in the thumbnail, and a small T appears in the upper-right corner of the thumbnail in Clip Viewer mode.

Figure 20-17
Clips with titles have a T marker

▼ **Note**

Getting the title attached to the correct slide thumbnail can be a little confusing. When you drag a title to the timeline, the clips part and make a hole for the slide. Whether you place the slide inside the hole or drop it on the clip to the left or right of the hole, the result is the same. It puts the text over the first clip to the right of the hole. The clip that gets the title shows up in the iMovie monitor as you're dragging the title. That's a clear indicator.

After you attach a title to a slide, you cannot go back and make any changes to that title, such as changing the text, the effect, or the typeface. To change anything about the title, you need to delete it and start over. To delete the title, click the titled slide thumbnail and press the Delete key or choose Edit ➜ Clear. This actually deletes the titled slide, and you'll find your original slide (without the titles) in its place. When you add titles, iMovie actually creates a whole new slide and puts it on top of your original image, so you only see the titled version of the slide. Deleting the titled version leaves the original slide, ready for you to try again.

Another disconcerting aspect of adding a title is that if the title extends across multiple slides, the first slide in the sequence simply disappears from the timeline. You *can* see the second slide in the timeline — complete with the title text — but not the first slide. Even odder, when you click the thumbnail of the second slide, you see the first slide in the preview window. In fact, there is no way to see the second slide (the one visible in the timeline) in the preview window after you add the title. I guess Apple is messing with us.

... AND SO MUCH MORE!

iMovie has many more features than I could begin to cover here. Hey, I have to save the good stuff for the iMovie book! Go play around. Select a couple of slides (Shift+click) and toy with the transitions to get from one slide to the next. Maybe you've got some video clips to go with the slides. Add those in there as well. Who knows? You may just find that you've got the video bug.

Occasionally, you will find that iMovie does have its limits. Remember at the top of this chapter when I was saying iMovie let you make the Chili's bacon cheeseburger of slideshows? When you get a more discerning palette for the best quality tools you can get your hands on, move on up to Apple's Final Cut. That's definitely more in the steakhouse category than in the burger joint category at this level. It's not nearly as easy to use as iMovie, but you'll have the freedom to do anything you can think of and do it well. But that's a topic for another book....

21

Creating an iDVD Slideshow

In This Chapter

Selecting albums to include in the DVD slideshow

Choosing and applying a theme to your slideshow

Setting the order and duration of the slides

Adding music and motion to your slideshow

Configuring and burning the DVD

iLife's been good to us so far, so let's check out its other sibling, iDVD. iDVD can create a slideshow on a DVD that will play in your entertainment center. This one even gets its own button in Organize mode in iPhoto. iDVD doesn't have quite the level of control we had with iMovie in the last chapter, but it does give you a simple way to build a slideshow that plays back on about any DVD box right there in the living room; and hey, if Grandpa doesn't have a DVD player, scrape up the $50 and get him one just so he can watch the DVD you're sending him. I just checked Walmart.com and they have one for $43.86 right now, so there's not much excuse.

That's the beauty of a DVD slideshow: You don't need a computer or Internet connection to view it. If I'm not mistaken, I believe that pretty much means we've now covered everybody on the planet in one way or another, except for blind people. iLife does a lot for $50. Feeding your photos straight into a person's brain is a bit beyond Apple's capabilities at the moment, but I hear they're working hard on the problem.

When you make the DVD, you can even include the original photographs on the disc; after your friends watch the DVD on television, they can put the disc in the computer and have access to the full-resolution files if they want to print them out.

SELECT THE PICTURES

The first step of creating an iDVD slideshow is to select the albums you want to include in iPhoto. Oh yeah, we're back in iPhoto for this step. Unlike iMovie, which had full access to all your photos and music, iDVD needs to have the content sent to it from iPhoto. You must pick entire albums, so you may want to build special albums for this purpose. You can choose several albums (⌘+click or Shift+click to select multiple albums), but the opening page gets pretty crowded if you select more than about eight albums for the DVD.

After you choose the albums to include, make sure you are in Organize mode and click the iDVD button. After a few minutes, iPhoto launches iDVD and displays the iDVD main screen (see Figure 21-1).

 Tip

If the theme music that plays in the iDVD main screen is driving you crazy while you figure out what to do next, click the Motion button to shut the music off. Just make sure to turn the Motion button back on before burning the DVD.

Figure 21-1
The iDVD main screen appears after you pick some albums and click the iDVD button from iPhoto

Note

You may have noticed that the album titles from iPhoto have followed you over here in the form of captions for your buttons. Nice eh?

Before going any further, you should set a few items to ensure that the resulting slideshow displays properly on a TV set. First, choose Advanced ➜ Show TV Safe Area. With this setting activated, iDVD outlines in red the area that will display properly on a TV set (see Figure 21-2).

To ensure that the DVD is burned using settings that work well for viewing on a TV set, follow these steps:

1. **Open the iDVD Preferences dialog box.** You do this by choosing iDVD ➜ Preferences.

2. **Click the Slideshow button in the toolbar.**

3. **Click the Always scale slides to TV Safe area checkbox.**

Red outline

Figure 21-2
The red outline shows how much of the iDVD screen is visible on a TV set

CONFIGURE THE MAIN TITLE PAGE OF YOUR SLIDESHOW

The main title page is what comes up when you first put the DVD in to play it. This is where your *buttons* go that take you to your individual slideshows. The buttons in Figure 21-3 just use the text you see stacked to the right. Each of those album titles is a separate button. Take a peek at Figure 21-4. That one has picture slots as well as the album title text. iDVD provides 44 themes in v4.0.1. When they put out an update, they tend to sneak in more themes. It's a good kinda sneak. Some of the themes are better suited for your slideshow than others. To create the opening title page for your slideshow(s), click the Customize button to open the Customize pane. iDVD displays a list of themes for the title page in this pane (see Figure 21-3).

iDVD comes with several sets of themes, such as 4.0 Themes, 3.0 Themes, and Old Themes. Choose a set of themes to work with from the pop-up list above the theme thumbnails. To choose a theme and preview it in the main

Figure 21-3
Click the Customize button to access the controls for customizing your slideshow

iDVD window, simply click the theme in the scrolling list. Any number of themes work for a DVD containing only a single album slideshow, and there are even some good ones for a DVD containing multiple album slideshows. Feel free to go through and click on every one of them if you want so you can get an idea of what you have available to you. It's best to switch the pop-up menu at the top of the list to All and then just go down the list. Figure 21-4 shows one of my favorite multi-album slideshow themes. To pick this

theme, select 3.0 Themes from the pop-up list and click Portfolio Color from the theme thumbnails.

 Note

The row of buttons across the top of the Customize pane are the *pane selection buttons*. You use these buttons to switch that side pane between the Themes, Settings, Media, and Status panes.

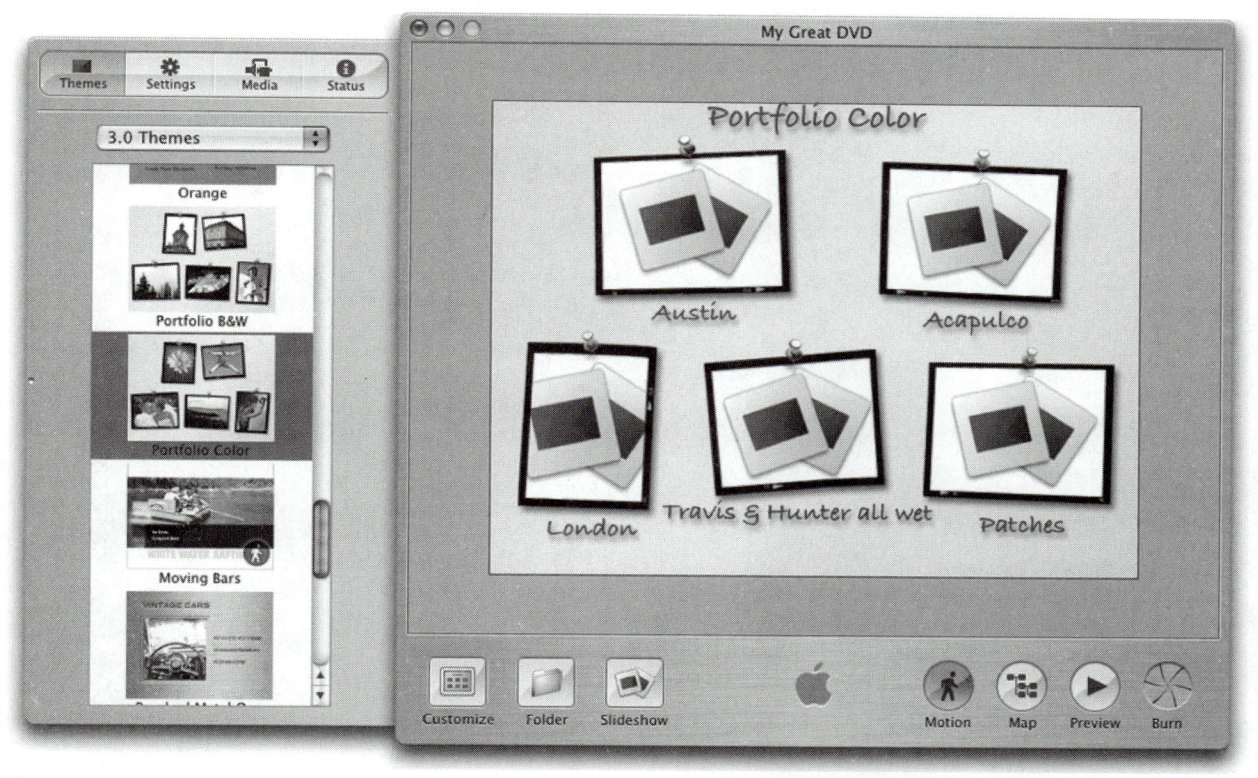

Figure 21-4

Choose a theme with multiple images when your DVD will contain slideshows from multiple albums

Frame up your button picture

Some themes (such as the Orange theme) have a frame in which you can place a photo. To add a photo to this frame, follow these steps:

1. **Click the Media button in the drawer.**

2. **Pick Photos from the pop-up list just below the drawer.** This displays a list of albums (and the photo library) in the upper part of the Customize pane. The lower part of the Customize pane shows the images from the selected album.

3. **Add an image to a frame.** Simply click and drag the image from the Customize pane to the frame (see Figure 21-5). If the title page has multiple frames, you use the same technique to fill each frame with a photo.

For themes that support one photo frame for each slideshow — such as the Portfolio Color theme — use this easier way to add a photo to a frame:

1. **Click the frame to display the Slideshow slider (see Figure 21-6).**

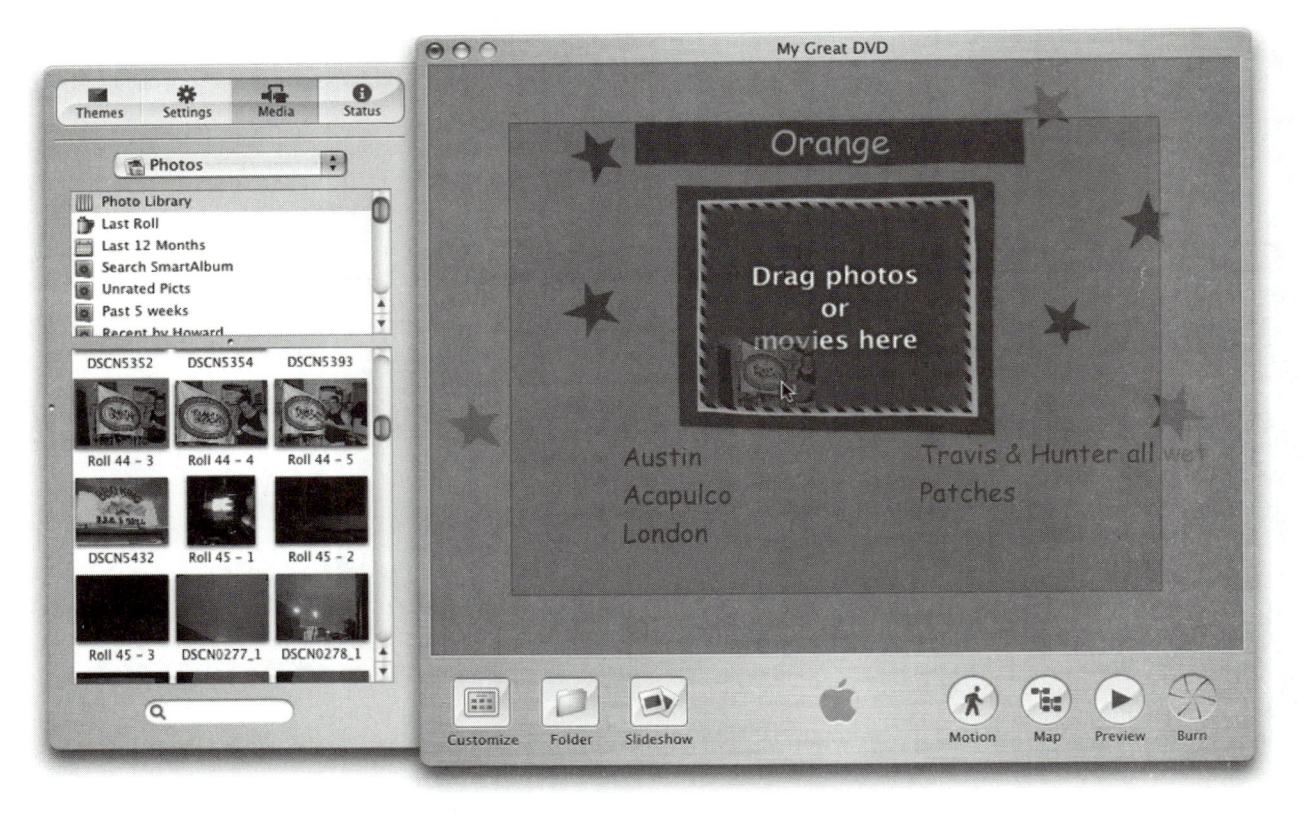

Figure 21-5
Click and drag a photo from the Customize pane to a frame in the title page

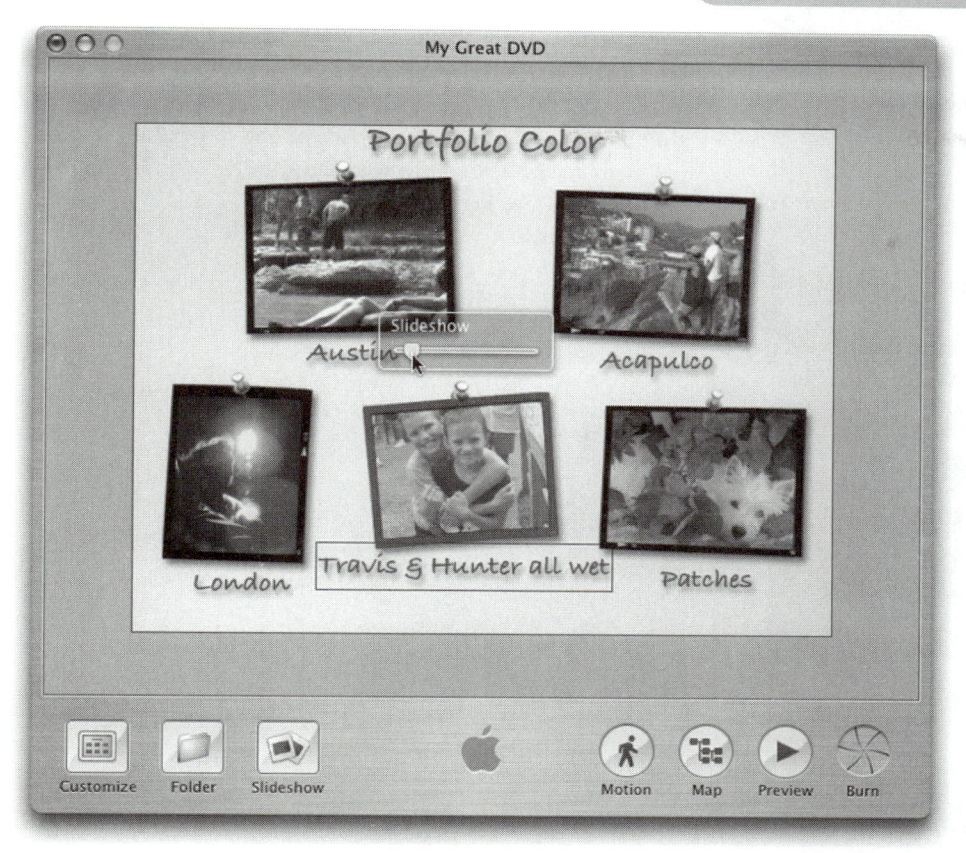

Figure 21-6
Use the Slideshow slider to choose an image for a slideshow's frame

2. **Click and drag the slider.** As you drag, images from the album display inside the frame.

3. **Stop dragging the slider when you see the image you want to use.**

▼ **Tip**

You can use the Left and Right Arrow keys to step through the images in the slideshow one at a time. This makes selecting the exact picture you want to use easier.

You can move the text and any photo frames on the title page: Just click and drag the text or a slideshow photo frame. If you find that the text or photo frame snaps back to its original location, click the Settings button in the drawer, and click the Free Position option in the Button section near the bottom of the Customize pane. This enables you to position the text and photo frame pretty much anywhere on the page — including overlapping one photo frame with another.

Changing text and titles

The default text associated with each slideshow is the album name, but you can change that by clicking in the text box, selecting the text, and typing the replacement text (see Figure 21-7). You can also use the same technique to modify the theme title text (such as Portfolio Color). This is a great way to add a title to the DVD main screen.

To customize the text and shape of the slideshow photo frames on the main screen, click the Settings button in the drawer (see Figure 21-8).

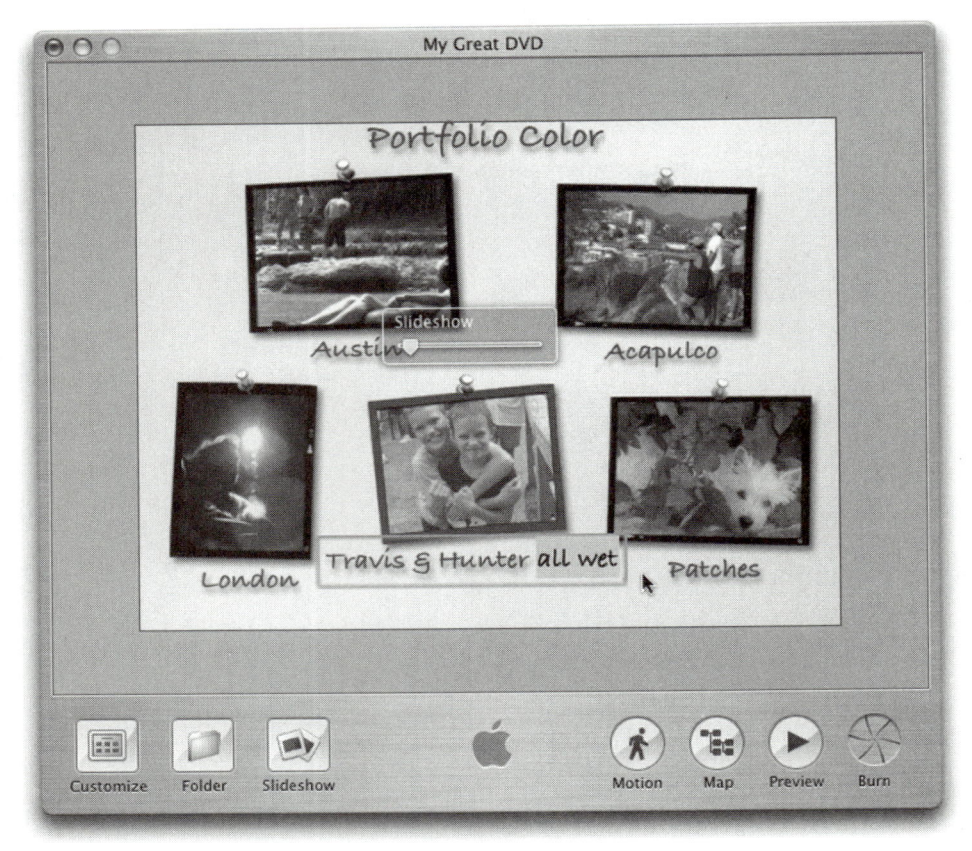

Figure 21-7
Edit the text for each slideshow using standard text-editing techniques

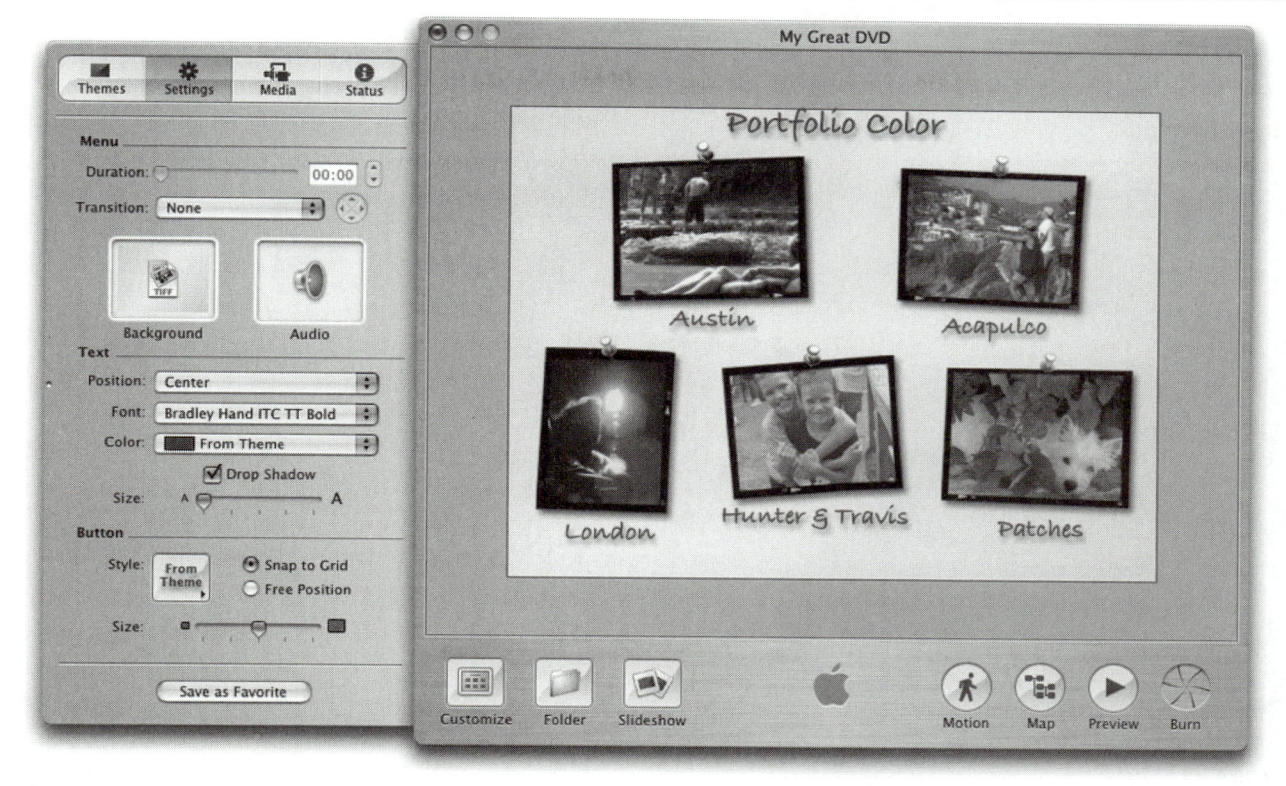

Figure 21-8
Modify the fonts and buttons using the Settings version of the Customize pane

With the Settings options selected, you can modify the following items:

- **Set the main title position.** Use the Position pop-up list in the Text section to pick the position of the title from the list or remove the title completely (by choosing No Title). Choose Custom to allow you to click and drag the title anywhere on the page.

- **Change the title font.** Click either the main title or one of the album titles you want to change. Pick the font you want from the Font pop-up list in the Text section.

 Note

When you select a slideshow title and make a change to the font family, color, size, or shadow, all the slideshow titles change. You can't change just a single slideshow title.

- **Change the title color.** Click either the main title or one of the album titles you want to change. Click the Color pop-up list in the Text section to pick the title color from a list (see Figure 21-9).

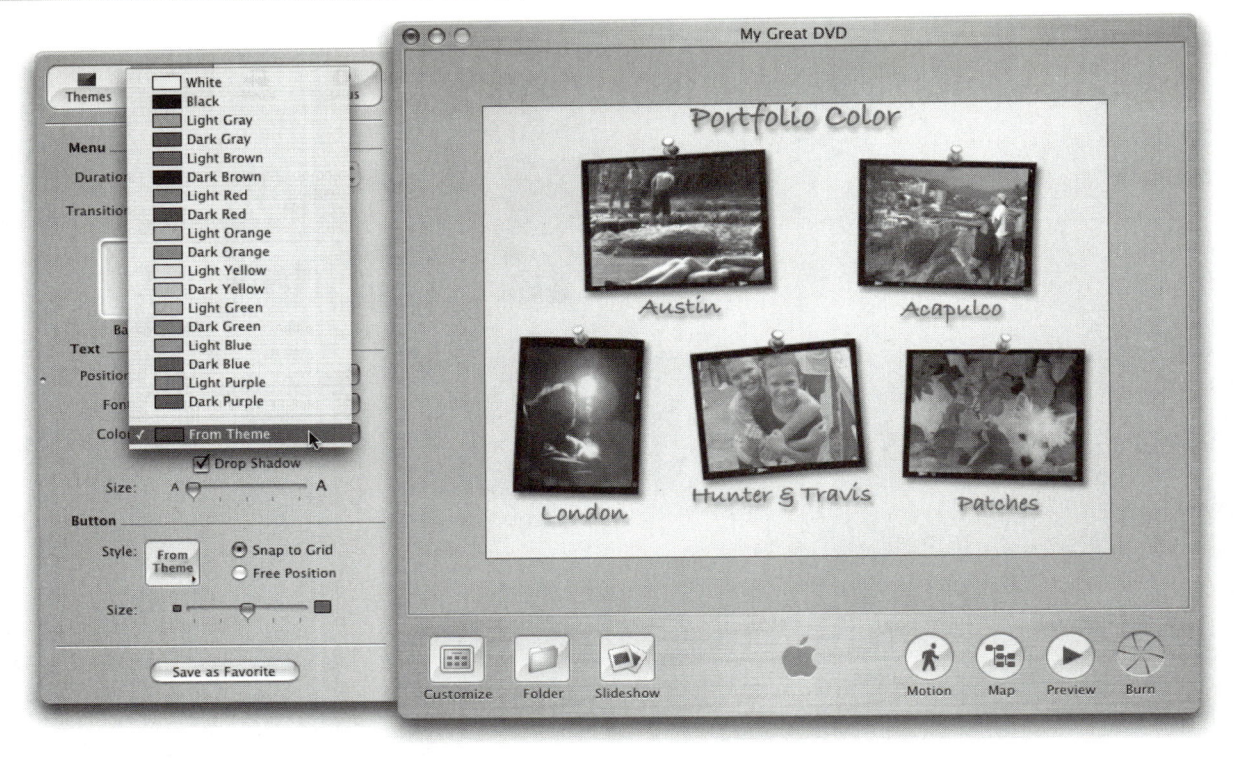

Figure 21-9
Use the color pop-up list to pick a title color

- **Change the title size.** Click either the main title or one of the album titles you want to change. Use the Size slider in the Text section to change the size of the title.

- **Specify a drop shadow for the titles.** Click either the main title or one of the album titles you want to change. Click the Drop Shadow checkbox to add a drop shadow to the title; clear the checkbox to remove the drop shadow.

- **Pick a transition between slides.** Select the transition between slides from the Transition pop-up list. You can configure some transitions for a direction. For example, you can set the Mosaic transition to begin at the top, bottom, left, or right; to specify this parameter, click the four-headed arrow button to the right of the Transition pop-up list.

- **Change the shape of the slideshow photo frames.** Click the Style button in the Button section to display a list of photo frame shapes (see Figure 21-10). Choose the shape you want from this list. Go ahead. Pick the heart. You know you want to! *(Awwwwww! Das jus so cuuuute!)* Okay, now pick a more manly selection if you feel the need. Figure 21-11 shows a set of oval photo frames. The "From Theme" option just picks the default shape the theme designers picked in that theme.

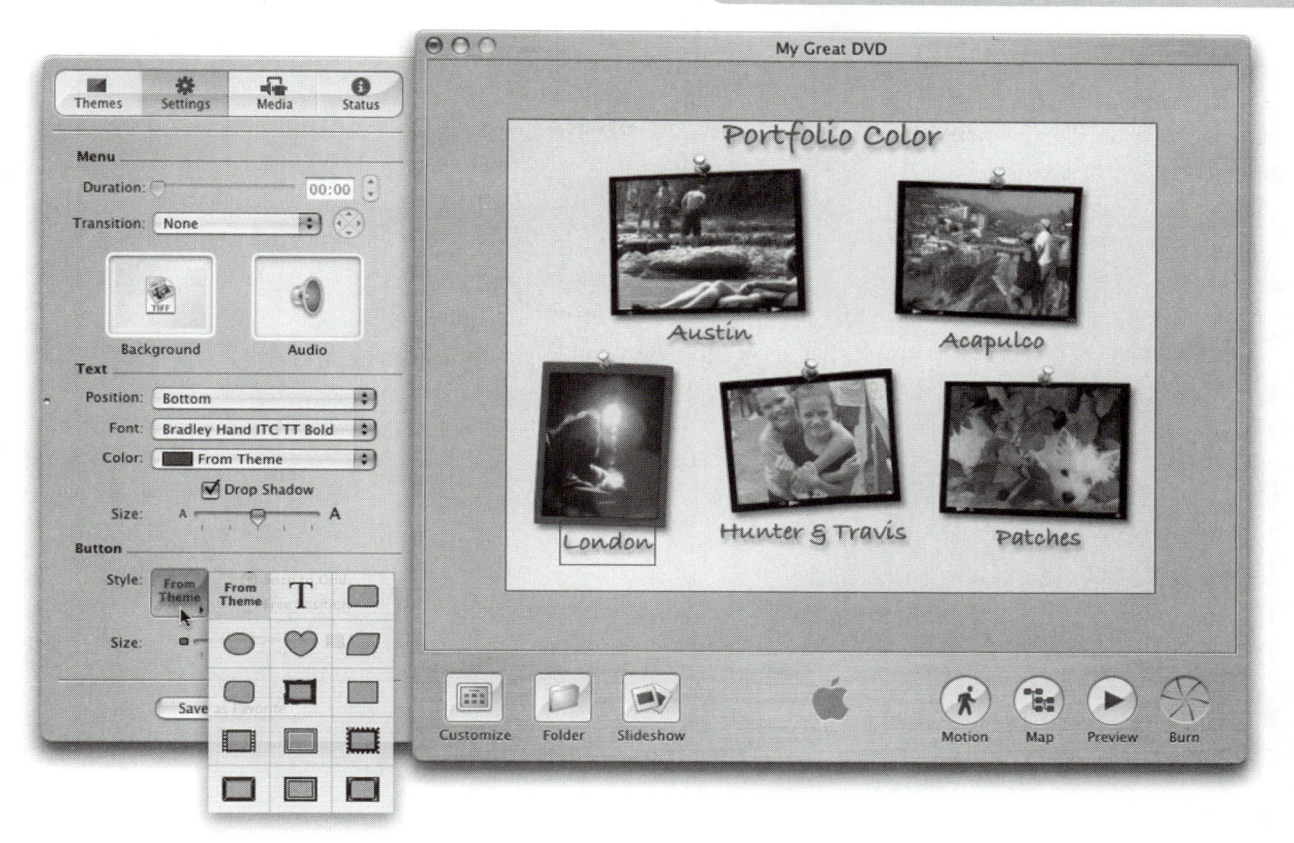

Figure 21-10
Pick a slideshow photo frame shape from the button shape list

- **Change the button size.** Click and drag the Size slider in the Button section of the Customize panel to adjust the size of the photo frames.

Menus need tunes too!

While you're fumbling around with the remote trying to decide what slideshow to watch, your DVD can be serenading you with a selection from your iTunes music library. It gives your menu pages a little more personality than a silent picture. Follow these steps:

1. **Click the Media button in the drawer.**

2. **Pick Audio from the pop-up list (see Figure 21-12).** This displays the contents of your iTunes library.

3. **Drag either a playlist from the top section of the panel or a song from the selected playlist to the main title screen.**

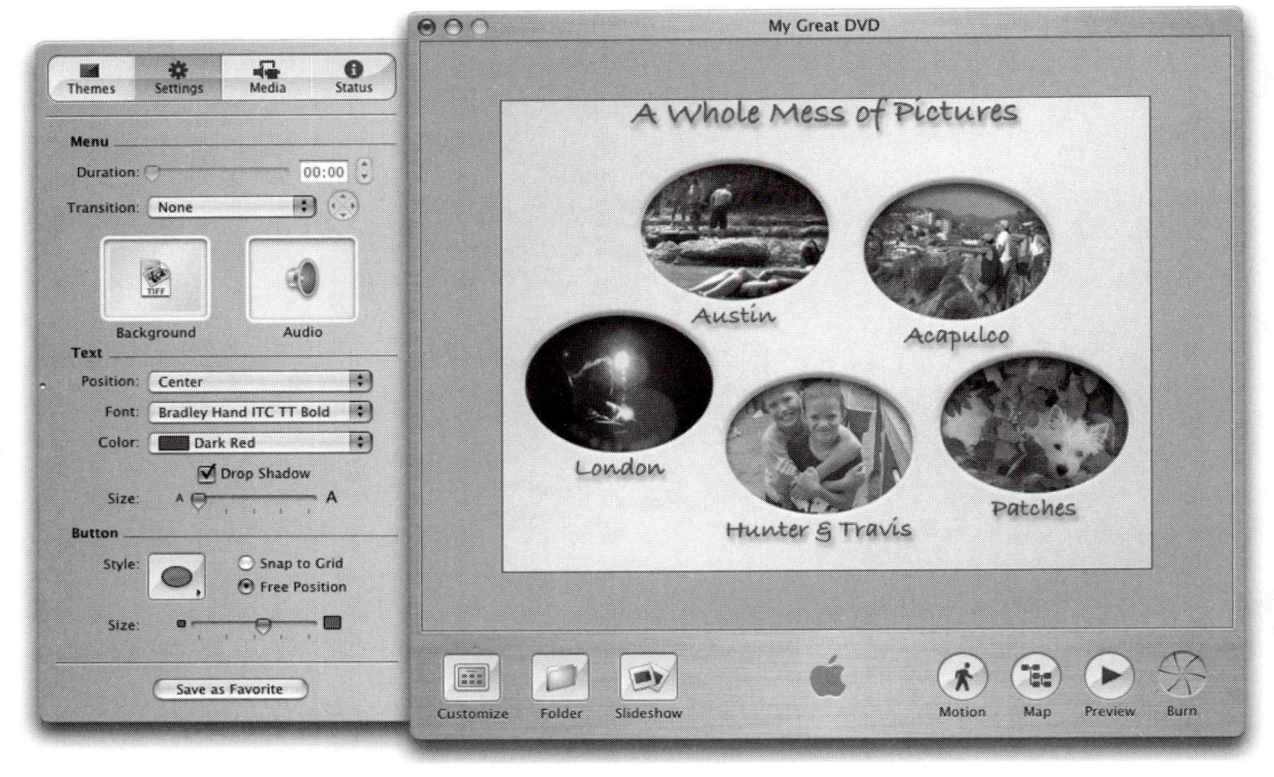

Figure 21-11
A different photo frame shape can dress up your main title page

4. **Click the Settings button in the drawer to switch back to Settings.**

5. **Use the Duration slider to set how long the tune should play (up to a maximum of the song length).** To actually hear the song, make sure the Motion button is activated (the button is green when activated).

One thing to keep in mind is that you can only assign one music *selection* to each menu page. Since you can assign a *playlist* as a music selection, that's right, you can apply multiple music cuts which will play in sequence! That's the silver lining. Now for the cloud. The duration of a menu can't go past 15 minutes. I just tried to assign the entire album *Who's Next* to a menu and it only gets through *Baba O'Riley*, *Bargain*, and *Love Ain't for Keepin'*, but it cut out about 2 minutes through *My Wife*.

Another creative use here would be to record your own audio file to use as the menu page. Use iMovie to record your own voiceover or combine it with music and export

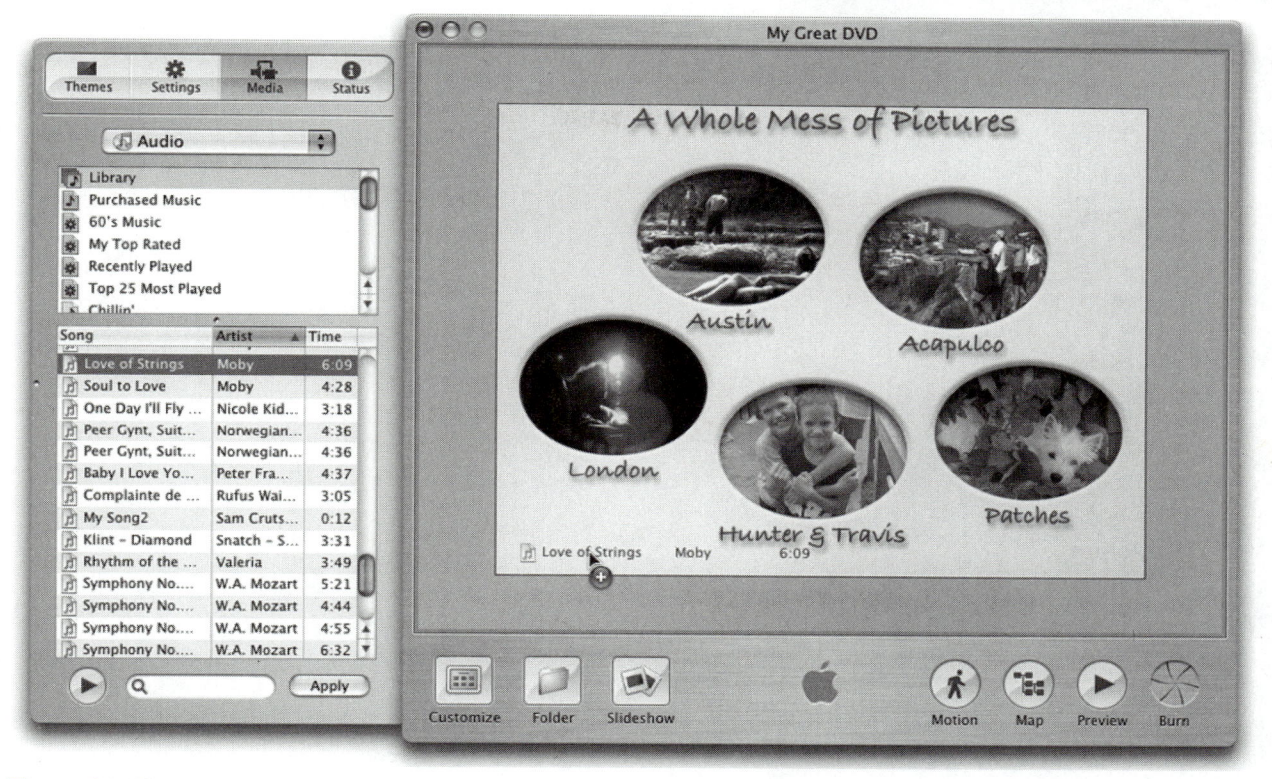

Figure 21-12
Add music to the main title screen from the Audio drawer

that into iTunes and it will be able to be used here. I actually got that idea from a couple of fish named Marlin and Dory who kept telling me to pick a button already and watch their little Finding Nemo cartoon.

TWEAK YOUR SLIDESHOWS

After you finish with the main title screen, you can configure the individual slideshows. This is where you tell the DVD all the specs for each individual photo album.

Double-click the slideshow to switch to the Slideshow screen (see Figure 21-13). To return to the main title screen, click the Return button.

Rearrange and remove slides

You can rearrange and remove slides from the slideshow. To rearrange the slides, click and drag to set the new order. As you drag the slide, you'll see a dark line like what you see in Figure 21-14 when you're between slots, but when

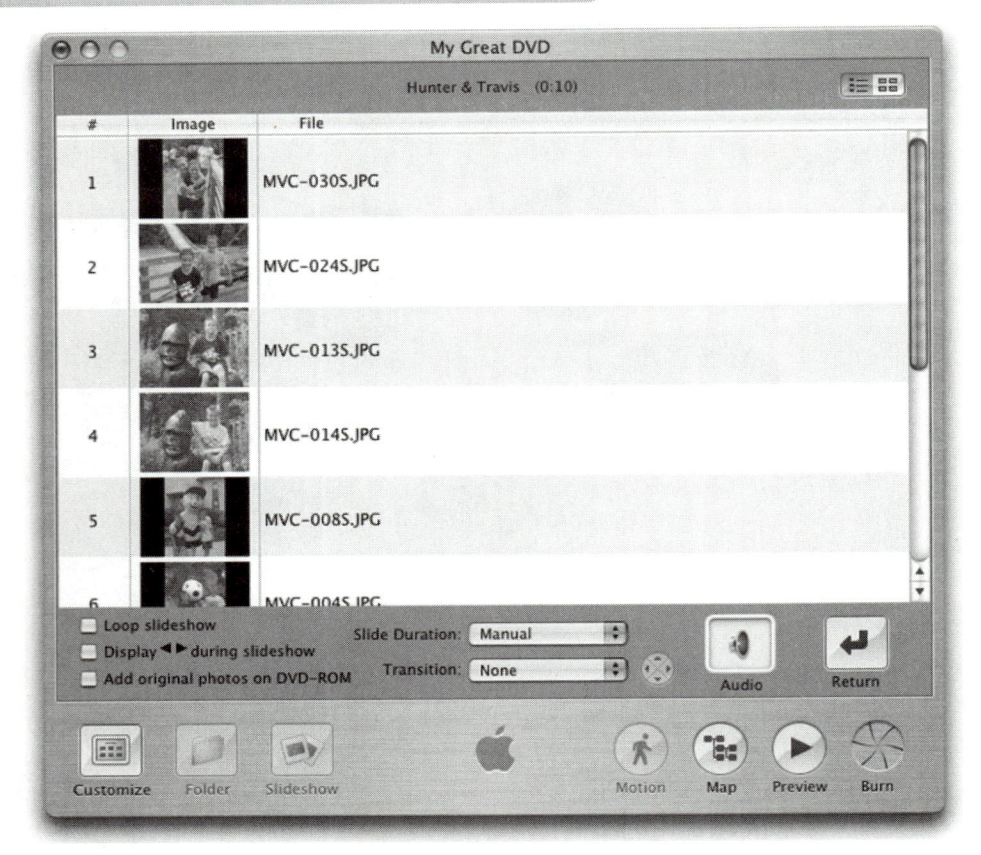

Figure 21-13
Configure an individual slideshow from the Slideshow screen for that album

you're directly over a slot, a dark rectangle appears around the slide before which the dragged slide will be placed. To me it's just easier to aim with the line target since there's no real confusion about what will happen when you let go; not that you're going to launch any missiles or anything if you drop a photo in the wrong place; I'm just saying it's a tad confusing.

To remove a slide from the slideshow, select it and press the Delete key, or choose Edit ➡ Delete.

If you want to see more slides on the screen, switch from the thumbnail list shown in Figure 21-14 to a more compact view (see Figure 21-15). To switch back and forth between these views, use the pair of controls in the upper-right corner of the iDVD screen.

 Note

You can rearrange the slides in this view as well: Just click and drag a slide to its new position. The existing slides rearrange automatically.

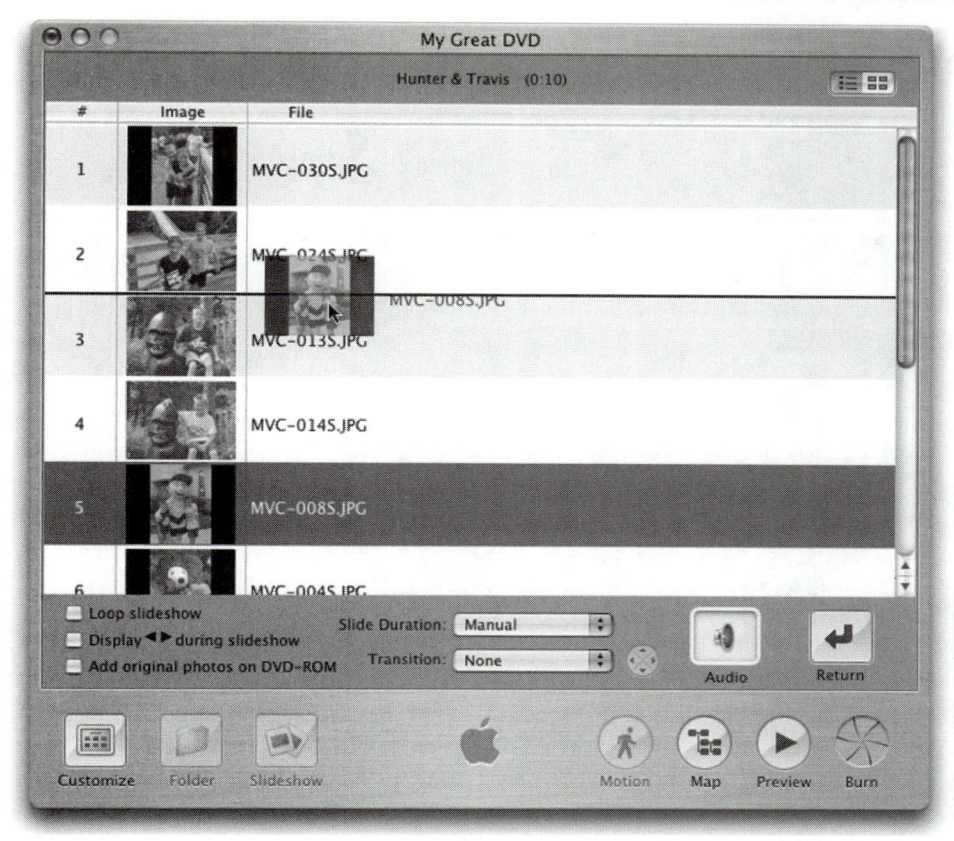

Figure 21-14
Click and drag slides to rearrange the order

Adding and deleting a music track

You can also add a music track to a slideshow by following these steps:

1. **Click the Media button in the drawer.**

2. **Pick Audio from the pop-up list.** This displays a list of music from your iTunes library.

3. **Click and drag a playlist or a song to the Audio well (just to the left of the Return button).** The

Audio well displays an icon representing the format of the music (refer to Figure 21-15 for an example of the MPEG4 icon).

You can purchase music from Apple's iTunes Music Store and then use those tracks on your DVD. That MPEG4 icon with the lock usually indicates a music cut from the iTunes Store. To remove a song from the slideshow, click and drag the Audio well out of the iDVD window. The Audio well icon changes to show a speaker icon, indicating that no music is attached to the slideshow.

Figure 21-15
View more thumbnails on the screen with this arrangement

▼ Note

By default, each slideshow inherits the music track of the album from which it was created. Because each album has a default music track ("Minuet in G"), each slideshow also has a default music track. If you don't want a music track, you have to discard the default track as described in the last paragraph. In addition, if you leave the music as "Minuet in G," the option to set the slide duration to fit to the audio is unavailable (a bug?).

Setting buttons, slide duration, transitions, and other options

Finally, you can set the following options from the Slideshow screen:

- **Display forward and back arrows during the slideshow.** Click the Display ◀▶ during slideshow checkbox to show these arrows on the screen. When you preview the slideshow, clicking one of these arrows jumps to the next or previous slide immediately.

- **Include original photos on the DVD.** Click the Add original photos on DVD-ROM checkbox if you want to make the *full-quality photo files* available on the DVD. The slideshow versions of the photos are lower resolution, suitable for viewing on a TV screen, but not for printing.

- **Set the slide duration.** Use the Slide Duration pop-up list to set the amount of time each slide is on the screen (1,3,5, or 10 seconds). If you added a music track to the slideshow, click the Fit To Audio option so that the slideshow finishes when the music does. The Manual option becomes available (and the Fit To Audio option becomes unavailable) only if the slideshow has no music track associated with it.

- **Loop slideshow.** If you want the slideshow to loop continuously, click the Loop slideshow checkbox. When the slideshow finishes, it loops back to the beginning and starts over.

- **Transition.** You can override the slide transition defined in the main title screen's preferences by setting a slide transition for the individual albums. Choose the transition you want to use from the Transition pop-up list. If necessary, use the four-headed arrow button to configure the transition.

PREVIEW THE SLIDESHOW

You should preview the slideshow to make sure everything works as expected before you burn the results to a DVD. To preview the contents of your DVD, make sure the Motion button is activated and click the Preview button. iDVD displays the main title screen and a player window that simulates a DVD control (see Figure 21-16). You can move between the different slideshows using the arrow keys on the control. Click the enter button in the center of the arrow keys to select a slideshow.

The rest of the buttons on the controller work just like their counterparts on a real DVD controller. These buttons include pause and stop buttons, a volume control slider, and buttons to move to the next or previous slide. To exit the preview, click either the Preview button again or the exit button on the controller. To return to the main title screen (so you can pick and view another slideshow) click either the title button or the menu button.

BURN YOUR DVD

To burn your slideshow onto a recordable DVD, make sure the Motion button is activated and click the Burn button *twice*. The first time opens the little shutter, and the second actually starts the process. iDVD prompts you for a blank DVD if you haven't inserted one already (I like to wait until prompted). After that, iDVD gets busy and burns the DVD for you. Simply eject the DVD when iDVD informs you that the disc is ready.

USE THAT WHOLE ILIFE

You've pulled in your photos with iPhoto, added music from iTunes, and made sweet slideshows in iMovie and now iDVD. About the only thing we haven't used is GarageBand. I won't be covering that one here because it's two degrees of separation away from iPhoto: You'd have to create your music in GarageBand and export the resulting song over to iTunes, at which point you can use it as your accompaniment in any of the other iApps.

Hopefully, you can now see why all this stuff came in one box: It's all connected tighter than Tony Soprano.

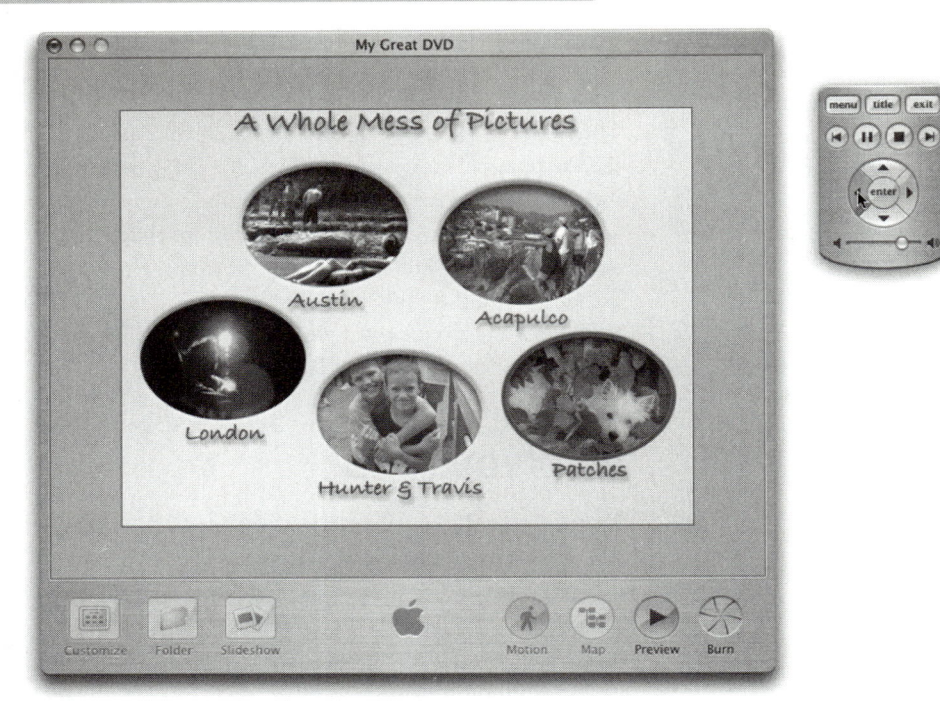

Figure 21-16
Use the simulated DVD controller to preview your slideshows before you burn the DVD

PART VII

Odds 'n Ends

Working with iPhoto Libraries

Okay. Due to some late editorial juggling and a publishing deadline that I heard whoosh past and crash into a tree several days ago, this chapter is more of a chapter-ette. It's no less informative than any other chapter; it's just a bit shorter. It's the Joe Pesci chapter. The Danny DeVito chapter. All the talent and attitude, but 1/3 less.... Oh never mind.

By default, iPhoto keeps all of its files in the Pictures folder of your home directory, under iPhoto Library. In that folder, iPhoto keeps everything it needs. Benefit from my pain: *Keep your mitts out of this folder*. iPhoto handles everything in there and if you go mucking about in it, you'll just bring trouble to your door. Don't delete pictures from there. Don't move anything out of there. Don't add things there from the Finder, thinking they'll show up in iPhoto. Changing anything in this folder is like somebody putting your shoes in the oven, but not nearly as funny because iPhoto has no sense of humor about such pranks.

For the most part, iPhoto only has the one library for everything; it *can* have different libraries (if you know the secret handshake), but iPhoto is only able to work with one library at a time. Using multiple libraries comes in handy if you want to keep certain pictures totally separate from other pictures. If you're a rocket scientist with lots of pictures of various covert new propulsion systems you're designing, it may be a good idea to *not* have those pictures in with your pictures from the Rocket Science Jamboree when your good friend, the international super spy, comes over to chat about, oh, *things*. You'd want to have those pictures in a different library on a removable drive you can stow in the anti-super-spy safe.

Another reason to have different libraries is that when the iPhoto Library gets past a certain size, the program starts to bog down. You can use a fresh library to get a clean start.

UNDERSTAND THE IPHOTO FOLDER STRUCTURE

When you run iPhoto for the first time, the program creates a directory structure in the Pictures folder of your user folder, starting with a folder called iPhoto Library (see Figure 22-1).

Inside the iPhoto Library folder, iPhoto creates a folder structure for storing images according to date:

- At the first level is a set of folders sorted according to year — one folder for each year.

- Inside each year folder is a set of folders sorted according to month.

- Inside each month folder is a set of folders sorted according to day.

- Inside each day folder are the image files (see Figure 22-2).

The day folders also contain some support folders:

- The Thumbs folder contains thumbnails of the images.

- The Data folder contains housekeeping data.

- The Originals folder, created after you edit an image, contains original copies (that you can revert to if necessary) of any edited images.

The iPhoto Library folder also contains support folders:

- The Albums folder contains album data.

- The iDVD folder contains data for creating DVD-based slideshows.

▼ Note

Do *not* mess with any of the files inside the iPhoto Library directory, especially the support files and folders. If you do, you may foul up iPhoto so bad you'll have to rebuild the library from scratch. Copying one of the images inside the day folders is safe, but that's about it.

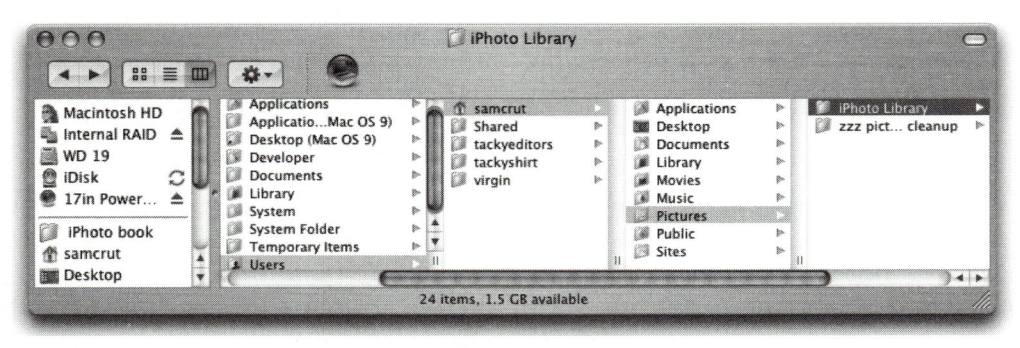

Figure 22-1
Click the Home button to navigate to your Users folder, and then open the Pictures folder

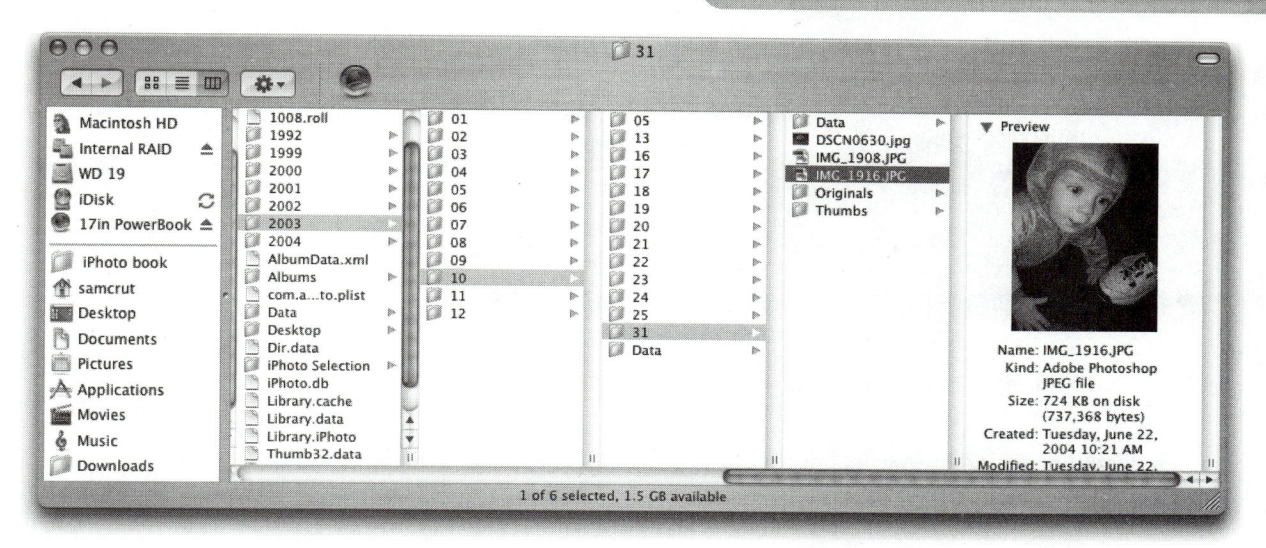

Figure 22-2
View the folder structure down to the image files

SUPER SECRET LIBRARY SWITCHER

As I mentioned in the introduction, iPhoto initially looks for a directory called iPhoto Library. If iPhoto doesn't find that folder, a dialog box comes up (see Figure 22-3) asking whether you want to create a new directory or find an existing directory. Of course, because you're a good boy or girl and you're not messing with the iPhoto Library folder, you'd never actually see this box.

Here's where I get really tricky: Quit iPhoto if it's currently running. Now launch it again while holding down the Option key. This tells iPhoto to pretend not to see your iPhoto Library so you can point the program to another library or tell it to create a brand new iPhoto Library.

Don't worry. If you change your mind and decide not to create a new iPhoto Library, press Quit and then launch iPhoto without the Option key; the program launches just like normal.

If you choose to create a new library, iPhoto asks you to choose the name and location for the iPhoto Library folder and then creates the folder with the proper structure. This folder *can be* in your Pictures folder with the other one but with a different name, or it can be on an attached FireWire hard drive. The folder can even be on a separate computer over the network if you don't mind iPhoto running slowly. Anywhere you can create a folder, you can create an iPhoto Library. Until you change it again, that new library will be your default every time you launch iPhoto. If you remove the external drive, or if you aren't mounted to the server where you stuck the new library, iPhoto simply brings up that same warning again.

If you choose Find Library, you get the standard Open window where you can navigate to the folder to use as the iPhoto Library. The folder does have to be an actual iPhoto Library folder. If it's not, you can click that little blue Open button until the cows come home; if iPhoto doesn't like what it sees, it waits for you to come to your senses and find it something it *can* eat.

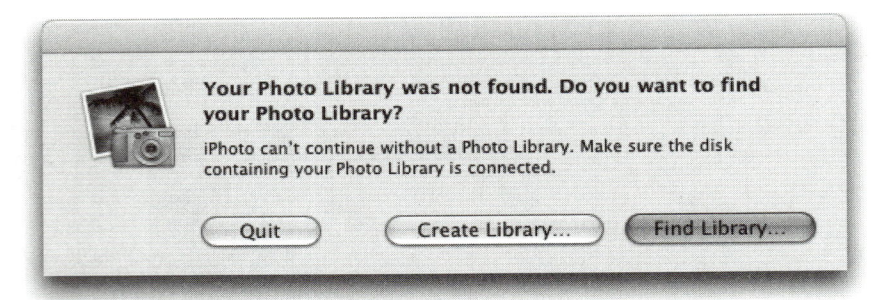

Figure 22-3
Oops! iPhoto can't find its library, so it asks what you want to do

My brother has four libraries on his system, but that's because he's been using iPhoto since it first came out; and prior to v. 4, if you had over 1,000 photos on a computer with a G3 processor, using iPhoto was like trying to walk through waist-high chocolate pudding, but without the tasty side effects. Now that he's running iPhoto v. 4, he's started to work from inside just one library.

Using multiple libraries has some major drawbacks: You can't drag stuff between them. Instead, you have to toss the pictures out to a folder, quit iPhoto, Option+boot it, switch libraries, and then import the pictures from your temp folder. Oh! Oops! Forgot to delete the picture from the other library. Now you have two copies.

You can see where this juggling can get a bit nerve-wracking.

PERILS OF POKING AROUND

At some point you may come to the conclusion that your photo collection is taking up way too much of your hard drive. Back in Chapter 14, I talked about how to back up your pictures to CD or DVD. After you back up those pictures, make sure you delete the pictures using iPhoto (not the Finder). If you use the Finder to delete the pictures, iPhoto still thinks they're sitting in the warehouse waiting to be pulled up. You'll have an incredibly annoying thing I call

"iPhoto Ghosts." They're pictures that aren't with us any more, but they still haunt our photo albums and picture collections. iPhoto still shows the picture. It's a thumbnail remnant, so it's usually fuzzy; but if you zoomed the picture to fill the window, the thumbnail may be pretty decent looking, good enough to make you think the picture's still there. When you try to edit the photo, BWAHAHAHAH, there's nothing there. (Sound Cue: Spooky Wind.)

I thought I was better than iPhoto. I mucked around in the iPhoto Library to try to delete a bunch of duplicate pictures I accidentally imported twice. I ended up with hundreds of pictures that had a good file and an iPhoto Ghost as well.

You'll get a different sort of phantom if you save files directly into the iPhoto Library structure where you think they should go. *Don't do that!* It doesn't work. You simply end up with a file sitting in your iPhoto Library folder, totally ignored by iPhoto.

Like I mentioned earlier, the iPhoto folder is broken down by shoot date. If you go digging around and find pictures that are in the wrong folder according to what date you remember taking them, you may think you can just change the name of the folder to the right date. *Don't do that!* Change the date on the picture(s) *from inside iPhoto* in the Info pane or with the Batch Change contextual menu.

Are you sensing a trend here? Treat the iPhoto Library folder like a snooty art gallery. Pretend that touching anything in there will set off alarms and mobilize a bunch of security goons to come whack you on the knuckles and say, *"Don't do that!"*

REBUILDING THE LIBRARY

If you've already thrown a monkey wrench into your iPhoto Library prior to my warning to you, or for those of you who broke it even after I warned you, there's still hope. Well, it may not actually be your fault. Sometimes computers just get cranky and need an attitude adjustment.

You can rebuild the iPhoto Library.

Just boot up iPhoto while pressing Shift+Option. That brings up a window asking you if you're sure you want to rebuild the database. Clicking Yes creates a whole new catalog of your pictures, but your old iPhoto Library is left intact. Everything in your old iPhoto Library folder is imported into the new folder and put in the right place. This should catch any pictures that are in the folders but not showing up in iPhoto for whatever reason. It also gets rid of any extraneous files that are left over from previously deleted images.

On the downside, your photo roll structure is most certain to be wiped out. Some other issues involving disappearing keyword assignments have been reported here and there.

This process can take a *looooong* time if you've got a lot of pictures; and because it copies every picture to the new folder, you have to have enough drive space available to house both the old and the new libraries. Afterward, you can delete the old iPhoto Library folder from your Pictures folder, but I recommend you work with the new library for a bit and see if you'd rather just revert back to the previous one.

The rebuild strikes me as a quick and dirty addition to iPhoto to help out with certain corruption issues, and it lacks the finesse I personally expect from my Mac; so for me, rebuilding is not a maintenance routine I'd jump into lightly.

But hey, if you've got the drive space, there's no harm in giving it a try. Like I said, it's nondestructive. Your old structure is still there to revert back to now that you know the super secret library switcher (Option+launch iPhoto).

The iPhoto Library folder has a sort of siren call to people like me. We get a kick out of the fact that there's a folder on our hard drive for *every single day* that we've ever taken a picture with our digital cameras. Yeah, it's something you can do with a Smart Album or whatever, but sometimes it's just faster to go into /iPhoto library/2002/10/31 and see what I was doing or where I was on my birthday a few years ago. Oh. Heh. Did I say 2002? Uh, no. That picture isn't for this crowd. I'm just glad eyebrows grow back. Leave the fire eating for the fire-eaters. That's what I always say. Now.

Anyway, the reason most people used to have separate iPhoto libraries has pretty much been taken care of by iPhoto v4's steel reinforced database upgrade from the previous version. It handles thousands of photos much better now. You're not *forced* to keep your collection below a wimpy threshold, but hey, this is America! We have a little thing called choice. We can choose to split up our libraries... into... (sigh). Sorry. It's an election year and that means that I'm getting swamped with, um, *flag* waving on every channel. It was bound to slip in at some point.

Oh, those of you in other countries can choose too – the library thing anyway.

PART VIII

Bonus Chapters from Andy Ihnatko

Automating iPhoto with AppleScripting

Have you ever stopped to thank the folks who built your car for putting in pedals and a steering wheel? You should. Think about how tough it'd be to manhandle that thing through downtown Boston if you had to haul out a socket wrench and crank the nut on the steering column every time you wanted to make a left turn. Because the people at Apple have a similar commitment to the user experience, when they designed iPhoto they were nice enough to toss in a user interface for free. Menus, buttons, windows... you've got the whole schmeer.

But the user interface isn't the only way you can interact with iPhoto. AppleScript is a system-wide resource that allows you to access the features of nearly any Mac OS X application directly. Instead of making things happen by clicking buttons and menus, you write a *script* of actions that you'd like the app to perform automatically. AppleScript isn't for everybody — it's a simple programming language that reads like plain English. It's a fun programming language, but it's still a programming language. Regardless, it's worth knowing about. If you learn a little bit about AppleScript, you can download and use some of the slick iPhoto scripts that are floating around on the Web. And if you learn more than a little bit, you can take a tedious 12-step process and reduce it to a single mouse click.

MEET APPLESCRIPT

I can't teach you all about AppleScript, but, hopefully, you'll walk away from this chapter with enough of the groundwork to start exploiting iPhoto's scriptability. AppleScript isn't a stand-alone app or a utility. It's a fundamental part of Panther's architecture, just as intimate as the mechanism that prints files or draws windows and menus. It's a superhighway that allows every piece of software running on your Mac — including the OS itself — to interact with each other and work together. If AppleScript causes the Mail app to check for new mail, it doesn't do anything so unsophisticated as send a mouse click to the Mailbox menu's Get New Mail item. It actually communicates with the code lurking *inside* Mail.

WHAT MAKES APPLESCRIPT SO GOSH-DARNED SUPER?

I'd like to think that at this point in the book, the mere fact that you're slobberingly enthusiastic about AppleScript should be reason enough for you to march straight into your child's public school, tear down all those pictures of losers like George Washington and Abraham Lincoln, and replace them all with shots of Sal Soghoian and Chris Espinosa, Apple's Iron Man and Captain America of AppleScript.

THIS OLD SCRIPT

So AppleScript is like the general contractor on a big home-remodel project. It can do things on its own without having to control other applications at all, but in everyday use its typical function is to hand tasks off to specialists, make sure they have what they need to get the job done, and make sure that all these individual tasks are done in the specified sequence without any errors.

Some of you might have been skipping around the book and haven't developed the sense of blind, robotic faith that has caused everybody else to acquire that slightly glazed look of contentment and buried individuality that's caused so much comment around the post office recently. So here's what makes AppleScript so special:

- Every Mac OS X app can be controlled through AppleScript to one extent or another (more on this later). It's a fundamental system resource.

- It's powerful and flexible enough that it can do most anything. Calculate the volume of a cone? Sure. Take 40 documents from your local drive; download 20 more from eight other people scattered all over the world; assemble all this content into a 100-page, full-color report; transmit this report to a shop for printing, binding, and delivery; and email digital copies to four department heads? A tad more ambitious, surely, but well within AppleScript's capabilities.

- Writing AppleScript is a basic skill that you can exploit elsewhere. Not only can you use AppleScript in simple automation projects, but also if you ever get the itch to start writing software for real, most of the popular Macintosh development systems (REALbasic, Revolution, Apple's XCode system) can use your AppleScripts without any additional conversion or transmogrification. So, if you've spent a month gradually turning a three-line convenience script into a sophisticated productivity solution, you're probably about 80 percent of the way to turning it into a rock-solid commercial app.

- With most programming languages, the code you write is as simple to read and understand as one of those customizable message signs that still sits outside the gas station seven years after the owner lost the last vowel in the set. No programming language is trivial to learn, but anybody can read a working script and get an immediate sense of what it does and how.

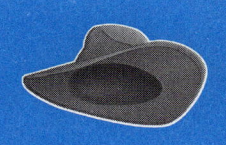

EASIER THAN ORDERING IN A FRENCH RESTAURANT

No, really. Let's say you want your AppleScript to make a list of every file in a selected folder whose file type is a JPEG Image. What would the AppleScript for that be? Here it is:

every file in (select folder) whose file type is "JPEG Image"

If *that* doesn't leave you agog, then your agogulator is long overdue for its scheduled periodic maintenance.

But is there anything about AppleScript that will make me want to, you know, drop my mouse, stomp outside, and go chuck rocks at birds? Well, in the interests of fairness, I need to point out that:

- **Application support of AppleScript is spotty.** Making sure that an application can be controlled by AppleScripted instructions is the responsibility of the app's developers, and frankly, many of them feel that they have enough on their hands ensuring that their new fuzzy-logic search-and-replace routine doesn't have the ability to one day become self-aware and lead all the machines in an uprising that will result in humanity becoming a slave race mining selenium and tungsten under the emotionless, unpitying steel heels of emotionless overlords. So, some apps (particularly those published by Apple itself) support AppleScript with all the zealotry of a member of alt.nerd.obsessive who's just read a public message claiming that the USS *Enterprise* could probably beat the *Millennium Falcon* in a battle. But others only support the four bare minimum AppleScript commands mandated by Apple: run, open a document, print a document, quit.

- **The documentation really stinks.** Apple doesn't do enough to provide users with AppleScript tutorials. And because every application supports AppleScript in its own individual way, the fact that you've mastered the AppleScript skill of creating a new document in TextEdit doesn't necessarily mean you've picked up any of the skills you'll need to create a new outgoing email in Mail.

- **Debugging stinks, too. At least in places.** In plush, cushy development systems like REALbasic, when you make a mistake with your code, the system clearly flags it and specifically explains the nature of the problem, and it might even suggest a solution. AppleScript tells you "TextEdit got an error: NSCannotCreateScriptCommandError" and you should feel lucky it doesn't toss a derisive "*Duh!*" at you before hopping back on its skateboard and zipping away.

- **AppleScript's easygoing approach to English and syntax can often be a double-edged sword.** With a language like C or even Basic, the code has either been written correctly (the way that causes your project to build and run successfully) or incorrectly (the way that causes your computer to do nothing except repeatedly remind you of what a dipwad you are until you finally rewrite your code The Correct Way). In AppleScript, there are often several ways to achieve the same results. This is great, because programmers can develop a style that makes the most sense to them, personally, but if you're starting to learn AppleScript by looking at other people's scripts, it can give you fits. Some parts of the script have to be entered verbatim. Other parts are a matter of personal preference. Your mission, Mr. Phelps, is to learn to distinguish between the two.

DEFINITIVE ARTICLE

The word "the" illustrates everything that's good and everything that's frustrating about AppleScript. Early on, the language's architects (who wanted AppleScript to sound like English, remember) realized that without any "the"s, the line "set the title of the window to 'Utopia Limited'" would look like it was being spoken by Frankenstein's monster. People don't *like* Frankenstein's monster — he's misunderstood, yes, but come on, the dude's done some nasty stuff — so they decided that *the* is optional in a script. AppleScript will just *bloop* right over it. Good. But in rare instances, omitting a "the" will cause a script to fail. Or, *including* a "the" will cause the script to fail. It's entirely the fault of whoever it was who wrote the AppleScript features of the app you're trying to script for, not Apple's. But that's extremely cold comfort.

USING SCRIPTS

"I'm sold," you're saying. "I'll take a dozen in assorted flavors." So how do you use AppleScript in your day-to-day life of home, work, and worship?

You can get started by using AppleScripts that have been thoughtfully written for you by Apple and by other users. You'll find a folder named AppleScript inside your Applications folder. It contains lots of useful sample scripts, along with documentation and a couple of scripting utilities.

There are three different kinds of script files. You can see what their Finder icons look like in Figure 23-1.

ONWARD FROM HERE

If you want to see what some *non*-Apple employees have been doing with AppleScript, skip ahead to the end of this chapter, wherein I list a number of online scripting resources. Many of them have enormous hoards of useful scripts available for free download.

- **Script Files.** These are akin to AppleScript documents. This format is used for scripts that you're still tweaking because while you can run them by double-clicking them, they can't run unless the Script Editor application is running as well.

- **Applets.** These are the standard, useful form of script. The AppleScript code has been saved as a Macintosh application — albeit one without a slick Macintosh user interface — so this script can run all by itself without any assistance from Script Editor.

- **Droplets.** These are a special form of applet. You can run them by double-clicking, but you can also drag and drop a file or a folder of files onto them. Doing this runs the droplet and tells it, "Whatever it is that you do, I want you to do it to all of *these* files."

Applets and Droplets are examples of compiled scripts. That is, for the purposes of speed and flexibility, the plain-text AppleScript instructions have been transmogrified into something considerably closer to the hobo's stew of numbers and addresses that a CPU is used to working with. You can still open them in Script Editor and edit their AppleScript code — unless the author decided to keep the code under wraps — but they'll run considerably faster than plain old Script files.

Figure 23-1
Script Files, Applets, and Droplets: The three faces of AppleScript

Launching scripts yourself

You can put Applets and Droplets anywhere you'd put an application. Keep 'em in the Dock, where you can easily launch them; put them on the Desktop or in the toolbar of your Finder windows so you can drag files and folders onto them. And like any other app, you can even have Panther launch them every time your Mac starts up by setting it as a Startup Item.

Mac OS X gives you another way of running scripts: the Scripts menu. This is a menu-let that you can install in your menu bar by double-clicking the Install Script Menu app found in your AppleScript folder. The Scripts menu looks like Figure 23-2.

By default, the Scripts menu comes populated with the dozens and dozens of utility scripts that were placed on your hard drive when you (or Apple) installed Mac OS X.

 Tip

Take a minute or two to walk through all those submenus and see what's there. There are some real gems to be found, including a whole collection of scripts that will apply modifications to a whole series of file names in the Finder.

The Scripts menu is populated from two sources: the Scripts folders located in your Home directory's personal Library folder, and your Mac's system-wide Library folder. Just drag in any Applet, Droplet, or script file. Scripts in your personal folder are yours and yours alone; any scripts you put in the system-wide folder will be available to any user. The scripts pop into the menu immediately (see Figure 23-3) and sink to the bottom of the list.

If you don't give a toss for any of those utility scripts, just click Hide Library Scripts and the menu will only show your personal stash.

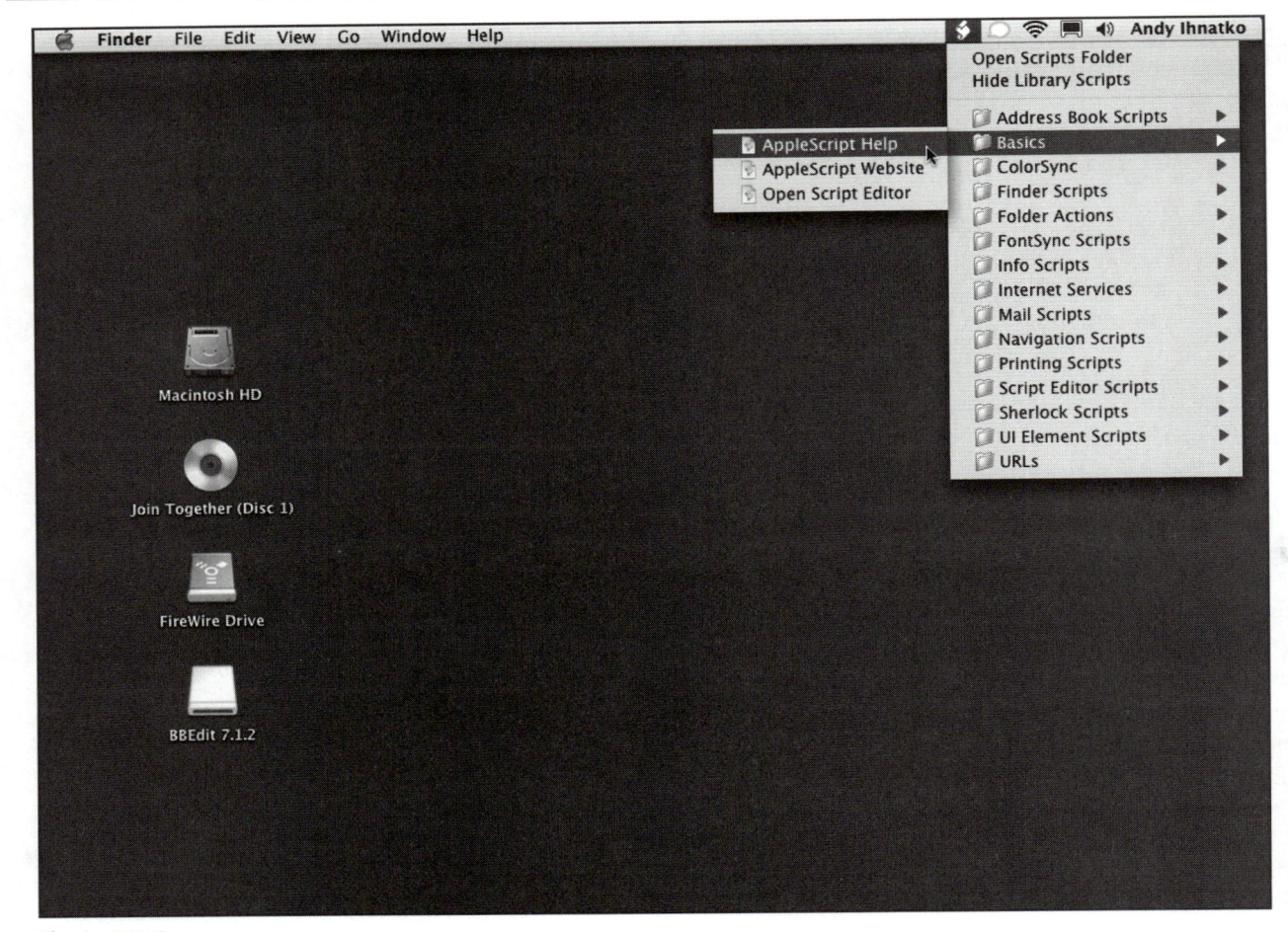

Figure 23-2
The Scripts menu

Attaching scripts to individual applications

A great many apps (including many of Panther's built-in apps) take advantage of AppleScript to increase their flexibility and power. The folks who wrote the Mail app, for example, couldn't possibly have thought of *everything* that *everybody* would *ever* want to do with mail. Even if they did, they all work in California. It's usually way too nice outside to stay cooped up inside bashing out code all day.

Mail can be scripted like any other Mac app, but it also can run scripts as part of its automatic mail filtering system (see Figure 23-4).

I've written an AppleScript that takes a specified message, converts it to text, and then installs it in my iPod's Notes folder so I can read it while I'm sitting in my doctor's office waiting for my weekly injection of sheep collagen. By attaching this script to a Mail rule, any time Mail

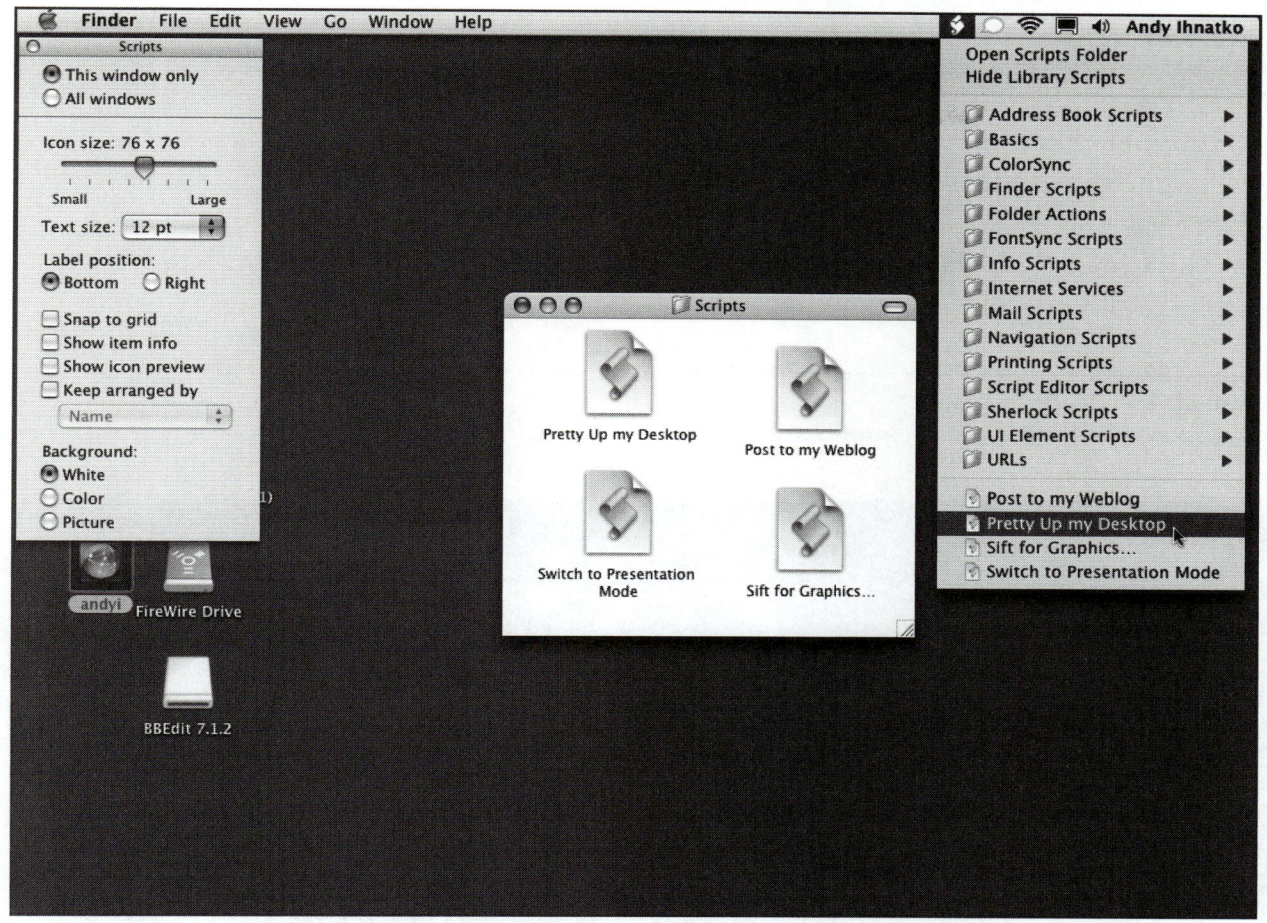

Figure 23-3
A few custom scripts in the Scripts menu

receives email digests from the Tony Danza Fanscene Message Board I belong to, it's automatically slurped onto the iPod.

That's just a single example of an app that can run an AppleScript automatically whenever a certain condition is met. They're all over the place. Go to System Preferences and click in the CDs & DVDs panel. It lets you dictate what Panther should do whenever a disc is inserted. There

are obvious things you'd want to do when you insert a disc of a certain type (audio CDs are opened in iTunes, photo CDs get handed off to iPhoto), but you can also tell Panther to run an AppleScript. That's handy for customizing Panther's response. I wish iTunes could display editorial information about a CD, as other players can. If it bugs me *that* much, I can write a script that opens the disc in iTunes, gets the name of the album, and then opens a Google page on it.

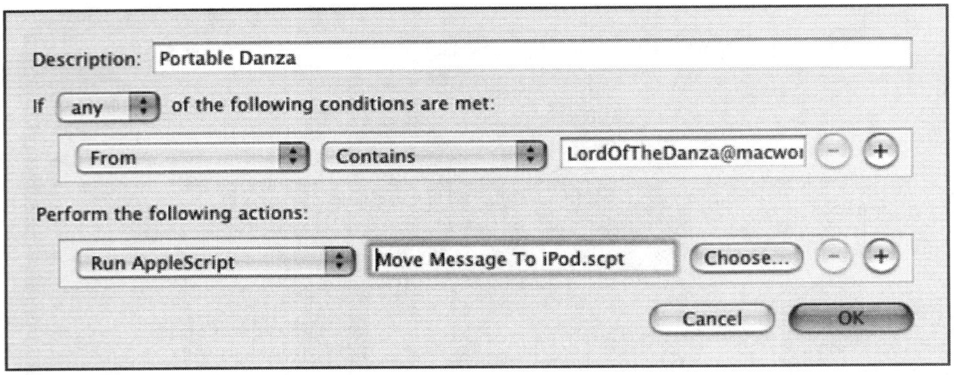

Description: Portable Danza

If [any ▼] of the following conditions are met:

[From ▼] [Contains ▼] [LordOfTheDanza@macwor] (–) (+)

Perform the following actions:

[Run AppleScript ▼] [Move Message To iPod.scpt] (Choose...) (–) (+)

(Cancel) (OK)

Figure 23-4
A Mail filter rule that triggers an AppleScript

BAD CRAZINESS

I've read the previous example and it's possible that you might come away thinking I'm not the harbinger of intense, brooding super-cool that would provoke comment among the likes of Sean Penn or Johnny Depp. So I will confess that the Mail script I *really* wrote is one that takes advantage of both Mail's scripting features and that of an app called XTension (www.shed.com). This app works with cheap home automation hardware and allows the Mac to both turn lights and appliances on and off and accept input from motion and temperature sensors.

Because I live the life of the sensitive artiste (and, again, I have that whole brooding thing going on), I often leave the office for a few hours to breathe a little fresh air. Depending on what I've got cooking, I may or may not check my email immediately when I get back, which can have serious repercussions if something important has come in when I had no idea that anything important might be coming in.

So here's what I did: I got my disco strobe light (It was a gift. *It was a gift.*) out of the closet, plugged it into a home-automation box, and wrote a three-line AppleScript for XTension so that any app could turn it on. I attached this script to a Mail rule so that the strobe activates whenever an email arrives from one of my editors, and voilá! When I pull into the driveway and see through the windows that there's a full-on rave in progress in my office, I head straight upstairs and check my email. Or, admittedly, I pull back out of the driveway again and hope that my assistant (either one of the two goldfish; doesn't matter) handles it. Either way, attaching scripts to mail actions is a useful feature.

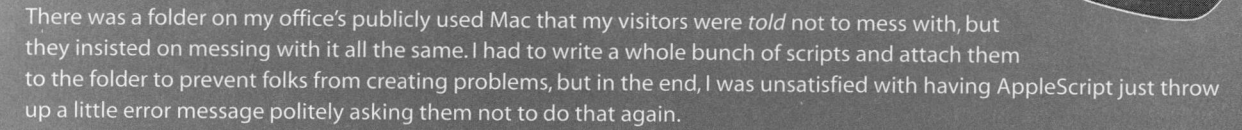

DO YOU FEEL PRODUCTIVE? WELL, DO YOU, PUNK?

But that's *productive.* Brrrrr! How about something stupid? Get a load of Figure 23-5.

There was a folder on my office's publicly used Mac that my visitors were *told* not to mess with, but they insisted on messing with it all the same. I had to write a whole bunch of scripts and attach them to the folder to prevent folks from creating problems, but in the end, I was unsatisfied with having AppleScript just throw up a little error message politely asking them not to do that again.

So I bought a repeating-action suction-cup gun at the toy store, fitted it with the door-lock actuator from an old car, gave it 12 volts of battery power, and wired it into a little interface box that allows a Mac to interact with electronics. And yes, the box is AppleScriptable.

The first visitor who tried to monkey with the folder got a polite warning. The second time resulted in three darts in the back of the head, fired from concealment behind a potted plant placed there for that specific purpose.

I haven't worked as a system administrator in quite some time. I think it's because I was just so dashed effective at my job that I set an impossibly high standard for others to follow. Plus, I kept stealing photocopiers, and if I'd known that was the boss's daughter, I sure wouldn't have encouraged her to drop out of law school and start a pottery business. Hindsight is 20-20, you know.

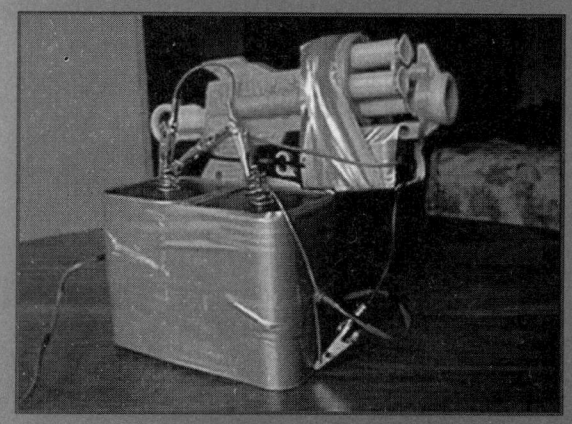

Figure 23-5
AppleScript applies a corrective action

It's just another way of turning Just Any Mac into a Mac that's specifically been dialed into your personal needs and preferences.

Attaching scripts to folders

One of AppleScript's ginchiest features went away temporarily during the transition to Mac OS X, but now it's back: Folder Actions. Just as Mail can run a script whenever a Mail Rule senses that a specific condition has been met, you can attach a script to a specific folder and have it run whenever any or all of the following things happen:

- The folder is opened.

- The folder is closed.

- An item is added.

- An item is removed.

- The folder's window is moved or resized.

And here I encourage you to just lean back in your chair — get out of bed first and move to your desk if need be because I like the visual of people leaning back with their hands folded behind their heads staring thoughtfully at the ceiling; c'mon, *work* with me, here — and consider the implications of this. Here's why AppleScript skills elevate you into a power user. For example, why bother publishing photos to your Weblog *by hand?* Attach a script to the folder that leaps into action whenever a new JPEG is added and uploads it to your Web site automagically.

You can attach a script to a folder through the folder's contextual menu. Folder Actions is a system-wide service that's disabled by default, so your first job is to turn it on. Control-click the folder to bring up its contextual menu and select Enable Folder Actions from the bottom of the list.

Select the folder's contextual menu a second time and you'll notice that a few new items have been added (Figure 23-6).

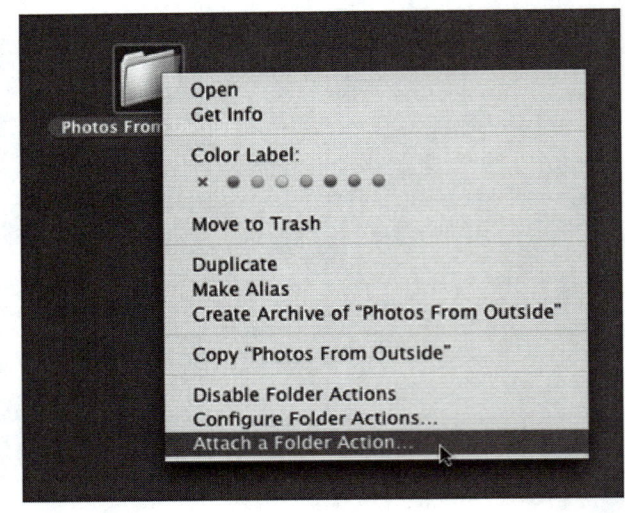

Figure 23-6
Setting up Folder Actions via a contextual menu

Clicking Attach a Folder Action will bring up a standard Choose File dialog. You can select any script anywhere on your hard drive, but by default, it points to Scripts ➜ Folder Action Scripts, located in your Mac's system-wide Library folder. There, you'll find a number of useful built-ins. Select add – new item alert.scpt.

 Tip

If you want to create a Folder Action Script that's available to all users of this Mac and not just you, be sure to copy it into the default folder.

This script is a useful thing to attach to your Drop Box. Every time someone on the network puts a file in your Drop Box, the script activates and alerts you (Figure 23-7).

Figure 23-7
Hail, Folder Actions! For now I know that Lenny has sent me the file he promised

You can attach multiple scripts to a folder. Removing scripts is just as straightforward: Activate the folder's contextual menu, go to Remove a Folder Action, and select the script from the submenu.

Apple, who loves you and only wants what's *best* for you and your siblings, has also provided you with the Folder Actions Setup utility (Figure 23-8).

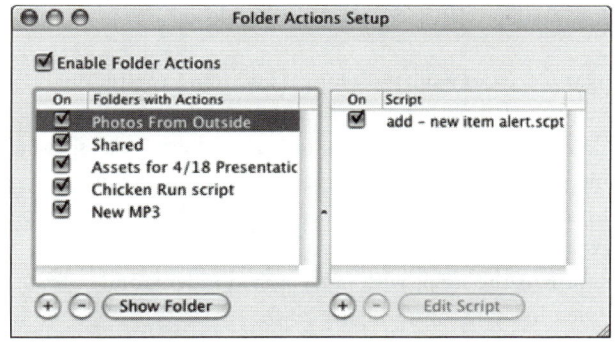

Figure 23-8
The Folder Actions Setup utility

As you add more and more scripts to more and more folders, a management utility such as this becomes more and more necessary. At a glance, it shows you which folders have scripts attached to them, and allows you to temporarily disable or enable them with a handy click.

PLEASE, ORGANIZE ME

And here I say, "Thank the Great Gor of Ranxeron-9." I'm what you'd call a power user, which means that I've customized my Mac's operations to such an extent that I barely have half an idea of what's going on three-quarters of the time. I kept losing files in my Pictures folder once. It turned out that I had attached a script a week earlier to automatically process hundreds of photos that were coming in across the network, and I'd forgotten to turn that script off when I was done.

I choose to see this as a sign of my power and prestige. Do you think Donald Trump has half a clue what goes on inside his offices? Of course not. We're Big Picture men, too busy steering empires (his, an international real-estate and entertainment conglomerate; mine, a dual-processor G4 tower) to waste time on trivial details.

CREATING YOUR OWN SCRIPTS

So what features are Scriptable? Nearly every app supports at least four basic AppleScript commands:

- **Run:** Launches the app

- **Open:** Opens an item, typically a document file

- **Print:** Prints an item, again, typically a document

- **Quit:** Fold; pack it in; give up hope; take your ball and go home; you know... *Quit*

Anything above and beyond that is up to the ambition and commitment of the developer. It's a crapshoot of delight and disappointment. It's the *good* apps that keep you committed to AppleScript.

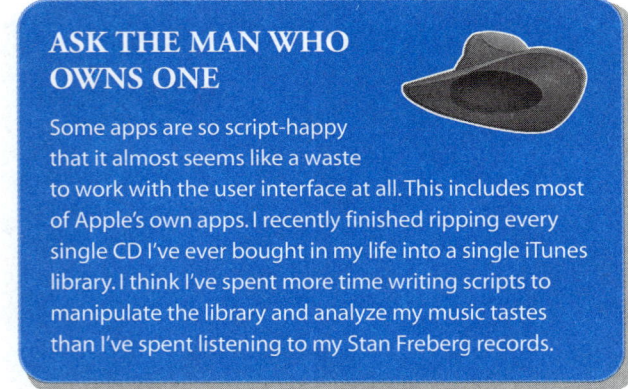

ASK THE MAN WHO OWNS ONE

Some apps are so script-happy that it almost seems like a waste to work with the user interface at all. This includes most of Apple's own apps. I recently finished ripping every single CD I've ever bought in my life into a single iTunes library. I think I've spent more time writing scripts to manipulate the library and analyze my music tastes than I've spent listening to my Stan Freberg records.

Script Editor

Script Editor is the app you'll use to record scripts, edit existing ones, write brand-new scripts of your own, and crack open your applications to see just how scriptable they are. You'll find it inside your AppleScript folder, which awaits you inside Applications. Figure 23-9 shows you a typical script-editing window.

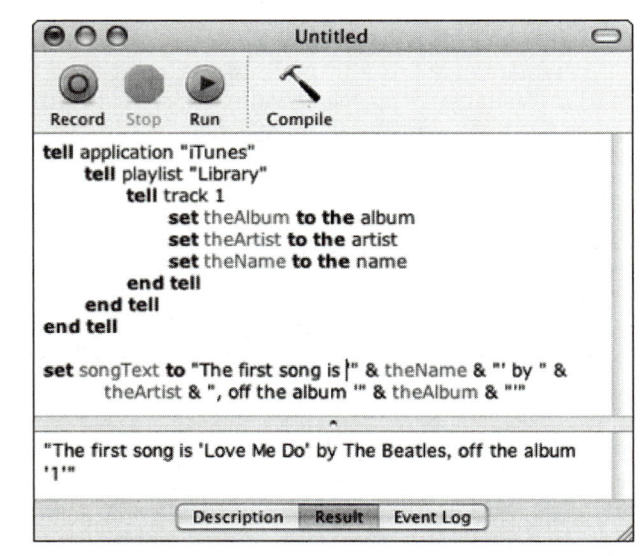

Figure 23-9
The Script Editor, with a simple script up on the lift so I can finally do something about those brake pads

This is Script Editor's entire interface, or near enough. Apart from Saves, Opens, and Prints, you'll never touch the menu bar at all. Here, give it a shot:

1. **Create a new script by pressing ⌘+N or choosing File ➜ New.**

2. **Type the following code in the editing window:**

```
say "Greetings, Professor Falken."
delay 1
say "How about a nice game of chess?"
```

3. **Click the Run button.** There you go. You're now a programmer. I bet your skin's a half a shade paler already.

If you were watching the window carefully, you noticed that the Stop button enabled itself while your script was running. Clicking that sucker terminates the script in midrun, a very useful feature when the script that you *thought* you told to look through your entire hard drive for Microsoft Word documents and copy duplicates onto a blank CD and then burn it actually winds up emailing those boudoir photos you had done at the mall to everyone in your 1,100-person address book.

As you start to work with longer and more complicated scripts, you'll probably start making regular use of the Compile button. Essentially, it double-checks your spelling and grammar. If something you've typed doesn't make sense as AppleScript, it flags it for you and does its best to explain what the problem is. If everything's flawless, it reformats the script with fancy nested indents and type styles, like you saw in Figure 23-9.

Underneath the code section of the window exists a little pane of information. It can display three different things, depending on which of those three tabs underneath it has been clicked:

- **Description.** It's a good idea to describe your script and what it does. You're going to start writing a lot of scripts (No, really; I've paid a large man $30 to come over to your house and beat the snot out of you if you don't. So, time's a-wasting.), and without attaching notes to these things, it becomes really easy to forget why you bothered to write a particular script in the first place.

- **Result.** That's a debugging tool. When a script runs to the very end, the results of the last operation it performed are displayed in the Result tab. You can see an example in Figure 23-9. The last thing this script did was build a sentence out of the information it retrieved from iTunes. Thus, this sentence winds up in the Result tab.

- **Event Log.** This is an even more sophisticated debugging resource. At the root of a gas engine is combustion. At the root of national-level politics are unresolved childhood inadequacy issues. And at the root of all Mac software are events. These are the molecules of what goes on behind the scenes — the actual activities that software has to carry out to make things happen. Script Editor can maintain an Event Log that keeps track of everything your script did during execution and what the immediate result was, step by step by step.

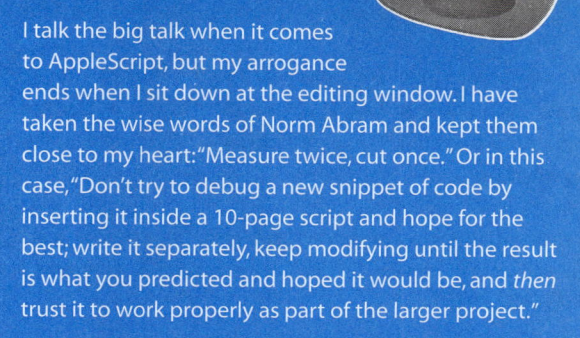

RESULTS ARE ALL THAT MATTER

I talk the big talk when it comes to AppleScript, but my arrogance ends when I sit down at the editing window. I have taken the wise words of Norm Abram and kept them close to my heart: "Measure twice, cut once." Or in this case, "Don't try to debug a new snippet of code by inserting it inside a 10-page script and hope for the best; write it separately, keep modifying until the result is what you predicted and hoped it would be, and *then* trust it to work properly as part of the larger project."

If the Result tab were a woman and I were a man of considerably greater means, I'd be buying it a condo and visiting it on the side.

With the current version of Script Editor it's impossible to stop the script in midrun to see if the line `set theArtist to the` artist evaluated properly. But if I click into the event log, I can see that this line of script returned the text The Beatles just as it should have. It's an essential tool when you need to learn precisely *where* a script went off the rails. You can fine-tune the behavior of the Event Log through the History tab of Script Editor's preferences.

Ah, yes; I seem to have overlooked the Record button. Well, let's just clear that out of the way so you can move on.

Recording scripts

A seldom-used AppleScript feature is recordability. When Apple first thought up AppleScript, it was hoping that every app's actions could be recorded. Click Record, switch to the app, perform a complex action, then return to Script Editor and stop recording. All of the AppleScript code necessary to duplicate that action would be created automatically.

NO NUDES

Sending those photos of you in your unmentionables wouldn't ordinarily happen. AppleScript doesn't make mistakes like that. But if there's one thing more powerful than AppleScript, it's karmic justice. Yes, *you*, the lady in the pink raincoat I encountered outside the video store this morning. That was *my parking space* and you knew it. Well, who's laughing *now?*

Well, that was a great idea, but few apps actually support recordability. And iPhoto isn't one of them. But it's simple enough to learn, and who knows, some of the apps you would like to script *alongside* iPhoto might be recordable.

Let's toss in a ringer for our example: the Finder. It's eminently recordable and as an environment for mind-numbing, repetitive behavior it gives secondary education a real run for its money.

I often organize my windows in a specific way that lets me reorganize my hard drive's clutter quickly. Regardez, Figure 23-10:

What you see is a master column view of the whole hard drive up top, and windows of subfolders arranged on the bottom. But it's a pain to create and arrange these windows manually, so I'm going to record a script that does it for me. Follow these steps to play along:

1. **I create a new script file in Script Editor by pressing ⌘+N or choosing File ➜ New.**

2. **Click the Record button.** The Stop button activates.

3. **Go to the Finder and create the four windows (as shown in Figure 23-10).** Click around in them until

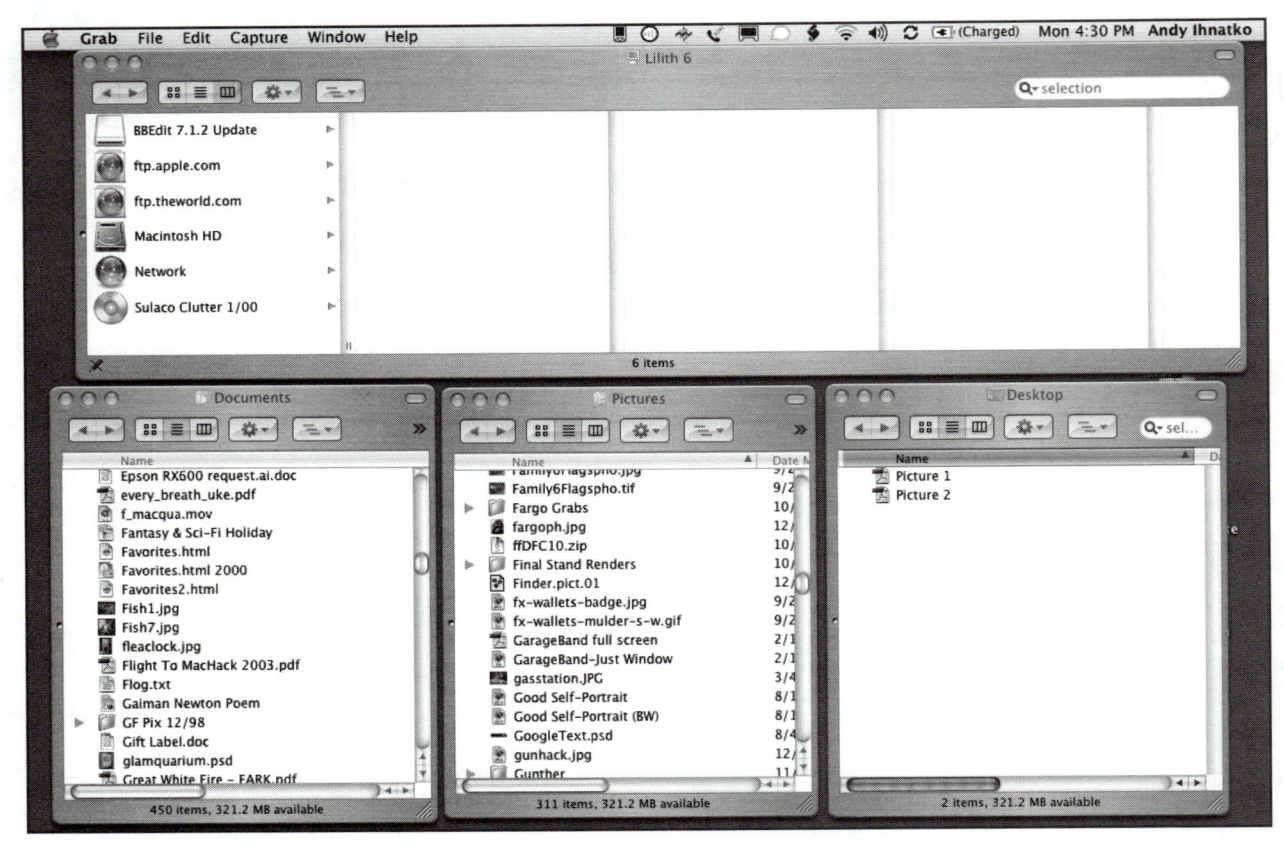

Figure 23-10

What my Finder screen looks like when I'm trying to beat poor, defensive Chaos into Order with a motorcycle chain

they're displaying the folders you want to examine, and change their views to the styles you want (my preference is one set to Columns and the rest set to Lists).

4. **Go back into Script Editor when the windows are just the way you like them.** Notice that the script window is now jam-freakin'-packed with script.

5. **Click the Stop button.** The final result appears in Figure 23-11.

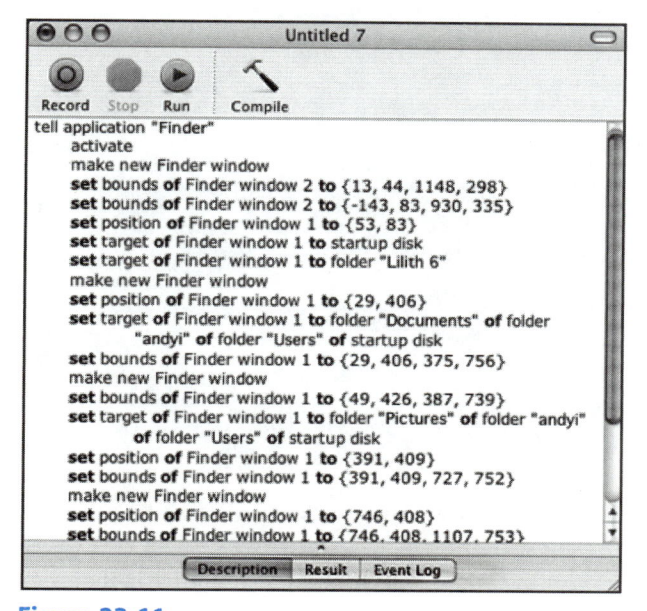

Figure 23-11
A successfully recorded AppleScript

Woo-hoo! Just imagine having to type all that yourself! Recording scripts *rules!!!*

Not so fast, Skeezix. Why don't you try something even simpler, such as recording all the steps of using the Finder to connect to an FTP server? Go ahead. I'll wait here.

Uh-huh. You wound up with something like Figure 23-12, didn't you?

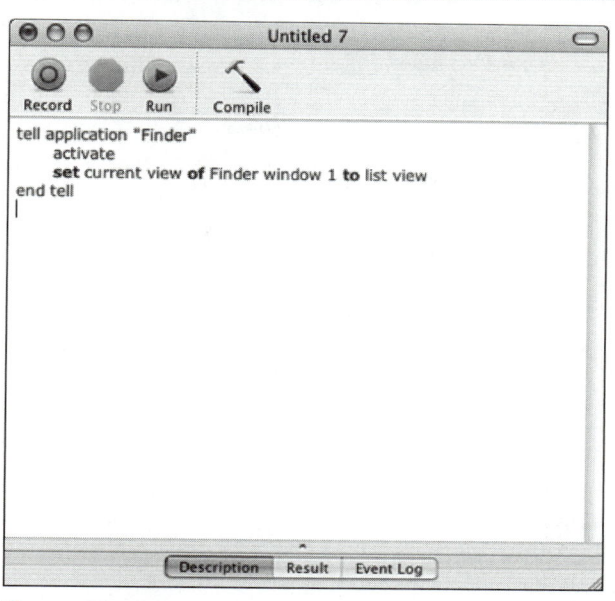

Figure 23-12
A stinky recorded AppleScript

The only thing it actually recorded was that thing at the very end, when you finished logging on to the FTP server and you changed the window's view from Icon to List. See what I mean? Spotty and unpredictable. Recording scripts isn't *totally* useless, but once you've picked up some scripting skills, you'll practically never use it.

Well, the Finder window thing went well at any rate. I might want to actually use that script later. Which dovetails nicely into the next section.

Saving scripts

Saving a script has a couple of quirks, compared to saving document files in other applications. No big surprise. In a sense, you're building software here, so you have to decide how this new software is going to be deployed, you know? Figure 23-13 shows Script Editor's standard Save dialog box.

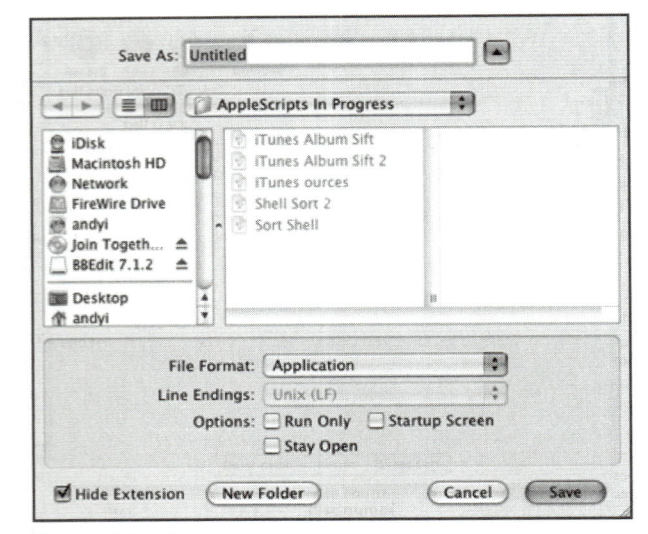

Figure 23-13
The Script Editor's Save options

- **Application.** The most *useful* form for your finished script. It'll run whether or not Script Editor is present and it can run as a drag-and-drop utility if you've scripted it properly.

- **Script.** If you're still working on your script — or if you're coauthoring it with another scripter — you might want to save it as a Script file instead. It's slower and not quite as versatile as an application, but it's a little easier for a scripter to work with.

- **Text.** It's a file containing nothing but words. No formatting, no other data at all. It's useful for publishing purposes and when you need to read your script on an OS that doesn't support AppleScript (such as a PDA or a Windows notebook).

You also have three options available to you:

- **Run Only.** Normally, a saved Script, even one that winds up as an application, can be opened in Script Editor and modified. If you want to protect your code from tampering or theft, click this option.

THESE AREN'T THE DROIDS YOU'RE LOOKING FOR; MOVE ALONG

It's been a long day. I barely had lunch. All day long, the FedEx and UPS delivery people and the mailman have wondered why I've been so brusque with them instead of engaging in the usual 20 minutes of neighborhood gossip, play-by-plays of recent surgeries, and so on. I mean, I haven't been shirking off and I haven't sandbagged a *single thing* in all my years of working on this book.

So can we *please* just pretend you never saw those two Bundle options? Trust me, you don't need to know how to use 'em. A bundle is a special format that lets you enclose files and resources along with the script. For example, if your script normally takes about eight minutes to complete its task, maybe you want to have it play *American Pie* to keep the user entertained while he or she waits. If you save the script as a bundled application, you can stick the MP3 file right inside the app, so everything's in one nice, convenient package.

- **Startup Screen.** Sure, *you* know what this script does, and know how to use it. But will everybody else? Clicking this option will take the text you wrote in the Description tab of the script window and package it as a startup screen that appears whenever the script is run.

- **Stay Open.** Scripts normally run once and then quit. Clicking this option causes the script to stay open and active. There's a special kind of AppleScript code called an idle handler that takes advantage of this. If it's *incredibly important* that iTunes is always up and running (it has to be available to serve music to all the other Macs in your house, for example), you can write a script that checks every 10 minutes to relaunch it if it doesn't appear to be in the list of running apps.

Give the script a name, click Save, and you're golden.

Tip

Remember, if you want this script to appear in the Scripts menu, save it in Library ➜ Scripts inside your user folder. If you want the script to appear in the Scripts menu of all of the other Mac users of that machine, save it in the system-wide Library folder (click on the hard drive icon in the Finder to see it).

Examining AppleScript dictionaries

Script Editor has another function on top of building, debugging, running, and saving scripts: It lets you examine an application's *scripting dictionary* to learn how it can be controlled via AppleScript.

As I pointed out earlier, the strength or the weakness of an app's scripting support is up to the developer. Any functions or capabilities that are specific to the app have to be *provided* by the app. And they also have to provide AppleScript programmers with documentation explaining what these app-specific functions and data types are.

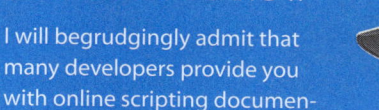

ME GOTTA GO NOW

I will begrudgingly admit that many developers provide you with online scripting documentation, and there's often a whole page of sample AppleScripts on their Web sites. All the same, keep your expectations low. The scripting dictionary is the only thing you can absolutely count on, and a scripting dictionary helps you understand AppleScript about as much as an English dictionary helps you to understand the lyrics to *Louie, Louie*.

The word documentation has to be used loosely. They write up a list of data types the app can recognize and deal with and a list of functions the app can perform, and make this list available to you, eager young space cadet, within the application itself in the form of a scripting dictionary.

Script Editor can open and read these dictionaries. Just choose Open Dictionary from the Script Editor's File menu. Script Editor will present a list of all installed apps. Pick an app like iPhoto and you'll see which of iPhoto's features and functions are available in AppleScript (see Figure 23-14).

GET A BIGGER HAMMER

In the end, reading through an app's scripting dictionary is useful to the extent that it'll give you a sense of the app's capabilities. If you wanted to write a script that automatically changes your Mac's Desktop to the most recent photo whose keyword is Family, you'd hope to find "set desktop photo" somewhere in iPhoto's scripting dictionary.

But that doesn't mean you can't write the script. Ever since Mac OS X 10.3, there has been an AppleScript feature called GUI Scripting. It's a system by which a script can send keystrokes and mouse clicks to an app and manipulate its user interface the same way a user can.

So while iPhoto's scripting dictionary doesn't let you do something as esoteric as set a selected photo as your Desktop, you can do it by having GUI Scripting send a phantom mouse click to the Desktop button in iPhoto's main window.

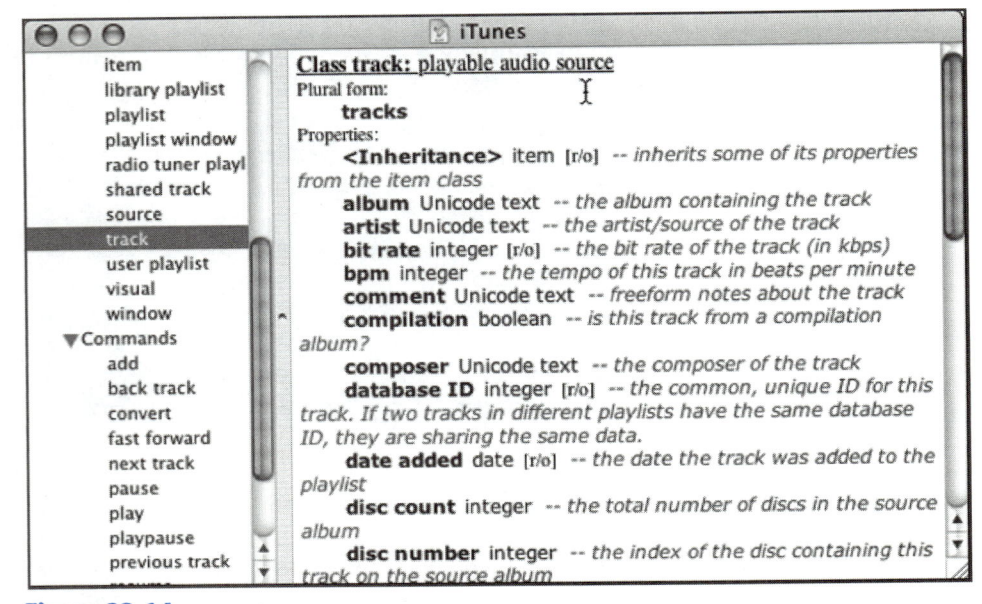

Figure 23-14

iPhoto's scripting dictionary laid bare

A scripting dictionary is organized into classes and commands. Classes are a sophisticated construct of modern computer science but the word thingamabob just about covers it. This list contains all of the thingamabobs that this app has been specially trained to deal with. In iPhoto's case, you've got albums, photos, and keywords. Commands are things that iPhoto can do to and with those thingamabobs.

Learning AppleScript: Resources

Time and space prevent me from including a full primer on the AppleScript language. And when I say time and space I of course mean money. This is simple, Einsteinian physics, people. Einstein said that time and space were merely vibrational manifestations of matter, and to us, nothing matters more than money. Slip us another three bucks and I'll be all over this whole primer thing; but otherwise, nothin' doing.

So instead I'll steer you toward other resources. The best way to learn AppleScript is to examine a script that (a) already exists, and that (b) works. Over time, you'll wind up working your way through all of the sample scripts Apple left for you in the Scripts menu. Scroll around until you see a script that seems to do something interesting, open the script file in Script Editor, and play with the code.

You'll *absolutely* want to go back to wherever you tossed your Panther install discs and get out Disc 4, the Developer Tools CD. I can confirm for you that this disc contains hardcore, supergeek resources and references so potent that even now, just reading about them causes calcium deposits to form around your neurons simply as a defensive measure. But on this disc lurks a complete set of AppleScript documentation and reference materials that'll help explain the basics of writing AppleScript all the way through the intermediaries.

GREAT ARTISTS STEAL AND CHEAT ON THEIR WIVES

(Although that second thing has nothing to do with their success as artists.)

No kidding. I've written plenty of AppleScripts that use Mail to create and send an email, but the central nugget of that code is always the lines I found in one of Apple's samples from the Scripts menu. Remember, kids, it's only thievery if you feel guilty about it.

Joking, joking. Apple's scripts say explicitly that you're free to recycle these samples as you see fit. Plus, this is exactly what AppleScript's framers originally intended: learning by example.

Some other places to go for AppleScripting information:

- **Apple's iPhoto Scripting Page (www.apple.com/applescript/iphoto/).** This is a logical starting point. It contains a big collection of downloadable and installable samples.

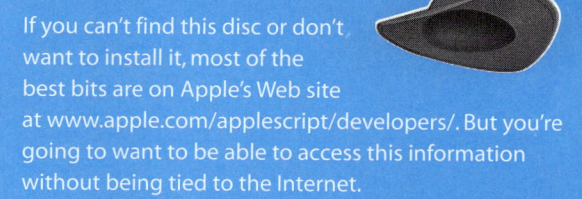

DISC? WHAT DISC?

If you can't find this disc or don't want to install it, most of the best bits are on Apple's Web site at www.apple.com/applescript/developers/. But you're going to want to be able to access this information without being tied to the Internet.

Note that I didn't end that sentence with the term "trust me," though I could have. But I've already used it once and Andy Ihnatko doesn't go around begging for respect. Do you hear me?

- **The AppleScript-Users Mailing List (www.lists.apple.com/).** This is a public mailing list that's chock full of seasoned scripting experts, newbies who've yet to write their first tell block, and everyone in between, all asking questions and swapping techniques. AppleScript is full of land mines that require the sort of lateral thinking that leads to madness, greatness, or the annual redesign of the federal tax code, and only someone who's been there can explain how AppleScript works and, more importantly, why it sometimes doesn't.

- **MacScripter.net (www.macscripter.net/).** This is hands down the best AppleScript information and education resource outside of Apple. What the hey, throw Apple in there, too. At this writing, MacScripter contains more than 1,300 sample scripts in every conceivable category for your benefit and edification. It attempts the impossible task of documenting every major Mac app's level of scriptability. There's also a busy, busy, busy message board where newbie questions are always welcome. MacScripter has succeeded in building a real community.

Okay. So once again, *why* devote a whole chapter to Apple-Script? Because as far as I'm concerned, every book on every Mac subject should have a chapter on AppleScript. If I had a Mount Rushmore for Mac OS features, Apple-Script would be right up there in the Teddy Roosevelt position. It's like the Lost Ark of features. It's the source of unspeakable power, and yet, for most users, it's in an unmarked packing crate inside an immense warehouse that nobody ever visits.

With the next edition of the Macintosh operating system (10.4, Tiger), automation will only become more important. A whole new resource will amplify AppleScript with the addition of a whole second system for automating your Mac. But instead of writing scripts, you'll build visual diagrams of what you want your Mac to do. Take a CD of photos, add them to iPhoto's library, tag them all with a certain keyword, choose nine of them at random, convert them to 640-x-480-pixel JPEGs, and upload them to your photo site. All with just one mouse click.

Even if you don't have Tiger, and even if you never use AppleScript directly, you'll be able to abuse, impress, and intimidate strangers simply by explaining what it is and why it's so keen. And the most important currency of any technology isn't speed or efficiency — it's arrogance. Don't knock it until you've tried it, friends.

Twenty iPhoto Questions from Aunt Estelle

There are two unavoidable occupational hazards that come with being the person in the room who has an insatiable interest in technology: One, very little chance of any second-base action until you're two years out of college at the earliest, and two, you're constantly being hit up for answers and advice. It comes from your friends, it comes from your relatives. As soon as you've proven to both that you're an immense sap, they start scoring points with *their* immediate social circle by passing your phone number and email address around. "Call at any hour of the day or night," they say. "S/he is bound to be home and eager for human contact, given that the last time they experienced the touch of nonplatonic love was in 1993."

Dopes. Ingrates. Do I even *need* to point out that as recently as 2000, a woman at a New Year's party kissed me full on the lips after I loaned her $80 for cab fare?

At any rate, the more you learn, the more powerful and far-reaching your guru aura becomes. I do have an Aunt Estelle who sends me common, odd, or just plain interesting questions on all subjects, but the following queries are a typical selection from my Inbox. Feel free to cut and paste them as you acquire your own personal Aunt Estelles.

Do I Really *Have* to Use iPhoto?

Naw. The Macintosh operating system has an app called Image Capture (located in the Utilities folder of your Applications directory) that automatically slurps a camera's contents onto your hard drive whenever it senses that one has has just been plugged in. Image Capture can even hand off all those photos to another program, or run each one through an AppleScript.

But you're going to want to use iPhoto, even if you've been underwhelmed by the app. It's true that iPhoto doesn't have a lot of the kinds of features that appeal to professional photographers, but as a quick and easy way to get pictures onto your hard drive, it's great. As a quick and easy way to locate a photo of your brother-in-law Anniston carving the traditional roast dolphin at last year's big Earth Day barbecue, it's terrific. And the fact that it stashes all of your photos in one location where every other Mac app can access them — whether it's iMovie, iDVD, or the front end for a special sort of machine that turns any JPEG file into needle-ready tattoo art — makes iPhoto a world-beater.

Just Where the Devil Are My Photos? I Mean, for *Real,* Man!!!

Yeah, even I find it just a *little* annoying that I have to play "Mother, May I" with iPhoto before the app gives me my original image files. But iPhoto keeps all of your files nicely organized by date. Head for your Pictures folder and look for a folder titled iPhoto Library. Open that puppy and you'll find a folder for every year, and a folder for every month, and a folder for every day.

How Do I Get Photos *out* of iPhoto?

Wow. I mean... well, *wow.* One, two, three questions, and they've all been pretty negative about iPhoto. This isn't *like* you, Auntie.

The main meat of this book offers plenty of details on exporting photos out of the iPhoto Library, but it boils down to three different methods:

- **The "I trust my software to do everything for me" approach.** Select the photos (or an entire album) and choose Export from iPhoto's File menu. iPhoto creates new copies of all of the photos in the group, resizing them or changing their file format at your command.

- **The "I'm a self-assured and confident Macintosh power user" approach.** Just drag the pictures from the Photo Library into a Finder folder or a Finder volume. iPhoto duplicates these pictures into the destination. If you cropped them or adjusted their image settings, the copies will retain those changes, but they'll be copied in their original file format and at their original size.

- **The "I've seen 'Colossus: *The Forbin Project,*' '*2001: A Space Odyssey,*' and other fine documentaries and I know that the only way to prevent Skynet from becoming self-aware and crushing all of Humanity under the merciless steel heels of a race of time-travelling superandroids is to do everything myself" approach.** Switch to the Finder, navigate to the folder containing your images (see previous question), and copy them just as you would any other files.

Hey, Who's the Girl Standing Next to You in This Picture on Your Web site?

Which one?

The Redhead.

No, I meant "which picture?"

The One at the Flea Market.

Oh. That's my friend Michelle.

I'm So Mad at Myself. I Went Out and Bought a 6-Megapixel Camera, and Now I'm Reading about 8-Megapixel Ones!

First off, never be mad at yourself. You should always be mad at the *industry,* even when they did absolutely nothing wrong.

Second, don't be overly dazzled by megapixels. An 8-megapixel camera isn't necessarily better than a 6- or even a 4-megapixel model. The only thing that more megapixels *automatically* give you is the ability to crop and enlarge more or less to infinity. If that's the only photo of Uncle Chewy where he has a flattering and winning smile, but it's a shot of him ogling the stripper at Cousin Mel's bachelor party, there's enough detail in a high-resolution image that you can easily turn it into a flawless head-and-shoulders portrait. And when he's made deacon at your church and they print his portrait in the *Sunday Missalette,* nobody will guess that just outside the borders of the photo, a seminude policewoman is cuffing someone to a pole.

Among all cameras 4 megapixels and above, the most important thing affecting the quality of your pictures is the software in the camera — the internal code that looks at the data flowing in from the image sensor and decides what the right exposure and color balance should be. The array of user features (like the number and variety of scene modes) is a close second. If you're happy with your 6-megapixel camera, use it in good health.

My Camera Can Take Pictures in a Couple of Different File Formats. Which One Should I Use?

All cameras use JPEG as their default storage format. It's universal and extremely flexible, and you shouldn't *not* use JPEG mode unless you can think of a dashed good reason. Herewith, I present some of the Dashed Good Reasons:

If your camera gives you the option of TIFF, the Dashed Good Reason is that when you're shooting something very, very subtle — like a majestic cloud-swept tropical sunset suitable for use in an antihistamine advertisement — JPEG's tendency to compress picture information means that the brilliant smooth transition from cobalt blue to purple to fire-red may be marred by a few blocky-looking patches. Almost all cameras that support TIFF use an "uncompressed" version of the file format, which means that although the pictures you shoot may take up four times as much space on your storage card, they'll look as natural as possible.

But most cameras let you adjust the level of JPEG compression, and to be honest, you'd have to work very hard to take a picture where compression artifacts are even noticeable. There's another common camera mode that's actually way more handy than TIFF: RAW mode. If you've shot more than, say, six pictures over the course of your life, you've certainly had a moment later where you thought, "Dang..., my sister Perforata's face is too dark. I wish either I or the camera had been smart enough to overexpose this shot a little."

RAW mode gives you the magical ability to go back in time and turn on the camera's "+2 overexposure" feature. In JPEG mode, after you click the shutter, the picture's been taken and that's it. You can tweak things using iPhoto's exposure settings, but that's like the guy at the photo lab taking the negative and making it lighter during the printing process. In RAW mode, your camera doesn't try to make sense of the data coming in off of its image sensor. Instead of turning that pile of numbers into a JPEG image, it just stashes the data itself into a file. The camera's manufacturer provides a special app that takes that raw data and turns it into an actual image file, and during the process you can tell it, "When you interpret the data, pretend that I pushed the camera's Overexpose button and that I set the white balance to Cloudy/Overcast."

Obviously, this app won't allow you to pretend that you remembered to use a flash or that you were careful enough to make sure nobody in the photo was blinking, but it's as close to a "do-over mode" as you're going to get until Doc Brown's flux capacitor technology is mature enough for consumer products.

I always keep my camera in JPEG mode and switch to RAW when I'm shooting something terribly important (but only if it's okay that I get fewer shots per card, and can afford to wait longer for each shot to record).

So How Long Have You and Michelle Been Dating?

We're not dating, actually. We're just good friends.

How Do I Add Non-Digital Photos to the iPhoto Library?

If you have old prints, you can just scan them in. These days, top-quality scanners are so cheap that if you have one on the left side of your desk and you're thinking of sliding it over to the right side, you can just buy a second scanner and stop worrying about it. A scanner works almost exactly like a photocopier except when you click the Scan button, the image is dumped into iPhoto instead of onto a sheet of cheap letter-sized paper.

If you have slides, the process is trickier. Plenty of scanners are set up to process slides — some of these models *only* process slides — but they're usually very, very pricey. Unless you have a huge pile of slides and transparencies to add to your library, you're better off phoning some of the one-hour-photo shops and film labs in your area to see if they offer slide-scanning services. Ask them if they do it on-site: If your slides are really precious, you don't want them to be mailed off to New Jersey.

Kodak and other big processing services also offer digital options as part of their standard film-processing service; that is, you hand over your film and you get back a CD of digital images as well as an envelope of prints and negatives. It's a handy way to get many of the benefits of digital without having to lay out $500 for a new camera. Just ask about the resolution of the digital images. Some operations give you tiny files that are suitable for the Web but useless for making future prints.

Your Uncle Chewy Is a Lying, Two-Timing Jerk and I Need to Remove Him from All of My Family Pictures.

Yyyyyyes, and I see you've already started by gouging his face out of your wedding picture with a fork. Well, some alternative techniques may yield far more subtle results. Alas, I'm not aware of any software that has a one-click "De-Jerkify" button, and this sort of elaborate image manipulation requires a sophisticated image-editing app like GIMP (you can get a free download from www.gimp.org) or Adobe Photoshop (available from www.adobe.com, but more or less the exact *opposite* of free).

If you want me to teach you how to remove people from a photo, I'm going to ask for some more money first. But essentially it comes down to covering up the newly minted ex-husband with elements from the photo's background. If he's standing in front of a wall, that's perfect. If lots of people are behind him, you'll have to paint in the missing parts of Auntie Goat's dress.

I was there at that barbecue and I can advise you to try not to make her look quite so hippy. That thick belt was definitely a fashion mistake.

Chapter 9 discusses some photo-editing options in more depth.

I Emailed Your Mom a Picture of Your Nephew D'Artagnian and Your Dad Says It Looks All Blocky When He Prints It Out.

(Wait... I'm spending hours of my day answering questions from total strangers, and my own *father* won't pick up the phone and ask me for help?)

Anyway. It's because you were polite and did the right thing. When you email someone a photo, it's proper etiquette to send them a small, screen-resolution file — 400 pixels wide, say. Otherwise you're choking his or her Inbox with huge files. But there isn't nearly enough information in that image to make a decent print.

When you use iPhoto's Email feature, you're asked how big you want the photo to be. If you want to send something big enough for people to make their own prints with, click Original for the size.

I'm Almost Ready to Just Take This Camera Back to the Store and Get a Refund. I Press the Shutter and by the Time the Thing Actually Takes the Picture, the Bird's Flown Off or the Goal's Been Scored or the Senator Has Desperately Thrown the Bedspread Up over Himself and His Campaign Manager.

Two answers to this one: First, there's nothing you can do about it. In a film camera, the shutter opens and closes in 1/500 of a second and the photons do the rest. A digital camera has to write a 2-megabyte file to disk, and that takes time.

Second... well, actually, there *is* something you can do about it: Take the camera back and buy another one. Some cameras have shorter wait times than others. My favorite digital is currently the Nikon D70, which is ready for another shot the instant I take my finger off the shutter button. Camera makers are only too familiar with the delay problem, and so the better models have a buffer that the camera dumps photos into if the storage device is currently busy. You may be able to squeeze off three or four shots before this buffer is full, and then you'll have to wait for those photos to be written out. Read your camera's manual. It may have a "burst" mode that you didn't even know about.

You can also invest in a better storage card. The El Cheapo cards work perfectly fine, but if you're willing to spend a 30% premium, you can buy one that can slurp in data a lot faster. It's not an ungodly improvement in speed, but it may be the difference between taking four shots in a brief span of seconds and taking five.

You and Michelle Look Pretty Cozy Together.

Yes. We've been friends — did I say that she's a *friend?* — for about seven or eight years.

If I Want to Put My Photos on the Web, Do I Need to Have a .Mac Account?

Naw. A .Mac account is by far the quickest and easiest way to "publish" an iPhoto album online, but it's not your sole option. iPhoto's Export feature (under the File menu) has a tab for Web Page. Clicking it saves the selected photos or album as a set of Web pages that you can then upload to a Web server.

And there's the rub: You need to stake out some personal space on the Web to post your pictures. Many ISPs set up a free personal Web site for you as part of their service. If not, you'll have to make your own arrangements, which will cost you between $9 and $20 a month. Beware: There can be huge surcharges if your Web site becomes incredibly popular. If a million people visit to see your photo of a 72-year-old Elvis cleaning pools in Fresno, it's going to cost you.

Instead, you may want to look into free photo sites like www.ofoto.com or www.shutterfly.com. You can upload as many photos as you want (in full resolution), arrange them into online albums, and go through the photos on the Web. The sites also offer printmaking services, making them a boon if you're surrounded by freeloading friends and relatives. So when someone asks you for three copies of that photo you took of him or her with Erik Estrada, you can just give out the URL of your Shutterfly gallery. There your friends can order prints and enlargements right from the Web site. It's their money and Shutterfly's time.

Is There an Easier Way to Go Through the Pictures I've Taken and Decide Which Ones to Keep and Which Ones to Toss?

The problem of quickly going through 100 photos and tossing out the 20 or 30 totally worthless ones is a central part of the Digital Experience, and I admit that I don't like the clumsy way iPhoto normally handles it.

A semi-hidden feature makes it all good, though. After you've imported your photos, click the Slideshow button, click the Display slideshow controls checkbox, and then click Play. A translucent toolbar appears at the bottom of every image, enabling you to immediately trash the current image. You can also assign the image a rating and rotate it 90 degrees in either direction.

One note, though: Disk space is cheap and CD-Rs are even cheaper. So the only reason for actually deleting an image is if the image is, indeed, too blurry to make anything out (or if you were wearing unusually tight jeans that day and when you stuck the camera in your back pocket, you wound up wedging the shutter button).

I Love Making Web Galleries, But I Want to Create My Own Gallery Styles.

At this writing, iPhoto doesn't allow you to create customized galleries, which is a big shame because not all of the preloaded ones are going to be perfect for everyone. I'm especially disappointed because when I make galleries, I don't want to just quip "Hyde Park, London; Westminster Abbey way off in background," which is about the longest caption iPhoto allows. I want to write a paragraph or two explaining where I was and what was going on.

My usual tool for putting my iPhoto albums on the Web is iView MediaPro (www.iview-multimedia.com), a commercial app designed to manage all kinds of media files. iView MediaPro can indeed turn a folder of images into Web pages, but (a) it uses a simple template format and (b) if you understand HTML (or understand third-party tools that can generate HTML files for you), you can easily create gallery pages that look exactly the way you want. iView also allows me to annotate to my heart's content.

If you want a simpler and cheaper solution, Galerie, a free download from www.myriad-online.com, builds galleries automatically and offers 10 times more options than iPhoto.

You and Michelle Have Been *Friends* for Seven Years and You Still Haven't Moved the Relationship Forward?

What do you mean? There's nothing weird about having female friends. I don't understand why you're still going on about this.

The Photo Looks Great on My Screen, But It Looks Lousy When I Print It.

You're sort of banging your head against a problem of consumer hardware and software. If you were a professional photographer, your monitor would have a little doohickey either stuck onto it or built right in that constantly checks what's being displayed and makes sure that the monitor's color settings are consistent and match a predefined standard. That way, whether you're sending the image to a $200 printer sitting next to the computer or to a $70,000 color press, you know that the red you've just added to this lady's dress is the same red that will appear in millions of copies of *People* magazine.

Consumer gear has color-management systems. Apple's is known as ColorSync — but ColorSync can still be a hit or miss proposition. You pretty much have to resign yourself to making a print and then making adjustments manually.

Nope, That Wasn't It.

What are your paper settings? Your print driver adjusts the color on the fly to make up for limitations or quirks of individual kinds of paper. So if you're using expensive glossy photo paper but the print driver *thinks* you're using cheap inkjet paper, all the colors will come out bleedy and funky-looking. In iPhoto's Print dialog box, click the Advanced Options button; your printer's driver should then give you a paper-selection option in one of the pop-up menus. Look for "Print Settings."

Still No Good.

Um... well, is one of your ink cartridges old or running low? If you see streaks or dramatic shifts in color, it's usually one of the ink cartridges. When you installed your printer's software, you probably also picked up a utility that lets you check the levels of all of your inks and clean the print heads if necessary. Try that.

Hang On... No, I'm Having the Same Problem.

Then I don't know what to say, and I swear if not for the fact that I live almost 40 whole miles away, I'd jump in the car and drive over to check it out personally. As it is, I'll give you the advice that I gave myself after Kodak's self-service digital-photo kiosks started popping up in all the drugstores: Desktop photo printing is something you do only on special occasions. The kiosk makes glossy, durable, professional prints in just a few minutes for well under the price of a postage stamp. So unless you're doing something incredibly artsy, using the kiosk rather than your printer just makes more sense.

Just export the pictures from iPhoto at their original resolution, slap them onto a CD-R or a memory card, and head on out. You need more Q-Tips, too, so hey, two birds with one stone.

I Just Want You to Be Happy. I Know Your Mother Is a Little Worried That You're Not Married Yet.

Why? So Michelle and I can be as happy as you and my ex-Uncle Chewy? I'd continue this argument, but I need to get back to work. I'm working on the shot of the family Bicentennial cookout, and your gouge marks took out part of Great Grampa's left ear.

25

You Got 'Em...Use 'Em: Digital Camera Features

As a guy who takes great pride in knowing that I have more microprocessors on my person than any other organic life form in the room, I can't say something like "I think digital cameras have way too many features" without suffering a major loss of face (as well as a reflexive series of dry heaves), so I'll just go ahead and lie.

A friend of mine emailed me yesterday complaining that digital cameras have way too many features. When he was a kid and he fell in love with photography, it wasn't because the camera had dozens of knobs, buttons, levers, lights, and indicators: It was because he quickly realized that if he was the one *taking* the family pictures, he wouldn't have to be *in* the family pictures. Oh, and the whole "magic of coalescing a continuum of events into one static, yet moving, image" deal. That, too.

He has a point. He's also twigged to a maxim of photography that's been true ever since the days when prosperous salesmen of spats and celluloid shirt collars would take scandalous boudoir photos in which women exposed their ankles: A thousand advanced technical features can't compensate for a photographer who didn't *think* before clicking the shutter.

That said, even a moderately advanced digital camera has enough processing power to cause the thing to fall under Asimov's Three Laws of Robotics. Still, you shouldn't be intimidated. Simply pushing the button and trusting the camera to do its job without any human intervention is a good instinct, but there are common features that you absolutely shouldn't ignore. Oftentimes, they're the difference between shooting so-so photos and coming home with ones that demand to be hung on the wall.

EXPOSURE COMPENSATION

When it comes to determining the correct exposure, a film camera really doesn't work very hard at all. A rudimentary image sensor takes a quick look at the overall brightness of the scene, the camera's microprocessor takes a guess, and then it crosses its fingers, knowing that if it made the wrong decision, hey, the guy in the mini-lab will be able to make up for it by printing the photo lighter or darker.

As in all other aspects of photography, digitals are way ahead. I mean, honestly, it's like comparing The Jetsons' hovercar to a medium-sized Idaho potato with the word "Ferrari" written across it in felt-tip pen. Most digital cameras take each picture twice, more or less. The first time, it captures the whole image to map out all of its brights and darks. It uses that reconnaissance mission to choose the picture's final exposure, based on the need to bring out the details hiding in the shadows while avoiding "blowouts" of intense light. All this is by way of explaining that your digital camera usually does a jim-dandy job of determining exposure. Even if you're a professional photographer with 20 years' worth of experience, you should *still* leave the exposure choices up to the hardware.

DISPOSABLE CAMERAS ARE ALL LIARS

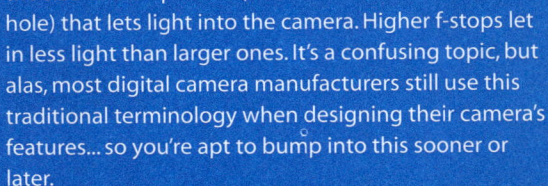

Ever wonder how the film companies can sell you a focusing, automatic-exposure disposable camera for just nine dollars? Simple: They can't. Their focus is hard-set to infinity, meaning that anything five feet away or farther will be acceptably (if not perfectly) in focus, and the camera uses the same exposure with every single picture, whether you're on the beach in bright sunlight or in the dim, purple lighting of one of the VIP rooms at a Hollywood bar. The camera relies totally on the photo-processing lab's ability to boost or mute the lighting when it makes your prints.

"F-STOP"? WUZZAT?

The *f-stop* (it's an ancient and traditional photographic term) is the size of the aperture (the hole) that lets light into the camera. Higher f-stops let in less light than larger ones. It's a confusing topic, but alas, most digital camera manufacturers still use this traditional terminology when designing their camera's features... so you're apt to bump into this sooner or later.

This is also, incidentally, why some lenses are stamped "f 2.8" in proud, white letters. That's the largest aperture this lens is capable of. Remember, smaller f-stops mean larger openings, which means that a lens with a maximum aperture of f 2.8 can let in a lot more light than one whose max is f 4.5.

Still, that microprocessor isn't quite as good as the human eye. It's a *nice* photo of a classic car, but if it were just a little darker, the deep, rich colors of the paint would have had a little more punch. Or maybe your three friends have three vastly different skin tones, and you need to make the shot brighter to avoid losing the highlights in the darkest face. Exposure compensation to the rescue. You're not losing the benefits of the camera's sophisticated software. You're just telling the camera, "That's nice, but I want you to make the scene just a little darker." Or lighter. It's up to you.

Typically, the exposure compensation feature is indicated by a little +/- symbol. It'll give you a selection of numbers based on traditional f-stops, plus or minus .3, .7, 1, 1.5, or 2 stops. If the shot was too bright, typically -.3 or -.5 will correct it nicely. You'd rarely need to make a more drastic compensation than that in either direction.

BUT WHY NOT JUST USE THAT "BRIGHTNESS" THINGAMOBOB IN IPHOTO?

Because. That's why.

Oh, all right. You want the *original image* to be as perfect as possible. Don't be seduced by all the things you can do to a photo in iPhoto and Photoshop. Yes, you can twiddle a slider and make an image a little brighter, but that control doesn't magically transport you back to Disneyworld to reshoot the picture. You're just fixing a defect, and the results will never be as good as a photo that had been shot correctly to begin with.

Adjusting a Brightness slider can make a photo darker, but it won't restore the subtle blues in the sky that were overexposed into dull white. It won't correct the lackluster intensity of that red barn. It won't erase that comment you made to your friend's wife that was perfectly innocent but, you now realize, could have been misconstrued as a crack about her weight. There are limits to what software can do for you.

Exposure compensation is so handy that many photographers leave it on all the time, forcing the camera to make every photo .3 of a stop darker. There's solid reasoning behind that. When a digital makes a mistake, it's usually by making the shot too bright. But before making this sort of unilateral decision, you should take lots and lots of photos to see if your specific make and model of camera needs the added intervention.

MANUAL FILL FLASH

Normally your camera only activates the flash when the scene is too dark to shoot with available light. But there are plenty of situations in which adding a pop of flash turns a snapshot into a professional-looking image:

- **Taking pictures of people in bright sunlight.** The flash will soften all of the dark shadows in their faces.

- **Taking pictures on a cloudy day.** The flash will prevent colors (of objects within its range) from becoming washed out and uninteresting.

- **Shooting a street scene.** The flash will prevent items in the foreground from getting lost in the background.

It actually sounds as though I'm telling you to leave the flash on all the time. Hmm. Maybe I am. So I should qualify all of that by saying that abusing your flash is a good way to create stiff, artificial-looking photos in which natural light has been banished from the scene like leather goods from a vegan's wardrobe. Still, fill flash is always worth considering, and when you're shooting pictures of people, it's almost always worth trying.

IT'S EVEN GOOD WHEN IT'S NO GOOD AT ALL

The limitation of fill flash is, of course, distance. Most built-in flashes have a range of only about 8 feet, which is why snarky photographers always laugh at the spectators during the Super Bowl halftime show. The TV blimp shows sparkles popping all over the stadium, representing thousands of people who are apparently trying to take flash photos of something happening on the field 400 feet away. (Hey, Ansel Adams. Did it ever occur to you that those cameras' flashes are firing automatically? People shouldn't judge. Except for all the people who, I'm sure, have told you that your tie looks like it came off a ventriloquist's dummy.)

If I'm taking pictures of people or other animals standing well out of range, however, I will indeed turn on the flash. Why? Because while it's not strong enough to illuminate the creature's face, it's probably strong enough to put a little highlight in the glossy surface of the eyes. That little twinkle really livens up the shot because the eyes are usually the first thing you look at.

MANUAL WHITE-BALANCE

Adjusting the color balance of an image is a forgotten art in the world of digital. If you grew up with film (let's just pretend you were born before 1996), you're probably at least aware of the filters that serious photographers had to screw onto their lenses to compensate for the color of artificial lights. Fluorescent lights make everything too green. Incandescent lights make everything yellow. On overcast days, everything's de-saturated. Et cetera.

We tend to forget about these problems because if a photo is too green, we can more or less push a button in Photoshop that says, "Less green, please." Usually it isn't even that complicated. Desktop software has an almost comically simplified button that reads, "Fix this picture," and if there's more green or yellow in the scene than the software has become accustomed to encountering in photos taken in Earth's atmosphere, it fixes them automatically.

But remember the lesson so wisely and skillfully imparted during the bit about exposure compensation: You get only one chance to get a picture right. You can make corrections later, but that's just repairing damage. Your shots will look so much better if the damage never happened. So mosey on over through your camera's white-balance (or color) menu. You might have to look deep inside your camera's "utility" or "setup" menu to find it, but most cameras have some sort of white-balance feature. There you'll find half a dozen built-in programs that help the thing deal with all sorts of different lighting conditions. Your camera *wants* you to take good pictures and it *wants* to help you, but it *can't* help unless you *want* help.

You're looking for something in your camera manual with words like *indoor, outdoor, incandescent, fluorescent,* and *color temperature,* and of course, *white-balance* is a dead giveaway.

You said it yourself to your drunken Uncle Herb (except you probably said "stop being such a stinkin' bum" instead of "take good pictures"), and now I'm saying it to you. Spend a little time experimenting with your camera's different white-balance settings. I admit that some cameras take this concept to obsessive extremes (I swear that one camera I've used had a setting for "tree shade"), but you ought to know how your own camera will handle different types of artificial light.

Movie mode

Many cameras can shoot QuickTime video as well as photos. Up until recently, I consistently derided those features. The resulting video was grainy and contained only half the frames per second of "real" video. Plus, you were limited to just short clips. "Bring the right tool for the job," I'd say, insisting that video should be shot by video cameras, not by two men in a camcorder costume.

But I'm mature enough, humble enough, and evolved enough to admit when I'm wrong.

 Note

And apparently, I'm also arrogant enough to take an admission of short-sighted ignorance and somehow turn it into something that makes me look good.

Modern cameras can shoot QuickTime videos that are nearly the same quality as VHS, and with modern memory cards that are both dirt-cheap and high in capacity, you can shoot half an hour of video on a $100 card. But that's

not the only reason why I want you to use this feature. You should use this feature because *nobody* is manufacturing a digital camera with an honest-to-God ultrawide-angle lens. Whether your Winnebago has brought you out to the Grand Canyon or your $140,000 in donations to a political party has brought you inside the Oval Office, you can't take it all in with one snapshot. You *could* carefully take a series of photos and assemble them into a panorama later on, but that's very time-consuming to shoot, and a lot of trouble to stitch together.

Instead, switch your camera to Movie mode and slowly pan the room. When you return home and are showing off your snaps to the family, you'll be able to give them a sense of being there that you would never have managed with a still picture.

AND DIGITAL CAMERAS *DO TOO* WORK AS VIDEO CAMERAS

I'll admit that once I started using my digicam's video features, I started shooting a lot more video than I used to. Even more than I do with my real video cameras. A MiniDV camcorder shoots at near-DVD quality in flawless stereo sound, but I almost never take it with me when I travel. I hate camcorders. I honestly do. Still cameras are great because they only tie you up for about 1/500 of a second at a time. If you're using a camcorder, well, *great*. Instead of watching the changing of the guard at Buckingham Palace in person, you're watching it through a tiny LCD video screen. No thanks.

But my digital camera is *always there* with me, so I don't need to make the overt gesture of dropping a camcorder in my bag every morning. Plus, I gotta admit that there are plenty of times when there's something I just *have* to get on video. I recently was driven through LA late at night by a friend who grew up there and really knows all the sights. I sure couldn't take pictures — not nearly enough light — and besides, I would have lost all that great commentary. So I whipped out my digital camera and got nearly all of it on QuickTime. It's not as good as what I'd have shot with a real camcorder, but I'm not making a PBS documentary. I'm just capturing the experience.

Besides, a digital camera is very much in tune with my attitude regarding the best way to shoot video. Camcorders encourage you to just keep the tape rolling, which means that the hour long tape's dang-near worthless until you sift through it in iMovie and cut it down to a humane six minutes or so. But the nature of digital camera video is to shoot specific, short clips. Each scene is a morsel in and of itself. Even when you assemble those QuickTime files together in iMovie, the moviemaking process moves much faster because you picked your moments carefully and didn't shoot any more than you needed to.

Self-timer

The self-timer doesn't just allow you to click the shutter and then run into the shot and be one of the 11 dudes breaking the record for most people stuffed into a Mini Cooper. You should also think of it as an electronic tripod. When you want to shoot a picture of a big, dark place (like the inside of a church, or a landscape during sunrise), you can't just hold the camera. The shutter has to stay open for a good long time, and camera shake will blur the shot.

Ideally, you would have brought a tripod to stabilize the camera, but failing that you can just set the camera on a stable surface, start the self-timer, and then take your hands away. Ten seconds later the shutter will open and close without any jabbing or wobbling on your part.

I WANNA HOLD BY HAND

If you're unsure about whether or not it's possible to hand-hold a shot without blurring the image, there's a handy rule of thumb: The inverse of the focal length of the lens is the longest shutter speed that you can safely shoot by hand. Somewhere in the manual for your camera (or in its advertising), the manufacturer will list the focal range of your zoom, in 35mm terms, that is "3x zoom lens (40mm-110mm film equivalent)." This means that at its widest setting, you can shoot long, 1/40 of a second exposures without using a tripod. But if you're shooting your daughter's Christmas recital, you've got the camera zoomed all the way in, and the LCD screen says the camera has selected a shutter speed of 1/60 of a second, you're hosed. You should have brought a tripod.

Alternative resolutions

You own a 6-megapixel camera. You *paid* for a 6-megapixel camera. Why the devil would you *ever* want to use it to take 3- or (oh, holy mother of God) even *2*-megapixel images?

Because you've been shooting all day, you only have six shots left on your one memory card, and there's still half the wedding reception left to go. Come on, the maid of honor isn't even slightly drunk yet! And you just know she's going to chase after those rented swans and tumble into the pool fully-clothed. Don't you think there should be a photo of that, just to ensure that she never ever ever lives the sorry incident down?

Remember, every 6-megapixel shot takes as much room as four 3-meg images or six 2-meg images. And a 3-megapixel image still has enough resolution for a perfect 5 x 7 print or a croppable 4 x 6.

Raw mode

You can fault film cameras for many things, but simplicity isn't one of their failings. You've got a lens, you've got a frame of light-sensitive film, and you've got a barrier between the two. Push the shutter and a window opens exposing the film to light. That's it. The image is recorded.

A digital camera is phenomenally complicated. Light hits a CCD or CMOS imager and then the fun has only begun. The camera takes the whopping pile of numbers that the image sensor blasts out and then it processes the data just like the guy at your local processing lab would process your unexposed film. If you've told the camera that you want it to increase the exposure by half a stop and correct for fluorescent lighting, it'll make the necessary changes. Then it'll convert the resulting data into a JPEG file, compressing the image as it does so, and write it to the memory card.

If your camera has a RAW storage mode, you can tell it to just take the data from the image sensor and write those numbers (the "raw data," hence the term) to a file. Don't do any post-processing. Don't turn it into an image file. Don't do nothin'. The result is a file that can't be viewed and can't be printed. It's data that only low-level imaging hardware can understand.

"But Andy," you patiently explain, "my Aunt Lolly isn't a piece of imaging hardware. She's a 58-year-old marketing manager. If she's going to look at a snapshot of my new baby, she needs to see, you know, an actual *photo*." Well, that's why the CD that came with the camera includes a utility for transmogrifying that data into a standard image file.

So what's the point? RAW mode seems to insert a needlessly complicated extra step into the proceedings. Actually, it brings two huge advantages. First, the raw data hasn't been compressed. The JPEG format is wonderful, but it's what's known as a "lossy" format. In order to reproduce the image in the smallest possible file size, the algorithm throws out details that it deems unimportant. The difference is unnoticeable in nearly every photo you take, but note the word *nearly*. If you're shooting a magnificent cloudless ocean sunset, JPEG might let you down. The color of the sky is a muted yellow at the horizon and an indigo blue at the top of the frame, and it's a seamless, airbrushed transition in between.

JPEG has trouble with that sort of thing. If you look closely at a JPEG version of this scene, you'll see that the sky actually has subtle bands marking areas where the compression algorithm looked at the 90 subtle colors present in that arc of sky and decided that 30 would probably do just as well.

I hasten to say that unless you've gone and told your camera to compress images as tightly as it possibly can, you'll almost never see any compression problems with your images. Still, it's good to know that RAW mode is there if you need it.

The second advantage of RAW mode is that it really allows you to go back in time and reshoot something. Remember, the data isn't a picture until it's analyzed and converted by a piece of desktop software. The better camera companies give you software that doesn't just convert the file into a JPEG or a TIFF, it also gives you access to many of the camera's exposure features. Wish you'd hit the exposure compensation button? Well, go ahead. Tell the app to add half a stop. Dang, I forgot that everyone was standing near a mercury lamp. No prob. Click the Color button and tell the software to correct for it. Not all cameras come with great RAW software. Some do little more than ask you whether you want to turn the file into a JPEG or a TIFF. But the great ones are real lifesavers.

I should take a moment to reassure you that JPEG is a great format and there's no reason to abandon it. You *want* compressed files. Otherwise, you'd only get a tenth as many photos on each card. But whenever I take a true, once-in-a-lifetime photo (like when the whole extended family gathers from eight different states, presenting the first opportunity for a true family group photo in two decades), I switch the camera to RAW.

And, of course, this just swats at the surface of what your camera can do. But these are features common to nearly all decent digital cameras, and knowing how they work will make you a much happier person when it comes time to pick up your prints.

The last lesson of the day is that the difference between good pictures and great ones isn't always the difference between a $1,000 camera and a $100 one. It's often the simple difference between a user who sat down one evening and read the entire manual straight through, and one who didn't. It's the difference between a user who

HATS OFF TO THE UNCOMPRESSED

This is also a good spot for me to pimp your camera's "uncompressed" image mode. Usually you'll only find it on higher-end cameras. "Uncompressed" uses either the TIFF (Tagged Image File Format) or an uncompressed flavor of JPEG, and as the name suggests, it isn't a "lossy" format. Every detail that the camera sees goes into the file.

I meant what I said about JPEG being (more or less) the visual equal of any other image file format. The format won't stand up to laboratory scrutiny, but if you stick with your camera's default compression settings, it's nearly impossible to put two 8 x 10 prints side by side and tell which one was shot in compressed JPEG and which was shot in uncompressed TIFF.

There's one caveat, though, and it comes into play when you open that JPEG, make some edits, and save it again. Then a month later, you open it, make some more changes, and save it again. Three months later, another change, another save. And now the image looks like it's been through the laundry. Well, it has: Every time you save a JPEG, it's *re-compressed* and the JPEG compression algorithm throws out a little more info. It's hard to notice at first, but as you run through more and more iterations, it becomes a big problem.

The way around this problem is to *never modify the image file that came out of your camera*. That's your "negative." You want to make changes? Make them to a *copy* of the original file. If an image is particularly important, re-save it to an uncompressed format, such as Photoshop (PSD).

spent two weeks trying every single feature at least once, and the user that knows where the shutter button is and that's it. Because when push comes to shove, it'll be the difference between a user who's aware that the camera has a special shooting mode titled "Child's orchestra performing in early evening late in the year, in a performance hall that doubles as the school gym and cafeteria" and a user who simply trusts that the camera's Automatic mode is all-seeing and all-knowing and probably should be entrusted to manage his or her retirement portfolio, too.

As an author of computer books, I hate to say, "Read the manual." It's very bad for business, you understand. But the only thing more compelling than my lust for filthy riches is my commitment to serving you, the reader.

Index

K

Ken Burns Effect, 325–327
keyboard shortcuts. *See also* selection
rectangles
   accessing context menus, 111
   bullets, 290
   bypassing iPhoto Library, 353, 354
   computer screen snapshots, 228
   copyright symbol, 290
   "curly" quotes/apostrophes, 290
   em dashes, 290
   rebuilding iPhoto Library, 355
   rotating images 1/4 turn, 156
   running slideshows, 170–171
   selecting images
      in film rolls, 70
      in Finder, 47
      multiple albums, 332
      thumbnails, 100
   switching between before/after edits,
      132
   switching between Edit windows,
      112
   undoing edits, 132
keywords. *See also* comments; titles
   assigning to photos, 100, 102
   check mark "keyword", 105
   versus comments, 101
   creating, 98, 100
   defined, 98
   deleting, 99–100
   displaying in Organize mode,
      102, 103
   editing, 98–99
   overview, 105
   photo searches using, 102–104
   printing, 193
   removing from photos, 104–105
   updating, 99
Keywords dialog box, 100, 102, 104

L

landscape-oriented images, 30, 122, 127
laser printers, 173, 175
Last Roll film roll, 60–61

Last 12 Months collection, 61
LCD displays, 5, 9
letterbox format, 122, 164
light, combating uneven, 10–11
locking book layouts, 284
locking screen savers, 230–231

M

.Mac accounts, 238, 239, 261, 384
.Mac Slides, publishing, 238–242
Macromedia Fireworks, 153
Mail Photo dialog box, 218–220
Mail program options, 30–31
memory cards
   16MB cards, 9, 42
   card readers, 42–43, 44
   ejecting, 41, 44
   importing images from, 42–44
   large-capacity cards, 9
   MSC mode and, 41
   naming, 40
   speed, 43, 383
   xD cards, 208–209
microphones, 321
movie mode in cameras, 390–391
Movie Settings dialog box, 224
movies, QuickTime, sharing photos as,
   221–225
MSC (Mass Storage Class) mode, 41
music. *See also* audio
   in iDVD slideshows, 341–343, 345
   in iMovie slideshows, 322–325
   in iPhoto slideshows, 168–169

N

N-Up printing feature, 195–197
naming. *See also* titles
   albums, 76, 78
   HTML naming issues, 259
   iMovie slides, 319
   memory cards, 40
   shared albums, 35
   Smart Albums, 82–83
narration in iPhoto slideshows, 170
netiquette, 220

New Album dialog box, 74–75
New Smart Album dialog box, 82–83
NSTextView Info dialog box, 306,
   308–309

O

open shade, 10
Order Book dialog box, 303–304
Order Prints button, 19, 207, 210
Order Prints dialog box, 210–214
Organize mode. *See also* albums
   arranging photos
      by date, 62
      by film roll, 62
      overview, 62
      by rating, 62, 63, 64
      by title, 62
      using drag and drop, 62, 63
   changing views, 64–66
   defined, 17, 57
   displaying keywords, 102, 103
   Double-click photo options, 29–30
   Edit menu, 30
   entering, 58
   film rolls
      adding comments, 69
      arranging photos by, 62
      batch-changing titles, 94
      changing titles/dates, 68–70, 71
      creating from images in
         library, 70
      defined, 57, 58–59
      expanding/collapsing, 67, 69
      and importing folders, 67, 68
      Last Roll, 60–61
      Roll Info option, 91
      selecting all images in, 70
      sorting images by, 62
      toggling visibility of, 62
   interface, 17, 19
   Last 12 Months collection, 61
   Mail program options, 30–31
   ordering prints online
      adding shipping addresses, 213
      using Order Prints button,
         19, 207, 210